Ethical Foundations for Educational Administration

Christopher Hodgkinson is one of the most important contributors to the field of educational administration. This collection of essays opens up the philosophical foundations of ethical administration and leadership by reviewing his writings and exploring the ethical theories of major philosophers, as they apply to educational organisations today.

Ethical Foundations for Educational Administration is published in honour of the work of Christopher Hodgkinson. It is divided into two sections. The first comprises biographical essays and a critical evaluation of Professor Hodgkinson's work, focusing on his personal and intellectual contributions to a moral theory of educational administration and leadership. The second section looks at how moral philosophy can inform administrative practice. The work of a broad range of philosophers is discussed, from the pre-twentieth-century theories of Aquinas, Adam Smith and Kant to the pragmatists Peirce, James and Dewey and to contemporary ethics of Heidegger, MacIntyre, Bourdieu, Churchland and Thagard.

Christopher Hodgkinson's definition of administration as 'philosophy-in-action' is now famous within the field. This collection illustrates the essential truth of that maxim, showing that moral philosophy, approached in the spirit promoted by Hodgkinson, has both practical and critical purpose when brought to bear upon educational administration and leadership.

Eugenie A. Samier is Associate Professor of Educational Leadership and Administration at Simon Fraser University in British Columbia, Canada.

Professor Christopher Hodgkinson

Ethical Foundations for Educational Administration

Essays in honour of
Christopher Hodgkinson

Edited by Eugenie A. Samier
with Kristina Mihailova

RoutledgeFalmer
Taylor & Francis Group

LONDON AND NEW YORK

First published 2003
by RoutledgeFalmer
11 New Fetter Lane, London EC4P 4EE

Simultaneously published in the USA and Canada
by RoutledgeFalmer
29 West 35th Street, New York, NY 10001

RoutledgeFalmer is an imprint of the Taylor & Francis Group

© 2003 Eugenie A. Samier, selection and editorial matter;
individual chapters, the contributors

Typeset in Palatino and Gill by BC Typesetting, Bristol
Printed and bound in Great Britain by
Antony Rowe Ltd, Chippenham, Wiltshire

All rights reserved. No part of this book may be reprinted or
reproduced or utilised in any form or by any electronic, mechanical,
or other means, now known or hereafter invented, including
photocopying and recording, or in any information storage or
retrieval system, without permission in writing from the publishers.

British Library Cataloguing in Publication Data
A catalogue record for this book is available from the British Library

Library of Congress Cataloging in Publication Data
A catalog record has been requested

ISBN 0–415–29871–7

Contents

Notes on contributors	vii
Preface	xii
Acknowledgements	xvi

PART I
The life and work of Christopher Hodgkinson — 1

1 Through the looking-glass with Christopher Hodgkinson: Letters and lessons on life and leadership from Arcadia West — 3
   Peter Ribbins

2 Christopher Hodgkinson: A student's perspective — 29
   Donald Lang

3 The Gentleman with the Lamp — 38
   Derek J. Allison

PART II
Ethical foundations for educational administrators — 71

4 Editor's introduction — 73
   Eugenie A. Samier

5 Aquinas's notion of good in the context of educational leadership — 80
   Donald Lang

6 Morals and markets: Adam Smith's moral philosophy as a foundation for administrative ethics — 97
   Richard Bates

7	A Kantian critique for administrative ethics: An alternative to the 'morally mute' manager? *Eugenie A. Samier*	126
8	The new pragmatism and social science and educational research *Spencer J. Maxcy*	155
9	Heidegger's 'question concerning technology': Implications for responsible school leadership in an era of restructuring *Carol Harris*	178
10	Vice and virtue: The value of values in administration *William Foster*	199
11	Thinking through moral values: Putting Bourdieu to work within the field of education management *Helen M. Gunter*	212
12	Naturalising ethical judgement: A neuro-computational view *Colin W. Evers*	235
13	Greatness and service: Antinomies of leadership? *Peter Gronn*	253
	Bibliography of Christopher Hodgkinson's writings	276
	Name index	281
	Subject index	287

Notes on contributors

Derek J. Allison is Associate Professor at the University of Western Ontario. He is editor of *Reform and Relevance in Schooling* (OISE Press 1991). He has contributed articles on principalship to *Educational Administration Quarterly* and chapters on educational administration theory to the *International Handbook of Educational Leadership and Administration* (Kluwer Academic Publishers 1996), on CEOs and Boards of Education in *Effective School District Leadership* (SUNY Press 1995), and on secondary school administration in *Contemporary Educational Issues* (Copp Clark Pitman 1993).

Richard J. Bates is Professor of Education in the Faculty of Education at Deakin University, Australia. He has been Dean of the faculty, and is the first Professor of Education in Australia to have been awarded a personal chair (1985). He has also taught at the London Institute of Education (UK) and Massey University (New Zealand). His international reputation rests primarily on his contributions to the debate over the New Sociology of Education and on his work in developing an alternative tradition of theory and research in educational administration. He has published some sixty journal articles and books. Some of his most recent theoretical titles are *The Bird that Sets Itself on Fire: Thom Greenfield and the Renewal of Educational Administration* (OISE Press 1995), 'Critical theory and education administration' (in C. W. Evers and J. D. Chapman, *Educational Administration: An Australian Perspective*, Allen and Unwin 1995), 'On knowing: Cultural and critical approaches to educational administration' (*Educational Management and Administration*, 1993), 'Conflict, contradiction and crisis' (in M. Muetzelfeldt (ed.) *Society, State and Politics*, Pluto Press 1992), and 'Leadership and the rationalisation of society' (in W. J. Smyth (ed.) *Critical Perspectives on Educational Leadership*, Falmer Press 1989).

Colin W. Evers is a Professor of Education at the University of Hong Kong. Previously, he was an Associate Professor in the Faculty of

Education at Monash University. His teaching and research interests are in educational administration, philosophy of education, and research methodology. Ongoing research projects include the development of a systematic theory of educational administration, as well as of naturalistic conceptions of educational theory. In addition to some seventy papers, he is the author (with Gabriel Lakomski) of three books on educational administration: *Knowing Educational Administration* (1991), *Exploring Educational Administration* (1996), and *Doing Educational Administration* (2000), all published by Pergamon/Elsevier. The ideas in these books have given rise to discussions in three Special Issues of journals, notably *Educational Management and Administration* (1993), *Educational Administration Quarterly* (1996), and the *Journal of Educational Administration* (2001). He has also edited (with J. D. Chapman) *Educational Administration: An Australian Perspective* (Allen and Unwin 1995), and (with K. C. Wong) *Leadership for Quality Schooling* (Routledge/Falmer 2001). As well as serving on a number of editorial boards, he is currently the editor (with K. C. Wong) of the journal *International Studies in Educational Administration*.

William Foster is Professor of Education in the Educational Leadership and Policy Studies Department at Indiana University, Bloomington. He has extensively taught and researched in the areas of school leadership, critical theoretical perspectives on administration, organisation theory, and moral theory in leadership, and has been a Visiting Fellow at the Institute of Education, University of London. He has been on the editorial boards of the *Educational Administration Quarterly* and the *Journal of School Leadership*. He has authored or co-authored over seventeen chapters in books, twelve articles, and two monographs, including *Paradigms and Promises: New Approaches to Educational Administration* (Prometheus Books 1986).

Peter Gronn is Associate Professor of Education and Associate Dean (Teaching) in the Faculty of Education at Monash University. His research interests cover all aspects of leadership, with particular emphasis on learning leadership, the development of leaders, leadership models and types, and the connection between organisational culture, leadership and organisational learning. Recent publications include *The Making of Educational Leaders* (Cassell 1999), and a number of articles on leadership theory in the *Journal of Management Development*, *Educational Management and Administration*, *Educational Administration Quarterly*, and *Leading and Managing*.

Helen M. Gunter is Senior Lecturer in the School of Education at the University of Birmingham. She is the author of *Rethinking Education:*

The Consequences of Jurassic Management (Cassell 1997) and *Leaders and Leadership in Education* (Chapman 2001). She has contributed articles on school organisation, school leadership, and the development of the educational management field to the *Journal of Educational Management and Administration, Educational Review*, the *British Journal of Special Education*, and the *Journal of Educational Administration*.

Carol Harris, who began her career in adult education and music, is now Professor of Leadership Studies at the University of Victoria where she teaches organisation theory and philosophy of leadership. Her recent book, *A Sense of Themselves: Elizabeth Murray's Leadership in School and Community*, reflects her research interest in the intersection of school and adult education. Her articles appear in national publications of the *Canadian Journal of Education*, the *Canadian Journal for the Study of Adult Education*, and the *Canadian Music University Review*, and in international journals such as *Educational Administration Quarterly*, and *Arts Education Policy Review*.

Donald Lang is a retired officer (Military Psychologist) in the Canadian Forces, having held senior command and staff positions. He has lectured in administrative and leadership theory and philosophy, and management studies at Canada's military colleges, the University of Victoria, and the University of Ottawa. His dissertation, 'Values and Commitment: An Empirical Verification of Hodgkinson's Value Paradigm as applied to the Commitment of Individuals to Organizations' (1986) was completed under the direction of Christopher Hodgkinson. Among his recent articles on the philosophy of leadership are 'Values: The ultimate determinant of commitment and legitimacy' (in T. Wyett and G. Reuven (eds) *Legitimacy and Commitment in the Military*, Greenwood Press 1990), 'Transformational leadership is not charismatic leadership: Philosophical impoverishment in leadership continues' (*Human Resource Development Quarterly*, 1991), 'Organizational culture and commitment' (*Human Resource Development Quarterly*, 1992), and 'A new theory of leadership: "Realwert" versus apparent good' (*Educational Management and Administration*, 1999).

Spencer J. Maxcy is a Professor in the Department of Educational Leadership, Research and Counseling at Louisiana State University. He sits on editorial boards and is a reviewer for several educational reform and leadership journals. His most recent research interests centre on pragmatic philosophy and educational leadership theory. He has written extensively on schooling and culture. Recent contributions to educational administration theory include an edited re-release of John Dewey's three major education texts, *John Dewey and Education*

(Thoemmes Press 2002), a textbook, *Ethical School Leadership* (Scarecrow Press 2002), plus numerous articles, papers, and presentations. He is currently involved in a large-scale publishing project dealing with pragmatism and education, a textbook focused on educational policy analysis, and a long-standing sponsored research study dealing with the impacts of online educational leadership courses.

Kristina Mihailova is a recent MA graduate in Political Science from Simon Fraser University. Her background includes an MA degree in English (University of Sofia) with specialisation in stylistics and Elizabethan drama, and considerable experience as broadcaster, editor and translator. Her current academic interests are in the field of international relations, and she has examined foreign policy, post-communist development and regional integration in her Master's thesis, 'Bulgarian foreign policy in Southeastern Europe 1989–2000: From client state to regional activist'.

Peter Ribbins is Emeritus Professor in Educational Management at the University of Birmingham. During his twenty-five years there he held many senior posts including Dean of the Faculty of Education and Continuing Studies. He has also been a local education officer, a schoolteacher and, briefly, worked in industry. He has published some twenty-five books and over a hundred articles and chapters. Over the past twenty years he has edited two academic journals, *Pastoral Care in Education* and *Educational Management and Administration*, and two book series, for Blackwell and Cassell. He was involved in setting up the National Association for Pastoral Care in Education (NAPCE) and the Standing Conference for Research in Educational Leadership and Management (SCRELM) and is Chairman of the British Educational Leadership, Management and Administration Society (BELMAS). He has worked in many countries. His interest in moral and philosophical issues in educational management and leadership is long-standing.

Eugenie A. Samier is Associate Professor of Educational Administration and Leadership Studies at Simon Fraser University. Her research and writing interests are in administrative philosophy and theory, Weberian foundations of administration, theories and models of educational leadership, and comparative educational administration. She currently holds a Guest Researcher position at the Humboldt University of Berlin during research semesters from Simon Fraser University. Her most recent publications include 'Demandarinisation in the new public management: Examining changing administrative authority from a Weberian perspective' (in E. Hanke and W. Mommsen (eds) *Max Webers Herrschaftssoziologie. Studien zu Entstehung und Wirkung*, Mohr/

Siebeck 2001), 'The capitalist ethic and the spirit of intellectualism: The rationalized administration of education' (in *L'éthique Protestante de Max Weber et L'esprit de la Modernité*, Editions de la Maison des Sciences de l'Homme 1997), and several articles on organisational culture and values, and Weberian foundations of administrative theory and ethics in *Educational Management and Administration, Journal of Educational Administration*, and *Educational Administration Quarterly*.

Preface

One measure of the maturity of a discipline is having major contributors to honour through biographical works and Festschriften. Educational Administration has begun to achieve this status, evidenced recently, for example, in Peter Ribbins's co-editing of many of Thom Greenfield's more significant articles in *Greenfield on Educational Administration* (Greenfield and Ribbins 1993). This collection of essays, following the traditional mode of Festschriften, is written to celebrate the 75th birthday of another major thinker – and a friend of Thom Greenfield's – Christopher Hodgkinson.

Chris's impact has been of international scope in the English-speaking world of educational administration and leadership. Throughout his major works, *Towards a Philosophy of Administration* (1978), *The Philosophy of Leadership* (1983), *Educational Leadership: The Moral Art* (1991) and *Administrative Philosophy: Values and Motivations in Administrative Life* (1996), he has challenged the field, perhaps more than any other single individual, to examine its philosophical roots. He may perhaps be 'the more dangerous opponent philosophically,' as Greenfield noted in his discussion of Colin Evers and Gabrielle Lakomski's review of major theories in the field in *Knowing Educational Administration* (Greenfield and Ribbins 1993: 263). Chris's influence has taken two forms. First, he has provided a substantive foundation for educational administration by situating questions of value as central to theory and practice in place of managerial technique. Secondly, he has introduced to educational administrative theory major figures in philosophy and social and political theory whose works provide a touchstone in identifying and formulating the architectonics of a mature and grounded discipline. One can only hope that in a field necessarily professional and applied, this substratum prepared by Chris will make philosophical work in educational administration respectable over subsequent decades as both a scholarly pastime and academic qualification. And, as he intended, as necessary to administrative life, a quality captured in his often-quoted definition of administration as 'philosophy-in-action'. Greenfield summed up Chris's importance as demonstrating 'that a social science of organization can never replace an understanding of administration itself' for 'expressing the power of ancient and modern thought, revealing its essence in pungent human terms' and 'lead[ing] the way to deeper and deeper insights into [management literature]' (Greenfield and Ribbins 1993: 264).

As is also traditional in Festschriften, and to honour the recipient's work, a number of colleagues and former students tackle a topic that the recipient has contributed to most in the field – in this case, the problem of moral values in educational administration and their philosophical grounding. Mitchell maintains that Chris has gained widespread recognition for his work on values: for example, on the use of a value-audit in uncovering one's philosophy of leadership (1990: 69) and on redefining administration as 'philosophy-in-action', bringing the true nature of leadership into the humanities (1990: 155).

While Chris's particular philosophical orientation, strongly leaning towards a Platonist view of valuational theory in hierarchical form, has for some readers objectionable implications for social order, power and authority, his views have occasioned a necessary debate about the legitimacy of philosophy as a grounding discipline for administration. There are two reasons for his importance. First, the development of any field is contained in the liveliness of its critique and argumentation, which he has helped to generate and assist throughout his scholarly career. Secondly, those authors Chris has relied upon, such as Plato and Nietzsche, regardless of any particular interpretation he holds of their works, do provide a continuing meaningful position from which to deliberate upon the essence of administration, its greatest evils, and its greatest potential. For the moral dimension of administrative activity holds its greatest import for social value and human aspiration.

As with all truly influential theorists, Chris's contributions are not solely scholarly, but also personal. Thom Greenfield acknowledged his debt publicly in a conversation with Peter Ribbins (Greenfield and Ribbins 1993), recounting Chris's support at a time when Greenfield was suffering the approbation and marginalisation following his theoretical challenge to the field in the infamous International Intervisitational Programme (IIP) in Bristol in 1974. This was a time of great academic and personal vulnerability for Thom, discussed in Peter Ribbins's contribution to this volume.

My own motivations in initiating this Festschrift are also personal, and echo many of the sentiments expressed by Greenfield, and also by Don Lang, my fellow doctor 'sibling', in his recollections of Chris in 'Christopher Hodgkinson: A Student's Perspective'. In contacting those who know and have worked with Chris most closely in his intellectual ventures, I found no hesitation on their part to contribute to this project (and due to the wondrous properties of e-mail, the project was launched within 48 hours). The measure of respect for him is underscored by the fact that most of the contributors do not share his worldview, or his philosophical disposition in the field. Including this editor.

My own intellectual apprenticeship with Chris carries the same intertwining of effect and scholarly preparation. In a previous dedicatory essay on his 65th birthday and impending retirement, I characterised my graduate years with him as 'The voyage out of Walpurgisnacht' (1993). I have now had almost a decade to reflect on that relationship, in part intellectualised through work on mentorship theory, and have little to add to the initial impressions of that time. My apprenticeship included political lessons – how to navigate the shoals of academic sterility, and the perils of conflict and alliances – in addition to indefatigable critique of my intellectual development (nourished by a mutual love for Belgian chocolate). The only difference now is that, as I fulfil my own aspirations in academia, the debt I owe is much greater – and has transformed from being more deeply intimate to organisational and professional.

In closing this preface, I would like to pay homage in the most deeply felt way that I can. Paraphrasing, and altering only some of the contingencies, from the German philosopher Johann Gottfried Herder's recollection of Immanuel Kant (in Beck 1956: xxii), I dedicate this volume to Chris Hodgkinson:

> I have had the good fortune to know a philosopher. He was my teacher. In his prime he had the happy sprightliness of a youth; he continued to have it even as an older man. His broad forehead, built for thinking, was the seat of an imperturbable wit and joy. Speech, the richest in thought, flowed from his lips. Playfulness, wit, and humour were at his command. His lectures were the most entertaining talks. His mind, which examined Plato, Sun Tzu, the Bhagavad Gita and Upanishads, the Buddha, Aristotle, Machiavelli, Nietzsche, Wittgenstein, and Weil, and investigated the laws of nature of Planck, Einstein, Schrödinger, and Gödel, comprehended equally the newest works of postmodernism . . . and the latest discoveries in science. He weighed them all, and always came back to the unbiased knowledge of nature and to the moral worth of man. The history of men and peoples, natural history and science, mathematics and observation, were the sources from which he enlivened his lectures and conversation. He was indifferent to nothing worth knowing. No cabal, no sect, no desire for fame could ever tempt him in the slightest away from broadening and illuminating the truth. He incited and gently forced others to think for themselves; despotism was foreign to his mind. This man, whom I name with the greatest gratitude and respect, was Christopher Hodgkinson.

Vancouver, August 2002
Eugenie Samier

References

Beck, L. W. (1956) 'Sketch of Kant's life and work', in I. Kant, *Critique of Practical Reason*, New York: Macmillan.
Evers, C. and Lakomski, G. (1991) *Knowing Educational Administration*, London: Pergamon.
Greenfield, T. and Ribbins, P. (eds) (1993) *Greenfield on Educational Administration*, London: Routledge.
Mitchell, J. (1990) *Re-visioning Educational Leadership: A Phenomenological Approach*, New York, Garland.
Samier, E. (1993) 'The voyage out of Walpurgisnacht', *Journal of Educational Administration and Foundations* 8, 1: 62–64.

Acknowledgements

I would like to thank all the participants of this project for their cooperation and trust, and especially my research assistant, Kristina Mihailova, whose patience and good judgement contributed greatly to the success of this project. I would also like to thank Madge Hodgkinson for assistance in providing a recent photograph for the frontispiece.

The final preparation of the manuscript would not have been possible without the financial assistance of Simon Fraser University.

And, to HJG:

> Für dich nur schließen sich die Dichter ein
> und sammeln Bilder, rauschende und reiche,
> und gehn hinaus und reifen durch Vergleiche
> und sind ihr ganzes Leben so allein . . .
> Rainer Maria Rilke, from 'Das Buch von der Pilgerschaft'

Part I
The life and work of Christopher Hodgkinson

Chapter 1

Through the looking-glass with Christopher Hodgkinson

Letters and lessons on life and leadership from Arcadia West

Peter Ribbins

The first letter that I ever received from Christopher Hodgkinson was written in January 1992 at a time when he was looking forward to the prospect of retirement. In it, he warned me to 'Beware of getting into the *Through the Looking-Glass* condition where one has to run faster and faster just to stay put' (21.1.92).[1] In the years that followed, I have come to look forward to his wise and often witty advice. This has come in occasional face-to-face meetings but more often in over seventy letters from him, written mostly in his legible yet spidery handwriting.

In some respects, Hodgkinson was then, and remains now, an unapologetic Luddite. In an early letter he wrote: 'Please forgive this scrawl in response to your beautifully word-processed and lasered letter. One stands in awe of all that technology. But at least I don't need sand to blot this ink; the Japanese are to be thanked for that' (19.10.92). This was not the last such apology. Months later he was again inviting me to: 'Forgive the lack of typescript and ascribe it to archaism, senility, eccentricity, bloody-mindedness, pigheadedness, or some combination of the above' (9.7.93). And two years later: 'Peter Gronn's last lines to me were in obvious pen and ink. I draw great comfort from that because before his seduction into word-processing high technology he was a devout pen-and-ink man. I also note that some small resolution in the US is underway amongst a few ex-hackers who have seen the light and have formed a *Leadite Society*, dedicated to the use of the lead pencil. I know I'm preaching to the unconverted' (23.4.95). He concludes: 'I will stick to my technophobia. As best I can for someone wants to teleconference me into his class next month. Perhaps I could do it on a cellular phone while driving down the Pat-Bay highway and listening to the Ride of the Valkyries?' (15.6.97). As it happens, his latest letter, containing a postscript he describes as 'Hodgkinson's email', shows signs of repentance. In it he acknowledges: 'Yes, yes, I know. One of these days I'll have to succumb to being "wired"' (26.7.02). I wait with bated breath.

In important respects, even before I got to know him, he was, although not with regard to his aversion for certain kinds of technology, preaching to the converted. I had discovered his work more than a decade before I first met him. Someone had sent me 'A new taxonomy of administrative process' suggesting that: 'You might find this interesting.' I did. Meredydd Hughes, Hywel Thomas and I had been struggling with *Managing Education: The System and the Institution* (1985). Part of my task was to consider management and administration. I wrote:

> In a helpful paper . . . the Canadian philosopher Hodgkinson (1980) . . . distinguishes between two levels of activity. Administration, he claims, is a philosophy in action, which becomes activated in two ways: by means of *administrative* processes which are abstract, philosophical, qualitative, strategic and humanistic in essence, and by means of *managerial* processes which are concrete, practical, pragmatic, quantitative and technological in nature.
> (Hughes, Ribbins and Thomas 1985: xii)

I admired the precision with which Hodgkinson developed his argument.

Years later we met. Thomas Greenfield was the go-between. Between 1989 and 1992, as his health declined, we worked on *Greenfield on Educational Administration: Towards a Humane Science* (Greenfield and Ribbins 1993). In our conversations, the depth of his personal and professional regard for Hodgkinson was evident. I expressed a desire to meet his friend and Greenfield suggested that one way of doing this would be to teach a summer school at the University of Victoria. He proposed this to Hodgkinson and in 1992 it happened. The course I was to teach was in Hodgkinson's area so I wrote to him. Among other things, I was worried that although my interest in philosophy was long-standing, I saw myself as, at best, an enthusiastic amateur. His response was consoling. First, regarding those I would teach: 'Your students will be eager, enthusiastic, and very hard working.' Second, about the course programme: 'Absolutely nothing hard and fast. Everything set in blancmange.' Third, about its orientation: 'We interpret philosophy in a sense utterly alien from the pedantries of academic squiggle logic and linguistic atom-splitting. One thinks more of the ancient sense of practical wisdom.' Such whimsy, as I was to learn, can mask a depth of conviction. In what follows, I will draw on his letters, on our conversations, and on his own writings and the writings of others, to attempt a partial portrait of the public scholar and the private person. Selecting themes for this from amongst the many that could serve to focus such an account has not been easy. In compensation, locating his place and assessing his significance to the field of educational administration and leadership have been less difficult.

Early life and education

In an editorial introducing a special edition of the *Journal of Educational Administration and Foundations* (1993, 8: 3) devoted to his retirement from the University of Victoria (UVic) in 1993, Yvonne Martin, as friend and colleague, writes of Hodgkinson that:

> As a person he has been a sort of paradox. He is clearly very private, elegantly sartorial, somewhat detached, elusive, and latterly very provocative; yet always kindly, affectionate, humorous, and a delight at a section meeting. How has he influenced me personally? I strive to develop Chris' equanimity, humility, and generosity of spirit even in the clinches.
>
> (Martin 1993: 7)

At the time, when I could not claim to know him very well, I thought this assessment affectionate and accurate. A decade later, with the benefit of substantial and regular correspondence with him, I could not improve on it. Given this, what do we know of his early life and the influences that formed him as a man and scholar and shaped his career?

These were amongst the themes that I tried to explore with him in an interview undertaken for the purpose reported in my contribution to the special edition entitled 'Conversations with a *condottiere* of administrative value: Some reflections on the life and work of Christopher Hodgkinson' (Ribbins 1993). It soon became tantalisingly evident that by most criteria he has enjoyed an unusually interesting life. 'Tantalising' because it also quickly became apparent that he was going to be highly selective in what he would be willing to tell me of it. His response to some of my questions was sometimes cautious and occasionally gnomic. For example, when I asked him about his work as a professional economist he responded: 'I want to draw a veil around that experience' (Ribbins 1993: 16). More to the point, earlier in our conversation he had warned that: 'I am not going to give you all the details of my life and career for a variety of complex reasons' (Ribbins 1993: 14). Much later in our relationship, I began better to understand his reservations. In my studies of the lives and careers of school principals I had, following Sigmund Freud, and more specifically Manfred Kets de Vries (1989) and Howard Gardner (1995), long been interested in the ways a leader's early years shaped her or his personality (see Rayner and Ribbins 1999). In commenting on this, Hodgkinson managed to both offer and partially withdraw his imprimatur in three pithy sentences:

> I liked the way you worked in infancy and upbringing (in *Headteachers and Leadership in Special Education*). Although I can't quite go entirely

along with potty-determinism there's no doubt the formative years do set the course. Kets de Vries and Freud still have a lot going for them.

(3.5.99)

Rightly or wrongly, I have come to see the key words as: 'I can't quite go entirely along with potty-determinism'.

More importantly, the comment quoted is typical of the kind of supportive yet critical relationship that fellow scholars might expect from Hodgkinson – or as Greenfield has so much more elegantly put it, he offers 'the steel of intellectual argument and the hand of friendship' (Greenfield and Ribbins 1993: 274). The circumstance in which the comment was made was a small part of a substantial, and thoughtful, response to a three-level model for research into leadership, especially that of the school principal, that I had put to him (see Ribbins 1999). It gave me plenty to think about:

> I am thoroughly impressed as well as quite fascinated by your stimulating thoughts on methodology. *Pace* Nietzsche I have long maintained that (a) all autobiography is lies (one cannot help self-justificatory editing); (b) all biography is biased (one must reject the dogma of immaculate perception) and; (c) all ethnography is hypentical (the dogma in spades! All anthropology is not only incredibly tedious but also vacuous . . .) to combine these three lines of attack on the discovery of the truth in leadership seems *prima facie* a lost cause whether one calls it triangulation or contextualisation. But this is only *prima facie*.
>
> (5.10.95)

Having noted this, he went on to contextualise his own objection, noting that:

> But I talk of 'greats' and perhaps the very strength of your proposal lies in its dealing (generally) with 'non-greats'. As scope lessens perhaps command can increase. In any case I'm convinced that yours is the way – perhaps the only way to go – the quibbling is only about difficulties. And none ever said the truth came easily. In the end though we be thrust back into the arms of Nietzsche: 'There is no truth, only interpretations'. In that case let us get ever more sophisticated, ever more subtle, ever more *conscious* interpretations.
>
> (5.10.95)

All this notwithstanding, in our interview, his boyhood was described with dispatch and I have not learnt much more about this in the years that followed:

I have no shame about being born in Blackpool in Lancashire. I left at the age of 3 and have not been back. Then we moved to Eire where I was initiated into the mysteries of bilingualism and biculturalism and encountered nationalism in the form of early brushes with the IRA. We then moved to Scotland, to Glasgow, where I found myself fighting Scottish Protestants. After Scotland we seemed to travel all over the world including the place of your birth – India.

(Ribbins 1993: 14)

In her editorial, Yvonne Martin stresses this aspect of his early life, noting that: 'Before he began his career in education Christopher had extensive global travel and experience on all continents, spending protracted time in Asia, Australia and Latin America . . .' (Martin 1993: 7). Given this, he must have experienced schooling in a number of different cultural contexts but, to the best of my knowledge, other than in the enigmatic and oblique observations quoted earlier, he has said little about this. He has, however, been more forthcoming about his university education and its influence on his attitudes and thinking. Some of this, and in particular his continuing attachment to economics, I have found rather surprising.

Economics and philosophy

Summarising his experience as a student in higher education, Martin notes that he was 'educated at the University of London (Economics and Political Science, 1959) and the University of British Columbia (Educational Administration, 1968), spending a year at Berkeley' (Martin 1993: 7). In reflecting on this, Hodgkinson remarked that:

My maternal discipline is economics, which is enough to sour most people for life. But economics should be part of the curriculum for any education person, if only because you cannot understand the contemporary world without some grasp, however elementary, of economic logic . . . if you are going to do any of the social sciences, do economics. It helps in all kinds of ways. For example, if you want to understand organisations and their limitations.

(Ribbins 1993: 15)

I was surprised to learn this, although a closer reading of some of his work should probably have alerted me to this possibility. I can only say in mitigation that in our extensive correspondence, I can recall very few references to the 'gloomy discipline'. Of these, the most notable was the observation that:

> As an ex-economist I cannot help but intuit that the Chinese are next up for the rot to set in – after all, those chaps invented bureaucracy and corruption while we were still running around wearing paint. Still, the house of Globalism may not entirely collapse, just run up enough repair bills to keep us all broke.
>
> (29.11.97)

What his letters, and talk, are full of are references to philosophy. But, even on this, Hodgkinson's views, as he expressed them in our initial correspondence and subsequent published conversation, were, to me anyway, disconcerting. I had assumed his parent discipline to be philosophy. This may be understandable given the themes of his early publications (Hodgkinson 1975, 1978). On learning it was not, I asked if he regretted this? His response was bracing:

> I am not a philosopher, although, I have much truck with academic philosophy. I know the business from the academic side but am proud to be able to say that I have never taken a course in philosophy in my life . . . You don't need to have taken a course in philosophy to become a philosophologist – you only need a library card or paperbacks.
>
> (Ribbins 1993: 17)

In developing this view, Hodgkinson expressed a profound scepticism for much modern academic philosophy noting, for example, that: 'Surely there must be a special place in hell reserved for such pseudo-academics: some nice little spot where they can get together and talk Derrida-Lacan-Foucault' (25.1.96).

His views echo those so forcefully expressed by Bryan Magee in *Confessions of a Philosopher*: 'I was trained in Oxford philosophy without ever subscribing to it. I seem to have learned to do it as well as some practitioners, but I never believed in its validity *as a conception of philosophy* . . . My most deeply felt criticism of it is that it trains its practitioners in quickness and cleverness while precluding depth . . . I could never take seriously the view that the subject matter of philosophy was linguistic, and this was something that all the various forms of Oxford philosophy had in common' (Magee 2000: 42–3). For Hodgkinson, such contemporary academic philosophy, 'as far as the man in the street or the administrator at his desk is concerned, has largely withered on the vine. Its practitioners are into squiggle logic; they write for each other, they have become esoteric, they have lost relevance in much of their work' (Ribbins 1993: 19).

What, then, of the relationship between economics and philosophy? On this, I was once unwise enough to suggest to Hodgkinson that his work was essentially philosophical but did not seem evidently informed by economics. His response was:

> Yes to the first and no to the second. I have never quite figured this out but whilst economics is not philosophical, it is somehow fundamental to philosophy. You have PPE courses in the UK. That seems a happy triad. One I can buy into as good preparation for the administrator. Even so philosophy and economics are separated. Yet most great economists from Adam Smith, who . . . held a chair in moral philosophy, onwards have dealt in philosophical ideas . . . Even so, my labours have been in a vineyard I might dare call the philosophy of administration.
> (Ribbins 1993: 18)

To understand how this came about we need to know something about his career.

Career highlights

Before Hodgkinson took up his first post in education, he 'saw service as a communications officer for H.M. Government and various Commonwealth, Colonial and Foreign Services. In Canada he had experience in business administration, labour relations, and as an economist for the Canadian Federal Government' (Martin 1993: 7). In 1962 he was appointed to his first post in education, as a teacher of social studies in Hamilton Junior Secondary School in North Vancouver. This was not, it seems, a straightforward progression:

> I had a sneaking desire to try my hand at education, but it took time to overcome the resistance of those around me. They saw it as a dead-end, a low status occupation. I prevailed on the grounds that it was just an experiment. If I did not like it I could move on. But I did like it. So things led gradually but automatically to where I am now.
> (Ribbins 1993: 16)

It is not clear over whom Hodgkinson had to prevail, but as he describes it, 'my time in high school was one of the most fulfilling periods of my life . . . I enjoyed my time there – the young people I met were full of *bonhomie*, of the spirit of life, of youth and of innocence' (Ribbins 1993: 16). But he is realistic, 'I don't think I would have the energy to go back and teach in them now. Ten months of ten-hour days is somehow no longer such an attractive idea' (Ribbins 1993: 16). And, much as he enjoyed working in secondary schools, this did not inhibit him, seven years later, from segueing 'in easy stages from school teacher to university teacher' (Ribbins 1993: 16).

A key aspect of these 'easy stages' was a decision to undertake postgraduate studies in educational administration at the Universities of British Columbia (UBC) and Berkeley during the late 1960s. In explaining this, Hodgkinson referred again to his debt to economics:

> I did my dissertation on organisational values. So this is something I have been interested in since the outset . . . probably a heritage of my earlier studies. The study of economics disabuses you of the naïve idea that everything can be reduced to a desire for wealth . . . So economics gave birth to my interest in values . . . I wanted then, and I want now, to understand if I can, what makes people tick and what makes administrators tick.
>
> (Ribbins 1993: 15)

On completing his studies at UBC, he came to Victoria. At the time of his appointment,

> the education department . . . consisted of just one man. The year after I arrived he said he was going to retire . . . for a time I was on my own – a one-man department with no political or other support. I survived but not without learning a great deal about internal organisational (and presumably university) politics.
>
> (Ribbins 1993: 16)

If Hodgkinson has enjoyed thinking and teaching about administration, there is reason to doubt if he has cared much for being an administrator.

Being an administrator

Hodgkinson has not entirely escaped administration. Early in his career in education he was promoted to the post of departmental head of economics and history at West Vancouver Secondary School. He did not do this for long before moving to the Faculty of Education at the University of Victoria. Many years later, he retired as a full professor and loaded with academic honours. As Martin describes these, they include: 'Canada Council Fellow (1975), Visiting Professor at McGill University (1978), Distinguished Visiting Professor at the Ontario Institute for Studies in Education (1980), Social Sciences and Humanities Research Council of Canada Fellow (1982), Senior Research Scholar at the University of Cambridge (1982–83), Fellow of the Ontario Institute of Studies in Education (1985), and Lecturer at the Matsushita School of Management and

Government in Japan (1988). He was nominated for the Henry Luce Chair of Ethics and Public Policy at Harvard (1980)' (Martin 1993: 7). What is 'missing (from all this) is some comment on Chris' impact on educational administration at the University of Victoria and in British Columbia' (Martin 1993: 9) and beyond.

His institutional and local impact was profound: 'the educational administration team has been proud of its association with Professor Hodgkinson . . . His major ideas have become a unifying force in our programs in educational administration, and have helped to give them their distinguished characteristics . . . colleagues have recognised the worth of his contributions and have reflected them in their teaching to the benefit of our students' (Martin 1993: 9). But Martin also notes 'his disdain for "sordid managerial details"' (Martin 1993: 9). His leadership seems to have been intellectual rather than organisational. No doubt, from time to time Hodgkinson assumed administrative roles at the university, but Martin makes no mention of this.

In so far as he did, I suspect that Hodgkinson may not have enjoyed this much. Most of the evidence for this is indirect. But that it is so, is hinted at by both what Martin says and what she does not say. In addition, in one of his letters to me, his distaste for the exercise of administrative responsibility seems to be reflected in an account he gave of his experience as a chairperson.[2] As he put it:

> It confirms Caesar's notion that Gaul is divided into three parts only the parts here are those who give a damn, those who don't give a damn, and those who are incapable of giving a damn. Respectively, the damned, the damning, and the damnable.
>
> (8.6.97)

Now it could be that this unhappy experience might better be explained in terms of those who happened to be involved rather than as a necessary consequence of anything inherently undesirable about administering. But Hodgkinson's inherently inimical view of the lot of the administrator is more or less undisguised in a series of sometimes sceptical and occasionally sympathetic remarks he made to me regarding my term as the Dean of a Faculty. Three must serve to give a flavour of his views:

> I am not sure whether (being a Dean) counts as a world to conquer having seen a lot of people conquered by it . . .
>
> (21.7.93)

> Governing *in absentia* [I had told him I was worried about being away from the Faculty at a sensitive time] is a highly developed academic

art. Also, in the words of one of my mentors, it's difficult to hit a moving target.

(26.5.96)

As for yourself . . . I note that you are already in the Byzantine coils (of deanship). But you can always draw comfort from the undeniable truth that you are keeping other colleagues out of the job.

(7.8.96)

I am led to believe from all this, what I knew anyway from reading his work, that Hodgkinson's attitudes on such matters are unashamedly Platonist. Accordingly he regards administration as far too important to be left to those who are unduly eager to do it.

This notwithstanding, how useful are his writings to those who would administer? Most praise their accessibility and relevance. In a review symposium on *Educational Leadership: The Moral Art*, Colin Evers stresses their 'sheer readability, sustained by Hodgkinson's felicitous writing style, his taste for aphorisms, and his sure sense of the practical . . .' (Evers 1993: 261). But Richard Williams, then Professor and Executive Director of the Puget Sound Educational Consortium in Washington, writing from the perspective of the practising administrator, suggests its 'style doesn't fit very well within the schedules of busy administrators . . . (Its) message is far too important to limit it to academics . . . The challenge is . . . how this might be translated into more understandable text . . . while retaining the rich texture and vast intellectual sources that support the argument. As with practising the art of moral leadership, it won't be easy – but nothing worthwhile ever is' (Williams 1993: 258). Interestingly, Michael Marland, the only full-time practising administrator, albeit one who has published more books than most academics, contributing to the symposium, had no such reservations:

> In the busy days of a school head's life . . . the pressure to be methodical can too easily become the pressure to be mechanical. Hodgkinson is always practical, but his great strength as a thinker and writer is that he sees the inspiration in administration. It is very rare to be able to say of even very good books on educational administration as one can of this: it is inspiring.
>
> (Marland 1993: 263)

Arcadia West, Arcadia and elsewhere

Hired to teach educational administration at UVic, Hodgkinson had not expected an extended stay. As he explains:

> Calgary is to Edmonton as Victoria is to Vancouver. When I came, the conviction on the mainland was that Victoria was a backwater. A place where you read the obituary columns to check if you were still alive. A place where nothing happened. A place which did not compare with the mega-university of UBC. I shared those prejudices. It was with some reluctance that I came. I saw it as a stopping point before I went on to a grander career at a university in the USA.
>
> (Ribbins 1993: 17)

This was not, in the event, how things turned out. When several years later, with his reputation soaring in the wake of the publication of his influential books, Hodgkinson was approached by one of the most prestigious of American universities, he chose not to pursue this possibility. Had this option been available earlier in his career he might have taken a different course. As retirement beckoned, in accounting for his extended sojourn in Victoria, he identifies wryly two very different reasons for this:

> In those days the mobility of the university community was enormous. But soon after I got here the big freeze set it. I found myself cast away, washed up on a beach in Victoria. Ironically, now this place is regarded as almost as desirable as a south sea island. Like Gaugin, everybody wants to come to Lotus Land. Now people at UBC are fighting to get to UVic. The tables are turned.
>
> (Ribbins 1993: 17)

In many respects, and by background and by predilection, Hodgkinson is a worldly and cosmopolitan figure, but some of his deepest loyalties are fundamentally personal and local.

Although he enjoys travel, if not always travelling, and knows much about many countries, his devotion to Victoria and Canada, if conditional, is considerable. Thus, if for him 'Canada continues to be the ultimate politically correct nation – much to my distaste – but there is little I can do about it other than grumble' (18.3.01), in much of his correspondence Victoria is described either as 'Lotus Land', as above, or more commonly, as 'Arcadia West'.

> It's a shame you will miss AERA – not for AERA of course but for San Francisco. It used to be my favourite city but, like all the post-modern world, it has deteriorated. Victoria on the other hand, being resolutely pre-modern, seems to be improving.
>
> (5.2.95)

> Canada is spacious and the protoplasm is thinner on the ground – the traffic and the living is easy – but the emotional air is thinner and the

intellectual climate is definitely inferior to that of the upper reaches of the US and the UK.

(16.10.94)

If Victoria is 'Arcadia West', 'Arcadia' is England. Hodgkinson's affection for the country of his and his wife Madge's birth remains undiminished by time if not unaffected by history:

We are back in Arcadia West after an enjoyable holiday in the real Arcadia. Madge's brother . . . took us to Somerset (to Berrow near Burnham-on-Sea) where it was glory to walk six miles over golden sands and drink in the silence of a 16th century seaside church.

(4.9.94)

There's 'Cool Britannia'. I confess to some queasiness about this, and Tony Blair. He seems like the archetypal Yuppie – a sort of Puritanical Clinton. One thing about Bill Clinton – no one is ever going to accuse him of Puritanism.

(27.12.97)

Whilst he approves of the emotional and intellectual climate of the United States, albeit in its 'upper reaches', Hodgkinson is less enamoured of its politics: 'What can one do with a nation that gives a state funeral to Richard Nixon? *Mit der Dummheit kampfen Gotter selbst vergebens*! None of this is intended to be anti-American. On the contrary I'm an Americanophile' (27.7.94). He expresses a fondness for numerous other countries, usually accompanied with a barbed reservation: 'You will like Australia, I fancy, even if it is going Republican' (25.4.93). And, having noted the antiquity of their civilisation, he goes on to note of the Chinese that they 'are inclined to eat anything that lives and moves and can be lured near a wok' (21.7.93). Nor, despite his admiration of its great philosophers, do the Germans escape entirely. In remarking on the 'Teutonic style', he quotes a colleague as having said to him, '"In Germany there has to be plenty of words, otherwise it doesn't count." Nietzsche, most certainly, would not agree' (3.3.96). India, however, may be an exception: 'I am reading an amazing and enthralling novel by Vikram Seth that is called *A Suitable Boy*. I recommend it to you. Its about the India that we both know and love – a great masterpiece' (25.7.93).

In praise of retirement

If he loves India, Hodgkinson adores 'retirement'. Not for him the conclusion of a career spiralling from 'disenchantment' (Day and Bakioglu 1996) into 'divestiture' (Gronn 1999) that some discern. There is something of a conspiracy of silence about what retirement can mean for those of us who have made a life as academics in higher education. For this reason, but also because he has much to say about it that is wise and entertaining, I will treat this phase of Hodgkinson's career at some length.

Anticipating retirement

In all the time that I have known Hodgkinson personally, he was either anticipating the prospect of retirement or had actually retired. His letters are full of references extolling the virtues of this happy state and he rarely misses a chance to recommend it to others. He writes of this even more often than of the joys of philosophy, although for him this could be because the enjoyment of the one (retirement) has enabled the further pursuit of the other (philosophy). His first letter to me, having offered some advice, acknowledged that in doing so he was speaking 'with the smug self-satisfaction of the impending retiree' (21.1.92). Returning to this theme some years later he concluded that:

> My present prejudice, hardening by the minute, is if it comes to a clear-cut choice between liberty and luxury: choose the former. I used to subscribe to Sophie Tucker's wisdom that 'rich is better' but I'm coming around to the view that 'freedom is better still'.
>
> (27.12.97)

In understanding his attitude to retirement, a comment he made some years later seems relevant. This was underpinned by a sort of fatalism, one that stressed the need to make the most of things as they are and not to pine for what might be:

> How time slips away! At an ever-accelerating rate as one approaches the exit. Someone pointed out to me recently that it was a pity one could not save one's youth until retirement. On the other hand if one did have it, youth that is, I'm quite sure one would waste it just as uselessly at any point in the life-cycle. If there is a moral to all this I'm not sure what it is other than to accept the ancient fatuous and vacuous (but true) *Carpe diem*.
>
> (8.7.97)

Taken as a whole, however, his views on retirement are rather more ironic than this last, as in his report that: 'They gave me a plaque [at the Edmonton CASEA Conference in 2000]. You *know* you're dead when they start handing those things out' (25.6.00). But, he also has much to say about retirement that is a good deal more ebullient or reflective than this.

Understanding retirement

Hodgkinson's observations on this theme include a reflection on the general problem of retirement. This, he argues, 'speaking from experience' and also 'as an economist', is fundamentally *'psychological* not economic':

> Included in this, of course, is the problem of *role*. In academe we are blessed and cursed compared to other professions. On the one hand we over-identify with such self-images as scholar, teacher, administrator, intellectual, writer, etc. On the other hand we don't just cut out on retirement but extend the umbilical cord indefinitely if we so wish – gradually attenuating and adjusting to the new (shrinking) horizons. In this regard I've been lucky for the first few years were taken up with completing the last book and the connection with teaching is never truly severed.
>
> (3.8.98)

Having retired for almost a decade, he now feels in a position to propose a tentative natural history of retirement as follows:

> Observing my fellow retirees I have noticed a pattern. First, fine careless raptures and cruises (avoid cruise ships like the plague). Then golf, gin and grandchildren (the three 'G's'). Then depression. Then deep depression. Then loss of faculties and finally death. Not necessarily in that order. Quite a few of my younger colleagues have popped off. And horrific medical accidents occur. To all of which my maxim is *Dum vivemus, vivamus* (While we are living let us *live*). I include the translation in view of your having failed to master Greek while you had the chance.
>
> (12.6.01)[3]

Making the most of retirement

Hodgkinson also stresses the need to make the best of the opportunities that retirement allows for enjoyment, for furthering one's education, for taking on new projects, and for completing old ones:

> Enjoy retirement. Enjoy the sheer liberty of it, a liberty that I've employed to indulge in the purest Greek sense of a 'liberal education'. Except that my liberal curriculum has been largely a catch-up on the neglected *scientific* aspects of my education: such exotica as biology, astrophysics, anthropology, physics, maths, . . .
>
> (12.6.2001)

In fact, a belated self-education in science has in practice been only one of the many aspects of Hodgkinson's continuing programme of liberal education. This is a theme to which I will return shortly, but before doing so I should stress that his letters have been full of enthusiastic, if sometimes critical, reports on the reading he had been doing. In this context, I can do no better than to begin by endorsing his view that 'reading is the one pleasure that never fails' (12.6.01). But, on second thought, perhaps there are others?

In praise of reading

Hodgkinson's views on contemporary fiction in the English language could easily form the subject of a substantial chapter in its own right. This is not to suggest that I agree with all his observations. Thus, for example, in response to the torrent of texts recommended in his letters, I have occasionally suggested something in return. One such was Jane Austen. His reaction was somewhat equivocal, but I was glad to learn that Madge shares my devotion to this most incomparable of English miniaturists:

> We did see *Pride and Prejudice* and both liked it and I've bought a copy of *Emma* to read later . . . So you can conclude that we are doing our bit for the cause. Madge of course has read all of her and loved it . . . I'm a novice and still nurture suspicions of it all being high class . . . Barbara Cartland but I must concede that any fiction that's never been out of print for two hundred years must have *something*.
>
> (25.1.96)

His suggestions in this genre have been very varied. In reporting on them, I have had to be very selective. They have embraced best-sellers, for example, Jostein Gaarder's *'Sophie's Choice* – I may use it as a text for uneducated graduate students' – but have largely been drawn from the heavyweight end of the canon. He reserves his highest praise for Anthony Powell (*'A Dance to the Music of Time* . . . An overwhelming tour de force. The greatest novel of our century . . . You must read it. But take it very slowly. Let the surprises mount' (8.7.97)) and William Trevor ('I have just finished 1,000 pages of *Collected Stories* . . . I have always admired him as a great Irish genius, better than Joyce in my judgement but a hyper-realist and unrelentingly pessimistic' (7.5.96)). Amongst the others described appreciatively are Iris Murdoch (*'Metaphysics as a Guide to Morals* . . . rambling . . . but full of insights if you pick through the chaff' (5.2.95)), Pat Barker (*'Regeneration, Eye in the Door,* and the shattering *Ghost Road'* (3.3.99)), Tom Wolfe (*'A Man in Full* . . . You want to know America?

Read and weep or become a stoic' (25.6.99)), Frank McCourt ('*Angela's Ashes* . . . I know it's true and supposed to be tragic but it was the funniest book I have read. The classroom scenes alone were sidesplitting. To appreciate it, of course, one needs to know Holy Mother Ireland' (9.5.00)) and David Lodge ('I'm reading *Therapy* (a recommendation from Don Willower). There were parts in it that had me in an agony of laughter' (7.8.96)).

In praise of science and theology

This rich tide of advice has greatly benefited my own continuing liberal education. But I have also valued Hodgkinson's many suggestions for nonfictional reading and his observations on a variety of scholarly themes, particularly in so far as these are related to his own ideas and writing. Two examples must suffice to indicate the breadth and originality of this project. The first focuses on connections between science and religion. In some cases, this is oblique:

> Mathematics is not equivalent to numbers any more than literature is equivalent to words. In fact, like philosophy, it is not at all clear what mathematics is. Russell had a good time with this question. Given its numinous quality, a piety towards mathematics is at least as respectable as a belief in the bodily assumption of the Virgin Mary.
>
> (15.6.96)

In others it is more direct:

> I am glad to hear that you are reading the *Bhagavad-Gita* (the translation by Christopher Isherwood is best). You'll see how nicely it connects with cosmology in Chapter VIII. Very definitely Big Bang and Black Hole stuff. Interesting how the Dawkins and Hawkings of the world so strenuously resist any kind of theological interpretations or metaphors. What are they resisting?
>
> (19.10.92)

Some years on, he returned to this last theme:

> It has always intrigued me that Big Bang cosmology is perfectly accommodated in Vedantic philosophy. *The Bhagavad Gita*, for example, talks of the Day and Night of Brahman, a macrocosmic evolution and involution that fits with current notions of Bangs and Black Holes.
>
> (25.1.96)

Later still, seeking to locate himself in the discourse between philosophy and theology (rather than between science and theology), he concludes that he might best be described as a 'Nietzschean Vedantist'.

> Someone has given me the new Catholic Catechism and I am ploughing my way through it. Respectfully of course, but also trying to bridge the gap (chasm, gulf, void) between philosophy and theology. This is very difficult. As John Paul II constantly states, 'It is a great mystery'. If it is a mystery to him then what is it to the struggling laity? But to get back to [a mutual friend] another remarkable enigma: a devoutly religious Christian Freudian. It's hard to top that for an oxymoron. But then you might say that I myself am a Nietzschean Vedantist so (we) have something in common. To quote Emerson, 'A concern for consistence is the hobgoblin of small minds'.
>
> (21.12.96)

The second focuses on the merits of possible links between Hodgkinson's values-based theories, notions on free will and determinism, and ideas that draw from socio-biology and bio-ethics. At the time of his letter the relevance of all this to educational administration and leadership was just beginning to be debated within the field:

> I shall not prophesy but will resort instead to an esoteric philosophical maxim to which I deeply subscribe: Your being attracts your life. 'Being' here referring to something like one's essential nature, an essence that may not be accessible to one's conscious daily self. Yes, it is a form of determinism but – the nearer I approach the final exit – the more convinced I become that my philosophical focus on will is justified. And the more certain that we have very few degrees of freedom, if any. Or, to put it differently, we are far more mechanical (at the psychological level) than we realise. In sum, our illusions of choice are just that – choices are made for us; 'will' is the end product of a complex internal unacknowledged calculus – there's plenty of it, all right, but is it ever *free*? Paul Begley must be tuned in to this frequency also for the other week he couriered me a copy of Edward O. Wilson's latest book *Consilience*. I have been wanting to get to grips with Wilson, socio-biology, and bio-ethics for some time. This, of course, is a form of determinism with which I only partially agree. So long as there is *any* degrees of freedom then Type I and IIA values retain some legitimacy and possibility.
>
> (31.5.98)

Shortly afterwards, he reported that: 'I am now plunged into Wilson's book. It is very, very good and beautifully written even though I deny his thesis. It will motivate me to take up my pen and write again' (6.7.96). Two years later he described *Consilience* as providing

> me with a life's work . . . [It] is a hallmark of the new-scientism but behind Wilson lurk more dangerous characters such as Dawkins, and the arch-fiend . . . Daniel Dennett. The implications for the practice of educational administration are at the moment distant but the movement feeds into the general condition of postmodernism and nothing could be more real for the educator in an anorak than that.
>
> (29.11.98)

His ambition was 'to write the definitive polemic blasting evolutionary biology and all its offshoots out of the firmament'. Regrettably, he was to 'find after a lot of false starts and wasted effort that the job had already been done, over and over, by E.O. Wilson's disciplinary colleagues and others'. Even so, he concludes that: 'this too was an education' (12.7.01) and one which led him in an associated direction:

> I'm reading genetics. It's increasingly clear that we now have information overload. We know more and more about less and less. I find biology a horrific subject – wonderful but terrifying, and not conducive to peace of mind. My physician friend tells me it, and the art of medicine as well, is all about attitude. Apparently the correct professional attitude is roughly, 'You can't do a damn thing about it anyway, so relax'. I try. As Woody Allen says, 'Don't regard death as an ending. Think of it as a very effective way of cutting down on expenditures'.
>
> (23.10.01)

I have labelled Hodgkinson as something of a technophobe. To an extent this should be taken as tongue in cheek. What I do not suggest, as has been mooted, is that he is anti-science. On this, he has made his position perfectly clear:

> Not that science, as such, was the enemy. Who can ever be against science *qua* science? It is the greatest post-enlightenment achievement of the species . . . But it was the pseudo-quasi-rationalization and ideologizing of science, scientism, which was abhorrent: the scientists amongst us (and they are still very much amongst us) were our anathema in the same way that philosophologists were and are in philosophy proper.
>
> (Hodgkinson in press)

To the best of my knowledge, nobody has ever suggested that he is antiphilosophy.

In praise of philosophy

If, for Hodgkinson, reading is a pleasure that never fails, so too, it seems, is philosophy. As he puts it himself, 'I am happy and am consoled endlessly (like Boethius) by the pleasures of philosophy' (9.1.00). This may be so, but it is possible to discern an element of obligation in his attitude to philosophy along with the pleasure. Thus he writes: 'I am trying to read some cognitive science, AI stuff (e.g. Dennett, *Consciousness Explained*) and it is *not* fun. Sheer agony in fact, but I feel it my philosophical duty to critique and acquaint myself with enough' (26.4.94). But there are also indications that he regards other aspects of the philosopher's life as potentially more entertaining. On the one hand he takes his Socratic responsibilities seriously: 'I continue my task of corrupting the youth of Athens at UVic and generally, with Madge, enjoying increasingly the concept of retirement' (5.10.95). On the other it is evident that he still enjoys being provocative in his lecturing and writing when the opportunity occurs:

> We're off to Toronto . . . I shall, sort of, be representing the Antichrist. The OISE lot are having me in . . . the title of my main address is *Nietzsche, Postmodernism, and the Decline of Just About Everything*. It should be fun – poking the stick into the cage again – I'll let you know how it goes.
>
> (16.10.94)

> You old slave driver, my contribution to *EMA* is to be in your hands by August. Well, I'll try . . . The theme I am toying with at the moment is 'Administration and the Will to Power' or something like that. Naturally old Fred N. would have a part in it and it is a given that it would not be politically correct. Stop me now if that should violate the editorial canons.
>
> (25.1.96)

Nietzsche continues to occupy a good deal of Hodgkinson's attention. In recent years, he has sought to locate this in a wider context. As he puts it: 'I am glued (simultaneously) to Nietzsche, Heidegger and Wittgenstein. They all seem to be saying the same things. And not a bit of it politically correct' (no date, but 1996) and 'I am currently reading and re-reading Heidegger, Nietzsche and Wittgenstein simultaneously; I find this fruitful of insight and not without pleasure' (19.1.97). Some months later, he confessed to be 'still grinding away at Heidegger–Nietzsche–Wittgenstein with increasing esteem for H and less and less for W. N remains *numero uno*, or should I say *Nummer Eins*?' (8.6.97).

In praise of writing

If reading has occupied much of Hodgkinson's time in retirement, so too has writing. As the past few pages indicate, he has been engaged in several projects, not all of which have been pursued to completion. One that has is his latest book, published in 1996, on *Administrative Philosophy: Values and Motivations in Administrative Life*. As he described it: 'Much of the work if not all will be familiar to you but it is a consolidation of my thought over the years . . . it is a sort of *sedimentation*; a last "Message to Garcia", and no doubt "a voice crying in the wilderness"' (3.3.96).

His letters stress that writing such books does not get any easier, even in retirement. In compensation, the joy of final completion remains as keen as ever:

> The albatross of Pergamon grows heavier about my neck with each passing day. Still eight chapters (out of a possible dozen or so) are now done in first draft and, to quote Macbeth, 'I am in blood stepped in so far that, should I wade no more, returning were as tedious as go o'er'.
>
> (5.2.95)

> I am in the post-partim relief stage, having dispatched copies of the completed MS to Pergamon. This along with an astonishing little technobauble, a so-called disc not much larger than a dollar upon which is inscribed in infinite detail the entire magnum opus . . . Sort of like putting the Lord's Prayer on the head of a pin. Diminishing, rather, or is it simply putting all that agony into perspective.
>
> (25.1.96)

However, the pain of writing books is soon forgotten and so I was not surprised to hear five years later of another project. As he described it:

> I am about 100 pages into a very tentative and projected new book that might run to over 300 pages. Writing a book is like climbing a mountain, the higher you climb the less oxygen, the more fatigue, and the harder it gets. Even when you reach the summit you realise with horror that you have to come all the way down again.
>
> (12.5.01)

I do not know what this book is to be about and I did not enquire about the progress that he has made on it until after I had begun writing this chapter. The last I heard was that 'I am weighed down by the pregnancy of this book I told you about . . . it gives me no rest' (26.7.02).

Nor have I had the nerve to ask about an earlier idea that he once raised with me some years ago. As I recall it, the context was the production of a special edition, planned for the autumn of 1994, of the journal *Educational Management and Administration* dedicated to a discussion of Greenfield's only book. At the time Hodgkinson wrote:

> I had hoped (and still do) to write a piece connecting Greenfield and Wittgenstein and Postmodernism based upon your book. I can see how it could be done and how it might contribute but – given all my other retired commitments I don't see how it can be done in the time set.
>
> (4.1.94)

I am sure that I speak for many others when I say that I hope to be able to read this at some time in the not too distant future. Nobody is better qualified to write it. Why this should be so is touched upon in the next part of this chapter.

Hodgkinson and Greenfield

This is not the place to attempt a comprehensive account of the personal and intellectual relationship between Christopher Hodgkinson and Thomas Greenfield. However, given their seminal importance separately and together to educational administration, there is surely a strong case for such a study. I look forward to it.

What, then, do I hope to learn about Hodgkinson from Greenfield that cannot be achieved in any other way? Given that each is on record as describing the other in glowing personal and intellectual terms, Greenfield offers a holistic perspective on Hodgkinson that is potentially unique in its intensity and unmatched in its profundity.

By way of background, suffice it to say that Greenfield was one of the most controversial scholars our field has known. His career, in the wake of a paper he gave at the IIP in Bristol in 1974 that frontally challenged established thinking, and did so from a humanist and values-driven perspective, illustrates the risks of heresy (Gunter and Ribbins 2002: 392–394). His apostasy was resented most strongly in North America where, as he saw it, for much of the rest of his life, he was anathema to many. Against this backdrop, in two key paragraphs taken from a long conversation between us, reported in his only book, he acknowledges the scale of his personal and intellectual debt to Hodgkinson. In doing so, he tells us a great deal about Hodgkinson the man and Hodgkinson the scholar:

> The first person to support me here (in Canada) was Chris Hodgkinson . . . He came to me at a time I was very vulnerable. This was about

the time his book *Towards a Philosophy of Administration* came out. Chris's style means there are no secrets with him, nothing you can't talk about. We talked of the whole intellectual furore, my changing personal circumstances, my marriage dissolving. He would talk about everything, intellectual and personal, everything others avoid in disdain, disagreement or embarrassment . . . There were no others like him. Everything was on the table, no averted eyes, no sham, no pitying condescension. No rejection. Acceptance, but also no holds barred disagreements when it came to that. But always understanding and support. The first time I met him, he said something like, 'What's this I hear about your taking up the vices of the Ancient Greeks?' . . . He was, as I say, a great, friendly, and supportive hand, and there weren't many of them then.
(Greenfield and Ribbins 1993: 247–248)

What I have taken from Hodgkinson is his argument that a social science of organisation can never replace an understanding of administration itself. He deals with the existential relative of the administrative act as virtually no other writer does. He is a fine philosopher, insightful, expressing the power of ancient and modern thought, revealing its essence in pungent human terms. His knowledge of the management literature is profound and he leads the way to deeper and deeper insights into it. He is relentless that technique, ancient or modern, can never supplant the wilfulness of human action or release human agents from responsibility for it. If there are ideas from Hodgkinson that have influenced me most, they are the irreducibility of value choice and the unavoidability of human responsibility for that choice.
(Greenfield and Ribbins 1993: 264–265)

In what has passed, I have said a good deal about Hodgkinson the man. In what follows, I will build on Greenfield's assessment of Hodgkinson the scholar to locate him within the field of educational administration and leadership and evaluate him within the canon.

Situating Hodgkinson

Over the past year or so my colleague at Birmingham, Helen Gunter, and I have been putting a great deal of time into thinking through what might be involved in mapping the field of studies in leadership and in suggesting what one or more maps might look like. What we propose is about to be published in two major papers (Gunter and Ribbins 2002; Ribbins and Gunter 2002). The key concern underlying what we have to say is the fear that in recent times the field is at increasingly serious risk, in the face of growing political pressure to focus on what works, how this can be measured, and how it can be done. As applied to education, this has encouraged what we have described as a 'ring-binder' approach to the practice of leadership and the development of leaders. Such an approach tends to give excessive priority to research that is essentially *instrumental* and *evaluative* in character and to undervalue alternative ways of understanding leading and leadership including the *critical*, the *humanistic* and the *conceptual*. In the first of our papers we outline key aspects of these five knowledge domains and, for illustrative purposes only, locate the work of one or two key writers in each. In doing so 'we stress two points. First, that the whole of the scholarly work of few can be expected to fit exclusively within any one knowledge domain. Second, that much, even most, research is likely to span more than one domain' (Ribbins and Gunter 2002: 374).

Conceptual research, we argue, can be regarded as being concerned with 'issues of ontology and epistemology and with conceptual clarification. It also deals with complexities arising from values and conflicts in values. This type of research has a major concern for historiography and with how knowledge is produced and used' (Ribbins and Gunter 2002: 374). To date, the writings of few indeed can be located largely, let alone exclusively, within this domain. Among those who have contributed significantly to furthering our understanding of the conceptual, we identify Hodgkinson as arguably the paradigm case, given that over 'a long career, he has published little empirically based work, but has written extensively on philosophy, especially values, in leadership' (Ribbins and Gunter 2002: 374). In developing our ideas, we sought the advice of a small number of reviewers, including Hodgkinson. As with my three-level model of research, his response to our request, contained in a letter of 25 May 2002 was supportive, substantial and challenging. Stressing that 'Your enterprise is defensible and valuable in the very delineation of complexity', he nevertheless identified some problems with it and suggested solutions for some of these.[4] All this was done with his customary elegance, erudition and clarity.

> My fascination (with the Gunter collaboration) stems from a personal interest in mapping. It seems to me to go way beyond geography and is at the heart of philosophy and science. It seeks *understanding*, to make the complex simple, to reduce, to locate limits and frontiers and possibilities ... $E = MC^2$ is a map. It relates two unknowns with one known. The ultimate biological map is the genome of DNA. Paradoxically, now we have it we don't know what to do with it. The molecular biologists are already lobbying for a new map: the proteome that will reveal all about proteins and have the happy side effect of keeping biologists on the payroll for decades. Borges wrote a classic short

story on a fabulous society consumed with a passion for map making. The denouement was that the only solution to their problem was to have a 1 to 1 scale map where every piece of information was 'mapped' onto itself. This is not utterly fatuous. It is what viruses and DNA do within cells. But all this is getting off the topic a bit and you wisely recognise the difference between the London Underground classic and the Borges *reductio ad absurdum*. How difficult it is to reach any pragmatic middle ground, however.

(26.5.02)

It seems that what you, Helen and I are doing is what might be called matrix mapping rather than location mapping. And there is the risk of the homogenetic fallacy, of taking cells as being equally or similarly significant or important.

(26.5.02)

I endorse your categories of knowledge domains. Perhaps with some slight niggling at the back of my mind as to how discrete they are and where axiology fits in exactly. I have long been disturbed at some level by the epistemological emphasis that dominates our discourse. Thom agreed with me on this, I think even he was heavily into it.

(26.5.02)

Given these comments, and much else in this chapter, I would not locate Hodgkinson's work exclusively within the conceptual domain. As man and scholar he deserves a much more generous and catholic assessment. In the light of the last quotation above, where would Thom have located him? In the 'Foreword' to *Educational Leadership: The Moral Art*, Greenfield claims that the worst error made by most theorists about organisations and their administration

> is to conceive of them as somehow separate from life, love, sex, growth, conflict, accomplishment, decay, death and chance. The exclusion of values from administrative science, the exclusion of both human and the humane, the exclusion of passion and conviction in all their frailty and perseverance, in all their power and majesty . . .
> (Greenfield 1991: 6)

His friend and colleague, Greenfield argues, could not be accused of such veniality either in his life or in his work. I had thought this would be the last word. But this, surely, should go to Hodgkinson himself? There are many quotations from his letters that I might have chosen for this purpose. One last will suffice. It embraces the conceptual but goes beyond it. It is the wry, wise, authentic voice of the philosopher as humanist.

I was intrigued by your piety towards physics. But isn't that in the end a sort of piety towards mathematics (and God is a mathematician)? All the incomprehensible Hawkings stuff seems too abstruse. Maths – lost at one end in the macro-cosmos and at the other in quantum theory. The mystery to me is how it *does* cash out at the intermediate level of human life, where you and I are. It makes the anthropic principle theory very persuasive. On the other hand, at our messy social level of muddle and chaos and uncertainty we do have *art*, philosophy, religion and these surely are compensation enough.

(21.12.96)

Notes

1 All quotations from Hodgkinson's letters are cited as here.
2 He will regard this 'politically correct' term with polite derision.
3 This refers to a semester that I spent at the University of Cyprus in 1999.
4 His advice has enabled us to improve the papers but their imperfections remain our own.

References

Day, C. and Bakioglu, A. (1996) 'Development and disenchantment in the professional lives of headteachers', in I. Goodson and A. Hargreaves (eds) *Teachers' Professional Lives*, London: Falmer, pp. 205–227.

Evers, C. (1993) 'Hodgkinson on moral leadership', *Educational Management and Administration* 21, 4: 259–263.

Gardner, H. (1995) *Leading Minds: An Anatomy of Leadership*, New York: Basic Books.

Glatter, R. (1972) *Management Development for the Education Profession*, London: Harrap.

Greenfield, T. (1991) 'Foreword', in C. Hodgkinson, *Educational Leadership: The Moral Art*, New York: State University of New York Press, pp. 3–11.

Greenfield, T. and Ribbins, P. (1993) *Greenfield on Educational Administration: Towards a Humane Science*, London: Routledge.

Griffiths, D. (1995) 'Review of *Greenfield on Educational Administration*', *Educational Administration Quarterly* 31, 1: 151–158.

Gronn, P. (1999) *The Making of Educational Leaders*, London: Cassell.

Gunter, H. and Ribbins, P. (2002) 'Leadership studies in education: Towards a map of the field', *Educational Management and Administration* 30, 4: 387–417.

Hodgkinson, C. (1975) 'Philosophy, politics, and planning: An extended rationale for synthesis', *Educational Administration Quarterly* 11, 1: 11–20.

Hodgkinson, C. (1978) *Towards a Philosophy of Administration*, Oxford: Blackwell.

Hodgkinson, C. (1991) *Educational Leadership: The Moral Art*, New York: State University of New York Press.

Hodgkinson, C. (1996) *Administrative Philosophy: Values and Motivations in Administrative Life*, Oxford: Pergamon.

Hodgkinson, C. (in press) 'Was Greenfield on the left?', in R. Macmillan (ed.) *Theory and Inquiry in Educational Administration: The Greenfield Legacy*, Ontario: Althouse.

Hughes, M., Ribbins, P. and Thomas, H. (1985) *Managing Education: The System and the Institution*, London: Holt, Rinehart and Winston.

Kets de Vries, M. (1989) *Prisoners of Leadership*, New York: Wiley.

Magee, B. (2000) *Confessions of a Philosopher*, London: Phoenix.

Marland, M. (1993) 'Inspiration in administration', *Educational Management and Administration* 21, 4: 263–265.

Martin, Y. (2002) (Editorial) 'Honour in his own country and within his own house: On Hodgkinson's retirement', *Journal of Educational Administration and Foundations* 8, 1: 7–10.

Rayner, S. and Ribbins, P. (1999) *Headteachers and Leadership in Special Education*, London: Cassell.

Ribbins, P. (1993) 'Conversations with a *condottiere* of administrative value: Some reflections on the life and work of Christopher Hodgkinson', *Journal of Educational Administration and Foundations* 8, 1: 13–29.

Ribbins, P. and Gunter, H. (2002) 'Mapping leadership studies in education: Towards a typology of knowledge domains', *Educational Management and Administration* 30, 4: 359–386.

Williams, R. (1993) 'Review', *Educational Management and Administration* 21, 4: 255–259.

Chapter 2

Christopher Hodgkinson
A student's perspective

Donald Lang

This is a personal perspective of Professor Christopher Hodgkinson. It rambles as if there were a break in class and a few students gathered around asking about him. We talk about my first encounters, being a student, applying his work, his impact, and his prescription for the betterment of humanity.

Student meets God

I first met Christopher Hodgkinson in the fall of 1979. I was forty-two, a Lieutenant Commander in Canada's navy, just posted to Royal Roads Military College as academic staff. I had two personal missions to achieve. First, learn to swim (it might surprise some, but a lot of navy types don't know how to swim; treading water, however, is essential). This I accomplished and still to this day I thank the gym staff as I do my laps every once in a while. The other mission was purely cerebral. I wanted to have the best in the business endorse a piece of research dealing with commitment of individuals to organisations. I had always been intrigued why normal healthy youth would join a military college because, much like the Holy Roman Empire was at one time neither holy, Roman, nor empire, military colleges are not really military, nor academic institutions – a point of view bound to engender debate. Be that as it may, I had a 'proposal' on sheets of foolscap (four pages) outlining in cryptic format the what, how, and why – literature perspectives were obviously absent. I had no idea who Professor Hodgkinson was or what he was all about, but after an hour in his 'chambers', he agreed to take me on. And I've been a student ever since.

After eighteen years in the navy I had a pretty good idea of what constituted 'good' leadership. It was very simple really: to what extent would I put my life in the hands of my superiors? One quickly learns the 'good' from the 'not so good'. Chris assigned only two texts for me: his *Towards a Philosophy of Administration* (1978) and Chester Barnard's *The Functions of the Executive* (1968). I simply could not comprehend how these two authors, coming from such different backgrounds, could be so in line with my own experiences of what command and leadership entailed. When I look back at these texts, they are almost unreadable now, with all sorts of colour highlighting, asterisks, marks, and notes. To this day I am convinced that Barnard said everything there was to say about 'good' leadership. I am equally convinced that what Chris did to Barnard is similar to what Aquinas did to Aristotle. What follows are my thoughts about Chris's impact on me as an individual and how that translated into the world of the classroom.

Galileo Syndrome: Observe, measure

'Observe, Don, observe.'

Chris is a man of Propositions. There is one, however, that is not yet included specifically in his repertoire, but runs throughout his whole being as a teacher. It comes from that encyclopedic storyteller Daniel J. Boorstin via political scientist George Bailey (1990: 13): worse than ignorance is the illusion of knowledge. Bailey used it to illustrate the heliocentric–geocentric debate where for political and theological reasons Ptolemy was 'correct'. Chris's approach to teaching was very methodical: he simply asked questions that instilled a sense of curiosity – very Socratic. And his use of silence in the classroom was something I had never experienced. Truly, there were times when he just sat there looking at us, all twelve of us – he rarely permitted more than that in his classes. It was like he was reading our minds. Then there was the business with his self-developed shorthand. You'd say something and he'd be making these strange little markings on a folded sheet of paper. Through all of this he was forcing us to question everything, above all his own works and points of view. He was much like G. E. Moore that way, encouraging debate but especially ready to acknowledge he might not have all the answers. He was the antithesis of being dogmatic. All he asked was that we think correctly. Like Galileo, he challenged orthodox thinking. True, he was not in the 'measurement mode' of Galileo, but he certainly observed – observed insightfully – human conduct in general, and in leadership situations in particular.

'Read, Don, read.'

Not having been down the doctoral road before, I asked the obvious, 'What should I do now that I have been accepted as a doctoral student?' Seemed appropriate to me. All he said was, 'Read, Don, read.' That was all he said. So I asked the obvious again, 'Read what?' Big mistake. Like maybe I really shouldn't be in this programme because all he said was,

'Read what you don't know.' I just loved that response. He really did not elaborate too much – only muttered a few things in apparent annoyance and said, 'Come back in six months.'

At this point I have to tell you where I was coming from and what sort of mind-set I was in. Fred Fiedler had been making his annual visit to Royal Roads for many years as part of his salmon fishing expedition up northern Vancouver Island. My wife and I had come to know him and his wife quite well, such that we were regular visitors to Seattle. He is clearly at the top of empirical-based leadership and I was thoroughly taken with his department's policy for 'producing' PhDs. His line was clear: give me someone who is qualified for the programme and I'll produce a PhD in twenty-four months. He had big contracts with the US military – I got to know a few of their personnel quite well. So here I was, thinking, 'Twenty-four months – thirty at the outside.' There was a small problem, however. The University of Victoria did not have a comparable 'PhD producing programme' – it did not have any for that matter, as I was the first doctoral student of Chris's. So when Chris said 'read' and left the 'what' to me, I gave some thought to switching to the US military. But that was a non-starter because as much as Fred had a production line going – it made one think of fast-food operations – my analysis of what he was all about left a lump in my throat because values could not be incorporated in his work. I can still recall, clearly, Fred and Chris relaxing in the ward room following one of Fred's presentations (with his octants a-glow), discussing the place of values in leadership research. Fred agreed with everything Chris was about, but very politely said he could not use it because values could not be measured. In retrospect, it is not unfair to suggest that Fred measured but did not observe; Chris observed but could not measure. Galileo was alive and well.

In an operational setting

From personal experience, there was no doubt in my mind that values and value analysis could explain many of the difficulties associated with leadership and commitment. It is this significance that has led me to think that Chris's value paradigm has not really been grasped by many of his associates. There are two interdependent constructs in any value-laden problem which seemed obvious to me in an operational setting – for instance, while working as a referral agent within the military for personnel with all sorts of adjustment problems, or when I was with the policy group at the National Defence Headquarters in Ottawa. The two constructs deal with the *mechanism* of valuing and the *object* of that mechanism. At least that is how I have come to understand Chris's position on values.

What bothered me for the longest time was the constant reference to the subjective nature of values, that values were therefore personal. It was not sufficient simply to say that 'values are subjective' because that left the question of how any given value came to be a value. Specifically, does a value simply 'pop into one's head' or is there some sort of mechanism that causes that value to be? I opt for the latter. This makes sense when one gives thought to Chris's view that values are concepts of the desirable with a motivating force. If one applies this approach to any behavioural event, that behaviour is, to some extent, a consequence of a subjective value operating within the individual. And the only way that value can have an impact on one's behaviour is if some mechanism gives rise to that value.

This line of thinking was very helpful in my understanding of commitment, which – surprise, surprise – is a value-based phenomenon. Despite all the best efforts of traditional North American approaches to measure commitment, the bottom line is that an individual's commitment to an organisation can only be assessed in a one-to-one interview, with Chris's value audit forming the major line of attack. Even then, risks abound. One has only to think of the Kim Philbys to realise the likelihood of false positives, especially when using standard measures of organisational commitment. To identify any given value is only half the job; one must also search out the mechanism generating that value.

The beauty of Chris's value paradigm is that the universe of valuing – that is, the array of mechanisms – comprises only four elements, counting logic-based and consensus-based as separate entities. There are only four valuing pistons driving all of humanity. These four pistons are the genesis of value objects that are internal, personal, and subjective. Chris uses the word 'justify' to account for how one values whatever it is one values. 'Justify' is another name for mechanism.

In the armed forces, a common referral is a request for a change in occupation – from infantry to military police, for example. In this case the usual reasons include having a better lifestyle while still in uniform, developing a marketable skill for civilian life, or spending more time at home with the family. Part of the referral process is an in-depth interview, and it is here that Chris's value audit becomes alive, as it were. The bottom line in this sort of counselling is to get the individual to 'come to know' the psycho-philosophical dynamics involved, the 'justification' of the decision-making. More often than not, the individual leaves with a much clearer understanding of the forces generating the referral.

From another perspective, policy-making offers an analysis of valuing that comes from the nomothetic dimension, the reality of which is like trying to hold gravy in your hand. One particular instance still bothers me a little. It involved the use of psychological tests for Aboriginal recruits – a problematic issue for every reason imaginable. The Federal

Government of Canada initiated 'an equal opportunity program' to have better representation of Aboriginal peoples in the military; whether the Aboriginals wanted it was neither here nor there. Recruiters went to many areas north of the 60th parallel, and from all the chiefs came the same response: no special treatment was to be given to their people; they were to get the same treatment as other peoples 'south of 60'. Well, my position was very clear: no testing because we had no normative data for the proper use of such tests. The Ministry of Defence was not interested in the niceties of psychological testing, but I suggested that the Canadian Psychological Association might be. After much debate, the testing went forward, justified on the grounds of gathering normative data. Chris's value paradigm did much to help tease out the nuances of the major stakeholders.

My experiences in command and staff positions have convinced me that Chris's analysis of values has a high degree of utility. Furthermore, its powerful epistemological structure gives one a big 'comfort zone'. As an aside, there was a time when that horrendous MMPI (Minnesota Multiphasic Personality Inventory) was widely used simply because of its utility, even though we all knew it totally lacked any validity.

Amor fati

Nietzsche's formula for greatness in a human being – to *love* what comes one's way, planned or otherwise – is an apt characterisation of what Chris is all about because nothing throws him (I haven't seen any evidence to the contrary). Perhaps of all his propositions, 'work for work's sake' is his single greatest message. And of all my experiences as a student, it was his consistency in never forcing his views on me or other students that stands as a testimony to his greatness as a teacher. So when I was asked if I would like to teach courses in Philosophy of Leadership and in Concepts and Theories of Administration, I had my role model. Of course, philosophy-as-teacher is easier to grasp than teacher-as-font-of-knowledge. I was still in kindergarten – perhaps still am. Anyway, it was study-and-learn time. Over the years two perspectives of classroom life seemed to have stood me in good stead: technique and material. However, students might well give other views.

Meet and greet

Chris was always first in the classroom and forever impeccably dressed in smart coordinates of suit, shirt, tie, and especially shoes. My university days of the 1960s, studying psychology, had Profs in about as dress-down as was possible. The change of seeing Chris as if ready for a semi-formal cocktail party after class took some getting used to. And I was certainly not alone in this view. Several years ago I chaired a seminar in summer session with Chris, Gabriel Lakomski, Gary Holmes, and the late Geoffrey Isherwood as panel members. Our organiser and editor of this Festschrift, Eugenie Samier, was there too. It was Isherwood who leaned into my ear as Chris came into the auditorium, 'Here he comes, always dressed as the gentleman, which he always is.' (In a way, Gabriel stole the show, appearing with a baseball bat, 'ordering' the assembly to 'lighten up'). The point is that I had been bred in the necessity and significance of appropriate dress, especially shoes, and here was Chris, 'ready for parade'. I took this to be more than a habit with him; I saw it, and still see it, as a token of respect for his subject matter. I can say this with some confidence because on our numerous luncheons over the years his dress, at times, has been more relaxed. In effect, he 'dressed for battle', where his outward attire was a reflection of his disciplined and well-ordered mind.

Wittgenstein's Proposition 7

Chris was forever reminding us of being careful about what we said and could say. With this in mind he always had his class do personal case histories in order to bring some personal reality to the subject matter. I have done that with every class in Philosophy of Leadership and in Concepts and Theories in Administration. Quite simply, students are asked to think of some personal instance or episode involving a conflict of values, a conflict that relates to them personally, and not to worry about what values might mean. I have refined this to a conflict of values involving policy matters, work procedures, and personnel. Students are asked to provide the case histories within seven days so that I can get some picture of the concerns amongst the class. Also, students know that a major portion of their grading comes from applying course material to their individual case studies. In every class, without exception, there have been at least two who tell me that is the most difficult assignment they have ever done.

Most analyses of case studies emphasise Chris's value paradigm and views of leadership; others, praxis and leadership. Over the years, through informal chats with former students and without any prompting, many have volunteered to say that doing those case studies was one of the most personally rewarding exercises of their programme. This approach merely highlights Chris's concern that students grasp the nuances of values and leadership from within themselves as opposed to a passive mode of learning. Also, it is consistent with his understanding of what constitutes reality, where his subject matter is located in the world of ideas. Having said that, the students like his line about philosophy beginning in the dirt because they see their own case studies embedded thus.

In this way, they come to see the unavoidable tie of the world of ideas to that everyday world that besets us, a view so pointedly made by Marcus Aurelius, 'I shall meet with the busybody, the ungrateful, arrogant, deceitful, envious, unsocial' (1980: 199).

Gardening for truth and beauty

I have two hobbies, gardening and reading, and, oddly enough, they're quite closely related because gardening presents as many metaphysical puzzles as one can find in the library. I'm not quite sure how slugs come to be, let alone appear where they do. The question is not *if* we are related but to what extent. A truly wondrous event to behold is how that ugly dahlia tuber can produce such a remarkable flower. Can something sensually pleasing come from something sensually unpleasant? To extend the lines of thought: can good come from evil? Jung says it can. But how solid is his epistemology when he says, 'A psychic content is as real as a plant or an animal' (Jung 1966: 454–455)? Perhaps Chris ought to search out an R-IV (*à la* Abraham Maslow).

The beauty of composting is nature looking after itself. Societal composting forces the issues of what and why we are. Are we mere hosts for genes totally contravening Kant's second formulation of the Categorical Imperative? Does Adler have it right when he advocates our *raison d'être* is to rid ourselves of our imperfections? The passion fruit plant never ceases to amaze us because in the spring there are all these dead-looking stringy vines that you just want to cut out. But that would be a mistake because as summer comes, the vines come alive and new growth produces the most intricate and delicate blossoms, a phenomenon that resembles classroom reality. I have lost count of the number of times I thought I was pulling weeds when in truth they were flowers. A student told an enlightening story. Math was his subject; he loved it and loved teaching it. He also had to teach music, about which he knew nothing and hated teaching. Many years later he got a Christmas card from a former student; he had difficulty placing her. Through subsequent phone calls, she insisted he meet with her and her family, just to say hello. During their meeting she explained that she simply wanted to say thanks for instilling in her a love of music such that she was now an accomplished pianist in the city's symphony. He was simply dumbfounded. Never in his wildest dreams did music figure in anything. When we teach, what are we *really* teaching?

The Fourth Noble Truth: The way out

Chris is what teaching is all about. It is not so much that he knows his subject; he loves the challenge it presents, which is met with passion that infects his students. He conveys a sense of controlled urgency that humanity must come to understand the inescapable conclusion – above all else, philosophy is what gets us through the day, regardless how the day went. The cloak of Elmer Gantry dresses the trade literature on leadership – snake oil. But, how is the buyer to be aware if prevented from being informed about alternatives? Much of the professional literature on leadership must view humanity as automatons, even though the authors might cry foul. The evidence is clear: search for discussions on what Chester Barnard (1968: 295) singles out as being at the heart of his views on leadership – 'the old question of free will and determinism'. This is what Chris is all about as teacher – that humanity must be led by insightful analysis of what we are and why. Only philosophy can do this. And what upsets Chris most is that the Western world has put philosophy at the back of the classroom.

Chris's curriculum for the betterment of humanity would have philosophy at the top. He would not single out particular philosophies for inclusion or deletion. All he would insist on is that students think about what they are reading and how that impacts on humanity. His most difficult assignment would be for leaders and 'wannabe' leaders to lead themselves first. The difficulty lies in individuals becoming authentic – a rare commodity in leadership. But he is optimistic about the future of humanity and believes that education is the best medium through which to inculcate notions of authentic leadership.

Scholia

Chris loves to stretch readers' vocabulary – in any language. During one of our lunches he gave me a copy of his *Administrative Philosophy* (1996) with the following inscription, 'Dum vivimus vivamus sed vive ut vivas.' Latin is not one of my strong suits and despite consulting all sorts of texts I eventually had to confess that I was not sure I had it right – it's like when someone gives you a rare gift, and then you turn around and ask what it is. Anyway, from the Master himself: 'In order to really live we should live intensely while we do live.' And for Chris, 'Leve fit, quod bene fertur, onus.'

References

Aurelius, M. (1980) *The Meditations of Marcus Aurelius*, Connecticut: Grolier Enterprises Corporation.
Bailey, G. (1990) *Galileo's Children: Science, Sakharov, and the Power of the State*, New York: Arcade Publishing.
Barnard, C. (1968) *The Functions of the Executive*, Cambridge, Mass.: Harvard University Press.

Hodgkinson, C. (1978) *Towards a Philosophy of Administration,* Oxford: Basil Blackwell.
Hodgkinson, C. (1996) *Administrative Philosophy: Values and Motivations in Administrative Life,* Oxford: Pergamon.
Jung, C. G. (1966) *Collected Works,* New York: Princeton University Press.

Chapter 3

The Gentleman with the Lamp

Derek J. Allison

> ... we will not escape hierarchy and authority in any organization; the fundamental question then is what justifies a moral order and makes it worthy of obedience and respect.
>
> Thom Greenfield (1993: 224)

Christopher Hodgkinson is the gentleman in my title and, as all who know him will surely attest, he is most worthy of this old world honorific. The LAMP with which I have endowed him is a flexible acronym in which the first letters stand for Leadership, Administration and Management. The 'P' takes a range of referents including Personnel, Process and Practice, where LAMP refers in a general sense to People in Positions of authority in formal organisations and the distinctive activities that constitute their Profession. Hodgkinson's scholarship speaks to these applications of the acronym in a more powerful way than much of the broader literature of administrative and organisational theory. We can nonetheless adjust our LAMP to shed a more focused light on Hodgkinson's particular contributions by substituting other 'P' words, chief among which is, of course, Philosophy. Others include Policy, Planning and Politics, as well as Praxis, Preferences and Principles.

My title is modelled on a famous phrase from Longfellow's *Santa Filomena* in which he paid tribute to Florence Nightingale, the Victorian heroine who did so much to alleviate the suffering of wounded and sick soldiers during the Crimean war, and who went on, through her leadership, administrative prowess, and will, to revolutionise the organisation and practice of nursing. In a contemporary account predating Longfellow, she was described as a 'ministering angel' whose 'slender form glides quietly along each corridor ... with a little lamp in her hand, making her solitary rounds' (Macdonald, as quoted by Cook 1913: 236). It is not too fanciful an indulgence to imagine Hodgkinson similarly stalking the corridors of organisational and administrative thought, using his LAMPhilosophy to illuminate neglected corners and cast new light along more well travelled ways. What has he shown us? In what ways and to what extent has the light he cast helped us to better see, appreciate, understand? How strong and far does his light shine? What demons lurk within the shadows?

Full and proper answers can be given only by posterity. All that can be essayed now is a rough anticipation, and all that can be offered in this chapter is a limited appreciation derived from one person's inherently fallible understanding of Hodgkinson's writing within the context of selected themes of thought. As illustrated by the bibliography at the end of this volume, Hodgkinson has made a substantial contribution to the literature. His writing is rich, his scope wide, drawing together many skeins of thought as he weaves his arguments. A full account of his work, still less an assessment, cannot be squeezed into a single chapter. In consequence I have chosen to concentrate on two main themes permeating his writing, Hodgkinson's view of the LAMProcess and his treatment of values. In attempting this I seek not to praise or bury Hodgkinson. Some of what I have to say is laudatory, some critical, but I trust the observations and comments offered will be found reasonable.

The titles of Hodgkinson's four books, which form my main sources,[1] nicely stake out the domain of his inquiry. Hodgkinson's (1978) first book was *Towards a Philosophy of Administration*. The title of his most recent volume (1996), *Administrative Philosophy: Values and Motivations in Administrative Life*, suggests at least a tentative arrival. His two intervening books substitute leadership for administration, one in a general sense, *The Philosophy of Leadership* (1983), the other in a context, *Educational Leadership: The Moral Art* (1991). Taken in sequence these four titles suggest development and diversification over time. Such is indeed the case but many of the main themes, claims and arguments persist across all four volumes, much of the new material serving primarily to extend, amplify, illustrate or embellish. Two notable developments on which this essay pivots are the increasing attention paid to sociocultural aspects of values, and an important change in his treatment of leadership that appeared between his first and second books.

Values and their place in administrative action, theory and philosophy dominate Hodgkinson's work and his contributions in this area have attracted the greatest attention and generated the most interest. This is especially so in the field of educational administration, where his name is indelibly associated with his assertion that administrators inescapably deal in and arbitrate values. Although, as we shall see, his attempts at getting to grips with the philosophical and practical implications of this have been hobbled by weaknesses in his analytical machinery, Hodgkinson's contributions have played an undeniably central role in stimulating the current renaissance of values studies in (educational) administration, and the growing interest in ethics and morals which is a central part of this renewal (Ashbaugh and Kasten 1984; Begley 1999; Greenfield 1991; Willower and Forsyth 1999). As the epigraph from Greenfield reminds us, hierarchy and authority are inescapable realities in organisations, forming and framing the acts of administrators and the moral orders they help create and sustain, be they worthy or not. In each of his four books, Hodgkinson begins his discussion of this complex process by seeking to clarify the nature of administration and its relation to the elusive phenomenon of leadership. We shall follow him.

THE HIERARCHICAL IMPERATIVE

Leadership is a particularly vexing notion: it not only defies ready definition, it is what Hacking (1999) calls an elevator word, by which he means a word with high-level semantic content that makes implicit claims about the way things are or should be, thus automatically raising the stakes of discourse and enquiry. 'Philosophers keep on fussing with them' (Hacking 1999: 90) and they become the subject of endless books. 'Administration' and 'management' also have elevator-word qualities, but in a lesser key, as it were. For this and other reasons there has been and continues to be considerable confusion about the relative meanings of these three key terms and how they are to be best used when talking about and attempting to study those aspects of life to which they fuzzily refer. The problem is exacerbated by each having noun and verb usages as well as cognates. This allows, even encourages, superficially intelligible but essentially meaningless constructions such as the following: 'The leadership expects all managers and administrators to empower organisational members through their on-going leadership so as to manage administrative affairs and administer management activities effectively and efficiently.' Although obviously fabricated to illustrate the point, perhaps we would not be surprised to find such orgspeak lurking in actual policy manuals, or being trumpeted by a CEO communicating her vision in a video peroration to employees. We are less likely to find such egregiously contradictory and confusing usage in the scholarly literature, but this is not because widely agreed understandings of management, administration and leadership have been established. There is a broad consensus that attention should focus on the active meanings of these terms, that leadership is somehow qualitatively different from management and administration and that, nowadays at least, leadership is to be preferred over the other terms, although this is largely a matter of fashion than theory. Regardless, there is little consistency and less precision in the ways in which these three basal words are used within the literature. Nor is there much prospect of improvement, most contributors choosing to elide what we might call the LAMPuzzle. Hodgkinson is a notable exception.

The LAMPuzzle is more than just a matter of nomenclature. Hodgkinson likes to draw on Wittgenstein, especially his 'What we cannot speak about we must pass over in silence', which he quotes at least once in all of his four books. In *Educational Leadership*, he juxtaposes this quotation with Wittgenstein's 'The limits of my language are the limits of my world', explaining that 'much of the modern thrust of philosophy has been devoted to . . . the clarification of language' (Hodgkinson 1991: 49). Words are more than labels; they are invested with meanings that form and limit our understandings of the world. Lewis Carroll's (1970: 269) Humpty Dumpty declared 'When I use a word, . . . it means just what I choose it to mean – neither more nor less.' Stipulating meaning has obvious attractions, but as a Chinese proverb reminds us, 'the beginning of wisdom is to call things by their right names'. How might this be attempted when there is no agreed-on conventional usage, as in the case of the LAMPuzzle? What seems to be required is some externally informed justification. One common way forward is to examine etymology. We can also look for coherence with related concepts or some pertinent theoretical frame. As the philosophical analyses that led to the demise of logical positivism remind us, no word is an island, sufficient unto itself. Elevator words derive their implicit claims about the way things are or should be from the meanings, theories and/or ideologies that undergird them, and which they help construct.

Administration and management

Throughout his work, Hodgkinson draws a consistent distinction between administration and management. The former he views as 'dealing more with the formation of purpose, the value-laden issues, and the human component of organizations' (1978: 5), the latter as 'those aspects that are more routine, material, programmatic, and amenable to quantitative methods' (1996: 27). In three of his books he uses sets of semantic pairs to illustrate this distinction, as summarised in the upper part of Table 3.1. Hodgkinson (1996: 27) explains, 'These dimensions of action and experience are illustrative rather than comprehensive', cautioning they 'do not, of course, exhaust the manifold complexity of administration/management' (1991: 50). He does not dwell on the contrasts drawn when they first appear in his texts, but large parts of Hodgkinson's books are concerned with working out what he sees as important philosophical differences between concepts classified as administrative and their matching managerial counterparts, especially the Art/Science, Policy/Execution and Values/Facts pairs, and the implications that follow for the moral order of organisations and the ethical actions of administrators. The concept pairs in the lower part of Table 3.1 are intended to extend the contrasts drawn in Hodgkinson's original lists. Some, such as Abstract/Concrete, are used

Table 3.1 Differentiating administration and management

Administration	Management
Hodgkinson's original 1978 list:	
Art	Science
Policy	Execution
Values	Facts
Upper Echelons	Lower Echelons
Strategy	Tactics
Qualitative	Quantitative
Human	Material
Reflective	Active
Generalism	Specialism
Added in 1991 and retained in 1996:	
Upper Ranks	Lower Ranks
Philosophy	Action
Top Management	Middle Management
Deliberation	Detail
Extensions:	
Abstract	Concrete
Broader	Narrower
Longer time spans	Shorter time spans
Principles	Procedures
Command	Cope
Complexity	Simplicity
Consilience	Consistency
Holistic	Elemental
Organisation	Individuals
Synthesis	Thesis

Source: Derived from Hodgkinson (1978, 1991 and 1996)

by Hodgkinson in his discussions; others, some of which will be touched on later, are offered in an attempt to enrich the distinction being drawn.

Hodgkinson readily acknowledges that the allocation of meanings in Table 3.1 is sometimes inverted, with the conceptual emphases he associates with administration being associated with management in some usages. Still, he has etymology on his side, the root of management being the Latin *manus*, for 'hand', evoking notions of 'hands-on' manipulation. Administration finds its root in the Latin *ministrare*, to serve, to minister to, which is thoroughly consistent with Barnard's (1938) focus on executives seeking to reconcile employee interests and sentiments with organisational purposes, a theme which Hodgkinson, a good Barnardian, picks up and develops.

Some of the contrasts in Table 3.1, particularly Upper [Ranks]/Lower [Ranks] and Top Management/Middle Management are explicitly hierarchical. Contrary to much contemporary preference, Hodgkinson does not shy away from hierarchy, which he sees as permeating the conceptual and functional essences of administration and management and, as we shall see later, values. 'By and large,' he tells us, 'administrators in our terms will tend to be located high in the organizational status hierarchy while managers will tend to the middle and lower levels of supervision and responsibility' (1978: 5). While he singles out the status hierarchy here, it is clear that in his view 'administration subsumes management' (1991: 51), within communication, authority, responsibility and all other functional hierarchies in formal organisations. He clarifies this in various discussions of his P3M3 taxonomy (1983: 27; 1991: 63; 1996: 31). Administrators are viewed as creating policy through due attention to Philosophy, Planning and Politics, with managers being responsible for implementation through the functions of Mobilising, Managing and Monitoring.

> Here philosophy means that the organizational values and *raison d'être* are articulated by top level administration. At this level, the *idea* of the organization is formulated and it is done by philosophical means: imagination, intuition, speculation, hypothesis, argument, dialectic, logic, rhetoric, value analysis and clarification. This ideational level of administration is then translated into the *plan*, the next phase in the emergent specificity of the idea. Next the plan must be entered into the political process of *persuasion*; it must be sold to those key individuals and organization members who ultimately control the resources necessary to realize the plan. The level of idea has now shifted to the level of people.
> The whole process, still at this people level, now moves toward the mobilizing of the resources necessary to the realization of the plan. Implicit in this phase, which has now become more managerial than administrative but is still within the realm of art and politics rather than science, is the motivation of the human resources of the organization to the collective purpose. When this has been accomplished, organizational means are brought to bear on ends and events occur not merely in the realms of *ideas* and *people* but also in the realm of things. . . . Routines are established and adjusted. The quotidian work of the technical staff is organized. Finally, there is a need for monitoring, a phase which would include formal supervision, auditing, accounting, reporting and evaluation. . . .
>
> (Hodgkinson 1991: 63, his emphasis)

Hodgkinson readily acknowledges that this overly neat and implicitly optimistic account grossly simplifies matters, and in any instance the distinctions he draws between administrative activities and managerial modalities will be blurred and blended. He nevertheless maintains, 'The movement is always in the same direction: from ideas to things, from the abstract to the concrete, and always via the mediation of people' (1996: 32). Consequently, he concludes 'the central problem of administration is always that of motivation of action or, more precisely, the reconciliation of the interests of individual organizational members or clients with the collective interests of the organization' (1996: 32).

In sum, hierarchy provides the organisational, conceptual, and functional scaffolding for Hodgkinson's approach to administration. As he put it in Proposition 7.23 in *Towards a Philosophy of Administration*, 'hierarchy is the essence of universal order' (1978: 221). Although nowadays the brute fact of hierarchy is often regretted, even denied, in some quarters, formal organisations are indubitably hierarchical, as are all complex systems. When we say organisation, we say hierarchy. And when we say hierarchy, we advert to the sub and super ordering of functions that, in organisations, are vested in roles and responsibilities differentiated by rank. Given that formal organisations are conventionally understood to be purpose-oriented cooperative systems where the work of individuals and groups is authoritatively coordinated to achieve otherwise unattainable ends and outcomes, it is clear that policies and plans have to be decided in some fashion, coordination effected in some way, organisational members motivated somehow. On Hodgkinson's analysis, administrators located towards the apex of organisational hierarchies are primarily concerned with creating policy and motivating people, while middle-level managers handle (literally) the details. Hodgkinson further urges us to recognise, accept and seriously consider that administration is thus inescapably suffused with value considerations. Because of this, and because the decisions of administrators can have profound consequences for people within and without the organisations they administer, it follows that administration has inescapable moral implications. This hierarchically anchored account provides the conceptual core of Hodgkinson's view of administration as philosophy-in-action.

The analytical summary offered in the previous paragraph provides an initial, internally consistent justification for differentiating between higher and lower ordered decision-making and purpose-oriented action in formal organisations, regardless of whether we call the higher-level activities 'administration', as does Hodgkinson and as we will do here, or something else, as does Barnard (1938) with his executive functions, Simon (1945) with his upper administrators, Plato with his Guardians, or Fayol (1949) and Mintzberg (1973) with their managers. Hodgkinson recruits all of these authorities as well as Scott and Hart (1979), Thompson (1967), Vickers (1970) and others to support his views in various ways and to differing degrees. Barnard is one of Hodgkinson's particular heroes, and he draws on him extensively.[2] On Barnard's analysis, administrators coordinate the work of subordinate unit organisations (departments). Their main purpose is to integrate (reconcile) the work and the sentiments of individuals and sub-units into the overarching purposes of the organisation, which they also have a duty to form and re-form. As he put it, 'Executive work is not that *of* the organization, but the specialized work of *maintaining* the organization in operation' (Barnard 1938: 215, his emphasis).

Further support can be readily found in literature not specifically drawn on by Hodgkinson. The two superordinate levels in Parsons' (1960) institutional, managerial and technical levels of organisation map nicely onto Hodgkinson's administrative and managerial realms respectively. Weber's construct of a *Betriebsverband*, which provides the structural frame for his organisational analyses, is composed of three similar subsystems (Albrow 1970: 40; Weber 1978: 37). Weber's celebrated ideal-type account of bureaucracy was directly concerned with authority and action within the middle strata of *Betriebsverbände,* which he refers to as the administrative staff.[3] But while Weber's approach provides support for Hodgkinson's differentiation between higher and lower level administrative/management functions, nomenclature can once again confuse matters for, when translated into Hodgkinson's usage, Weber's bureaucrats are revealed as managers. It is in the governance subsystem in Weber's model of bureaucracy, with its monocratic or collegial head and the senior officials that advise and administer to them, where we find Hodgkinson's administrators.

Elliott Jaques' (1976, 1989) theory of requisite organisation provides additional independent support for Hodgkinson's approach. Jaques identifies important and consistent differences in the cognitive complexity of the work that has to be accomplished within extended organisational hierarchies. At lower levels, first-line managers and unit heads typically deal with concrete tasks and problems, the completion of which extends over relatively short time spans (from one day to a year or so). At higher levels, work becomes more cognitively complex and abstract with task completion extending over longer time spans. Jaques' research identified an important qualitative discontinuity at the two-year time span level. At and beyond this threshold, organisational tasks and problems become progressively more complex, general, abstract and integrative in accord with the administration/management distinctions drawn in Table 3.1. Here, then, is an empirically grounded theoretical demarcation between managerial and administrative action: discrete organisational tasks which have to be accomplished by coordinating the work of others over a time horizon of two years or longer appear as essentially administrative in Hodgkinson's usage, while those that can be accomplished within shorter time spans are managerial.[4] Jaques' theory appears unique in specifying time spans, but the general principle of administrative work and responsibility extending over longer time horizons is also recognised by Barnard, Thompson and Vickers. Barnard's comments on the formulation of purpose appear particularly pertinent:

> This involves a pyramiding of the formulation of purpose that becomes more and more general as the number of units of basic organization becomes larger, and more and more remote in future time. Responsibility for abstract, generalizing, prospective, long-run decision is delegated *up* the line, responsibility for definition, action, remains always at the base where the authority for effort remains.
> (Barnard 1938: 232–233)

The themes of thought and analysis discussed earlier reinforce Hodgkinson's claim that 'Administrators must be "specialists in generalism"' (1978: 89). 'The higher the positions in the line of authority,' observes Barnard (1938: 222), 'the more general the abilities required.' Jaques (1976: 149) points out that the military title of General first emerges at his two-year time span level, reflecting the conceptual essence of Hodgkinson's proposition. Just as Barnard's executives have responsibility for coordinating and instilling purpose in collections of subordinate unit organisations, Generals command brigades and larger units of combined arms composed of multiple specialised units which they are expected to coordinate and inspire, each and together. Competent management at lower, sub-unit, levels of organisation requires specific functional specialisation in, for example, accounting, marketing, nursing, teaching, scheduling, research, IT, artillery, logistics and the like. What is required at the administrative level is a concentration on the interests, purposes and problems that are common to the overall complex of organisational units: a specialisation in generalism. And just as large armies have echelons of generals – Brigadier General, Major General, Lieutenant General and (four star) General – administration at increasingly higher hierarchical levels (when they exist) is a matter of more general generalism. As Hodgkinson notes in various places, those with successful experience in high-level generalism seem able to 'pass easily from one complex organization to another. The general becomes a university president and ministers of state move from portfolio to portfolio or criss-cross the lines of public and private sector enterprise' (1996: 29). Generalism generalises.

In Hodgkinson's scheme, administrators make policy, but is this not the prerogative of governing bodies composed of elected representatives of various kinds? The answer is clearly yes, and as Hodgkinson bewails, this distinction can take the form of a 'powerful political dogma that is sometimes raised to ideological status in Anglo-Saxon cultures' (1978: 67). Yet while this dogma is rehearsed from time to time in editorials and other platforms of popular opinion, it has little support in the contemporary administrative or political science literatures (e.g. Allison 1983, Dye 1975, Pal 1992). Regardless of how we construe their relative roles, administrative officials and their political masters will normally both be involved in fashioning policy. For Hodgkinson it follows that politicians are *de facto* administrators (Hodgkinson 1978: 67). This leads him to identify two main classes of administrators, political and professional.[5] The first comes to his or her administrative duties through election or political appointment, the second through career advancement (Hodgkinson 1978: 69; 1996: 58). Administrators are thus revealed as amateur politicians *simpliciter*, and politicians – as amateur administrators. Policy-making embraces and engulfs both elected and appointed officials in the characteristically administrative actions and emphases sketched in Table 3.1.

Leadership

How does leadership, our initial point of departure, fit into Hodgkinson's scheme? In his first book, Hodgkinson approached the question with caution, even suspicion. Leadership, he told us, 'is a slogan word, eulogistic, blurring many levels of meaning'. Yet its very ambiguities 'make it a useful rhetorical instrument' for the ambitious who 'seek to appropriate many of the meanings inherent in the term' in ways that legitimate 'power, authority and rank'. Aspirants to administrative office (professional and political) 'claim that they, to a greater degree than their competitors, possess the qualities of leadership' (1978: 89). He concluded, 'the concept of leadership is complex indeed and . . . its facile usage among the naïve must be discriminated from its sense, reference and intent in administrative philosophy' (1978: 93–94). Hodgkinson's views on this point appear to be summed up by his (in)famous Proposition 6.4: 'The term leadership is an incantation for the bewitchment of the led' (1978: 219).

In his second book, *The Philosophy of Leadership*, Hodgkinson abandoned his initial cautious suspicion, rushing with unjustified haste to equate leadership with administration. He is quite clear about this, although he takes a while getting around to it, eventually declaring well past the mid-point of the book that 'It is now time to make explicit what has been implicit all along. Administration *is* leadership. Leadership *is* administration' (1983: 195, his emphasis). On my reading this interchangeable identity was not at all implicit in the preceding text, nor is the reciprocal identity of administration and leadership made any more obvious in his following two books where the claim is repeated (1991: 53; 1996: 78). In *Educational Leadership* he argues that because administrators tend to conceive of their role as that of a leader, 'For our purposes the term can *then* be used synonymously with administration' (1991: 53, my emphasis). He claims the validity of this can be checked by 'substituting "administration" for "leadership" wherever and whenever the latter term is encountered in the literature' (1991: 53). Applying this test to the nonsense illustration of orgspeak offered earlier makes the fabrication even more nonsensical, which perhaps bears him out! But what about Hodgkinson's Proposition 6.4, which becomes 'The term administration is an incantation for the bewitchment of the led'? Surely he would not want us to believe this? Indeed, the whole idea is pernicious, making the LAMPuzzle even more incorrigible and serving to undo all the good work Hodgkinson accomplished when distinguishing between management and administration.

Given Hodgkinson's differentiation of management from administration, it would seem that one of the more obvious implications of his move to equate administration with leadership is that management cannot be leadership. But he rejects this by claiming, 'Leadership extends from apex to base of organizational hierarchy. It pervades the organization. No one can escape leadership acts and leadership responsibilities any more than they can evade the administrative–managerial processes' (1983: 195–196; 1996: 78). Just what is meant by 'leadership acts and leadership responsibilities' here and how they differ from the 'administrative–managerial processes' is not immediately clear, but the intent is presumably to recognise that all members of an organisation can provide leadership, and are indeed expected to do so under appropriate circumstances, as is recognised, encouraged, or even demanded in various formal and informal normative media. In support of this, Hodgkinson cites a *Führerprinzip* of the Nazi military, which laid responsibility to lead on all officers and enlisted men. This is by no means unique to Nazism, the principle of distributed responsibility for leadership being something of a metavalue in military doctrine. In addition to the more obvious emphasis on leading troops, as nicely captured in the 'Follow Me' motto of the United States' Infantry, military commitment to the leadership principle seeks to create a doctrine that can preserve purpose and order when formal organisation crumbles in the heat of battle. Hodgkinson (1996: 79) cites the apt example of an 'NCO isolated with his men on the battlefield', but it could also be a handful of soldiers with no formally designated leader. In such instances, and also in times of crisis in non-military settings, leadership does not flow from or inhere in the hierarchy and obligations of formal organisation, but arises from the people and the circumstances, although in some instances (as in the military), it may also be encouraged by convention or formal indoctrination.

This points to a crucial difference between administration and leadership. Hodgkinson's differentiation between management and administration anchors administration in formal organisations, more specifically in the upper strata of larger, compound ones. But leadership is a far, far more diffuse phenomenon. Not only can we sensibly talk, as Hodgkinson does, about leadership being exercised by any member of an organisation at any level and even surviving the collapse of organisation, leadership can also be found in the absence of formal organisation. Street gangs, dissident academics, sewing circles, war parties, bridge parties, tea parties, can all have leaders. James MacGregor Burns (1978), who bequeathed to us his much misunderstood and misapplied theory of transforming leadership, also gave us his neglected but particularly pertinent notion of complete leadership acts (CLAs), 'that is, the process and achievement of intended change'. As he explains, CLAs are manifest not only in larger-scale activities such as building a new political party, a campaign against literacy, or in administering a complex organisation, but also in

> a mother consciously acting in such a way that her small son's sensitivity to others will be improved, a taxi driver deliberately setting an example of considerate driving, a Red Guard leader making sure food and drink are equally shared up on a work project in the country – all these are parts of the totality of the leadership process. Leadership begins earlier, operates more widely, takes more forms, pervades more sectors of society, and lasts longer in the lives of most persons than has been generally recognized.
>
> (Burns 1978: 427)

Just so. But we can go further. Wolf packs have leaders, so do coteries of prairie dogs, troops of baboons, and pods of killer whales. Not only is leadership not restricted to formal organisations, it is not unique to human kind. Indeed, we have good reasons to think our species would not have evolved to its current world dominance had it not been for successful tribal leadership among our hominid ancestors. 'We were small, we were vulnerable. We could have hunted large game successfully only in bands with certain, reliable leadership' (Ardrey 1966: 263).[6] Hodgkinson likes to remind us of the ancient heritage of administration, suggesting it is the oldest of professions (1983: 17). Leadership is much, much older, almost certainly predating the dawn of language. Indeed, the challenges faced by proto-human leaders when communicating to others what was to be done on the hunt, in the defence of the tribe, or when mounting an attack to seize territory, likely played a significant role in the emergence of language. As Hodgkinson correctly has it, 'Language is the basic administrative tool' (1978: 204, Proposition 1.22). Administration is indeed an ancient art and calling, but it cannot predate the emergence of (written) language, or the emergence of social organisations with the hierarchical depth to require complex, generalised, abstracted coordination, such as city states, large military formations, and pyramid construction enterprises.

The argument runs the other way as well, for surely administration is more than just leadership. Hodgkinson himself cautioned that 'it must always be remembered that the administrator role involves more than leadership' (1978: 191), and elsewhere he talks about the administrator as 'sometimes a leader, sometimes a statesman, sometimes philosopher, sometimes a judge' (1978: 178). We could explore this further by recruiting from the broader literature various lists of functions, activities, processes such as those proposed by Fayol and others, ranging from planning and budgeting, through decision-making, problem-solving, policy creation and the like. But let us just enlist Hodgkinson's hero Barnard, who identified the three broad, interrelated functions of executive work as being 'first, to provide the system of communication; second, to provide the securing of essential efforts; and, third, to formulate and define purpose' (1938: 217). But while Barnard did not equate his executivism with leadership in the way Hodgkinson does with administration, Barnard did assign particular importance to leadership, a point to which we shall return at the end.

One senses that Hodgkinson is not entirely satisfied with his decision to equate administration with leadership. The awkwardness of his position is illustrated by his retreat to using the term 'administrator-leader' when discussing what he calls 'solitaires', by which he means non-organisational leaders such as Marx, Christ, and Buddha. Charisma is the key concept here, and Hodgkinson considers this mysterious quality at length when discussing his Poet archetype (1983: 177–190; 1996: 215–222) which we will consider later. Elsewhere, he mentions Max Weber's treatment of charisma, but fumbles the important point, declaring Weber's 'analysis of leadership is a classification into the categories of traditional, rational and charismatic' (1996: 81). He corrects himself in a footnote (1996: 279, n. 34), explaining the reference is to Weber's famous typology of authority, not leadership, but he does not follow through on this key distinction. For Weber, the authority of charisma was the defining essence of leadership:

> From a substantive point of view, every charismatic authority would have to subscribe to the proposition, 'It is written . . . but I say unto you . . .' The genuine prophet, like the genuine military leader and every true leader in this sense, preaches, creates, or demands *new* obligations – most typically, by virtue of revelation, oracle, inspiration, or of his own will, which are recognized by the members of the religious, military, or party group because they come from such a source. Recognition is a duty.
> (Weber 1978: 243–244, his emphasis)

There is an intriguing parallel here between Weber's account of the origins of a leader's new demands and Hodgkinson's account of the first step in his P3M3 administrative taxonomy as quoted earlier. We shall return to this, but here we may note that the essence of the new obligation revealed by Weber's leaders will always challenge an established order: 'It is written, but I say unto you . . .'. In contrast, we can imagine the quintessential motto of Hodgkinson's managers will be 'It is written, and therefore . . .', or, in more technical specialised sub-units, perhaps 'The capacity/potential/limits of the system will only allow . . .'. As portrayed by Barnard, Jaques and Vickers, and in Hodgkinson's original distinction, administrators would likely say, 'It is written, but what else is possible?', or 'How can it be better written, or reconceived?', or 'What, now, should be written?'

It would seem then that leadership cannot be administration: leadership is too broad, old, ambiguous, and multiply manifest to fit within the more precise idea of administration as developed by Hodgkinson. Nor can administration be leadership, as we can have leadership without the specific obligations and responsibilities of administration. To maintain that each is the other impedes rather than helps in trying to discriminate the sense, reference and intent of these concepts in the doing of administrative philosophy. But it is possible to rescue Hodgkinson from his descent into Humpty-Dumpty-like stipulation. As noted, he has occasion to make use of the term 'administrator-leader' when he needs to focus more directly on those who practise their leadership 'within and on behalf of an organization' (1983: 197). This suggests that what he really had in mind when equating administration with leadership was that administration deals in, is associated with, is differentiated by, a particular kind of leadership. In any event, such an approach offers a potentially productive way forward. The general strategy would be to look for ways in which expectations for and the actual practice of leadership vary across organisational levels, positions, processes and other contexts. In the specific instance of the LAMPuzzle we would look for systematic differences in reasonable expectations for, theoretically informed accounts about, and philosophically defensible analyses of, leadership at the managerial level on one hand and in the administrative realm on the other. A more complete agenda would extend such enquiry to include expectations for and instances of leadership among organisational members on shop floors, in sales departments, secretarial pools, classrooms, officerless military units, nursing wards, sports teams and so forth. This inverts the way in which leadership has been most commonly studied in modern times, enquiry typically having been directed towards developing generic theories of leadership which could then be applied to specific roles and positions. This approach has been stunningly unsuccessful (see Richmon and Allison 2003). The alternative suggested here turns that approach on its head by anticipating that the way people lead varies across organisational (and historical, cultural and social) contexts. The term 'leadership' thus comes to designate the *qualities* that (systematically) differentiate how the acts and processes of leading are attempted and accomplished in different contexts. The first questions in leadership enquiry will be, who or what is being led and for what purpose? And we expect the form and nature of leadership to vary when the answer is a football team, a work group, a family, a mutiny, a revolution, a political party, a department, a platoon, or an army or some other complex, multi-unit formal organisation headed by administrators.

In one of his discussions of the dramaturgical aspect of administration, Hodgkinson observes 'the administrator must be aware that he is continually acting a part. This part is conventionally understood as that of the leader, and the role performance is continually monitored by a variety of audiences, even when the script must be improvised and the scenarios are totally obscure' (1983: 23). This puts the point discussed earlier nicely into focus, since comparing scripts followed by role incumbents and anticipated by their fellow cast members and audiences is one potentially powerful way of exploring meaningful differences in the way leadership is enacted in different roles and contexts. Not just specific scripts themselves, of course, but more interestingly the question of how the role incumbent and the whole ensemble come to know these scripts. Even so, we must be careful of the dramaturgic analogy, for it has the power to seduce us into once again confounding leadership with administration. Certainly administrators lead, and it would certainly appear that the ways they play their leading role are important, probably vitally so. But they play other roles too, and they also have important responsibilities backstage and offstage.

In sum, it seems reasonable to interpret Hodgkinson's attempt to equate administration with leadership as an overstatement of his case, attributable to his overriding interest in coming to grips with the distinctive ways in which administrators lead. His more detailed explorations of this shift the focus from LAMProcesses to LAMPrinciples, from organisations to values, from characteristics to character.

THE VALUE IMPERATIVE

Ribbins (1999) dubbed Hodgkinson's books the 'Victorian Quartet of values literature', a direct reference to Hodgkinson's home in Victoria, BC, otherwise known as Arcadia West. Yet Hodgkinson's anabasis into the realm of values does have something of a Victorian, or perhaps more accurately, an Edwardian, feel. More than a few of his assumptions and analyses are out of step with recent thinking in the philosophy of science and values, his ideas marching more with the thoughts of Moore, Hegel, Kant and Nietzsche, than with Foucault, Rorty, Hacking, or Margolis, accompanied, it almost seems, by the faint strains of brass bands playing on the promenade, rather than selections from a CD in a PC.[7] Whether this is the case or not, we need to consider Hodgkinson's approach to values before returning to the broader question of administrative leadership.

Facts and fallacies

'The world of fact is given, the world of value made' (Hodgkinson 1978: 220; and 1996: 133). From this basal claim Hodgkinson hangs all his lore and prophecy about values. This time etymology is not on his side, 'fact' coming to us from the Latin *factum*, to make.[8] What he wants to convey is the notion that significant aspects of reality are given to us by the world 'out there'. But as his various quotations from Wittgenstein go to show, we come to know the world by interpreting what appears to be given through language and theory. Through, as Weber had it, the 'perpetual process of reconstruction of those concepts in terms of which we seek to lay hold of reality' (1949: 105), or as Kuhn more recently expressed it, through 'the entities with which [a] theory populates nature' (1996: 201). As discussed at length by contemporary philosophers of science such as Hacking (1999), Latour (1999) and Pickering (1995), this applies to facts as much as to other conceptions. Facts are not given to us like pebbles on a beach, they are constructed by human artifice and artefact.[9] Nor are values made in the sense that Hodgkinson claims. They are given to us through the media of human culture *via* the dynamic processes of enculturation, socialisation and education, which forge our identity and infuse the world with meaning. We may and do choose some values over others, but characteristically and for the most part our values pre-exist us (Geertz 1973, Strauss and Quinn 1997). It is more the case then, that facts are made and values given. This reversal does not do serious harm to Hodgkinson's project, although it does provide the ammunition to blow some of his proscriptions about science out of the water, a point not at issue here. We can nonetheless proceed by agreeing with him that facts and values are inextricably interwoven in sociocultural reality, and thus in the fabric of life in organisations and the responsibilities of administrators.

One of the noteworthy developments in Hodgkinson's work is a growing recognition of the salience of sociocultural values. In *Towards a Philosophy of Administration* the focus was firmly on values as internal and, to a lesser degree, organisational phenomena, with only passing reference to 'Extra-organizational cultural values' (1978: 131). In contrast, his latest book offers and uses a well worked out typology of layers of value, the development of which can be traced through the two intervening volumes. Two versions of the model are actually presented. As is made clear in the accompanying text, the first version, aptly entitled 'The Administrative Value Field', is an 'extension and modification' of the venerable Getzels–Guba delineation of nomothetic (formal role expectations) and idiographic (individual personality) dimensions in organisations (Hodgkinson 1996: 44–46). Hodgkinson's expansion is a genuine advance that deserves to be widely noticed and used. The second version, entitled 'The Field of Value Impress', explicitly deals with five 'broad levels of value' as sources of values external to individuals (1996: 151). These layers of external values (which also appear in the first variant) are named and indexed as follows: V5 = Cultural ethos and Zeitgeist, V4 = Local and subcultural interpretation, V3 = Organisational values, V2 = Peer group (encompassing the informal organisation), and V1 = Individual. But while Hodgkinson recognises and accepts these enfolding layers of value, and while he acknowledges that values at higher levels are impressed on lower levels and their human constituents, he remains reluctant to accept both the formative effect and the objective status of sociocultural values to anything like the extent to which they are viewed in contemporary cultural realist and social constructivist approaches, clinging to his contention that values are made, not given. We will return to this.

Hodgkinson warns readers against committing various fallacies, chief among which is the naturalistic fallacy. But as Colin Evers (1985) pointed out, Hodgkinson consistently conflates Moore's original account of this fallacy, which is the error of assuming that good can be defined as if it were a simple natural property, with Hume's earlier stricture against getting an 'ought' from an 'is'. Hodgkinson adverts to both transgressions in all four volumes of the Victorian Quartet, but concentrates on the sin of Getting Ought From Is (GOFI), sternly warning that administrators 'must beware of the temptation to derive their subjectivities ("ought's") from their objectivities ("is's")' (1996: 124). For Hodgkinson this is more than faulty logic: it amounts to a typing error which results in values being improperly derived from facts (1978: 106; 1991: 90). Yet despite vigorous preaching of the GOFI doctrine by various proponents in addition to Hodgkinson, it has been demonstrated that we can indeed get to ought from is (e.g. Arrington 1989; Evers and Lakomski 1991: Ch. 8). We do not need to look into these logical arguments; what is of more interest here is Mark Holmes's (1986: 85) straightforward challenge to Hodgkinson: 'She is a teacher of 7-year olds in our local schools; therefore she should teach them to read'. Hodgkinson's response is revealing. 'The value premises in [Holmes's] example are there prior to the definition of teacher. . . . Once the values are set then one can, *of course, appear to* derive values from the value-loaded fact' (Hodgkinson 1991: 90, my emphasis). Indeed we can – but there is no 'appear to' about it. The meanings with which cultures infuse language ensure that nominative and descriptive terms will be saturated with value. Hacking's elevator words are powerful manifestations of this, but common everyday conversation is replete with examples, especially in organisations. We can readily expand on Holmes's example by pointing out whoever *is* the school principal *ought* to do 'all that is prudent, possible and permitted to ensure' that Holmes's teacher teaches her students to read (Allison and Ellett 1999: 198) – and we can readily imagine that if she were not doing this, then such an expectation would be being voiced by parents and in the school staffroom. Such expectations are embedded in our shared expectations for role incumbents: she is a mother; she ought to care for her child. He is a manager; he ought to possess requisite technical expertise. She is an administrator; she ought to provide (appropriate) leadership. And so on and so forth. While Hodgkinson recognises the possibility of this in his V5 to V2 layers of value impress, he tries to duck the implications for his fact/value and is/ought dichotomies by arguing that common concepts such a 'teacher' will bear 'different value connotations from culture to culture and from time to time' (1991: 91). True enough, but this is a red herring, since each of us lives and has our being in – and each administrator must decide and act within – a single culture complex at a single time. It is also the case, of course, that the normative conclusions people reach from their interpretations of everyday events and circumstances obviously cannot be taken as categorical or universal: they will always be contingent on the context within the culture. But this is precisely the domain in which administrators (and the rest of us) are located. In consequence, administrators who heed Hodgkinson's advice and cling to the GOFI doctrine will be denying the validity of everyday value discourse in their organisation, which he presumably would not want them to do.

Finally, we need to consider Hodgkinson's 'analytical model of the value concept' (1978: 110; 1991: 97), which he also calls his 'value paradigm' (1983: 38; 1996: 114). This is a typology derived from the four (and only four) grounds on which Hodgkinson claims values can be justified by those who hold them (1982: 37; 1991: 98; 1996: 117). Type III values are simple, idiosyncratic, self-justifying preferences for what is believed to be 'good' by an individual: what he or she desires. I prefer Scotch; my wife prefers port, and that is all that can be said on the matter, as there is no accounting for tastes (1996: 117). His remaining value types are justified with reference to conceptions of what is 'right' rather than 'good' in this hedonistic sense: the desirable rather than the desired (1996: 116). Type II values are justified on rational grounds, two subtypes being recognised: Type IIb values, where what is right is determined by social consensus or some aggregation of views, as through a legislative process or social norms and conventions. Type IIa values are justified through rational calculation of some kind, such as cost–benefit analysis. Both kinds of Type II values assume a social context within which heads can be counted, individual preferences aggregated (IIb), or expected consequences assessed with reference to 'a given scheme of social norms, expectations, and standards' (IIa) (1996: 117). Type I values are 'the ultimate level of value' and 'are transrational; they go beyond reason. They imply instead an act of faith or intent or will – a *conviction* manifested in the acceptance of a *principle*' (1996: 118, his emphasis). In addition to an implicitly assumed social context, Type I values have a metaphysical dimension and a 'quality of absoluteness' (1996: 118): 'They are often codified into religious systems . . . or . . . political ideologies' (1996: 120). In his accompanying postulate of hierarchy Hodgkinson declares, without argument, that 'Type I values are superior, more authentic, better justified, and of more defensible grounding than Type II. Likewise, Type II are superior to Type III' (1978: 116; 1996: 121). This is a remarkable claim, for in addition to stipulating levels of justification and authenticity, it appears as if values themselves are being ranked. This introduces an ontological problem that haunts the paradigm and bedevils Hodgkinson's use of it as an analytical engine.

Hodgkinson claims this scheme is 'philosophically robust' (1996: 181), but as a variety of commentators have pointed out, it is quite rickety (e.g. Evers 1985, Evers and Lakomski 1991, Lobb 1993, Willower 1998). This is not the place to dwell on its shortcomings, but notice must be taken of several important limitations. First, by limiting conceptions of 'good' to Type III values of hedonistic preference, the typology is powerless with regard to what might count, for example, as the 'good' exercise of leadership by an administrator. As such, the paradigm lacks the resources to differentiate between good and evil. Whatever is preferred at the Type III level is by definition 'good', and whatever is chosen by reason or force of will at levels II and I respectively is 'right', but only for the person making these choices. Hodgkinson tries to get around these problems by allowing Type II and I valuation to embrace normative standards and moral codes. However, this does not help because mere recognition of the social, moral and philosophical content of values that are valued by Type II and I valuation does not allow analysis of their relative moral worth. What is 'right' for Hodgkinson's chooser may well be condemned as evil by others. Ironically, by equating 'good' with innumerable individual preferences, the model also condemns us to endlessly committing the naturalistic fallacy as originally propounded by Moore, which is strange, given Hodgkinson's warnings about this sin.[10]

One of the more obvious problems with the model is how 'subrational' Type III values of Preference are reliably differentiated from 'transrational' Type I values of Principle. Both are by definition non-rational and, as Hodgkinson says, 'Type I values are Type III values writ large' (1996: 211). His most direct answer appeared in an article responding to Evers's (1985) original criticisms. Here he abstracts and makes more explicit key psychological 'correspondences' or 'faculties' incorporated into the schematic presentations of the value paradigm in his four books. They are emotion and affect at level III, reason and cognition at level II, and will and conation at level I. In accord with the postulate of hierarchy, this is summarised as Will > Reason > Emotion: 'So long as the faculty of will can be discriminated from the faculty of emotion then the paradigm holds', declares Hodgkinson (1986: 14). This drives home the dynamic of individual choice underlying the model, with value status being set by the grounds on which an individual is considered to hold a particular value. The key analytical question in Hodgkinson's scheme is thus why someone holds a given value: is it a case of emotion, reason or will? Because this can change, an individual's values can be transmuted, mutated, transvalued: what was initially an emotional preference for some valued state can modulate into reasoned justification or be transformed into a transcendental commitment and vice versa. Hodgkinson's value paradigm is thus very much concerned with motivation, as he acknowledges through his various discussions of parallels between his paradigm and the theories of Maslow and Herzberg (e.g. 1978: 117–120; 1996: 129–131). Indeed, it often seems to work better as a theory of motivation than value.[11]

In his most recent book, Hodgkinson compares his typology to Weber's constructs of instrumental and value rationality, concluding 'the Weberian interpretation is supportive of the value paradigm as given' (1996: 132). These constructs form part of Weber's broader typology of social action, which also recognises affectual and traditional (habitual) bases for social behaviour. The affectual maps onto Hodgkinson's Type III level of preference. Action and orientation to action based on habit is not directly recognised in Hodgkinson's paradigm, but given that much of such behaviour flows from conformity with social and cultural conventions in Weber's analysis, it seems very similar to Hodgkinson's IIb type of value attachment. Contrary to Hodgkinson's interpretation, his Type I value commitment looks very similar to Weber's value rationality, where action is described as being 'determined by a *conscious belief* in the value for its own sake of some ethical, aesthetic, religious or some other form of behavior, independently of its prospects for success' (Weber 1978: 25, emphasis added). Pulling this together, Type III value attachment maps onto Weber's affectual bases for social action, Type IIb onto Weber's traditional/habitual bases, Type IIa is Weber's instrumental rationality (*zweckrational*), and Type I value commitment Weber's value rationality (*wertrational*).

As noted earlier, Hodgkinson sometimes refers to Type I, II, and III values as if the hierarchy of superiority was somehow inherent in the values themselves. When outlining his 'homogenetic' fallacy he explicitly claims that 'values are themselves amenable to hierarchical analysis' (1996: 124), although the examples he gives to illustrate this rest on different levels at which individuals subscribe to similar values. A particularly intriguing case occurs in a discussion of the 'moral character' of organisations where Hodgkinson asks 'Is the organization, say, elitist (Type I), productive (IIA), politically correct (IIB), hedonic (III)' (1996: 169). Here Hodgkinson appears to be classifying organisational cultures according to differences inherent in values themselves. But how can political correctness, for example, *be* IIb? As we all know from personal experience, some individuals can most definitely subscribe to such values at the Type I level, and presumably an organisation staffed entirely by such people would be characterised by shared normative commitments at this level. But what are the implications for organisational culture if some (many) members of the organisation subscribed to such values only at the IIb or even III level? Obviously the 'official' culture as proclaimed in mission and vision statements and the like could formally commit the organisation to a politically correct value set. But as Hodgkinson takes pains to point out, organisations cannot value; only people can (e.g. 1996: 176). As he presents it, Hodgkinson's value paradigm only allows for Type I preference or Type II or III commitment *by* individuals *to* whatever values they choose. In the examples given and elsewhere, Hodgkinson appears to commit what we might call the paradigmatic fallacy of assigning hierarchical levels to values independent of a valuing agent.

In any event, we are left with the reality of organisational (V3), social (V4), and cultural values (V5). These are values that exist in the sociocultural world and can be known objectively but are not necessarily subscribed to by any given individual at any level in the paradigm. Hodgkinson clearly accepts the reality of such values in his levels of values impress schema as discussed earlier. His four organisational metavalues of maintenance, growth, effectiveness, and efficiency are also described as applying to collectives, not to individuals. He acknowledges the problem that arises by recognising the following paradox:

> While the individual alone has the only real *experience* of value and in the end the individual alone, by force of will or force of preference, has the sole *capacity* to take value action yet this individual is the constant recipient of value-determining forces beyond his control or beyond his ken.
>
> (Hodgkinson 1996: 153, his emphasis)

This is more than just a paradox: it highlights a fundamental limitation in Hodgkinson's approach. The important point, as he acknowledges, is that values can be and are determined in ways that do not depend on individual emotion, reason or will. As Hodgkinson says, the cultural 'value impress is inexorable and inescapable' and 'Organizations are always culturally determined' (1996: 153). Administrators, as hierarchically superordinate framers of policy, forgers of purpose, and coordinators of the general interest in all its complexity have the power to influence the culture of their organisation and, by their actions and inactions, vest their organisation with value. Which brings us back to leadership.

Responsible leadership

Hodgkinson gets a great deal of mileage out of his value paradigm, using it to construct a range of additional analytical models and to deconstruct various administrative scenarios. He seems to press it into service at every possible juncture, as well as at some impossible ones. In this respect he appears to have an authentic Type I commitment to the paradigm, whereas an arm's-length Type IIa engagement would perhaps be more appropriate and probably more fruitful. Here we will limit ourselves to a brief consideration of how he uses the paradigm to address the qualities of administrative leadership.

Thom Greenfield, a close colleague of Hodgkinson, helped teach us that organisations are not conscious entities that independently decide courses of action and choose values: they have their being in and act on the world by and through people. Building on this, Hodgkinson portrays organisations as 'moral primitives' (1996: 178) with his organisational metavalues of maintenance, growth, effectiveness and efficiency, as well as other sociocultural norms taken for granted, imbuing, or perhaps better, infecting, fields of action and decision with 'elemental, primitive, unsophisticated, and even inhumane' expectations (1996: 179). In the absence of countervailing forces, the people who are the organisation can become infected with, caught-up in, bewitched by these metavalues to such a degree that they displace more humane moral codes. Decisions become dominated by the assumed interests, needs, realities of The Organisation; actions are justified by sacrifice to the Corporate Gods which displace the common good. The impress of social interests outside organisations can readily amplify this tendency. In private enterprise, unreflective commitment to 'enhancing stockholder value' spurs blind pursuit of the organisational metavalues, while in the public sector, administrators are often exhorted, or nowadays even compelled, to 'do more with less'.

Given their location at the apex of organisations, and their functional power and influence over organisational purpose and process as discussed in the first section of this chapter, administrators have the potential to modulate the press of both external demands and internal metavalues through their decisions and dispositions, for good or ill. Hodgkinson and Barnard agree that because of this, the character of any organisation's chief office-holders is crucial. 'Insofar as organizations are moral orders the values of their leadership makes them so', says Hodgkinson (1996: 177), echoing Barnard's 'Organizations endure, however, in proportion to the breadth of the morality by which they are governed' (1938: 282). An important part of the answer to the question Greenfield posed in our epigraph lies here: by virtue of their position, authority and actions, administrators have the potential to create moral orders that are worthy of obedience and respect. Even if they fall short of this difficult goal, as many do, their power to form and reform the moral order of an organisation constitutes a central quality, perhaps the defining quality, of administrative leadership.

Hodgkinson explores this central issue using a set of four ideal type characters developed from his value paradigm, which he calls archetypes. The first of these, the Careerist, is highly ambitious, power-hungry, ultimately self-centred, obsessed with visible success as measured by progress up organisational hierarchies and access to perquisites of office. The Careerist character has a 'rugged amorality' evident in a willingness to work around moral conventions rather than abide by them (1996: 93). Careerists are often regarded as good leaders as a result of their drive, initiative, and ability to attract followers or, perhaps more accurately, satellites. Careerists' preoccupation with self and pursuit of success for personal rewards embodies an essentially Type III level of valuation. In Hodgkinson's second archetype, the Pragmatist, 'the ordinary narcissism of the careerist' is 'modulated or sublimated through identification with group values and group interests' (1996: 96). Pragmatists are highly attuned to social sentiments and attentive to group opinion, to which they typically orient decisions and from which they are prone to draw moral and ethical principles. The parallel to Type IIb consensus valuation is evident. Pragmatists' leadership forte lies in coalition formation, consensus building, and the 'art of the possible'. Hodgkinson underlines the Pragmatists' authentic commitment to collective sentiments by suggesting that a Pragmatist leader sufficiently at odds with official policies would be inclined to 'assist the followers to mutiny' (1996: 99).

His third archetype, the Technician, embodies Type IIa rationality. Technicians are portrayed as 'pre-eminently rational-cognitive and rational-legal' with 'values that are primarily those of intellect and logic – intrinsic vales subserved by the extrinsic values of dispassion, impartiality, efficiency, effectiveness, planning' (1996: 222). He notes that Technicians' moral vision will typically extend beyond their organisation and they will characteristically be little concerned with self-interest, advancement or public recognition. Hodgkinson readily acknowledges that his Technician character is much like Weber's ideally typical bureaucrat, noting that the archetype also embodies central notions in the terms 'professional', 'expert', 'technocrat' and 'mandarin'. He explains that he decided against using one of these titles because of the pejorative semantic moss they have gathered.[12] Even so, one regrets his choice of Technician, with its limiting connotations. Perhaps Architect would be better: or Polyarch to capture the expertise of generalism, or Consul in honour of Ancient Rome's chief administrators. Regardless, Hodgkinson seems to have had some difficulty warming to the task of describing this archetype, which appears bland, colourless, faceless, reminiscent of Simon's 'moral cipher', which Hodgkinson so deplores (1978: 20; 1996: 36). Not so with his fourth and final archetype, the Poet, which is offered as the embodiment of Type I valuation. Hodgkinson waxes at length here, in awe of the charisma that is the defining essence of this archetype. Indeed, his treatment of the Poet archetype in his latest book is entitled 'charisma'. On Hodgkinson's account, the Poet 'goes beyond the limits of normality' and promises a new order (1996: 218). 'It is written, but I say unto you . . .', as we noted earlier. History attests that true charismatics have a mysterious but very real power over others and because of this, Hodgkinson correctly views this archetype as potentially dangerous, citing Hitler as an example. 'There is no aspect of administration more dangerous than that which forges the link between power, charisma, and men' (1978: 291, Proposition 6.431; 1996: 85, Proposition 68). By definition in Hodgkinson's scheme, a Poet's values will inhere in the new obligations demanded by his[13] revelation, intuition, or will. These values are deemed right because the Poet believes in them and expects others to do so. Whether a Poet's Vision will be good or evil cannot be anticipated in advance of the revelation he brings, or perhaps of the consequences that follow. As such, Poets can have no defining moral code because the morality they preach will inhere in the Vision they reveal which, by definition in Weber's account, will be at least subjectively new to potential followers. Hodgkinson nonetheless holds that the Poet 'becomes a *moral* leader, calling followers beyond their petty rationality, the bourgeois comforts, their prudential insecurities' (1996: 216–217, his emphasis). True enough in the sense that the Poet seeks to bind others to the obligations he reveals, be they good or evil. But Careerists, Pragmatists, and Technicians can also seek to bind others to their values and moral precepts, which are more readily predictable. And if any of these become administrators, they will be invested with the authority and other sources of power and influence that can be used to do this. As true charismatics, Poets do not need the authority granted by established office to bend others to their will: their authority is given by their charisma.

Consonant with Weber's use of ideal type models, Hodgkinson takes care to explain that his archetypes are abstractions for which there will be no exact empirical analogues. The objective is not to produce painstakingly accurate representations of reality, but to abstract key features that can further conceptual analysis. Specific individuals will usually be amalgams of several or all archetypes in various degrees. We would expect all actual and aspirant administrators to be ambitious to some degree, but only in Careerists would ambition and self-advancement dominate. Consistent with the machinery of his value paradigm, Hodgkinson also claims that higher archetypes subsume the defining characteristics of lower ones.

Hodgkinson's archetypes further his analysis well. Without reviewing the pertinent points directly, the values, interests and abilities associated with the Careerist appear well suited for managerial work and leadership at the Managing and Monitoring levels of his P3M3 model,[14] while Pragmatists seem well fitted for work and leadership at the Mobilizing and Motivating levels. Both have the potential to appear promotable to higher levels. Yet while the characters and leadership strengths of Careerists and Pragmatists appear well suited for managerial responsibilities, they seem less well matched to administrative positions where Planning and Philosophy dominate. It appears implausible that a Poet would ever work his way up though the hierarchy of a complex organisation to an administrative level position. If this should appear likely, Hodgkinson sensibly warns those tempted to appoint a Poet to high office to beware – 'to be *aware*' of the dangers (1996: 222). Charismatics are more likely to establish their own organisation *pace* Weber, or to seize control of an existing organisation directly. The prospect of truly Poetical leadership of an organisation sufficiently complex to require administration thus appears thankfully remote under normal circumstances. A more likely possibility is for a successful Careerist to clothe him or herself in a cloak of manufactured charisma as a means of enhancing prospects for promotion or election. The groups successfully managed by Pragmatists are likely to try to do this to their leader in an attempt to increase his or her chances of further promotion or election. In either case, should Pragmatists or Careerists attain the heights of professional or political administration, we may anticipate they will present themselves and whatever manufactured vision they come to espouse wrapped in a mantle of ersatz charisma.

We are left, then, with Hodgkinson's seemingly bland yet proficient Technician as the apparent heir to administrative posts, and thus the challenges of administrative leadership. When compared to the forms of leadership associated with Careerists, Pragmatists and Poets, this seems bland indeed.[15] But this need not be so if we apply the value paradigm differently. I submit that when constructing his Poet archetype Hodgkinson not only committed what was called the paradigmatic fallacy earlier, he also conflated authority with motivation. Weber's classic analysis treats charisma as one of his three sources of authority, which he takes care to keep analytically separate from his four bases of social action, which were briefly described earlier. The charismatic subscribes to the values he reveals at a Type I level, that is, he believes in, is committed to, fully engaged with, these values. He demands that others adhere to them and when they do so this legitimises his authority over them. But whatever conceptions of the desirable may be revealed by a charismatic, they cannot, by themselves, *be* Type I values. To claim such is to commit the paradigmatic fallacy. Nor will those who follow a Poet necessarily subscribe to the revealed values at a Type I level; they may value them out of a rational consideration of their self-interest (IIa), because others espouse them or out of habit (IIb), or as a matter of preferential convenience (III). In short, the transcendental power of Hodgkinson's Poet comes from his charismatic authority and not from the inherent transcendental quality of his revelation.

Once we recognise this, we can place the Poet archetype aside and view charisma as the sociocultural wild card that it is, accepting Weber's view that charismatic authority involves 'surrender to the extraordinary' (1978: 954), rather than participation in the ordinary.[16] We can also see that Hodgkinson's other three archetypical characters can subscribe to the values that distinguish them at any of his levels of valuation. A Careerist may so sincerely and completely believe in his or her abilities and self-interest that the Type III origins of these become transvalued into a Type I commitment to personal advancement. Similarly, a Pragmatist can subscribe to group interests and consensus with Type I fervour, Type II calculation or consensus, or a Type III preference. Put this way, we have a prima-facie case for Technicians who have a Type I commitment to their defining values of instrumental rationality.

Here is where the apparent blandness of Technician leadership can become vitalised. As Greenfield observed in his final paper from which our epigraph is taken, the essence of the matter is Service, the capitalisation being deliberate. Not service to the organisation with its culture and metavalues as such, but Service to the idea of what the organisation stands for, what it ought to be, and how members or clients should ideally participate in its life and work (cf. Hodgkinson 1996: 223 and 227, Proposition 231). Unlike the Poet, or for that matter Careerists or Pragmatists, Technicians who are authentically engaged with their defining values at the Type I level will not demand or necessarily expect others to embrace their ideals. On the contrary, they are more likely to keep both the details and the level of their commitment private.[17] Theirs will be a personal vision rather than the publicly proclaimed 'vision statement' so beloved of managerial consultants, political spin-doctors and leadership shamans. Because their hierarchical position and their duties give them power, sometimes great power, over others, administrators' personal visions of and for their organisation will inevitably have moral content. Hodgkinson adverts to this in his reference to administrative morality being 'private in genesis, public in effect' (1996: 176), and when he muses on the possibility of a 'leadership ethic of personal and private honour (moral integrity) . . . which may even be deliberately *secret*' (1996: 268, his emphasis).

In Barnard's treatment, administrators' personal conceptions of what is desirable in and for their organisation will form part of their personal moral code. As a consequence of the position they hold, the problems with which they are confronted, and the decisions they must make, he holds that administrators' moral codes will necessarily be complex (1938: 270–272). Barnard further holds that fidelity to one's personal moral code, especially in the face of adversity, is the defining essence of responsibility. Hodgkinson draws on both of these observations, although his treatment is less enthusiastic than might be expected (cf. 1978: 178–179; 1983: 204; 1991: 128–129; 1996: 177).[18] Hodgkinson seems to prefer the notion of commitment rather than responsibility (1991: 156; 1996: 245), but it is much the same thing, given that he treats commitment as 'a sort of internalized set of self-expectations' (1996: 245). As we have seen, administrators must necessarily be concerned with reconciling multiple demands and Hodgkinson aptly framed this as the central problem of administration (1996: 32). As viewed by Hodgkinson and Barnard, the specific challenge of administrative leadership is to reconcile these competing demands while remaining true to one's personal moral code and the private vision for the organisation that it contains. More specifically, the responsibilities of administrators require them to satisfy their organisation's metavalues (generic and specific) and associated environmental demands and developments while attending to the human interests of the people through which the work of the organisation is coordinated and accomplished. Administrative leadership adds to this the infusion of purpose, ideals and values grounded in the administrator's personal moral code and nourished by his or her private vision of the organisation. At heart it is a matter of being personally responsible for one's public responsibilities (cf. Hodgkinson 1991: 127).

This is a daunting challenge. When the demands are complex and pressing, administrators will obviously be tempted to adjust or compromise their moral standards. As Lord Acton said, 'Power corrupts'. Both Hodgkinson and Barnard recognise that avoiding such temptations will be exceedingly difficult, and that failure will not be unusual. Hodgkinson appears to think that success is essentially a matter of individual will. Barnard sees responsibility and creativity as the crux of the matter, the key being to find, invent, create solutions that satisfy multiple demands while not compromising the administrator's moral code. As he said,

> The creative aspect of executive responsibility is the highest exemplification of responsibility . . . few can do it long, except on the basis of personal conviction – not conviction that they are obligated as officials to do it, but conviction that what they do for the good of the organization they *personally* believe to be right.
>
> (Barnard 1938: 281, his emphasis)

Neither Barnard nor Hodgkinson offers a list of virtues to define or prescribe the ethics of administrative leadership. If we resist being bewitched by Hodgkinson's Poet and accept the Technician archetype with a Type I engagement to the defining values as being best suited for administrative leadership, then we have good grounds for believing both Barnard's ideal executive and Hodgkinson's best case archetype will not hold or subscribe to implicitly objectionable morals. In Barnard's case, he explains that the moral complexity of his executives is to a large extent a product of integrating the pertinent legal, social, technical and professional codes that impinge on the office (1938: 273). Hodgkinson's principle of subsumption implies that Type I committed Technicians (henceforth Polyarchs) will be attuned to social norms, conventions and group sentiments, but not preoccupied with these, unlike the Pragmatist. In both cases, then, we may legitimately expect Polyarchs to be aware of and orient their actions to standards of moral conduct endorsed by key reference groups. Burns's (1978) treatise on leadership both supports and augments the themes developed here. His account of transactional leadership is very similar to the type of leadership associated with Hodgkinson's Pragmatist archetype, but Burns (1978: 75) highlights the importance of what he calls the modal values of 'prudence, honor, courage, civility, honesty, fairness' in the successful practice of transactional leadership, values that would seem central to Hodgkinson's Pragmatist. Although it is missed in some interpretations, Burns carefully steered clear of the bewitchment of charisma leadership when developing his account of transforming leadership (Allison and Cunningham 1998). For Burns the defining quality of transforming leadership is raising others to higher levels of morality, especially as represented by his triptych end values of equality, justice and liberty. While neither Hodgkinson nor Barnard commits himself to such specificity, Burns's whole approach is very much in accord with theirs.[19]

In the conventional wisdom, the greatest leadership challenges for administrators come in times of crisis, when the very future of the organisation is at risk as a result of implacable external demands, deteriorating internal conditions, or some combination of the two. But crises are not always so evident. Barnard points to the handling of exceptional cases where the administrator's decision will be viewed within the organisation as setting an important precedent as one of the most difficult leadership challenges (1938: 279). Hodgkinson reminds us that the day-to-day stuff of administration is a stream of 'matters to be dealt with', problems to be solved, issues addressed, opportunities explored, decisions taken, meetings attended, letters written, interviews held, and so forth (1996: 247). Each of these quotidian acts offers opportunities for administrative leadership, opportunities to incrementally promote the administrator's personal vision for the organisation and to be true to his or her moral code. This is how moral orders worthy of obedience and respect are ultimately created in organisations: case by case, act by act, decision by decision, each guided by private responsibility to public responsibilities.

Envoi

Hodgkinson's LAMPhilosophy provides us with an internally consistent and externally supported portrayal of administrative action and casts valuable light on the qualities of managerial and administrative leadership. He has also brought us to an improved comprehension of the mystery of moral orders in organisations, but limitations in both his value paradigm and his applications of this typology leave much in the shadows. In one of Barnard's closing remarks on creativity, which Barnard saw as the essence of responsible leadership, he observed 'Cooperation, not leadership, is the creative process; but leadership is the indispensable fulminator of its forces' (1938: 259). Hodgkinson's work has had something of a fulminating effect on the appreciation and study of values in administration, and thus the problems of ethical administrative action and moral order in organisations, but much remains to be done. Let's get on with it.

Notes

1 While most of my quotations from his work are taken from Hodgkinson's latest (1996) book, I have also drawn freely on his other volumes. In some cases, page citations are given from several of his books to illustrate the persistence of key ideas and claims. The absence of multiple citations should not be interpreted as implying that the idea or quotation referred to appears only in the cited source.
2 This is widely recognised in the field but I did not appreciate the extent to which Hodgkinson echoes and seeks to amplify Barnard until I read their works side by side when working on this essay. Hodgkinson could be reasonably regarded as Barnard's modern-day prophet. This is another of Hodgkinson's notable contributions, as Barnard's work deserves to be rediscovered and given more attention than it currently receives in the *en passant*, seemingly obligatory, comments made in most textbooks.
3 See his section titled 'Legal authority with a bureaucratic *administrative staff*' in Chapter III of *Economy and Society* (Weber 1978: 217, emphasis added).
4 See Allison (1996) for a more extended discussion, as well as Allison (1989), Allison and Allison (1993) and Allison and Morfitt (1996), which provide support for the existence of Jaques's levels of abstraction and cognitive complexity in school systems, findings from the last two studies cited suggesting that the work of school principals approximates the two-year time span horizon, making them administrators in this sense at least.
5 He also identifies collegial administrators as a distinct class, the type case of which is the university department head. This refinement is ignored here in the interests of economy.
6 Note how Hodgkinson's 'validity test' of substituting administration for leadership produces a quite incongruous result here.

7 See Hodgkinson's useful summary of streams of philosophical thought in the final chapter of his most recent book (1996: Chapter 13), and his broadly warm treatment of the first set of luminaries cited here (although he doesn't mention Moore).
8 For completeness, 'value' finds its root in the Latin *valere*, to be strong, as do valiant, valid, valence, avail and evaluate. Interestingly, given our topic, the Old English *wealdan*, to rule, and *wieldan*, to govern, share this heritage.
9 What appear as invariant (as far as we think we know) regularities commonly referred to as laws are another matter. Still, these are codified and expressed using human-made concepts. As best we know, light travels at 1.80 tera furlongs per fortnight.
10 As defined by Moore, the naturalistic fallacy is committed when one attempts to define 'good' with reference to some natural object or state. We end up doing this with Type III values as follows: If and only if Chris prefers tea, then tea is good. Chris does prefer tea. Tea is therefore good. As Moore points out, this is fallacious because there are more things than tea that are good, as can be demonstrated by asking 'is tea all that is good'. I am indebted to Walter Lobb (1993) for this point.
11 This is not intended to imply that the paradigm *is* a typology of motivation rather than values, but to suggest that it might be better applied as such.
12 This seems to be the natural fate of words of power, that is titles and descriptive labels for people in high authority.
13 The male pronoun is used consciously here to reflect Hodgkinson's suggestion that charisma may well be (primarily) a male phenomenon (1996: 217).
14 Hodgkinson develops the match between his archetypes and the P3M3 taxonomy in his various ways in his last three books.
15 Note that by recognising those other types of leadership, Hodgkinson's own scheme provides a rebuttal to his claim that administration is leadership, as discussed earlier.
16 This is not to deny the reality and the sheer power of charismatic authority. History obviously attests otherwise. The point I've been trying to establish is that when it arises, charismatic authority, by definition, always seeks to destroy or at least displace established orders, moral or otherwise. For this and other reasons it is inherently unstable and congenitally unsuited to the form and process of modern organisations. To see this, imagine what it would be like if the chief administrator of your organisation was Attila, Buddha, Jesus, Gandhi, Moses, Hitler, or Charles Manson.
17 Mintzberg's (1973) research and that by others provide empirical support for administrators' private visions for their organisations. See Allison (1996: 524–529) for a brief review.
18 Why this should be so is not clear. In his earlier work he sometimes seems in awe at Barnard's treatment of executive leadership and morality (e.g. 1978: 95–96), but in his later books he appears almost tolerant in a somewhat distant fashion. Both stances may be fuelled by a reluctance to embrace the elitism that can be easily read into Barnard's views (cf. Hodgkinson 1978: 13). Evers and Lakomski (1991: 100–101) politely accused Hodgkinson of elitist leanings. While he observes in various places that governance by a (competent and moral) elite has its attractions (e.g. 1978: 94; 1996: 107), and he considers his Technician archetype to represent 'rule by the *best*' (1996: 223, his emphasis), he nonetheless shies away from endorsing this view. This is strange given his well known willingness to tilt at other politically correct windmills, especially as his philosophy of administration shows us

we should strive to ensure that those best prepared and suited for the responsibilities involved should be our administrators. Provided there is no overriding social privilege operating that excludes worthy candidates on particularistic grounds, this is not elitism. Still, as Hodgkinson recognises in his various discussions of LAMProfessionalism, our current knowledge is inadequate for the establishment of a justifiable meritocracy based on reliable credentials.

19 In addition to his transactional and transforming types of leadership, Burns also sketches, but does not develop, a third type which could be called tyrannical, where the leader is preoccupied with personal gratification. This produces a pleasing parallel to Hodgkinson's archetypes as adapted here, Tyrannical matching Careerist, Transactional Pragmatist, and Transformational Polyarch.

References

Albrow, M. (1970) *Bureaucracy*, New York: Praeger.

Allison, D. J. (1983) 'Policy and the practice of educational administration', *Canadian Administrator* 23, 1.

Allison, D. J. (1989) 'Exploring the work of school chiefs: The case of the Ontario Director of Education', *Alberta Journal of Educational Research* 35, 4: 292–307.

Allison, D. J. (1996) 'Problem finding, classification and interpretation: In search of a theory of administrative problem processing', in K. Leithwood, J. Chapman, D. Corson, P. Hallinger and A. Hart (eds) *International Handbook of Educational Leadership and Administration*, vol. 1, Dordrecht, NL: Kluwer Academic Publishers.

Allison, D. J. and Allison, P. A. (1993) 'Both ends of a telescope: Experience and expertise in principal problem solving', *Educational Administration Quarterly* 29, 3: 302–322.

Allison, D. J. and Cunningham, A. (1998) 'Transformational leadership and the principalship: Much ado about nothing?', Paper presented at the annual conference of the Canadian Association for the Study of Educational Administration, Ottawa, Ontario, May (ms. available from allison@uwo.ca).

Allison, D. J. and Ellett, F. S. (1999) 'Evers and Lakomski on values in educational administration: Less than coherent', in P. Begley (ed.) *Values and Educational Leadership*, Albany: State University of New York Press.

Allison, D. J. and Morfitt, G. (1996) 'Time span of discretion and administrative work in school systems: Results of a pilot study', *Journal of Educational Administration and Foundations* 11, 1: 8–37.

Ardrey, R. (1966) *The Territorial Imperative*, New York: Dell Publishing.

Arrington, R. L. (1989) *Rationalism, Realism and Relativism: Perspectives in Contemporary Moral Epistemology*, Ithaca, NY: Cornell University Press.

Ashbaugh, C. R. and Kasten, K. L. (1984) 'A Typology of operant values in school administration', *Planning and Change* 15, 4: 195–208.

Barnard, C. (1938) *The Functions of the Executive*, Cambridge, MA: Harvard University Press.

Begley, P. T. (ed.) (1999) *Values and Educational Leadership*, Albany: State University of New York Press.

Burns, J. M. (1978) *Leadership*, New York: Harper and Row.

Carroll, L. (1970) *The Annotated Alice*, Harmondsworth: Penguin.
Cook, E. T. (1913) *The Life of Florence Nightingale, vol. I, 1820–1861,* London: Macmillan.
Dye, T. R. (1975) *Understanding Public Policy*, Englewood Cliffs, NJ: Prentice-Hall.
Evers, C. W. (1985) 'Hodgkinson on Ethics and the Philosophy of Administration', *Educational Administration Quarterly* 21, 4: 27–50.
Evers, C. W. and Lakomski, G. (1991) *Knowing Educational Administration,* Oxford: Pergamon.
Fayol, H. (1949) *General Industrial Management*, London: Pitman.
Geertz, C. (1973) *The Interpretation of Cultures: Selected Essays by Clifford Geertz,* New York: Basic Books.
Greenfield, T. B. (1991) 'Foreword', in C. Hodgkinson, *Educational Leadership: The Moral Art*, Albany, State University of New York Press.
Greenfield, T. B. (1993) 'Science and service: The making of the profession of educational administration', in T. Greenfield and P. Ribbins (eds) *Greenfield on Educational Administration: Towards a Humane Science*, London: Routledge.
Hacking, I. (1999) *Social Construction of What?,* Boston: Harvard University Press.
Hodgkinson, C. (1978) *Towards a Philosophy of Administration*, Oxford: Basil Blackwell.
Hodgkinson, C. (1983) *The Philosophy of Leadership*, Oxford: Basil Blackwell.
Hodgkinson, C. (1986) 'Beyond Pragmatism and Positivism', *Educational Administration Quarterly* 22, 2: 5–21.
Hodgkinson, C. (1991) *Educational Leadership: The Moral Art*, Albany: State University of New York Press.
Hodgkinson, C. (1996) *Administrative Philosophy: Values and Motivation in Administrative Life*, Oxford: Pergamon.
Holmes, M. (1986) 'Comment on "The Decline and Fall of Science in Educational Administration"', *Interchange* 17, 2: 80–90.
Jaques, E. (1976) *A General Theory of Bureaucracy*, London: Heinemann.
Jaques, E. (1989) *Requisite Organization: The CEO's Guide to Creative Structure and Leadership*, Arlington, VA: Cason Hall.
Kuhn, T. S. (1996) *The Structure of Scientific Revolutions*, 3rd edn, Chicago: University of Chicago Press.
Latour, B. (1999) *Pandora's Hope: Essays on the Reality of Science Studies*, Cambridge, MA: Harvard University Press.
Lobb, W. M. (1993) 'Hodgkinson's value model: A question of ethical applicability', unpublished M.Ed thesis, University of Western Ontario.
Mintzberg, H. (1973) *The Nature of Managerial Work*, New York: Harper and Row.
Pal, L. A. (1992) *Public Policy Analysis: An Introduction,* 2nd edn, Toronto: Methuen.
Parsons, T. (1947) 'Introduction', in M. Weber, *The Theory of Social and Economic Organization*, New York: Free Press.
Parsons, T. (1960) *Structure and Process in Modern Societies*, Glencoe, IL: Free Press.
Pickering, A. (1995) *The Mangle of Practice: Time, Agency and Science*, Chicago: University of Chicago Press.
Ribbins, P. (1999) 'Foreword', in P. T. Begley and P. E. Leonard (eds) *The Values of Educational Administration*, London: Falmer Press.

Richmon, M. J. and Allison, D. J. (2003) 'Toward a conceptual framework for leadership inquiry', *Educational Management and Administration* 31, 1: 31–50.

Runciman, W. G. and Matthews, E. (eds and trans.) (1978) *Max Weber: Selections in Translation*, Cambridge: Cambridge University Press.

Scott, W. G. and Hart, H. D. K. (1979) *Organizational America*, Boston: Houghton Mifflin.

Simon, H. (1945) *Administrative Behavior*, New York: Macmillan.

Strauss, C. and Quinn, N. (1997) *A Cognitive Theory of Cultural Meaning*, Cambridge: Cambridge University Press.

Thompson, J. D. (1967) *Organizations in Action*, New York: McGraw-Hill.

Vickers, G. (1970) *The Art of Judgment*, New York: Basic Books.

Weber, M. (1949) '"Objectivity" in social science and social policy', in E. Shils (ed.) *The Methodology of the Social Sciences*, Glencoe, IL: Free Press.

Weber, M. (1968) 'Science as a Vocation', in S. N. Eisenstadt (ed.) *Max Weber on Charisma and Institution Building*, Chicago: University of Chicago Press.

Weber, M. (1978) *Economy and Society*, G. Roth and C. Wittich (eds), Berkeley, CA: University of California Press.

Willower, D. J. (1998) 'Values and valuation: A naturalistic inquiry', in P. Begley (ed.) *Values and Educational Leadership*, Albany: State University of New York Press.

Willower, D. J. and Forsyth, P. B. (1999) 'A brief history of scholarship in educational administration', in J. Murphy and K. Seashore Lewis (eds) *Handbook of Research on Educational Administration*, 2nd edn., San Francisco: Jossey-Bass.

Part II
Ethical foundations for educational administrators

Chapter 4

Editor's introduction

Eugenie A. Samier

The purpose of this collection is to build upon and extend the ethical foundation of educational administration laid in part by Christopher Hodgkinson, and guided by Greenfield's estimation of his influence in this regard. 'If there are ideas from Hodgkinson that have influenced me most, they are the irreducibility of value choice and the unavoidability of human responsibility for that choice' (1993: 265). Hodgkinson's approach contrasts strongly with the two most common forms of approaching ethics in educational administration teaching and scholarship – the dubious practice of telling 'war stories', and presenting uncritically existing codes, policies, rules and procedures – both of which enforce compliance, the former to organisational politics and the latter to organisational norms. Neither of these is a substitute for the moral judgement necessary to ethics. It was Hodgkinson's contention that administration can, and should, be grounded in philosophy.

This collection was conceived as an attempt to address the continuing problem of theoretically grounding educational administration in an area most underdeveloped and contentious. In the spirit of intellectual enquiry, that is, its debating and argumentative tradition, a spectrum of essays on ethical foundations for administrative decision and action in an educational setting have been assembled to contribute to this foundation.

While the problem of a normative foundation for administration had preoccupied some theorists, such as Dahl (1947) in the immediate post-World War II period, it was not until the Minnowbrook conferences in the 1970s and 1980s that a concerted effort was taken by a number of American public administrative theorists to define a value-laden administrative ethic in contrast to the prevailing ethos of a 'value-free science of administration'. The focus, though, was predominantly on reconciling democratic values with bureaucratic necessity in producing a new 'ethic' of public administration in the US (Garofalo and Geuras 1999: Ch. 1).

An examination of ethical foundations has become a greater preoccupation in administrative theory in response to the New Public Management (NPM), sometimes referred to as 'reinventing government',[1] which has introduced greater marketing, state control and special interest group pressures to the civil service. As Kellough argues, many of the changes brought about by NPM in fact place greater discretion in the hands of administrators, sacrificing principles of responsibility for efficiency and productivity imperatives (1999: 665, 668). This view is shared by Maguire, who reviewed recent government reports in Canada, Norway, the UK, New Zealand and Australia, noting that the changed roles of administrators and increased public scrutiny make new and increased ethical demands (1998: 26–27).[2] For Preston (1999), an important consequence of these current administrative reforms, apart from the introduction of public sector ethics programmes in government globally in the 1990s, is the erosion of ethical standards through a politicisation of the senior civil service. Menzel (1999), in reviewing many critics of the NPM for ethical implications,[3] also concludes that NPM proponents are mostly silent on this issue.

However, ethics in public administration is not only a problem of the NPM, but of administrative theory generally. Rohr was able to write in 1978 that the ethics of bureaucracy, as a field of enquiry, was insufficiently developed to allow for an 'established literature capable of being ordered, summarized, and presented in a way that is meaningful to the uninitiated' (1978: 4). This situation changed dramatically as an increasing interest and growing body of literature on ethics in public administration developed in the 1980s,[4] occasioned partly by the aftermath of Watergate in the US,[5] and increasing public dissatisfaction with the public sector in many Western jurisdictions accompanied by consistent 'bureaucrat-bashing' by many politicians. Menzel reports in 1995 that only in the preceding decade had empirical research on public sector ethics begun to grow, yet it remained 'limited and disjointed' in its cumulative findings (1995: 381). Despite Menzel's disappointment over an underdeveloped empirical contribution, the theoretical body of literature on administrative ethics has mushroomed in the past two decades to support regular academic conferences on the topic, a recognised group of administrative ethicists, the first *Handbook of Administrative Ethics* (Cooper 1994), while the sub-field of administrative ethics has been institutionalised in academic bodies.[6]

The expansion of administrative ethics literature is reflected in the inclusion of ethics courses in MPA programmes in the 1980s and 1990s. However, as Menzel points out in his recent survey, while ethics education seems to have made at least a modest improvement in the ethical thinking of graduates, there is no evidence to indicate that any particular ethical school – Aristotelian, Kantian, utilitarian – matters in both sensitising administrators to moral issues or in better equipping them to reason morally (1997). Nor are ethics courses a requirement for graduation in more than 25 per cent of programmes (Menzel 1999: 9). Burke critiques what he calls the 'traditional moral theorizing' in public administration, which

> simply present[s], case-like, the range of practical problems and then permit[s] the morally perplexed free rein to pick and choose from a 'cafeteria of moral principles' in which competing moral theories end up being treated as equally valid, and since they often yield incompatible solutions they render morality meaningless.
> (Burke 1983: 1112)

In other words, ethics in administration literature is dominated by relativism. Denhardt (1988) has also argued that public administration curricula should provide a more philosophically rigorous grounding from which to understand moral precepts and problems relevant to administration: the relationship between means and ends, choosing the lesser evil, the harm principle, cooperation in evil, the principle of double effect, and the difference between motive and intent.

The development of ethics in public administration is mirrored in the educational administration field. As early as 1979, Gibson was able to determine that a new phase had begun by 1970, which he called a period of 'critical consciousness' following the descriptive-analytic period of 1900 to 1950 and the theory movement period of 1950 to 1970 (1979: 33). Gibson highlights Thom Greenfield's challenge to prevailing theory in the mid-1970s – this was to be followed shortly by Chris Hodgkinson's debut, and the appearance of articles arguing for the establishment of a philosophical foundation. The 1980s and 1990s in education administration have seen a flourishing interest in ethics including such authors as Hannah (1980), Farquhar (1981), contributors to Sola's collection of readings (1984), Strike, Haller and Soltis (1988), Beck (1994), Evers (1992), Kirby, Paradise and Protti (1992), and Sergiovanni (1992). What is missing, though, are systematic and detailed studies of the ethical groundwork major philosophical figures can contribute.

The philosophical contributions of the participants in this project to an ethical foundation for educational administration are organised chronologically by the main subject of the essay. The first three, by Don Lang, Richard Bates, and Eugenie Samier, demonstrate the perennial relevance of pre-twentieth-century philosophers to educational administration. Lang's discussion of Thomas Aquinas (1225–1274) focuses on the role of the 'good', and its relationship to intention, will and reason in administrative moral judgement. Of greatest relevance to administrative and leadership morality is the ability to distinguish real from apparent good: the former leading to perfection and higher order principles, and the latter to evil, often in the form of 'right' compliance with rules, regulations and policies. Bates's review of Adam Smith's (1723–1790) economic theory is most timely, given the current New Public Management turn to market models for the public sector, including education, in many countries. Countering many errant portrayals of Smith and popular mistaken notions of his view of market forces, Bates demonstrates that he was seeking to find a role for economics in encouraging moral behaviour. Necessary to Smith's approach is a concept of justice that through jurisprudence establishes a moral responsibility for government in ensuring the welfare, security and liberty of all. Samier's treatment of Immanuel Kant (1724–1804) is developed to demonstrate the direct and practical applicability of the categorical imperative, in its three formulations, to administrative reason and action, in contrast to the common presentation of Kant in administrative theory. Embedded in his notion of ethics as a means of achieving a politically just society are respect for individuals and the autonomy of will in moral freedom. Contained in Kant's moral system is a critique of systems and organisations that inhibit or suppress morality, such as administrative culture, professionalism, administrative training, and traditions of administrative research and theory.

The early part of twentieth-century philosophy is represented by Spencer Maxcy's discussion of pragmatism as it evolved from the writings of Charles Sanders Peirce (1839–1914), William James (1842–1910) and John Dewey (1859–1952), and Carol Harris's discussion of Martin Heidegger (1889–1976). Maxcy reviews four strands of pragmatism – scientific, political, romantic and critical – for the foundation they provide to social justice. Critical pragmatism, which emphasises critical self-reflection oriented towards a desire to reform and reconstruct social and cultural life on a moral yet practical foundation, is demonstrated by Maxcy to contain valuable elements of the three other forms without their possible negative effects. Harris explores the relevance of Heideggerian ethics in a modern technological world, and in regions where neo-liberal social and educational policy has placed great emphasis on economic values. Using four concepts embedded in Heidegger's ontology – enframing, concealment, freedom and agency – Harris demonstrates what ethical conditions are required for educational leaders to create the communities predicated upon empathy, care and the social good.

Contemporary ethics is represented by the contributions of William Foster, Helen Gunter, and Colin Evers. Foster argues for the moral alternative Alasdair MacIntyre (1929–) provides to the dominant positivistic theory of the first half of the twentieth century. MacIntyre conceives of morality as embedded in the virtues of character rather than 'value-addedness', and bureaucratic/instrumentalist orientations as necessarily corruptive of moral language. Of administrative relevance is MacIntyre's argument that virtues are best produced in community, largely inimical to most modern conceptions of administration. Gunter applies Pierre

Bourdieu's (1930–2002) theory of practice and notion of habitus to an intellectual history of educational management in the UK by examining how those participants shaped their professional identities, chose professional practices, and adopted the values upon which ethical dilemmas were dealt with. What is portrayed is the creation of a dynamic, ever-changing living space within which purpose, theory, practice and morality are constructed and debated at the intersection of academic and practitioner lives. Moral purpose among the network of intellectuals in educational management, from a Bourdieuian perspective, is produced through contested legitimacy, cultural power, and struggles over language within the field, as well as the imposition of market forces through government-driven policy causing competition among the members, and is therefore a continuous structuring process. Evers selects as representative of a naturalistic view of ethical judgement, the work primarily of Paul Churchland (1942–) and Paul Thagard. This entails the use of a natural science framework, grounded in empirical psychology, that provides a cognitive model for moral reasoning. Combining Thagard's neuro-computational model for ethical decision-making with Churchland's theory of moral knowledge acquisition, Evers constructs a normative theory of moral learning that meets the epistemological criteria of coherentism.

Peter Gronn's essay, concluding the collection, examines the current forms in which two essential notions of the idealist tradition, service and greatness, have become bifurcated in the twentieth century, often developed as mutually contradictory values, each with a strong inherent moral disposition. As exemplars of this opposition, he discusses Robert Greenleaf's conception of leadership, characterised as a 'collectivised guardianship role for trustees', and Christopher Hodgkinson's view of leadership as not only value-driven, but a morally ambiguous 'great man' theory derived from will. Their attempts to recapture idealism are placed within the growing interest in establishing ethical standards for educational leaders in various policy documents and programmes.

Notes

1 Occasioned by Osborne and Gaebler's *Reinventing Government* (1992) that typifies this ethos.
2 Maguire's article is in a collection of papers presented at a conference on ethics and accountability of the European Group of Public Administration, held to 'investigate ethics for the public service, taking into account the actual development in governance and new public management' (Hondeghem 1998: 1).
3 See Menzel 1999: 5–6. Among those he references are Terry (1998), Frederickson (1997) and Gawthrop (1998).
4 Some of the earlier authors include Rohr (1978), French (1983), Chapman (1988) and Denhardt (1988).

5 To this, in the US alone, one could add a number of subsequent scandals: Iran-Contra, savings and loan, HUD, and Ill-Winds – although Rohr argues that the frequently mentioned Watergate scandal is a 'false start' for a discussion of administrative ethics since it was not a problem involving the career civil service (1978: 7–8).
6 See Goss (1996) for a survey of contributors, and Cooper (1998: xi–xvi) for an overview of developments in the US field.

References

Beck, L. (1994) *Reclaiming Educational Administration as a Caring Profession*, New York: Teachers College Press.

Burke, J. P. (1983) 'Book review of Peter A. French, *Ethics in Government* (Englewood Cliffs: Prentice-Hall, 1983)', *American Political Science Review* 77: 1112–1113.

Chapman, R. (1988) *Ethics in the British Civil Service*, London: Routledge.

Cooper, T. (ed.) (1994) *Handbook of Administrative Ethics*, New York: Marcel Dekker.

Cooper, T. (1998) *The Responsible Administrator*, 4th edn, San Francisco: Jossey-Bass.

Dahl, R. (1947) 'The Science of Public Administration: Three Problems', *Public Administration Review* 7, 1: 1–11.

Denhardt, K. G. (1988) *The Ethics of Public Service: Resolving Moral Dilemmas in Public Organizations*, Westport, CT: Greenwood Press.

Evers, C. (1992) 'Ethics and ethical leadership: A pragmatic and holistic approach', in P. Duignan and R. MacPherson (eds) *Educative Leadership*, London: Falmer Press.

Farquhar, R. (1981) 'Preparing educational administrators for ethical practice', *Alberta Journal of Educational Research* 27, 2: 192–204.

Frederickson, H. G. (1997) *The Spirit of Public Administration*, San Francisco: Jossey-Bass.

French, P. (1983) *Ethics in Government*, Englewood Cliffs: Prentice-Hall.

Garofalo, C. and Geuras, D. (1999) *Ethics in the Public Service: The Moral Mind at Work*, Washington, DC: Georgetown University Press.

Gawthrop, L. G. (1998) *Public Service and Democracy*, Chappaqua: Chatham House.

Gibson, R. O. (1979) 'An approach to paradigm shift in educational administration', in G. Immegart and W. Boyd (eds), *Problem-Finding in Educational Administration*, Lexington, MA: D. C. Heath and Company.

Goss, R. (1996) 'A distinct public administration ethics?', *Journal of Public Administration Research and Theory* 6, 4: 573–597.

Greenfield, T. (1993) 'Educational administration as a humane science: Conversations with Thomas Greenfield', in T. Greenfield and P. Ribbins (eds) *Greenfield on Educational Administration: Towards a Humane Science*, London: Routledge.

Hannah, W. (1980) 'Toward administrative philosophies', *Journal of Educational Administration* 18, 1: 114–131.

Hondeghem, A. (ed.) (1998) *Ethics and Accountability in a Context of Governance and New Public Management*, Amsterdam: IOS Press.

Kellough, J. E. (1999) 'Reinventing public personnel management: Ethical implications for managers and public personnel systems', *Public Personnel Management* 28, 4: 655–671.

Kirby, P., Paradise, L. and Protti, R. (1992) 'Ethical reasoning of educational administrators: structuring inquiry around the problems of practice', *Journal of Educational Administration* 30, 4: 25–32.

Maguire, M. (1998) 'Ethics in the public service – current issues and practice', in A. Hondeghem (ed.) *Ethics and Accountability in a Context of Governance and New Public Management*, Amsterdam: IOS Press.

Menzel, D. (1995) 'Through the ethical looking glass darkly', *Administration & Society* 27, 3: 379–399.

Menzel, D. (1997) 'Teaching ethics and values in public administration: Are we making a difference?', *Public Administration Review* 57, 3: 224–237.

Menzel, D. (1999) 'The morally mute manager: Fact or fiction?', *Public Personnel Management* 28, 4: 515–527.

Osborne, D. and Gaebler, T. (1992) *Reinventing Government: How the Entrepreneurial Spirit is Transforming the Public Sector,* Reading: Addison-Wesley.

Preston, N. (1999) 'Ethics and government: Preliminary considerations', *Australian Journal of Public Administration* 58, 4: 16–18.

Rohr, J. (1978) *Ethics for Bureaucrats*, New York: Marcel Dekker.

Sergiovanni, T. (1992) *Moral Leadership: Getting to the Heart of School Improvement*, San Francisco: Jossey-Bass.

Sola, P. (ed.) (1984) *Ethics, Education and Administrative Decisions: A Book of Readings*, New York: Peter Lang.

Strike, K., Haller, E. and Soltis, J. (1988) *The Ethics of School Administration*, New York: Teachers College Press.

Terry, L. (1998) 'Administrative leadership, neo-managerialism, and the public management movement', *Public Administration Review* 58: 194–200.

Chapter 5

Aquinas's notion of good in the context of educational leadership

Donald Lang

Thomas Aquinas's notion of good is linked to educational leadership for several reasons. To begin with, it is so difficult to find a meaningful treatment of good in the context of leadership that one might well conclude that 'good' leadership, as distinct from 'right' leadership, especially in education, is of minimal interest. Of greater significance, however, is the fact that organisation members cannot be reprimanded or punished for doing what is right, where doing right is following procedures, policies, rules, regulations. This is not so with doing good, to which any whistle-blower can attest – the most notable case being Dr Nancy Olivieri, the medical researcher at Toronto's Hospital for Sick Children who recently disclosed her concerns about a drug whose clinical trials she was working on. Unfortunately, blind adherence to doing right has the nerve-racking effect of reducing leaders to automatons. One never gets hurt playing it safe, doing it by the book – indeed, the prospects for promotion are enhanced. But trying to do good can be career-costly.

An analysis of Aquinas's notion of good is presented first, followed by linking the good to values, then to leadership in general, and then to educational leadership. A thought from Daniel J. Boorstin guides this endeavour: 'I distrust single explanations of anything, including the meaning of truth.'

Thomas Aquinas on good

Thomas Aquinas's philosophical psychology (Aquinas 1952, 1956) gives us the most lucid and intelligent treatment of good, for which he readily acknowledges the philosopher's influence. So, in a sense, it could be viewed as an Aristotelean–Thomistic analysis of good, which draws on four key concepts:

1 *Transcendence of time.* When Aquinas discusses good, no time-dependency is involved. Whatever he says about human beings applies to those at the beginning of humanity, to all those alive today,

regardless of psychological or medical condition, and to those of the future, to the very last one.

2 *Movement*. This is clearly one of his most powerful concepts, and it is something we witness on a daily basis. While all beings *qua* beings exist as they are, they have within them the potential to exist in another way: trees might become statues or houses, water can freeze or become steam, foetuses can become adults – the list goes on. It is critical to understand that not all beings can become whatever other beings might wish for.

3 This introduces the notion of *agreement*. Whether Aquinas actually discussed 'silk purses and sows ears' is not really relevant, but his notion of agreement certainly covers it. No being can become what does not exist within it, *in potentia*. One cannot get a silk purse from a sow's ear, or a tulip from a dahlia tuber.

4 *Perfection* is the fourth key concept. All movement from one state of existence to another, where the *intention* is to maximise or enhance what exists *in potentia*, is movement to perfection or a perfective state. States of perfection are *goods*. Clearly, there are as many 'goods' as there are states of existence. 'To be' is a good. What exists *in potentia* is a potential good. Also, with equal clarity, some 'goods' are better than others – thus the obvious link to Hodgkinson's value paradigm and the justification of what constitutes 'better'.

Good

The psychology of Aquinas is evident in current notions of instincts, drives, and motives: 'Now, the essential meaning of good is that it provides a terminus for appetite, since, "the good is that which all desire"' (Aquinas 1956: 38).[1] This, of course, leaves the door wide open to all sorts of interpretations. But Aquinas insists that if the key concepts noted earlier be kept in mind when discussing different assumptions of what good means, the outcomes will always be the same: good refers to what exists and to the state of perfection of any given being. That which inhibits or negates any being to achieve what exists *in potentia* is *evil*. Here it is appropriate to invoke the concept of 'intention' because Aquinas links perfection and intention this way: 'Now, it is a good thing for matter to be perfected through form, and for potency to be perfected through its proper act, but it is a bad thing for it to be deprived of its due act' (Aquinas 1956: 42). The latter phrase of that quotation is of the utmost importance, particularly in the domain of moral good and moral evil, because depriving a being of what it is capable of becoming – that is, perfecting itself – cannot be intelligently discussed without the key concept of intention. 'Evil', in Thomistic language, is 'simply a privation of something which a subject is entitled by its origin to possess, and which it ought to have'

(Aquinas 1956: 48), a point of view that C. G. Jung, among many others, dismissed as utter nonsense.

The moral dimension

Apprehension is another familiar concept – one shared with all sentient beings – which involves matters of understanding or judgement-making based on sensory information processing. We see it all the time with animals. Apprehension is linked to intention in such a way that what is apprehended becomes the goal or the end of the intention process. At this juncture, we readily admit that errors are easily made – have you ever made apple pie only with Ritz Crackers? A soya bean hamburger? Apprehension plays a critical role in moral good and moral evil because it interacts with two uniquely human attributes: the potential to reason and the potential to will. Both reason and will are qualified as 'potential' merely to convey what we already know: there are degrees within which any given human being – from cases of severe psychological or medical handicap to the most enlightened minds – can reason or will. This, of course, is what courts consider in evaluating suitability to stand trial, captured in the concept of responsibility.

The mechanics of going through moral-laden situations include apprehension, intention, reasoning and willing; defects in any of these reduce the level of moral responsibility. These four components can be collapsed into two, where reason includes apprehension and will includes intention. The entire operation, as if through histological analysis or a Lewinian 'freezing a moment in time', goes as follows. Reasoning includes apprehension, judgement as to whether what is apprehended is attainable, deliberation on the means to attain that, judgement on the choice of means, an 'order' to proceed, and evaluation. Operations of will include desire for what is apprehended, intention to achieve what is apprehended, 'agreeing' to evaluate the means set up by reason, 'agreeing' to the selected means, executing the 'order' from reason. Clearly, all this is beyond the realm of objective analysis but its epistemology is strong and, perhaps of equal importance, it is highly useful in teasing out the nuances of moral good and moral evil. Furthermore, many of these concepts have been extensively examined by the noted researchers of decision-making, Irving L. Janis and Leon Mann (1977).[2]

Real versus apparent good

The dichotomy of real versus apparent good provides us, without doubt, with the most meaningful approach to a question so commonly asked: why is there so much evil in the world when everyone says they are doing good? This issue is clearly addressed by Aristotle (1980: 4): 'The object of rational wish is the end, i.e., the good or apparent good'. Real good is that which perfects a being. Apparent good is that which negates perfection in a being. It is this notion of apparent good that helps explain the feeling (or belief) that humans can will evil. If one accepts as a basic premise that 'the good' is what is intended in human behaviour, then its opposite cannot be what is intended. The unintended cannot be the intended. This is where the concept of the 'apparent good' becomes relevant because, for whatever reason – cultural, physical, psychological, medical – humans believe, think, or feel that their essence is 'the good'. What amounts to ultimate good through ultimate sacrifice leading to martyrdom is terrorism from the other side – evil most horrid. No amount of natural science will ever explain away such contentious phenomena, but education with specific contents addressing the nature of real versus apparent good will make a difference.

Cause of evil

An overarching Aristotelean–Thomistic concept is causality: for every effect there is a cause, even though Aquinas acknowledges chance happenings (Aquinas 1956: 40, 46). In the non-moral sense of evil, 'non-good' or evil is caused by a defect or imperfection within the specific being affected. Aquinas's common example for that is blindness, which is an evil caused by defective or imperfect sight organs. Were he our contemporary, he might have singled out chromosome 16 with protein 2 as the defective agents causing Crohn's disease. The same idea holds true for all other instances where 'things go wrong', be they cars breaking down, diseases, you name it. In the context of moral evil, the cause is faulty, defective or imperfect reasoning, which is precisely what courts examine. It is this defective reasoning that gives rise to apparent good. Defective reasoning is best exemplified by individuals who fail to recognise that their actions against another – or themselves – impede, prevent, or thwart the betterment of that individual. If the intention is otherwise, then there is no moral evil because moral evil requires intent.

Good from other perspectives

What follows are a few insights into the ideas of others who have contributed much to our understanding of the nature of good.

Moore, Russell, Whitehead

G. E. Moore's well known position that good is indefinable but universally known – as is the colour of yellow – makes it difficult to account for the evil around us. Nonetheless, he raises the issue of the reality of good and evil in his reply to H. J. Paton. Specifically, Moore makes it clear that neither a rational will nor existence is a necessary precondition for the reality of good: 'even if nothing at all existed . . . a scarlet thing would be red' (Schilpp 1968: 617). Bertrand Russell, who uses the colour red to convey much the same idea as Moore, advocates that good exists on its own account and that our knowledge of good is confined to our experiences and imaginations (Russell 1992: 219). And in the context of the Socratic–Euthyphro debate he states: 'A thing is "good", as I wish to use the term, if it is valued for its own sake, and not only for its effects' (Russell 1954: 51). Whitehead provides quite a different treatment of the notion of good when commenting on the trinity of Truth, Beauty and Goodness, where Goodness cannot be considered an aim of art, of which the other two are, 'For Goodness is a qualification belonging to the constitution of reality, which in any of its individual actualisations is better or worse. Good and evil lie in depths and distances below and beyond appearance . . . the real world is good when it is beautiful' (Whitehead 1964: 267).

Chinese, Indian, Japanese perspectives

Harmony is the pervasive theoretical and practical principle guiding thought and life in the Chinese worldview, where philosophy takes precedence over religion. While all people are 'created equal' and perhaps potentially may stay so, in actuality the latter is not the case. 'Qualitative and personal criteria seem to take precedence over actual individuality and equality. Only the sage, it seems at times, is a genuine individual – and very few attain this status' (Moore and Morris 1967a: 6). This, of course, is the world of Confucian *jen*, the 'perfect individuals' who in establishing their own character also establish the character of others. 'The superior individual brings the good things of others to completion and does not bring the bad things of others to completion. The inferior individual does just the opposite' (Confucius 1992: 16). This makes one think of Alfred Adler, with his emphasis on social interest and the need to rid humanity of its imperfections.

In Indian thought, 'to be', not 'to do', is of supreme importance, which is perhaps best captured in religion taking precedence over philosophy. This presents a reversal of the Chinese position noted above: 'Ethics, though considered of absolute importance in life, is, nevertheless, considered to be subordinate to spiritual realization' (Moore and Morris 1967b: 15). This is the territory of *Bhagavad-Gita*, the 'living Bible of Hinduism to this day' (1967b: 6), where the concluding chapters discuss 'the good person' in the context of work. From here we can establish a direct reference to Professor Hodgkinson's principle of work for work's sake, not for the attachments that go with it.

The Japanese mind-set is best characterised as a negative Socratic dictum: 'It is the examined life that is unfit to live, because it is not *life*' (Moore and Morris 1967c: 289). Where good might be embedded in religion, the Shinto worshipper is interested in the spiritual experience devoid of any intellectual input. Indeed, there is no rigid intellectual foundation for life: it is accepted as is, and Absolutes play no part. There are three principles of the ideal good: simplicity, purity and sincerity.

William James and John Dewey

William James might well have been from any of the three Eastern orientations noted earlier, except for his die-hard emphasis on science. His well known stance on the existence of free will, for example, is for the world of metaphysics, not science. Good is tied to moral-laden issues: 'A moral question is a question not of what sensibly exists, but of what is good, or would be good if it did exist' (Roth 1969: 207). And 'sensibly' refers to the senses, not to 'what makes sense'. Then again, he goes to the heart – the organ – to have it master will and reason:

> The question of having moral beliefs at all or not having them is decided by our will . . . if your heart does not want a world of moral reality, you head will assuredly never make you believe in one . . . science can tell us what exists; but to compare the worths, both of what exists, and what does not exist, we must consult not science but what Pascal calls our heart.
>
> (Roth 1969: 207)

However, the last line belongs to the poet in William James, with a Kantian flavour: 'Whether a God exist, or whether no God exist, in yon blue heaven above us bent, we form at any rate an ethical republic here below' (Roth 1969: 179).

The nature of good for John Dewey was – and still is – a hotly debated issue between fact and value, science and personal philosophically laden end-values: 'Complete bifurcation between rationalistic method and an empirical method has its final and most deeply human significance in the ways in which good and bad are thought of and acted for and upon' (McDermott 1973: 577). But, ideals, ends and absolutes are non-starters for Dewey: 'We recur to our fundamental propositions. Morality is connected with actualities of existence, not with ideals, ends and obligations independent of concrete actualities' (McDermott 1973: 721); social acts are in reality moral acts even if no moral thought is considered (Dewey 1906: 415).

Nietzsche – of lambs and birds of prey

Friedrich Nietzsche likes to remind us that there are only interpretations of facts, and perhaps this holds true for good as well. He slices through those who would pontificate on good and evil, so often encountered in the very halls of supposed pristine purity. The physical and psychological carnage of 'men of God' bespeaks of his twofold prehistory (Nietzsche 1986: 45). Is he not right on the mark with his concept of power? 'What is good? – All that heightens the feeling of power, the will to power, power itself in man. What is bad? All that proceeds from weakness. What is happiness? – The feeling that power increases – that a resistance is overcome' (Nietzsche 1968: 2). Walter Kaufmann summarises the Nietzschean good that few of us can attain: *'The good man is for Nietzsche the passionate man who is the master of his passions'* (Kaufmann 1974: 280).

Kant: To be in awe of starry heavens above and moral law within

With Kant, the essence of good switches from passions to the mind: there is no room in a Kantian life for excitement, joy. Indeed, 'Freedom and autonomy à la Kant involve emancipation from our individuality and subjectivity' (Kaufmann 1980: 111). Only the will, the practical reason, can be good without qualification, and it is its very act of willing that makes it thus. However, in the context of relationships with objects of the will, different types of good emerge: arbitrary good (warfaring, good for killing rats, can also kill humans despite its potential beneficial side), purposeful good (health is good for happiness), and obligatory good (doing one's duty).

Thomistic good and values

The ideas of Milton Rokeach (1973) and Christopher Hodgkinson (1996) have dominated the field of values in the second half of the twentieth century, where the former is psychologically oriented and the latter philosophically so. Rokeach favours terms like 'preferred end states' and 'preferred means to preferred end states' instead of Hodgkinson's usual term, 'desirable'. While both interpretations are quite similar conceptually, Hodgkinson's notion of values is rooted in an Aristotelean–Thomistic view of what it is to be human. That is, values for Hodgkinson derive from sub-rational, rational and transrational domains.

If values are considered as some form of 'movement' or as generating some form of 'movement', then some sort of goal must be involved. That is, the organism is 'moved' to a goal. Furthermore, this goal – whether it be immaterial or material – is a good. Of critical importance is the nature of this good, which may be either real or apparent, a qualifier for sentient beings only.

Human beings function through the subrational, rational and transrational. These domains generate uniquely related values, which means specific goods tied to each of them. That is, the 'good' associated with quenching a thirst is of a different type from the 'good' associated with learning to surf the Internet, while both are different from the 'good' associated with a spiritual experience. It is the nature of these different 'goods' that is missing in virtually all value-related literature. It has been commonly accepted that values, by and large, justify one's behaviour. But that is only partially correct; it is the good associated with the specific value-type that actually justifies behaviour. Whatever value-based behaviour exists, it does so because of a perceived good to be attained. Thus the Socratic–Euthyphro debate ends in that we value something because it is good, not the other way round.

The good that is valued may be real or apparent. What distinguishes the human being from other life forms is the notion of responsibility, and it is this notion that determines real good from apparent good. To be responsible implies reason leading to choices from amongst a number of options, and it is in relation to this that we have become conditioned to have 'right' as the criterion for choosing. We really like to think that we are doing good in what we do, but the ultimate criterion is the right. And the explanation is relatively simple: it is easier to acquiesce to rules, regulations, policies and all the rest of what 'right' entails. In the course of human behaviour real good occurs when the intention is to enhance, to perfect what others have within them to become.

Thomistic good and leadership

Two irritants of leadership must be disposed of before any meaningful discussion can take place. They are those bothersome things that students seem to have problems resolving to their satisfaction. The first pertains to the minimum number of individuals for leadership activity to occur. The other deals with idol worship, which can be a blessing or a curse, depending on what side of the fence one is located. Reason has little chance dealing with such leaders despite society's obvious need for them.

Leadership as $N = 1$ activity

Clarification is needed on James MacGregor Burns's statement that

> 'One-man' leadership is a contradiction in terms. Leaders, in responding to their own motives, appeal to the motive bases of potential

followers. As followers respond, a symbiotic relationship develops that binds leader and follower into a social and political collectivity.

(Burns 1978: 452)

Hodgkinson's position for the past thirty years has been the opposite to the assertion in Burns's opening sentence. Yet, Burns himself appears to concur with Hodgkinson in the second sentence of the quotation above, that is, 'responding to their own motives'. This is of some significance because either leadership is an activity wholly and solely a matter of followership, or it involves someone in addition to followers. Clearly, the latter is the case and that 'other' is the leader. However, that leader must have some sense of direction because of response to his or her 'own motives'. Another way of considering 'own motives' is movement to some goal, be it immaterial or material. This, of course, is what values are all about, being guideposts for behaviour. But the goal has to be a 'good' in the eyes of the leader, if for no other explanation than values are concepts of the desirable, where desirable is either a real good or an apparent good.

At its barest minimum of meaning, leadership implies movement to some sort of goal. When goal-attainment is perceived as requiring others, all that has changed is the dynamics of the leadership movement. This view applies to all sentient beings. (All this might well change if one begins to ascribe some type of conscious quality to stem cell activity.)

Birth of the noble savage

There is a tendency to equate the great with the good, but this could be problematic for leadership studies. Alexander the Great is a leader we have tended to idolise, propped up as some sort of god. Why not? The qualifier justifies it. But here is what noted military historian Sir John Keegan has to say about Alexander the Great: 'His dreadful legacy was to ennoble savagery in the name of glory and to leave a model of command that far too many men of ambition sought to act out in the centuries to come' (Keegan 1991: 91). Savagery is, of course, still with us and makes sense only in the context of apparent good. While we tend to think of savagery in politically corrupt states, there is now increased awareness of psychological savagery, especially in the context of child abuse, in supposedly more civilised parts of the world. There are idols of the educational process that differ from Alexander only in terms of time.

More 'how' than 'why' of leadership

The 'how' and 'why' of leadership are conceptually independent and logically distinct, where right justifies the former and good the latter. It is readily acknowledged that when one is asked, 'Why are you doing that?' the answer is often, 'Because it is the right thing to do'. Thus right affects good, as so stated. It is much easier to deal with 'right' leadership because all that is involved is following some rules – be they 'rules of leadership' or 'organisational rules'. 'Good leadership' is entirely different because it forces an analysis of 'why'. So if the question is repeated with the same answer, the next phase would be to force the respondent, or oneself, to deal with the uncomfortable realisation that rules, regulations, policies, procedures and the like are what determines good. But, in the order of existence, both real and apparent good precede right. Yet our penchant for 'getting it right' – the 'how-to' of leadership – saturates the academic community with such force that only rarely do 'whys' surface, as in the works of James MacGregor Burns, Christopher Hodgkinson, Thomas Sergiovanni.

These how-to works can be grouped according to their focus on science, business, psychology and politics. The best representatives of the 'science of leadership' are Bernard Bass (1998) and Fred Fiedler (1967). Bass has introduced the term 'pseudotransformational' to describe leaders who *appear* to be authentic transformational leaders but in reality are not; what they do is pursue their own agenda. In contrast, authentic transformational leaders transcend their self-interest to the greater good of others. For our purposes, apparent good guides the pseudotransformational leader, and real good the authentic. And if Bernard Bass were to be giving the class on leadership, here is what he would say:

> For too long, leadership development has been seen mainly as a matter of training, as such, and skill development. But leadership – particularly transformational leadership – should be regarded as an art and a science likely to be enhanced with quality education process.
> (Bass 1998: 86)

This obviously begs the question as to the 'why' of leadership, and by implication the question about the difference between real and apparent good. Fiedler's work spans some forty years and, with his rigour for science, good can only be seen as mission achieved.

The best exponent of the 'business of leadership' sub-field – Stephen Covey – is in a class all by himself, but honourable mention should be given to Peter Senge. Both produce marketplace leadership material, and educators are on their top-client lists. One quotation from each illustrates the dangers involved. Covey, discussing his Habit 7 that includes the spiritual dimension, states: '[It is] your core, your center, your commitment to your value system' (Covey 1989: 292). One must be careful here because any commitment that is religion-based has the potential for inflaming behaviours that are, by definition, faith-based. As is all too well known, such behaviours do much to inspire others beyond their own perceived limitations. If Senge were giving the class, he'd say: 'Not only is being a good parent a training ground for being a learningful manager, but being a learningful manager is also good preparation for parenting' (Senge 1994: 312). From personal experience in the classroom, many educators have problems with this attitude, which only highlights the necessity for leadership courses that deal with issues of values and good.

If Paul Hersey and Ken Blanchard were giving the class as representatives of the psychology of leadership sub-field, here is what they would say in the context of transformational leadership:

> We define transformational leadership as a deliberate influence process on the part of an individual or group to bring about a discontinuous change in the current state and functioning of an organization as a whole. The change is driven by a vision based on a set of beliefs and values that require the members of the organization to urgently perceive and think differently and to perform new actions and organizational roles.
>
> (Hersey, Blanchard and Johnson 1996: 525)

The quotation may sound like a script for the Hitlers of the world, an antithesis to what Burns had in mind. In fact, however, it merely points out how doing what is right can be anything but good.

The Art of War (Sun Tzu 1971) and *The Prince* (Machiavelli 1981) are clearly the world's best leadership documents for those who care not a wit about realising the potential of others, *for the benefit of others*. They are what Kant had in mind when he penned his second formulation of the Categorical Imperative.

The 'how' of leadership is essential for success because failure is guaranteed for those who do not know how to lead. But overexposure can persuade educators to conclude that is all there is to it. To think of the 'why' necessitates an entirely different approach to leadership. It deals with notions of good, that is, determining in what context good exists in what is happening. It deals with thoughts that might have been going through Alfred, Lord Tennyson's head when he penned: 'Their's not to make reply / Their's not to reason why / Their's but to do and die'.

Thomistic good and educational leadership

Of the three concepts central to leadership studies – ideology, culture and climate – ideology has received the least amount of attention, and culture the most. This is quite likely due to preoccupation with the 'how' of leadership, captured in the operational terms of culture and climate. Culture, generally accepted to mean 'the way things are done around here', includes all those accepted beliefs about how organisational life is governed, while climate refers to observable behaviours (Hoy and Miskel 1996). But these phenomena are effects of organisational ideology, of the *raison d'être* of an organisation. Ideology deals with ideas and principles; it explains the 'why' of an organisation and what it stands for (Lang 1986). In sequence, individuals have ideas to achieve goals that they cannot attain by themselves alone. Hence, they form an organisation, in the Barnardian sense. However, these ideas must be made manifest with guiding principles of conduct – the culture that constitutes social reality. But this reality also needs a catalyst to 'move members to stated goals' – the observable behaviours of what leaders do. Thus leaders, regardless of how they might be described, are catalysts, actually *doing* things such as using verbal reinforcements to make members feel that what they are doing is important.

It is from the above perspectives that leadership curricula for educators must be geared to what education stands for. The 'how' of leadership, which is indispensable, is not a problem because course requirements are more than adequately met with a mixture of readings by Bass, Fiedler, Hersey and Blanchard. It is the teaching of the 'why' – the evidence of good embedded in acts of leadership – that needs fine-tuning in that the only substantive studies available are from Burns, Hodgkinson and Sergiovanni. Furthermore, leadership issues raised by Colin Evers, T. 'Bar' Greenfield, Peter Gronn and Gabriele Lakomski have become part of the 'why' solution, but they do not deal comprehensively with the concept of good in a leadership context.

There are three possible explanations for the omission of good in leadership studies and programmes. One is the unconscious linking of good to right. That is, if the 'right' procedures, or ideas, are followed, then they must be good. Or the issue of good has become entrenched in a G. E. Moore-like thinking, in part supported by the general acceptance that good, like art, is a matter of personal taste. Finally, good has become so tied up with morality and religion that any critical analysis of good gets entangled with concepts transcending the rational, as in 'Can we be good without God?'[3]

A submariner's perspective

Incorporating the notion of good in educational leadership requires rethinking what leadership *really* is. It is unfortunate that Peter Gronn and Gabriel Lakomski did not have the opportunity to meet the late Alastair Campbell Colquhoun Mars, DSO, DSC (Bar) and discuss leadership, because they had a lot in common. Alastair Mars is 'Mr Submarines' of World War II.[4] Amongst other notable events, he spent over a thousand days at sea in command of British submarines, having survived fifteen depth-charge attacks. After the war he was dismissed from the Royal Navy via court martial on the quarter-deck of *HMS Victory* for disobeying a lawful command (posting to an instructor staff position). Mars authored several fiction and nonfiction books, including *British Submarines at War, 1939–1945* (1971), which became standard reading for NATO submariners. In 1980 he penned his views of leadership – and they had to be on one page. To go beyond that meant his views were not in focus.

Here is what he had to say on this subject in a personal communication to the author on 28 March 1980:[5]

> The quality of leadership in officers is difficult to describe and hard to get at. One often hears of 'born leaders' but I would say there is almost no such thing and most of that ilk were, in fact, born bullies with too much power and that they drove rather than led. Leadership of highly intelligent individuals has to be learnt and acquired. The following ideas constitute only my own and could be so easily challenged. FIRSTLY – manners for 'manners maketh the man.' Always be courteous and never lose your temper. SECONDLY – Example. No one can be anywhere near perfect; but set the best example you can . . . and be kind to women. For, as you must know your juniors, so will your juniors know you, even into the innermost recesses of your private life. This does not mean being prude, only kind. THIRDLY – be fatherly (certainly without letting anyone know it – for that they will really resent). You should regard the men under you as your family, and that goes for their wives and children. When you feel that all of your men in any trouble will come to you for advice, then you are *theirs*. If you do not know the answer, admit it and say you will find out. In this respect there are always your own Seniors, Doctors etc. to advise you. For instance, a man might not want to approach such paragons directly. If he does it through you, then you must do your best; for you have his trust which is greater than loyalty . . . and the latter is thin on the ground today. FOURTHLY – no sarcasm in anger. It is the lowest form of wit. FIFTHLY – power. You may rise to have great power. Never use it. The use of power so often results in the loss of power. If a man must be punished, then punish him with as little as possible, and remember the effects that punishment may have on his family. SIX – fear. If you are afraid, mask it. The smell of fear, or fear on the face of an officer, usually leads to panic and that is, of course, disaster. Fear is the eighth – and worst – 'deadly sin.' SEVEN – command. Your men must obey implicitly. If you give a wrong order, it can be countermanded without any disgrace. But a slackly given and slackly obeyed order is almost impossible to cancel. EIGHT – determination, last but of the utmost importance. You must show by your face

and by your actions that you are quite and absolutely determined to achieve your objective. They will follow you without hesitation.

One can readily sense common threads of thought with Gronn and Lakomski: leadership is learned behaviour; leadership as an activity; separation of leadership from headship; the very meaning of leadership as social conscience; authority versus power. This statement comes from an authentic warrior talking to young officer cadets. (I have many times wondered what he would have said to an Educational Administration class.) Although the military was his frame of reference, his ideas fit all organisations. Indeed, the whole tenor of what he wrote is sound philosophy for all academic institutions and the administrators who lead them. Without question submariners are thoroughly trained, as was Mars himself. However, his views on leadership have nothing to do with training but everything to do with education, where education exists to produce an informed and enlightened citizenry for the betterment of all, all neatly captured in things we often neglect: manners and example. For manners are about treating others with respect and dignity, and demonstrating through example is how such behaviours are reinforced. Surely one of the main objectives of education is creating future conditions to maximize what exists within us, *in potentia*. This involves nothing more than the notion of *movement* noted above and where the manifestations are goods.

A Kantian perspective

Educators who are concerned with matters of 'how' at the expense of the nature of good that is automatically embedded in what is going on run the risk of jeopardising future conditions to enhance and make real what others have within them to become. There is nothing new in any of this; it is the message Kant gave concerning the ultimate destiny of the human race. It is almost as if Kant were commenting on current affairs of state, as special representative to the UN concerning matters of education:

> The universal end of mankind is the highest moral perfection. If we all so ordered our conduct that it should be in harmony with the universal end of mankind, the highest perfection would be attained . . . How then is perfection to be sought? Wherein lies our hope? In education, and nothing else. Education must be adapted to all the ends of nature, both civil and domestic. Our present education, both in the home and at school, is still very faulty, in respect of discipline, doctrine and the cultivation of talent as much as in respect of the building of character in accordance with moral principles. We care more for skill than for the disposition to use it well.
>
> (Kant 1930: 252–253)

Conclusion

There are two fundamental interdependent concepts in Aquinas's notion of good. First, what is, is good. Second, good can be either real or apparent. Another concept is movement: all beings move or can be moved to other states of existence. When that other state of existence perfects being, then real good has occurred. When that other state of existence negates or impedes perfection, then apparent good has occurred. Apparent good is evil.

The essence of education is to move individuals to other states of existence that perfect those individuals, and other individuals as well. This movement can be a result of one's own initiatives or of those by others. The primary others are parents or significant others in the educational process.

How education occurs has overshadowed *why* education occurs. This is the same phenomenon as 'method determining what will/can be researched'. Perhaps it is this mind-set that drives the 'how' engine of education. This is a consequence of putting 'right' before 'good', where in the order of existence good determines right.

For those who might be described in conventional terms as leaders (parents, teachers), their role is to inculcate in children/students an awareness of what constitutes right and what constitutes good, and how the two are related. Much of this is put into perspective by Alfred Adler in his view of humanity's innate drive to overcome imperfections and achieve a sense of social interest. These goals are achieved through education, but those who do the educating had best be on guard: 'Too many children come to school with the feeling that the teacher is simply an employee of the state' (Adler 1927: 284). If the 'state' be enlarged to incorporate authoritative organisations, then doing right is not only highly predictable but desirable by both senior personnel and individuals themselves because doing good can be career-costly.

The intent of an educator should not be to convey the notion that right and good cannot coexist; they have to, if for no other reason than that all activity has good as its goal. That is, doing what is right will always be a good. What is advocated here is that the very notion of good needs to be seen in terms of real good and apparent good, from which perspective the two are conceptually distinct. Educational leaders need to be exposed to this sort of thinking, but this is unlikely to occur due to the dominant influence of the 'how' of leadership.

In the context of historical leadership research, military personnel were the object of analysis and it is from there that we have the basic 'how-to' building blocks of consideration and task structure. Yet in the eyes of one war-time submarine commander, his 'how' contains a lot of grounding for the 'why' of leadership: being mannerly and leading by example.

Manners – treating others with respect and dignity regardless of station – might just well be the medium through which real good and apparent good can be separated. And then actualising the difference by example will at least place the 'why' of leadership on a par with the 'how' of leadership.

Notes

1 The quotation within the quotation is Aristotle's, found throughout his *Nicomachean Ethics* (1980).
2 In their work Janis and Mann examined the following: appraising the challenge, surveying the alternatives, weighing the alternatives, deliberating about commitment.
3 See, for instance, Tinder (1989), Chamberlain (1996) and Buckman (2000).
4 His passing was noted in the *Sunday Times* (14 March 1985) and *Contemporary Authors* (vol. 116, p. 305).
5 Alastair Mars was a guest of Royal Roads Military College in Victoria, British Columbia (Canada) in March 1980, where he gave a series of talks to cadets. This script on leadership is virtually as he wrote it in a personal communication to the author. Mars was a bit of both Crocodile Dundee and Indiana Jones; he loved audiences, storytelling, and being the centre of attention – the definitive dinner guest. He was born in 1915 and educated at Dragon School, Oxford, before going to Royal Naval Colleges in Dartmouth, Greenwich. In 1950 he ran unsuccessfully as Liberal candidate in the general election.

References

Adler, A. (1927) *Understanding Human Nature*, trans. Brian Wolfe, New York: Greenberg Publishers.
Aquinas, St T. (1952) *The Summa Theologica*, vol. 1, Toronto: Encyclopedia Britannica, Inc.
Aquinas, St T. (1956) *On the Truth of the Catholic Faith (Summa Contra Gentiles)*, Providence, New York: Doubleday.
Aristotle (1980) *Nicomachean Ethics*, Oxford: Oxford University Press.
Bass, B. (1998) *Transformational Leadership: Industrial, Military, and Educational Impact*, London: Erlbaum Associates.
Buckman, R. (2000) *Can We Be Good without God? An Exploration of Behaviour, Belonging and the Need to Believe*, Toronto: Viking Press.
Burns, J. M. (1978) *Leadership*, New York: Harper and Row.
Chamberlain, P. (1996) *Can We Be Good without God? A Conversation about Truth, Morality, Culture and a Few Other Things that Matter*, Downer Groves: InterVarsity Press.
Confucius (1992) *Analects*, Hong Kong: Chinese University Press.
Covey, S. (1989) *The 7 Habits of Highly Effective People*, New York: Simon and Schuster.
Dewey, J. (1906) *Democracy and Education*, New York: Macmillan.
Fiedler, F. (1967) *A Theory of Leadership Effectiveness*, New York: McGraw-Hill.

Hersey, P., Blanchard, K. and Johnson, D. (1996) *Management of Organizational Behavior*, 7th edn, Upper Saddle River: Prentice Hall.
Hodgkinson, C. (1996) *Administrative Philosophy*, New York: Elsevier Science.
Hoy, W. and Miskel, C. (1996) *Educational Administration*, 5th edn, New York: McGraw-Hill.
Janis, I. L. and Mann, L. (1977) *Decision Making: A Psychological Analysis of Conflict, Choice, and Commitment*, New York: Free Press.
Kant, I. (1930) *Lectures on Ethics*, London: Century.
Kaufmann, W. (1974) *Nietzsche: Philosopher, Psychologist, Antichrist*, 4th edn, Princeton: Princeton University Press.
Kaufmann, W. (1980) *Discovering the Mind: Goethe, Kant, and Hegel*, Toronto: McGraw-Hill.
Keegan, J. (1991) *The Mast of Command: A Study of Generalship*, London: Pimlico, Jonathan Cape.
Lang, D. (1986) 'Values and commitment: An empirical verification of Hodgkinson's value paradigm as applied to the commitment of individuals to organizations', unpublished Ph.D. Dissertation, University of Victoria.
Machiavelli, N. (1981) *The Prince*, Harmondsworth: Penguin.
Mars, A. (1971) *British Submarines at War, 1939–1945*, London: Kimber.
McDermott, J. J. (ed.) (1973) *The Philosophy of John Dewey*, vol. II, New York: Putnam Sons.
Moore, C. A. and Morris, A. V. (1967a) *The Chinese Mind*, Honolulu: East-West Center Press.
Moore, C. A. and Morris, A. V. (1967b) *The Indian Mind*, Honolulu: East-West Center Press.
Moore, C. A. and Morris, A. V. (1967c) *The Japanese Mind*, Honolulu: East-West Center Press.
Nietzsche, F. (1968) *Twilight of the Idols and The Anti-Christ*, Harmondsworth: Penguin Books.
Nietzsche, F. (1986) *Human All Too Human*, Cambridge: Cambridge University Press.
Rokeach, M. (1973) *The Nature of Human Values*, London: Free Press.
Roth, J. K. (ed.) (1969) *The Moral Philosophy of William James*, New York: Crowell.
Russell, B. (1954) *Human Society in Ethics and Politics*, London: Allen and Unwin.
Russell, B. (1992) *Logical and Philosophical Papers, 1909–13*, London; New York: Routledge.
Senge, P. (1994) *The Fifth Discipline: The Art and Practice of the Learning Organization*, New York: Doubleday.
Schilpp, P. A. (1968) *The Philosophy of G. E. Moore*, 3rd edn, London: Cambridge University Press.
Sun Tzu (1971) *The Art of War*, Oxford: Oxford University Press.
Tinder, G. (1989) 'Can We Be Good without God?', *Atlantic Monthly* 264, 6: 68–85.
Whitehead, A. N. (1964) *Adventures of Ideas*, Cambridge: Cambridge University Press.

Chapter 6

Morals and markets
Adam Smith's moral philosophy as a foundation for administrative ethics

Richard Bates

Adam Smith has a contemporary reputation as the prophet of greed. It is a wholly undeserved reputation. He was, in fact, as concerned about morals as he was with markets. As markets and morals are two of the major contemporary concerns among educational administrators (Chubb and Moe 1990; Hodgkinson 1991; Marginson 1997; Murphy 2002; Sergiovanni 1992, 2001), it would seem that a revisiting of the premises on which Adam Smith's work depends might offer at least a corrective to his undeserved reputation and, at best, some insight into relationships between morals and markets as they affect public institutions such as education and the work of those who administer them.

Smith's reputation depends primarily on his great work *An Inquiry into the Nature and Causes of the Wealth of Nations* (Smith 1976). Published in 1776, it almost immediately became a *cause célèbre* throughout Europe, at least in part because of its attack upon gross social inequalities founded upon the inheritance of wealth by the landed gentry (who because of their wealth saw no need to improve their lands and therefore the common good) and by the monopolistic practices of the mercantile class (whose trade and profits were protected by government regulation and who had no need therefore to attend to the common good). Markets were seen by Smith as a mechanism through which the immorality as well as the inefficiency of social, economic and political inheritances of the eighteenth century could be corrected. Indeed, the mechanism of the market, which was the focus of much of the *Wealth of Nations,* was seen as a mechanism for *moral* as much as economic discipline: a discipline, moreover, that had the capacity to transform unjust social and economic relationships (Alvey 1998, 2000; Coker 1990). As Sowell suggests:

> It is impossible to appreciate fully the thrust of Adam Smith's arguments concerning laissez-faire until he is regarded as very much, and very self-consciously, a social critic of eighteenth century society . . . The concepts of laissez-faire and consumer sovereignty had some quite radical implications in Smith's time. I do not want to portray

Smith as a radical in any of the twentieth century meanings of the term, but in eighteenth century Britain these were distinctly radical ideas, with radical policy implications.

(Sowell 1979, in Bassiry and Jones 1993: 623)

But this is not the picture of Adam Smith or 'the Market' presented in contemporary economics textbooks, where economics is entirely separated from the world of values, ethics and moral behaviour. As a number of contemporary commentators have pointed out, 'It is a widely held view today among mainstream economists that economics is free from any ideological, theological or moral philosophy' (Alvey 2000: 1231). Indeed,

The 'scientification' of economics . . . has led to a separation of economics from its ethical roots. The 'mainstream economics' of the 20th century fully accepts this separation. Economic theory is seen as a positive science which has to analyse and to explain the mechanisms of economic processes . . . Important as ethical valuations ('ought'-statements) may be, they should not form part of an economist's research programme.

(Rothschild 1993: 16)

Economic historians point to the effects of nineteenth-century German positivism and the increasingly inward and mathematical focus of economics under the influence of figures such as Jevons (1970). The result has been that in the twentieth century economics has rejected its historical roots and, along with them, any sense of moral responsibility. As Alvey puts it:

The notion of economics serving a moral end has been ruled out by positivism. Positivism ruled out moral philosophy . . . there was a rejection of a broad, interdisciplinary education of economists: at the same time, partly due to positivism, there was a considerable narrowing of the scope of the discipline itself . . . Once all the moral concerns of economics are stripped away, only rational calculation remains . . .

(Alvey 2000: 1246)

This process is much akin to the influence of positivism on the development of theory in educational administration (Bates 1980).

The adoption of such a position is not without its effects, as Alvey notes:

Modern economics stresses rational calculation, the baser material objectives, and scientific neutrality on moral issues. However, these foci can easily shift to something else. For example, Yezer et al. state

> that 'introductory microeconomics is based on assumptions of rationally selfish behaviour' (1996, p. 178). Note that self-interest has slipped to 'selfish behaviour'. But consider also what one of today's leading micro-economists, David Kreps, has to say: 'a sparse set of canonical hypotheses – . . . greed, rationality, and equilibrium – became the maintained hypotheses in almost all branches of [economics]' (Knapps, 1997, p. 59). Note that he has slipped from the 'selfishness' of Yezer et al. to 'greed'. The slip to the assumption of 'greed' is frequently made by economists.
>
> (Alvey 2000: 1232)

Moreover, the language and assumptions of contemporary economics appear to influence behaviour, in that economics students have been found in several studies to be more selfish and uncooperative than other students (Frank, Gilovich and Regan 1993; Marwell and Ames 1981; Lux 1990). As Alvey comments: 'By producing selfish and uncooperative individuals one may think that there is empirical evidence for the actual detachment of economics from ethics' (2000: 1232).

Such a result would have horrified Adam Smith, who spent a great deal of his academic life elaborating the ideas of his first great book, *The Theory of Moral Sentiments* (Smith 2002). First published in 1759, some seventeen years before *The Wealth of Nations*, this work grew out of the lectures that Smith gave while Professor of Moral Philosophy at Glasgow. It is a work concerned primarily with the sources of moral behaviour and the social mechanisms which encourage such behaviour. As Small pointed out in 1907, Smith's social analysis was a precursor in many ways to the development of 'modern sociology' (Small 1972).

More explicitly, Muller argues that:

> Though *The Wealth of Nations* is rightly regarded as the work that served the foundation of the discipline of economics, the seminal role of *The Theory of Moral Sentiments* in the development of sociology and social psychology is rarely appreciated. Readers familiar with the development of sociological theory will find that in that book Smith presents a conception of what Charles Horton Cooley was to call the 'looking glass self,' and that Smith's discussion of the 'impartial spectator' led to George Herbert Mead's distinction between the 'me' that reflects my perception of how others see me and the 'I' that is capable of judging the 'Me'. Indeed, behind what may seem the archaic language of *The Theory of Moral Sentiments* lies a theory of the development of conscience through the internalisation of norms, as well as a theory of how the morally developed individual is able to ascend from moral conformity to moral autonomy.
>
> (Muller 1993: 100)

It seems clear, through the works themselves and the work of contemporary economic historians, that the claims of some economists that Adam Smith founded modern economics by setting aside his concerns with ethics (elaborated in *The Theory of Moral Sentiments*) while developing his theory of market behaviour (elaborated in *The Wealth of Nations*) are incorrect. Rather than setting such issues aside, *The Theory of Moral Sentiments* sets the social and ethical context within which the economic behaviour discussed in *The Wealth of Nations* is to be understood and practised.

In *The Theory of Moral Sentiments* Smith argued that the 'chief part of human happiness arises from the consciousness of being beloved' (Smith 2002: 50) and that such consciousness brings about 'beneficent' behaviour which contributes much to social solidarity. Moreover, he also argued that benevolence brought benefits to the benefactor:

> No benevolent man ever lost altogether the fruits of his benevolence. If he does not always gather them from the persons from whom he ought to have gathered them, he seldom fails to gather them, and with a tenfold increase, from other people. Kindness is the parent of kindness: and if to beloved by our brethren be the great object of our ambition, the surest way of obtaining it is, by our conduct to show that we really love them.
>
> (Smith 2002: 50)

However, Smith also acknowledges that while society depends greatly on such benevolent behaviour, it can exist without it:

> All the members of human society stand in need of each other's assistance, and are likewise exposed to mutual injuries. Where the necessary assistance is reciprocally afforded from love, from gratitude, from friendship, and esteem, the society flourishes and is happy . . . But though the necessary assistance should not be afforded from such generous and disinterested motives, though among the different members of society there should be no mutual love and affection, the society, though less happy and agreeable, will not necessarily be dissolved. Society may subsist between different men, as among different merchants, from a sense of its utility, without any mutual love or affection . . . Society, however, cannot subsist among those who are at all times ready to hurt and injure one another . . . Beneficence, therefore, is less essential to the existence of society than justice. Society may subsist, though not in the most comfortable state, without beneficence; but the prevalence of injustice must utterly destroy it.
>
> (Smith 2002: 100–101)

In between Smith's considerations of ethics and the market therefore there lies a third major preoccupation – that of jurisprudence. Although Smith never published his planned book on jurisprudence (he burnt the draft of such a book just prior to his death), notes on his lectures on jurisprudence have survived and are published as his *Lectures on Jurisprudence* (Smith 1978). This book was to provide a necessary link between the ethical concerns of *The Theory of Moral Sentiments* and the economic concerns of *The Wealth of Nations*.

For Smith, jurisprudence covered both *morality* and *expediency*, which were bound together in the responsibilities of government.

Smith defined jurisprudence as 'the theory of the rules by which civil governments ought to be directed' (Smith 1978: 4). It is based upon and encompasses 'that branch of *morality* which relates to justice' and also 'those political regulations which are founded, not upon the principle of justice, but that of *expediency*' – in short, upon morals and markets (Smith 1978: 4). For Smith the issues of justice founded on morality (that is, those that are necessary for maximising individual virtue and social order) and those founded on expediency (that is, those necessary for maximising the common wealth of a nation) are intertwined. Both are founded on four fundamental virtues: prudence, justice, benevolence and self-command.

Smith's definitions of these virtues and their relationship to each other form the basis of his moral philosophy *and* his economics.

Prudence is argued by Smith to be a 'self-regarding' virtue, in that it is based upon the desire of men for the approbation of their fellows, that is, for the care and nurture of their reputation. It is a fundamentally *social* virtue in that the desire for approbation, while self-interested, is only possible within a social context. Thus, while caring for one's reputation is essentially a self-regarding and self-interested act, it is also a foundation for sociability. For Smith,

> The care of the health, of the fortune, of the rank and reputation of an individual, the objects upon which his comfort and happiness in this life are supposed principally to depend, is considered the proper business of that virtue which is commonly called Prudence.
> (Smith 2002: 249)

And again,

> In the steadiness of his industry and frugality, in his steadily sacrificing the ease and enjoyment of the present moment for the probable expectation of the still greater ease and enjoyment of a more lasting period of time, the prudent man is always both supported and rewarded by the entire approbation of the impartial spectator and of

> the representative of the impartial spectator, the man within the breast.
>
> (Smith 2002: 252)

Here, as Young suggests,

> Such a frugal and industrious person lives within his income, is contented, and witnesses a continual growth of his small accumulation of wealth. The parallel between this discussion of prudence in [*The Theory of Moral Sentiments*] and the description of the frugal man in [*The Wealth of Nations*] whose constant desire is to better his own condition is obvious. As is well known the desire to better one's condition is the source of savings which in turn generate capital accumulation and the expansion of the division of labour, the principle source of wealth of nations. Thus, the fundamental behavioural assumption of the economic theory of growth turns out to be the same thing as the desire to cultivate the virtue of prudence, which is rooted in the desire for approval.
>
> (Young 1997: 45–46)

The second of the fundamental virtues described by Smith is that of *Justice*. Here Smith takes the first principle of justice to be that of refraining from the harm of others:

> In one sense we are said to do justice to our neighbour when we abstain from doing him any positive harm, and do not directly hurt him, either in his person, or in his estate, or in his reputation.
>
> (Smith 2002: 318)

Moreover, following from this, Smith argues that it is a fundamental function of government to ensure that such hurts, where they occur, are punished. More particularly, it is the responsibility of government to ensure the 'internal security' of the people through a system of 'administration of justice' which will protect 'every member of society from the injustice or oppression of every other member of it' (Smith 1976: 687).

Here, Smith suggests that it is obviously in the best interests of the propertied class to support such a system for,

> Wherever there is great property, there is great inequality. For one very rich man, there must be at least five hundred poor, and the affluence of the few supposes the indigence of the many. The affluence of the rich excites the indignation of the poor, who are often both driven by want, and prompted by envy, to invade his possessions. It is only under the shelter of the civil magistrate that the owner of that valuable

property, which is acquired by the labour of many years, or perhaps of many successive generations, can sleep a single night in security . . . The acquisition of valuable and extensive property, therefore, necessarily requires the establishment of civil government.

(Smith 1976: 709)

But while this is an historical explanation of the emergence of civil law, Smith argues further that in *commercial* society, as well as the protection of life and property, the law must also provide for the enforcement of contract. For, without such enforcement the contracts on which exchange depends may well fail. And the freedom to enter into contracts which will be honoured is a basic freedom which, originating among friends and families, provides the basis for both freedom and honour among the wider society. Only a legal framework independent of wealth or politics is able to achieve this: 'upon the impartial administration of justice depends the liberty of every individual' (Smith 1976: 722–723).

The third fundamental virtue described by Smith is that of *Beneficence*. Beneficence, Smith argues, is a virtue engendered by our 'sympathy' or identification with others. In the first place our sympathy grows naturally within the family. Here, living together 'long and familiarly' engenders that 'delicious sympathy, confidential openness and ease' which characterises family relationships (Smith 2002: 260).

> After himself, the members of his own family, those who usually live in the same house with him, his brothers and sisters, are naturally the objects of his warmest affections. They are naturally and usually the persons upon whose happiness or misery his conduct must have the greatest influence. He is more habituated to sympathize with them. He knows better how every thing is likely to affect them, and his sympathy with them is more precise and determinate, than it can be with the greater part of other people. It approaches nearer, in short, to what he feels for himself . . .
>
> (Smith 2002: 257)

The sympathy on which beneficence depends extends outwards, as it were, to others with whom we have greater or lesser contact:

> After the persons who are recommended to our beneficence, either by their connexion with ourselves, by their personal qualities, or by their past services, come those who are pointed out, not indeed to, what is called, our friendship, but by our benevolent attention and good offices; those who are distinguished by their extraordinary situation; the greatly fortunate and the greatly unfortunate, the rich and the powerful, the poor and the wretched. The distinction of ranks, the

> peace and order of society are in great measure, founded upon the respect which we naturally conceive for the former. The relief and consolation of human misery depend altogether upon our compassion for the latter.
>
> (Smith 2002: 265)

Beneficence is, therefore, a major positive virtue for Smith, who saw it as vital to a happy society.

While he was especially concerned with the role of the state and its agents, the civil magistrates, in establishing a system of justice that secured life, property and contracts of exchange, Smith also saw a role for the state in ensuring a limited degree of benevolence:

> A superior may, indeed, sometimes, with universal approbation, oblige those under his jurisdiction to behave, in this respect, with a certain degree of propriety to one another. The laws of all civilised nations oblige parents to maintain their children, and children to maintain their parents, and to impose upon men many other duties of beneficence. The civil magistrate is entrusted with the power not only of preserving the public peace by restraining injustice, but of promoting the prosperity of the commonwealth, by establishing good discipline, and by discouraging every sort of vice and impropriety; he may prescribe rules, therefore, which not only prohibit mutual injuries among fellow citizens, but command mutual good offices to a certain degree.
>
> (Smith 2002: 95)

But beneficence stems not only from sympathy and civil obedience. Its main roots lie in our desire for approbation:

> What reward is most proper for promoting the practise of truth, justice and humanity? The confidence, the esteem, and the love of those we live with. Humanity does not desire to be great, but to be beloved. It is not in being rich that truth and justice would rejoice, but in being trusted and believed . . .
>
> (Smith 2002: 277)

The fourth major virtue Smith argued to be *Self-Command*. Even with knowledge and commitment to the virtues of Prudence, Justice and Beneficence, all comes to nothing if Self-Command is absent:

> The man who acts according to the rules of perfect prudence, of strict justice and proper benevolence, may be said to be perfectly virtuous. But the most perfect knowledge of these rules will not alone enable him to act in this manner: his own passions are very apt to mislead

him; sometimes to drive him and sometimes to seduce him to violate all the rules which he himself, in all his sober and cool hours, approves of. The most perfect knowledge, if it is not supported by the most perfect self-command, will not always enable him to do his duty.

(Smith 2002: 279)

And again,

> To act according to the dictates of prudence, of justice, and proper beneficence, seems to have no great merit where there is no temptation to do otherwise. But to act with cool deliberation in the midst of the greatest dangers and difficulties; to observe religiously the sacred rules of justice in spite both of the greatest interests which might temper, and the greatest injuries which might provoke us to violate them; never to suffer the benevolence of our temper to be damped or discouraged by the malignity and ingratitude of the individuals towards whom it may have been exercised; is the character of the most exalted wisdom and virtue. Self-command is not only in itself a great virtue, but from it all the other virtues seem to derive their principal lustre . . .
>
> (Smith 2002: 284)

One of the chief achievements of Smith was, in fact, to show how such virtues provided the foundation for what he called 'commercial society'. But more than this, Smith sought to explain how the pursuit of the approbation of one's fellows, while in itself a self-interested behaviour, led to the development of both commerce *and* society. Indeed, the search for approbation along with the propensity to barter constituted the basis of the 'invisible hand' that led to the efficiency of markets and the development of a benevolent society. Morality and markets are inseparable in Smith's cosmology.

Smith was a strong advocate of 'Commercial Society', which he saw as the fourth great stage of human history (following those of the Age of Hunters, the Age of Shepherds and the Age of Agriculture). He believed that the development of Commercial Society was historically inevitable and permanent, foreshadowing what Fukuyama (1992) has described as the triumph of capitalism and the death of history.

Smith's description of the development of commercial society begins with the emergence of the division of labour within the family. The specialisation that develops as a result of the division of labour leads to the exchange of gifts within the family on the basis of which a rough mutuality of value emerges – the basis of a 'pricing' mechanism or the 'natural price' of a commodity. Smith does not assume that the division of labour is the result of a conscious commitment to a particular form of social organisation, but rather that it originates perhaps in some principle of human nature, or, rather more interestingly, in close association with the emergence of speech and reason:

> This division of labour, from which so many advantages are derived, is not originally the effect of any human wisdom, which foresees and intends that general opulence to which it gives occasion. It is the necessary, though very slow and gradual consequence of a certain propensity in human nature which has in view no such extensive utility; the propensity to truck, barter, and exchange one thing for another.
>
> Whether this propensity be one of those original principles in human nature, of which no further account can be given; or whether, as seems more probable, it be the necessary consequence of the faculties of reason and speech, it belongs not to our present subject to enquire.
>
> (Smith 1976: 25)

Barter and speech are, therefore, tied together, the social use of language being fundamental to the processes of exchange and therefore to the establishment of markets. As Young puts it, 'Exchange is a social phenomenon and it appears that it arises out of an original principle in human nature which serves to help bind people together into social groupings, namely reason and speech' (Young 1997: 60).

Through the power of reason and speech, the 'benevolence' of transactions within the family is extended to those outside through the mechanisms of barter and exchange. Here, Smith makes a profound observations that in such exchanges benevolence is exchanged for self-interest and that mutual self-interest is what holds the exchange together:

> But man has almost constant occasion for the help of his brethren, and it is in vain for him to expect it from benevolence only. He will more likely to prevail if he can interest their self-love in his favour, and shew them that it is for their own advantage to do for him what he requires of them. Whoever offers to another a bargain of any kind, proposes to do this. Give me that which I want, and you shall have this which you want, is the meaning of every such offer: and it is in this manner that we obtain from one another the far greater part of those good offices which we stand in need of.
>
> (Smith 1976: 26)

Here, persuasion is added to the mechanism of exchange, where language becomes the mechanism of negotiation. Moreover, in such exchanges it is not only goods that are being exchanged but also reputation. Here, Smith insists that the requirements of exchange of more than a single act, require the display of particular virtues: probity and punctuality – especially in the payment of bills:

> Whenever commerce is introduced into any country, probity and punctuality always accompany it. . . . A dealer is afraid of losing his character, and is scrupulous in observing every engagement. When a person makes perhaps 20 contracts in a day, he cannot gain so much by endeavouring to impose on his neighbours, as the very appearance of a cheat would make him lose. Where people seldom deal with one another, we find that they are somewhat disposed to cheat, because they can gain more by a smart trick than they can lose by the injury which it does to their character . . . Wherever dealings are frequent, a man does not expect to gain so much by one contract as by probity and punctuality in the whole, and a prudent dealer, who is sensible of his real interest, would rather chuse to lose what he has a right to than give any ground for suspicion. Every thing of this kind is as odious as it is rare. When the greater part of the people are merchants they always bring probity and punctuality into fashion, and these therefore are the principal virtues of commercial society.
> (Smith 1976: 538–539)

Commercial society grows, therefore, out of benevolence within the family; through the giving of gifts of relatively equal value; to the process of exchange negotiated through the social mechanisms of language and reason; to a process of barter based on mutual self-interest; towards a self-regulating system of exchange based upon long-term relationships which engender the virtues of probity and punctuality. Morals and markets emerge together within a system of social as well as economic relationships.

Smith was, however, as Young (1997), Alvey (1998) and Rosenberg (1990) point out so clearly, also aware of the 'malevolent' potential of commercial society. While the benevolence of commercial society was part of what Weber might have called an 'ideal type', bringing forth sociable behaviour unintentional from the requirements of mutually beneficial exchange, it was also possible that human frailty would produce quite different results.

Ironically, it is the very capacity for speech and persuasion that is fundamental to the development of equitable exchange that also carries the potential for inequity:

> The desire to be believed, the desire of persuading, of leading and directing other people, seems to be one of the strongest of all our natural desires. It is, perhaps, the instinct upon which is founded the faculty of speech, the characteristical faculty of human nature . . .

> Great ambition, the desire of real superiority, of leading and directing, seems to be altogether peculiar to man, and speech is the great instrument of ambition, of real superiority, of leading and directing the judgements and conduct of other people.
>
> (Smith 2002: 397–398)

Such desires to lead and dominate can lead to serious distortions to the ideal of commercial society. For instance, the will to dominate can lead to slavery:

> The pride of man makes him love to domineer, and nothing mortifies him so much as to be obliged to condescend to persuade his inferiors. Wherever the law allows it, and the nature of the work can afford it, therefore, he will generally prefer the service of slaves to that of freemen.
>
> (Smith 1976: 388)

As in the sphere of production, so in the sphere of government:

> For though management and persuasion are always the easiest and the safest instruments of government, as force and violence are the most dangerous, yet such, it seems, is the natural insolence of man, that he almost always disdains to use the good instrument, except when he cannot or dare not use the bad one.
>
> (Smith 1976: 799)

As with the propensity of speech to lead to slavery and bad government, Smith saw that the division of labour on which commercial society was based could also have very negative consequences:

> The man whose whole life is spent performing a few simple operations, of which the effects too are, perhaps, always the same, or very nearly the same, has no occasion to exert his understanding, or to exercise his invention in finding out expedients for removing difficulties which never occur. He naturally loses, therefore, the habit of exertion, and generally becomes as stupid and ignorant as it is possible for a human creature to become. The torpor of his mind renders him, not only incapable of relishing or bearing a part in any conversation, but of conceiving any generous, noble, or tender sentiment, and consequently of forming any just judgement concerning many even of the ordinary duties of private life. Of the great and extensive interests of his country he is altogether incapable of judging; and unless very particular pains have been taken to render him otherwise, he is equally

incapable of defending his country in war. The uniformity of his stationary life naturally corrupts the courage of his mind, and makes him regard with abhorrence the irregular, uncertain and adventurous life of a soldier. It corrupts even the activity of his body, and renders him incapable of exerting his strength with vigour and perseverance, in any other employment than that to which he has been bred. His dexterity at his own trade seems, in this manner, to be acquired at the expence of his intellectual, social, and martial virtues. But in every improved and civilized society this is the state into which the labouring poor, that is, the great body of the people, must necessarily fall, unless government take some pains to prevent it.

(Smith 1976: 782)

One of the 'natural' outcomes of commercial society resulting from the division of labour was, therefore, that of social inequality. Smith's position here is somewhat ambiguous. He clearly saw inequality as a result of proper ambition resulting from the pursuit of self-interest. But the kind of degradation outlined in the preceding quotation was clearly unacceptable to him, as was extravagant excess at the other end of the scale:

Those great objects of self-interest, of which the loss or acquisition quite changes the rank of the person, are objects of the passion properly called ambition; a passion which *when kept within the bounds of prudence and justice*, is always admired in the world, and has even sometimes a certain irregular greatness, which dazzles the imagination, when it passes the limits of both these virtues, and is not only unjust but extravagant.

(Smith 2002: 202, emphasis added)

Moreover, the envy of great possessions is also a seriously corrupting passion:

The disposition to admire, and almost to worship, the rich and powerful, and to despise, or, at least, to neglect persons of poor and mean condition, though necessary both to establish and maintain the distinction of ranks and order of society, is, at the same time, the great and most universal cause of the corruption of our moral sentiments.

(Smith 2002: 72)

Social inequality is, therefore, both a source of incentive and admiration (as achievement earns the approbation of one's fellows) and a possible source of intellectual, physical, social and moral degradation and of the corruption of moral virtues.

What is clear from a close reading of the *Theory of Moral Sentiments* in conjunction with *The Wealth of Nations* and *Lectures on Jurisprudence* is that Adam Smith had a well developed theory of the interdependent relationships between morals and markets, between economy and society, and of the necessary structures of governance which could in some measure restrain the malevolent potential of commercial society, ensure just and equitable contracts and, indeed, insist on benevolent conduct towards the most needy. As Muller argues:

> Because Smith was so attuned to the role of social surroundings and of human models in the creation of morally decent character, he was particularly alert to the social sources of moral pathology in commercial society. In his recommendations to the legislator, Smith emphasized the need for social institutions that restrain egoism, and the dangers inherent in the emulations of the 'loose' lifestyles of the rich and powerful. If one task of the legislator was to maximize economic benefits by preventing the circumvention of the market, his other task was to maximize the moral benefits of commercial society by fostering institutions to counteract the characteristic moral hazards of that society.
>
> (Muller 1993: 139)

This is especially true of his views regarding education. Consistent with his ideas regarding the family as the primary context for the development of moral behaviour, Smith argues against the separation of children from their families for educational purposes:

> The education of boys at distant great schools, of young men at distant colleges, of young ladies in distant nunneries and boarding-schools, seems, in the higher ranks of life, to have hurt most essentially the domestic morals, and consequently the domestic happiness, both of France and England. Do you wish to educate your children to be dutiful to their parents, to be kind and affectionate to their brothers and sisters? Put them under the necessity of being dutiful children, of being kind and affectionate brothers and sisters: educate them in your own house. From their parent's house they may, with propriety and advantage, go out every day to attend public schools: but let their dwelling be always at home . . . Surely no acquirement, which can possibly be derived from what is called a public education, can make any sort of compensation for what is almost certainly and necessarily lost by it. Domestic education is the institution of nature; public education, the contrivance of man. It is surely unnecessary to say, which is likely to be the wisest.
>
> (Smith 2002: 260–261)

According to Smith, people of rank and fortune seldom want for educational opportunity either in terms of expense or available time:

> If (people of rank or fortune) are not always properly educated, it is seldom from the want of expence laid upon their education . . . The employments of people of some rank and fortune, besides, are seldom such as to harass them from morning to night. They generally have a good deal of leisure, during which they may perfect themselves in every branch of either useful or ornamental knowledge of which they may have laid the foundation, or for which they may have acquired some taste in the earlier part of life.
>
> (Smith 1976: 784)

Indeed, people of rank and fortune have the means to purchase education in universities or through travel. Smith has a low opinion of such 'education'.

Smith's unhappy experience of Oxford (where he spent six years of relative isolation) led him to the view that 'The endowments of schools and colleges have necessarily diminished more or less the necessity of application in their teachers' (1976: 760). The result was that universities were seldom at the cutting edge of new ideas. Indeed, they 'have chosen to remain, for a long time, the sanctuaries in which exploded systems and obsolete prejudices found shelter and protection, after they had been hunted out of every other corner of the world' (Smith 1976: 772).

This was particularly the case at Oxford, where the dons colluded with one another to avoid their responsibilities:

> If the authority to which he is subject resides in the body corporate, the college, or university, of which he himself is a member, and in which the greater part of the other members are, like himself, persons who are, or ought to be teachers; they are likely to make a common cause, to be all very indulgent to one another, and every man to consent that his neighbour may neglect his duty, provided he himself is allowed to neglect his own. In the university of Oxford, the greater part of the publick professors have, for these many years, given up altogether even the pretence of teaching.
>
> (Smith 1976: 761)

Here, as with other areas of commercial society, Smith advocates a strong dose of market economics, where teachers are paid directly by their students instead of clinging to the security of their sinecures. But the market is here, as elsewhere, conceived as not simply an improvement of efficiency, but primarily as a tool for achieving *moral* ends: of ensuring that teachers actually teach!

If there are problems with the education of the gentry, then there are also problems to be addressed among those with little rank or privilege. Indeed,

> The education of the common people requires, perhaps, in a civilized and commercial society, the attention of the publick more than that of people of some rank and fortune . . . They have little time to spare for education. Their parents can scarce afford to maintain them even in infancy. As soon as they are able to work, they must apply to some trade by which they can earn their subsistence. That trade too is generally so simple and uniform as to give little exercise to the understanding; while, at the same time, their labour is both so constant and severe, that it leaves them little leisure and less inclination to apply to, or even to think of any thing else.
> (Smith 1976: 784–785)

The solution to this problem, Smith argued, was a publicly funded universal education system for the lower ranks of society:

> But though the common people cannot, in any civilized society, be so well instructed as people of some rank and fortune, the most essential parts of education, however, to read, write and account, can be acquired at so early a period of life, that the greatest part even of those who are bred to the lowest occupations, have time to acquire them before they can be employed in those occupations. For a very small expence the publick can facilitate, can encourage, and can even impose upon almost the whole body of the people, the necessity of acquiring those most essential parts of education.
> (Smith 1976: 785)

Smith advocated a policy whereby education could become available to the broader mass of the people, on whom the division of labour could have the effects of both moral degradation and the neglect of education as children were sent to work in the factories. This was against the advice of other intellectuals such as Voltaire and very much against the views of the British upper classes, 'who feared that schooling would discourage deference' (Muller 1993: 150).

Part of Smith's advocacy of publicly funded education for the poor was derived from his ambiguous commitment to distributive justice and the claims of the poor on a fuller humanity. On the one hand, education was necessary to counter

> the gross ignorance and stupidity which, in a civilized society, seem so frequently to benumb the understanding of all the inferior ranks of

people. A man without the proper use of the intellectual facilities of a man is, if possible, more contemptible than even a coward, and seems to be mutilated and deformed in a still more essential part of the character of human nature.

(Smith 1976: 788)

On the other hand, the greater part of Smith's argument was justified in terms of the potential contribution of education to the moderation of those violent propensities that led to religious wars or revolutions. In particular, education could moderate those 'delusions of enthusiasm and superstition' that lead to religious wars. Similarly, education could be a bulwark against revolution by ensuring that individuals were 'more disposed to examine, and more capable of seeing through, the interested complaints of faction and sedition':

> An instructed and intelligent people besides are always more decent and orderly than an ignorant and stupid one. They feel themselves, each individually, more respectable, and more likely to obtain the respect of their lawful superiors, and they are therefore more disposed to respect those superiors.
>
> (Smith 1976: 788)

Thus, in education, as elsewhere, morals and markets, economy and society, private and public institutions, the interests of the individual and the state were inextricably linked.

The past thirty years have seen a significant re-emergence of liberal economics following the work of Hayek and his colleagues in the mid-twentieth century. Supposedly drawing on the work of Adam Smith, this school of thought advocates market solutions to social as well as economic problems. Taking as their text Smith's metaphor of the invisible hand, they argue that self-interest, rather than altruism, is the foundation of commercial society. Smith's great insight into the unintended consequences of exchange in producing simultaneously both individual benefit and social solidarity is developed by Hayek into an argument *against* solidarity and altruism. For Hayek, Smith's observation that 'It is not from the benevolence of the butcher, the brewer or the baker, that we expect our dinner, but from regard to their own interest' (Smith 1976: 26–27) becomes the foundation of an economic and social theory which pits individualism and competition against altruism and solidarity. Indeed, for Hayek the 'primitive' notions of solidarity and altruism are remnants of a previous tribal stage of civilisation: socialism. Moreover, for Hayek,

> Socialism threatens the survival of civilization because it encourages two moral instincts, solidarity and altruism which . . . are the two great obstacles to the development of the modern economy.
>
> (Gamble 1996: 28)

They are so because such notions imply criteria that are external to the market and which would provide a yardstick against which the results of market activity could be redistributed. However, the resultant intervention would be a constraint upon freedom, which Hayek holds to be the supreme value. The redistributions required by notions of social justice therefore infringe on the moral order of a market society.

> The cult of social justice tends to destroy genuine moral feelings. The demand that we should equally esteem our fellow men is irreconcilable with the fact that our moral code rests on the approval or disapproval of the conduct of others . . . the postulate that each capable adult is primarily responsible for his own and his dependants' welfare is incompatible with the idea that society or government owes each person an appropriate income.
>
> (Hayek 1973: 99)

According to Hayek, ideas such as social justice in fact corrupt the society of free men by allowing government to be captured by self-serving sectional interests:

> The whole history of the development of popular institutions is a history of continuous struggle to prevent particular groups from abusing the governmental apparatus for the benefit of the collective interest of these groups.
>
> (Hayek 1973: 6)

Hayek's position is summed up by Gamble:

> Hayek believes that in a market order there can be no such thing as social justice, because social justice implies that there is some superior criterion which can be applied to the outcomes of the market, a notion of just deserts or fairness, which justifies redistributing what the market has allocated. The notion of fairness belongs to pre-modern societies, however. Fairness implies that there should be a connection between individual merit (measured by effort and achievement) and reward. A market order breaks that link . . . Some of the least deserving individuals on conventional moral criteria receive the highest rewards, and some of the most deserving the least.
>
> (Gamble 1996: 47)

Hayek is willing to set aside concerns with social justice in favour of the 'spontaneous order' created by market activity. This order is entirely the outcome of market operation and is a profoundly unconscious outcome of collective engagement:

> The aim of market order . . . is to cope with the inevitable ignorance of everybody of the particular facts which determine this order. By a process which men do not understand, their activities have produced an order much more extensive and comprehensive than anything they could have comprehended, but on the functioning of which we have become utterly dependent.
>
> (Hayek 1983: 19)

For Hayek, market order is akin to the concept of competitive equilibrium through which supply and demand are supposed to be brought into a stable relationship through market operations. But as Ormerod, among others, demonstrates, 'there is not just one but many possible solutions to the equations which describe a competitive economy. In other words, there is not just one equilibrium in the economy, but many equilibria' (Ormerod 1994: 90).

If there are many possible equilibria, then the questions of which equilibrium is preferable and how it is to be achieved remain unresolved. They can indeed be resolved only according to criteria which exist independently of the market and which can be achieved only by interventions in the market. As Gamble comments:

> The concept of spontaneous order is one of the key concepts in Hayek's work. But what he fails to do is to demonstrate that spontaneous orders are always superior to made orders. There are many circumstances where it is reasonable to doubt that this is the case.
>
> (Gamble 1996: 39)

Again, as Kley (1994) also points out, it is difficult to see how spontaneous order will resolve the difficulties created, for instance, by natural disasters, epidemics or war. Again, it is not at all clear from Hayek's work just when a state of spontaneous order may be said to exist. Given the boom and bust cycle of market activity, at precisely what point in any cycle is spontaneous order achieved?

In reality, as Adam Smith argued, one of the main functions of government, beyond that of securing the order that allows markets to operate effectively, is that of intervening to ensure that the unwarranted excesses of commercial society do not entirely destroy the social order or the moral foundations of behaviour. As we have seen in his arguments regarding the role of publicly funded education in redressing the worst of the degrading and demoralising effects of the division of labour and reducing the possibility of revolutionary protests against an unjust social order, Smith argued that in effect 'the visible hand of the state would counteract the potentially stultifying effects of the invisible hand of the market' (Muller 1993: 152).

Those, like Hayek and Friedman, who advocate an unrestrained competitive individualism and the articulation of self-interest through unconstrained markets also argue that publicly funded education systems which pursue notions of equity and social justice – even in terms of access – are incompatible with the spontaneous organisation of the market and the freedom of the individual. Education should, rather, ensure the production of the competitive individual for the competitive society organised through competitive markets. Even democratic participation in political and social processes should be subordinate to such concerns (Marginson 1997).

This was especially the case in education, as Chubb and Moe (1990) argued. Beginning with their analysis of poor performance in American schools, they argued that the institutionalisation of democratic control in the governance of public education in America was the root of all that was wrong:

> the specific kinds of democratic institutions by which American public education has been governed for the last half century appear to be incompatible with effective schooling . . . The problem of poor performance is just as much a normal, enduring part of the political landscape as school boards and superintendents are. It is one of the prices Americans pay for choosing to exercise direct democratic control over their schools.
>
> (Chubb and Moe 1990: 2)

Moreover, the democratic control of schooling subordinates the interests of parents and students to those of the wider community:

> The fundamental point to be made about parents and students is not that they are politically weak, but that, even in a perfectly functioning democratic system, the public schools are not meant to be theirs to control and are literally not supposed to provide them with the kind of education they might want. The schools are agencies of society as a whole, and everyone has a right to participate in their governance. Parents and students have a right to participate too. But they have no right to win. In the end, they have to take what society gives them.
>
> (Chubb and Moe 1990: 32)

As an alternative, Chubb and Moe advocate the development of markets in schooling which foster responsiveness to consumer demand, freedom of choice between alternatives and the elimination of unwanted schools through 'natural selection' (1990: 32–33). Social considerations such as equity of access, the redress of disadvantage and general issues of social justice in the curriculum and treatment of children are set aside, as are the likely effects of such a system on the reproduction of advantage and disadvantage:

> The unequal distribution of income in society may bias certain markets in favor of the rich and against the poor. To the extent that these imperfections are serious, markets are less likely to generate the diversity, quality and levels of services that consumers want, and prices are likely to be higher than they otherwise would be . . . These imperfections cannot be eliminated . . . It is a mistake, however, to place too much emphasis on these sorts of imperfections . . .
> (Chubb and Moe 1990: 34)

What is important and cannot be emphasised sufficiently is the need for choice and for parents and students to be allowed to make whatever choices they wish between an array of alternatives; alternatives which are free from any governmental constraints:

> Each school must be granted sole authority to determine its own governing structure . . . The state must refrain from imposing structures or rules that specify how authority is to be exercised . . . the state will do nothing to tell the schools how they must be organised . . . The schools will be organized and operated as they see fit . . .
> (Chubb and Moe 1990: 223)

This decentralised authority extends to curriculum, teaching, hiring and firing, infrastructure decisions and so on. Public authorities will fund public schools but have minimal control over them. 'Each student will be free to attend any public school . . . regardless of district' (Chubb and Moe 1990: 221). Moreover,

> Public officials and their constituents would be free to take their own approaches to taxation, equalization, supplementary funding for the disadvantaged, treatment of religious schools, parent add-ons . . . thus designing choice systems to reflect the unique conditions, preferences, and political forces of their own states.
> (Chubb and Moe 1990: 225)

The underlying principles that justify this approach are, first, consumer choice and, secondly, the theory of the firm, both of which seem to approximate what happens in generalised models of industrial production and competition. However, when applied to education they do not seem to operate as intended.

First, in respect of parent/student (consumer) choice there are significant restrictions on choice. Some of these restrictions are a result of the 'imperfections' noted by Chubb and Moe, notably differences in wealth but also including location, mobility, and so on (Parker and Marganis 1996). But more important still is a fundamental property of successful firms who not only have strict controls on their internal production functions (what happens inside the black box) but also, and crucially, strict control over their inputs. In education this means that 'successful' schools can, because of excess demand, control their most significant inputs (pupils) who themselves contribute to the success of the school. So, rather than parents getting to choose the school they want for their children, certain schools get to choose the pupils (and parents) who will provide superior inputs and therefore increase the 'efficiency' of their production process (Ball 1994). Again, because the inputs of schools vary so greatly and the outputs are so varied it has been impossible for economists to develop adequate production functions for schools, which measure the 'value added' nature of their work (Easton 1999).

Despite the technical problems and social inadequacies of the 'market' approach, it still has an initial appeal to parents who want schools to be moulded in their own (rather than a more general public) image. Moreover, recent literature in educational administration and leadership argues the need for more attention to be paid to the social, ethical and moral dilemmas involved in educational management (Begley 1999, Grace 1995, Greenfield 1999, Goldring and Greenfield 2002, Sergiovanni 1992, Starratt 1991).

For example, the notion of the 'virtuous school' (Sergiovanni 1992) is built around distinctions outlined in research by Hill, Foster and Gendler (1990) between 'focus' schools and 'zoned' schools. Focus schools

> have clear, uncomplicated missions centered on the experiences they intend to provide their students and on the way they intend to influence their students' performance, attitudes and behaviour . . . [They] are strong organizations with a capacity to initiate action in pursuit of their missions, to sustain themselves over time, to solve their own problems, and to manage their external relationships . . . [Their] distinct characteristics set them apart, in the minds of their staff, students, and parents from other schools . . . each has a special identity that inspires a sense of loyalty and commitment. They are committed to education in its broadest sense, the development of whole students.

> They induce values, influence attitudes and integrate diverse sources of knowledge. They also transmit facts and impart skills, but mainly they try to mould teenagers into responsible, productive adults.
>
> (Sergiovanni 1992: 100)

By contrast,

> The zoned schools . . . emphasized delivering instructional and other service programs to students and following procedures. Instead of relying on strong social contracts, they allowed staff and students to define their own roles. They saw themselves primarily as transmitters of information and imparters of skills. Finally, they emphasized the tracking of students and offered a potpourri of curricular options, in an effort to find something for everyone. The emphasis seemed to be more on processes and treatments than on the substance of purposes, people and outcomes. These characteristics gave the schools a diffuse and ambiguous sense of identity as technical and instrumental organizations, rather than self-contained, free-standing entities.
>
> (Sergiovanni 1992: 100–101)

Sergiovanni sums up the character of the 'focus' schools in terms of the 'covenant' that exists in such schools between teachers, pupils and parents. He points to the fundamental features of covenants in providing

> the kind of morally based contractual relationship that can bond people together. Bonding relationships respond to the reality that emotion, values, and membership connections are important human impulses. They also acknowledge the aspect of human nature that places others before self-interest. Finally, they give needed meaning and significance to our work lives. These inclinations join covenant and virtue.
>
> (Sergiovanni 1992: 102)

So far, so good. And indeed, Sergiovanni echoes much of the emphasis that Adam Smith placed on the family as the primary 'covenantal' community within which the genesis of moral behaviour and mutual obligation inheres and which gradually develops into a broader understanding of trust and obligation in economic and social relationships.

However, this view of the moral dimension of schools as covenantal communities faces several problems, some of which Adam Smith foresaw. While agreeing that the well run family was the covenantal milieu within which early notions of moral and social responsibility were formed, Smith had a rather ambivalent attitude towards the religious communities which claimed to provide continuing moral guidance.

On the one hand he saw established religion as a system of sinecures, which sapped the vitality of the clergy:

> The clergy of an established and well-endowed religion frequently become men of learning and elegance, who possess the virtues of gentlemen, or which can recommend them to the esteem of gentlemen; but they are apt gradually to lose those qualities, both good and bad, which gave them authority and influence with the inferior ranks of people, and which had perhaps been the original causes of the success and establishment of their religion.
> (Smith 1976: 789)

On the other hand, along with his colleague David Hume, Smith saw the vitality of dissenters as 'highly pernicious [with] a natural tendency to pervert the true, by infusing it into a strong mixture of superstition, folly and delusion' (1976: 791). Indeed:

> Each ghostly practitioner, in order to render himself more precious and sacred in the eyes of his retainers, will inspire them with the most violent abhorrence of all other sects, and continually endeavour, by some novelty, to excite the languid devotion of his audience. No regard will be paid to truth, morals, or decency in the doctrines inculcated. Every tenet will be adopted that best suits the disorderly affections of the human frame.
> (Hume in Smith 1976: 791)

So, covenantal communities, like markets, in themselves neither comprise nor necessarily contain the constituents of beneficial moral and social capital. As Putnam argues, the 'social capital' of particular networks can have both positive and negative value for individuals and for society:

> we cannot assume that social capital is everywhere and always a good thing. Although the phrase 'social capital' has a felicitous ring about it, we must take care to consider its potential vices, or even just the possibility that virtuous forms can have unintended consequences that are not socially desirable . . . In short, we must understand the purposes and effects of social capital. Networks and norms might, for example, benefit those who belong – to the detriment of those who do not. Social capital might be most prevalent among groups of people who are already advantaged, thereby widening political and economic inequalities between those groups and others who are poor in social capital . . . Moreover, some forms of social capital are good for democracy and social health; others are (or threaten to be) destructive.
> (Putnam 2002: 9)

Putnam uses the Ku Klux Klan as an example of a 'convenantal' community with considerable social capital but with quite malign effects on the wider society. Other examples such as the Italian or Russian mafias or El Quaeda spring immediately to mind. Covenantal communities are not, of themselves, good things.

However, there is a tendency in education to see covenantal communities or communities of interest as the appropriate basis for the binding together of the members of schools into moral communities with shared values, purposes and goals, often around religious or ethnic identities, and to see this as a necessary foundation for 'effective' education.

Peshkin (1986) provides a detailed sympathetic but ultimately critical ethnography of such a school. It is one which clearly meets Sergiovanni's criteria of a 'virtuous school', but which is isolating in terms of the wider society:

> The academy epitomizes the case of a community successfully projecting its idiosyncratic outlook onto its school. More than just a community school, however, the academy is a 'communal' institution . . . Communal describes a community whose strong commitment to its own welfare inevitably places it in conflict with other communities that do not accept its doctrinal foundation. A communal school serves an internally integrative or community-maintenance function. That is, it simultaneously links believers together and separates them from non-believers. In its defensive capacity, the academy shields its students and beliefs from competitors by promoting dichotomies not only of we and they, but also of right and wrong. *We* follow God's truth in God's preferred institutions; *they* are the unfortunates of Satan's dark, unrighteous world.
>
> (Peshkin 1986: 282)

The result, as Smith realised *vis-à-vis* religious sects, is internal integration of a particular social group at the cost of wider social cohesion. In increasingly pluralistic societies the withdrawal of important sectors of society into the gated communities of exclusive covenantal groups (whether they be class-based, religion-based, or ethnically based) brings into question the relationship between education and the commonwealth to which Adam Smith was committed.

Sergiovanni, and many of those who are interested in the moral basis of education and educational leadership, acknowledge this problem but seldom reach more than a perfunctory answer, usually by stating their own beliefs and commitments and by suggesting that, for instance,

> In a democracy, the loyal opposition is committed to the same overarching values as the majority, but differs in its views of how the

values should be put into action and what the means of obtaining them should be. The relationship between majority and loyal opposition is characterized by mutual respect.

(Sergiovanni 1995: 143)

But this really won't do. It won't do because, as Gray (2000) points out, the search for a liberal consensus on the values that should underpin the behaviour and commitments of everyone inhabiting a liberal society is proving impossible. Consequently:

> If liberalism has a future, it is in giving up the search for a rational consensus on the best way of life. As a consequence of mass migration, new technologies of communication and continued cultural experimentation, nearly all societies today contain several ways of life, with many people belonging to more than one. The liberal ideal of toleration which looks to a rational consensus on the best way of life was born in societies divided on the claims of a single way of life. It cannot show us how to live together in societies that harbour many ways of life.
>
> (Gray 2000: 1–2)

The resulting problem is not resolvable by simply abandoning the battlefield in a dudgeon of moral relativism, for the fact is that we have little option but to live alongside and possibly even with each other regardless of our differences. Circling *our* wagons when we feel under attack from *theirs* is not a solution.

The solution might well lie in a variant of the tradition of liberalism: one concerned not with agreement on ultimate values and a single way of life, but upon constructing institutions that allow us a *modus vivendi* – a way of living together and profiting from our differences:

> Whereas our inherited conception of toleration presupposes that one way of life is best for all of humankind, *modus vivendi* accepts that there are many forms of life, some of them no doubt yet to be contrived, in which humans can flourish. For the predominant ideal of liberal toleration, the best life may be unattainable, but it is the same for all. From a standpoint of *modus vivendi*, no kind of life can be the best for everyone. The human good is too diverse to be realized in any life. Our inherited ideal of toleration accepts with regret the fact that there are many ways of life. If we adopt *modus vivendi* as our ideal we will welcome it.
>
> (Gray 2000: 5)

The point of such a position is to take the pressure off the need for conversion, cultural dominance or ethnic cleansing and to focus our attention on the problem of how to build institutions which will allow us to live together – a condition that we cannot avoid:

> The aim of *modus vivendi* cannot be to still the conflict of values. It is to reconcile individuals and ways of life honouring conflicting values to a life in common. We do not need common values in order to live together in peace. We need common institutions in which many forms of life can coexist.
>
> (Gray 2000: 5–6)

Building such institutions was one of Adam Smith's preoccupations. Indeed, he saw the market as an institution which cut across various ways of life, both local and distant, national and international; which linked different families together through the invisible hand that underlay the market. Commerce itself required certain habits and commitments – prudence, justice, benevolence, self-command – which were practised through trade, whatever the ways of life otherwise practised by the participants. Moreover, the role of government was to strengthen and guarantee such mutually beneficial practices and to punish departures from the procedures which facilitated market transactions.

Education was indeed one of the institutions by which such beneficial practices were to be encouraged – not as a means of enforcing a particular way of life, but as a means of equipping individuals to participate in the division of labour without being corrupted or demeaned by it, and by learning the moral and technical skills of production and negotiation required by commercial society.

For Smith, market society involved the building of public institutions which would allow for the development of commerce and an increase in the common wealth. Part of the purpose of achieving 'a plentiful revenue or subsistence for the people' was also to provide 'a revenue sufficient for the publick services' (Smith 1976: 428). Publicly funded (and possibly compulsory) education was one of those 'publick services'. Its intention was to build the skills and virtues – prudence, justice, benevolence and self-command – on which both morals and markets depend.

Despite the archaic language of Smith's writing, many of his concerns are quite contemporary: how to construct markets which are governed in such a way as to prevent corrupt behaviour and project the moral virtues of prudence, justice, benevolence and self-command; how to develop government interventions including appropriate punishments and civil law which would guarantee the proper operations of markets; how to gain sufficient revenue by which government might support essential 'publick services'; how to develop an education which would prevent the gross ignorance of the poor and guarantee the virtue as well as the skills of all ranks of society.

His answer was neither to abandon government in favour of market 'solutions' nor to abandon markets in favour of 'command economies', but to seek compromises which would ensure the vitality of markets within the context of a social order committed to the development and preservation of institutions which would encourage order, justice, benevolence, prudence and self-command. The challenges Smith articulated are still with us. His careful consideration of the balance required between morals and markets is a dilemma that is still with us. The consideration of both Smith's *Wealth of Nations* and his *Theory of Moral Sentiments* might well provide us with guidelines for the foundation of an administrative ethics for education as well as for the broader purposes of government. The development of such an administrative ethics is vital to the development of a truly effective education.

References

Alvey, J. E. (1998) 'Adam Smith's three strikes against commercial society', *International Journal of Social Economics* 25, 9: 1425–1441.

Alvey, J. E. (2000) *Adam Smith's Moral Science of Economics*, Palmerston North: Massey University.

Ball, S. (1994) *Education Reform*, Buckingham: Open University Press.

Bassiry, G. R. and Jones, M. (1993) 'Adam Smith and the ethics of contemporary capitalism', *Journal of Business Ethics* 12: 621–627.

Bates, R. J. (1980) 'Educational administration, the sociology of science and the management of knowledge', *Educational Administration Quarterly* 16, 2: 1–20.

Begley, P. T. (1999) *Values and Educational Leadership*, Albany: SUNY Press.

Chubb, J. and Moe, T. (1990) *Politics, Markets and America's Schools*, Washington, DC: Brookings Institute.

Coker, E. W. (1990) 'Adam Smith's concept of the social system', *Journal of Business Ethics* 9: 139–142.

Easton, B. (1999) *The Whimpering of the State*, Auckland: Auckland University Press.

Frank, R. H., Gilovich, T. D., and Regan, D. T. (1993) 'Does studying economics inhibit cooperation?', *Journal of Economic Perspectives* 7, 2: 159–171.

Fukuyama, F. (1992) *The End of History and the Last Man*, New York: Avon Books.

Gamble, A. (1966) *Hayek: The Iron Cage of Liberty*, Cambridge: Polity Press.

Goldring, E. and Greenfield, W. (2002) 'Understanding the evolving concept of leadership in education', in J. Murphy (ed.) *The Educational Leadership Challenge: Re-defining Leadership for the 21st Century*, Chicago: University of Chicago Press.

Grace, G. (1995) *School Leadership*, London: Falmer Press.

Gray, J. (2000) *Two Faces of Liberalism*, Cambridge: Polity Press.

Greenfield, W. (1999) 'Moral leadership: Fact or fancy?', Paper presented at the Annual Meeting of the American Educational Research Association, Montreal, Canada.

Hayek, F. (1973) *Law, Legislation and Liberty, vol. 1*, London: Routledge.

Hayek, F. (1983) *Knowledge, Evolution and Society*, London: Adam Smith Institute.
Hill, P. T., Foster, G. E. and Gendler, T. (1990) *High Schools with Character*, Santa Monica: Rand Corporation.
Hodgkinson, C. (1991) *Educational Leadership: The Moral Art*, Albany: State University of New York Press.
Jevons, W. S. (1970) *The Theory of Political Economy*, London: Penguin.
Kleer, R. A. (1995) 'Final causes in Adam Smith's theory of moral sentiments', *Journal of the Philosophy of History* 33, 2: 275–300.
Kley, R. (1994) *Hayek's Social and Political Thought*, Oxford: Clarendon Press.
Lux, K. (1990) *Adam Smith's Mistake*, Boston: Shambhala.
Marginson, S. (1997) *Markets and Education*, Sydney: Allen and Unwin.
Marwell, G. and Ames, R. E. (1981) 'Economists free ride, does anyone else?', *Journal of Public Economics* 15: 295–310.
Muller, J. Z. (1993) *Adam Smith in His Time and Ours*, New York: Free Press.
Murphy, J. (2002). *The Educational Leadership Challenge: Redefining Leadership for the 21st Century*, Chicago: Chicago University Press.
Ormerod, P. (1994) *The Death of Economics*, London: Faber.
Parker, L. and Marganis, F. (1996) 'School choice in the U.S. urban context: Racism and policies of containment', *Journal of Education Policy* 11, 6: 717–728.
Peshkin, A. (1986) *God's Choice: The Total World of a Christian Fundamentalist School*, Chicago: University of Chicago Press.
Putnam, Robert D. (2002) *Democracies in Flux*, Oxford: Oxford University Press.
Rosenberg, N. (1990) 'Adam Smith and the stock of moral capital', *History of Political Economy* 22, 1: 1–17.
Rothschild, K. W. (1993) *Ethics and Economic Theory*, Aldershot: Edward Elgar.
Sergiovanni, T. (1992) *Moral Leadership*, San Francisco: Jossey-Bass.
Segiovanni, T. (1995) *The Principalship: A Reflective Practice Perspective*, Boston: Allyn and Bacon.
Sergiovanni, T. J. (2001) *Leadership: What's In It For Schools?*, London: Routledge/Falmer.
Small, A. W. (1972) *Adam Smith and Modern Sociology*, Clifton: Augustus M. Kelly.
Smith, A. (1976) *An Inquiry into the Nature and Causes of the Wealth of Nations*, Oxford: Oxford University Press.
Smith, A. (1978) *Lectures on Jurisprudence*, Oxford: Oxford University Press.
Smith, A. (2002) *The Theory of Moral Sentiments*, Cambridge: Cambridge University Press.
Sowell, T. (1979) 'Adam Smith in theory and practice', in *Adam Smith and Modern Political Economy: Bicentennial essays on 'The Wealth of Nations'*, ed. G. P. O'Driscoll, Jr., Ames: Iowa State University Press.
Starratt, R. (1991) 'Building an ethical school', *Educational Administration Quarterly* 27, 2: 185–202.
Young, J. T. (1997) *Economics as a Moral Science*, Cheltenham, UK: Edward Elgar.

Chapter 7

A Kantian critique for administrative ethics

An alternative to the 'morally mute' manager?

Eugenie A. Samier

> Nothing straight can be constructed from such warped wood as that which man is made of.
>
> [The good will] dwells already in the natural sound understanding and does not need so much to be taught as only to be brought to light.
>
> In some affairs which affect the interests of the commonwealth . . . [some members] must behave purely passively . . . obedience is imperative.
>
> Every rational being exists as an end in himself and not merely as a means to be arbitrarily used by this or that will.[1]

It is apparent in these four quotations from Kant – on the concept of radical evil, the inherent capacity for goodness, obedience and loyalty due to government, and the universal principle of justice grounded in a concept of freedom – that either his ethics is flawed by fundamental contradictions, or it is sufficiently broad to encompass the complex tensions in human beings and their social relationships. These propositions can also be found in traditional English-language administrative theory, but in bifurcated, simplified and amoralistic forms: in Theory X and Theory Y, in the opposition of Tayloristic managerialism and human relations theory, and in the politics–administration dichotomy.[2] This excision of moral agency from administration has resulted in a condition Menzel calls the 'morally mute manager', a metaphor invoked to characterise public administrators as 'good men and women with good intentions who allow themselves to be seduced by a sense of duty as competent purveyors of neutral information. Thus, they become neither moral nor immoral actors. Rather they become moral mutes' (Menzel 1999: 6). It is this image of moral inadequacy and a proposed Kantian alternative that are the focus of this chapter.

While Kantian theory is not a common foundation from which to discuss administrative ethics in the English-speaking world,[3] it does provide an interesting, and perhaps even provocative, potential for raising questions about not only administrative theory, but the moral nature of administrative decision-making, judgement, and character. Through an elucidation and resolution of the opening four propositions, this chapter will explore a Kantian ethical foundation for administration grounded in the transcendental idealist[4] tradition and its implications for the practical demands of administrative life. It will also be explored as a foundation from which to critique conventional administrative theory.

Determining the relevance of Kant to administrative ethics involves addressing the following three underlying questions. First, what does a Kantian ethic bring that other approaches do not? That is, for example, does the problem of abuse of power appear clearer and more adequately resolvable? Second, what would it demand of administrators individually and collectively? This involves identifying the requirements of moral reasoning in the fundamental functions of administrative practice, of policy-making, organisational management, and obligations due to political masters. In other words, what kind and quality of judgement in meeting administrative demands and the good of others (e.g. political masters, colleagues and staff, and the general population) are necessary to morality? And finally, what are the impediments to morality, such as bureaucratic requirements, organisational politics, codes of professionalism, and administrative culture? It is my contention that a Kantian formulation of ethics is antithetical to many administrative imperatives, particularly those derived from, in Weber's terms, a legal-rational style of administration we commonly call bureaucratic, and therefore is unlikely to be acceptable instrumentally as a guide to decision-making and action.

The presentation of Kant in administration theory

It is interesting to note that Kant is referenced frequently in administrative and educational administration theory. The manner in which this is done is instructive in measuring the philosophical sophistication of the field and demonstrating a deeply held instrumentalism that has hindered a meaningful discussion of Kant, and ethics in administration generally. For example, in one text written exclusively on Kantian contributions to the field, Grundstein's *The Managerial Kant*, the portrait presented is that of a proto-systems theorist and apologist for bureaucracy (Grundstein 1981: 105, 118–120). Grundstein conflates the 'order' of reason in Kantian philosophy with bureaucratic rationality, exemplified in the writings of Chester Barnard, reducing Kantian reasoning to a 'regulative order' and 'mechanism with intelligence' (*ibid.*: 3–4) consistent with managerial principles. Kantian theories of desire, interest, will, reason, prudence, and personality are interpreted within a regime of organisational conformity: moral reasoning is likened to that of an automatonic switchboard operator regarding the code of her organisation as a universality of principle, or pure moral law, to which she submits her will (*ibid*.: 22). Grundstein misconstrues Kant's pursuit of moral reasoning as a means of attaining individual freedom; instead, he uses the dictum of obedience to moral law in a subjugated form more consistent with Barnard's concept of 'organisational personality' (*ibid*.: 30–31). He conceives of Kantian reason and moral law as impersonal functions conterminous with the necessity of organisational authority through mechanisms of prediction and control, rather than in the personal and individual terms Kant established (*ibid*.: 160). He also excludes Kant's 'crooked timber', or theory of radical evil – a much more fruitful source for a theory of politics and immorality in organisational life. An underlying assumption in this perspective is that management is as moral as it is regulative, a principle that commonly underlies administrative ethics.

Most references to Kant in administration are to the categorical imperative, but in most cases this is misunderstood, misapplied, or treated in a cursory fashion. Many use Kant as a representative of deontological ethics (frequently referred to, ambiguously, as the ethics of duty) in contrast to various types of consequentialism, such as utilitarianism or teleology (e.g. Foster and Greenwood 1996: 109–111). As some authors note, modern systems of administration are a combination of these two – the utilitarian deeply embedded in managerialism, and the deontological in constitutional and legal provisions (e.g. Lewis 1998). Woller, for example, refers to Kant's categorical imperative (that one should act as if legislating a universal law) to build an argument for universal rules in public administration, but he mistakes Kant's method by asserting that such universal principles are derived from empirical cases (1998: 92). Rohr dismisses Kant, virtually out of hand, for a perceived absolutist position deriving from a deontology divorced from *Realpolitik* (2000: 203–204). Sheeran criticises the categorical imperative for being an inadequate guiding ethical principle, as he equates the law of the categorical imperative with judicial laws of a state (1993: 7), further claiming that there is no evidence (presumably empirical) for its existence (1993: 66).[5] Chandler concludes an examination of deontological administrative ethics with a pragmatic situationalist criticism of the categorical imperative as inadequate in dealing with the 'moral ambiguity that is the stuff of administrative life' – itself better dealt with 'personally, courageously, responsibly, and creatively' (2001: 192).

More sympathetic presentations of the categorical imperative exist; however, they are only briefly alluded to or are underdeveloped. Warwick appeals to the categorical imperative as a model for constructing a 'Law of Procedural Reciprocity': 'Seek exceptions to established procedures only when you would grant the same right to others in comparable circumstances' (1981: 122). Wolf invokes it as an option in interpreting a standard such as equity (1981: 133). Zajac and Bruhn present the categorical imperative and related values of human autonomy, dignity, and self-realisation within a framework of a participatory duty to respect staff involvement in planned organisational change (1999: 710–711). However, they do not extend this principle to questioning the fundamental character, structure and purpose of the organisation. Fox's treatment, although presented briefly in a broad discussion of the potential value of philosophy for administrative ethics, stands out as conceptually well developed (2001). Garofalo and Geuras (1999) have also recently investigated Kantian ethics in some depth as a possible foundation. However, they try to resolve what they regard as a theoretical–pragmatic dichotomy between deontological and teleological ethics in an unsuccessful manner by proposing a synthesised unification theory intended to encompass the inherent oppositions without adequately representing the differences between utilitarian and Kantian courses of action.

Often Kant is appealed to indirectly. An example is Dorbeck-Jung (1998: 47–48), who introduces the Kantian primacy of reason over the rational from Rawls (1980), and the categorical imperative grounding in the principle of treating people as ends (instead of means) from Selznick (1992). Rohr and Stewart reference Kant passingly as relevant for an understanding of Rawls (Rohr 1978: 56, 1998: 20; Stewart 1991: 363), Stewart critiquing the tradition for an over reliance on reason as an assurance of ethical behaviour (1991: 365–366). Jos and Hines attribute Kohlberg's ethic of justice and post-conventional stage of moral development requiring independent, rational, and impartial choice-making through the application of universal moral principles partly to Kant – as transmitted through Rawls' liberal conception of moral judgement and the morally good person as one governed solely by a rational will (Jos and Hines 1993: 374).[6] Mitchell references Kant as representative of a moral tradition grounded in concepts of 'the Good, the True, the Beautiful', informing Bloom's critique of the malaise of relativism affecting all social actors, including civil servants (Mitchell 1999: 28–29).

Common (and briefly developed) critiques of Kant are that his work is too abstract and disconnected from organisational *Realpolitik* to be of use. For Thompson, Kant's volitional doctrine – that one is morally responsible only for what one intends – is too simplistic to account for the situations that administrators face (1981: 275–276). Brown argues that Kant's principle of respect for others is too abstract to be applied to particular cases and does not guide administrators in what obligations should be met (1981: 298). Burke includes Kant as a representative of one of the many moral approaches (such as consequentialism and Machiavellianism) in the field that are inadequate to the demands of administration, in Kant's case because responsibilities are derived from the dictates of personal morality (Burke 1983: 1112; also 1986: 162). For Burke, Kantian conscience and personal morality entail an absolutist moral position in which individual conceptions of unconditional duty supersede 'the demands of politics and the dictates and obligations of office' (1986: 162), and which do not take into account circumstantial considerations (1986: 180–182). Stewart argues that Kantianism focuses on the 'acts' that one ought to perform rather than the kind of person one should be, characterising it this way in order to distinguish it from the Aristotelian tradition of virtue ethics (1991: 363, as do Zajac and Bruhn 1999). Hitt represents Kant's position as 'rules ethics', 'determined by laws and standards' (1990: 99, 130–132), a position not unlike that of Rawls.

Positive, although simplistic, references to Kant are also common. For Weingartner, Kant is the *eminence grise* of moral reasoning (1999: xii). However, he discusses only briefly, and I would argue weakly, the obligational standard of Kantianism we must meet in behaving morally, as he concentrates on an apparent free rider for officials in meeting a threshold of moral duty when mitigated by limited ability or capability without seriously questioning administrative systems and practices (1999: 80). In other words, living up to the 'ought' is required only when one can comfortably operate within existing procedural and regulatory regimes. Gortner presents a scheme of questions by major political philosophers of administrative relevance first devised by Wayne Leys in 1952, that includes the moral idealist tradition of Kant and Plato, to demonstrate the perennial character of concerns in organisational life. As Gortner notes, despite changing contingencies 'there is little new under the sun' in political thinking and decision-making (1991: 85–87). A number of Kantian principles are implied through the sequence of questions he proposes for moral decision-making relating to various formulations of the categorical imperative. This scheme, though, is presented simplistically in a panoply of ethical traditions, eliding the inconsistencies and contradictions among them. Wittmer also presents Kant cursorily in an overview of ethical systems relevant for administration, identifying two formulations of the categorical imperative. Despite criticisms of Kantian ethics as 'abstract, vague, and unhelpful in specific situations', he argues that it can still provide guidance for administrators through its adherence to principles of 'duty to principle, consistency, and rationality' (Wittmer 2001: 502).[7] Luke and Hart follow suit in a survey of moral traditions focusing on Kant's categorical imperative and the necessity of having Good Will as a motivation to act out of moral duty (2001: 536).

In educational administration Kant has received a warmer, though less sophisticated, reception. Strike, Haller and Soltis discuss only one among the 'many wise things' Kant wrote about ethics, 'that the only really good thing is a good will' (1988: 103), which they associate with the capacity for empathy, and its joy and pain. In other words, they reduce ethical principle to affect. Thomas and Davis introduce Kant's imperative that individuals should be treated as ends in themselves, suggesting that this 'imperative' is contiguous with Sergiovanni's five tenets of the 'virtuous school' (Thomas and Davis 2000: 59–60). Maxcy associates Kant with the practice of developing a 'normative set of ordered principles to guide moral decisions', in contrast with virtue ethics (1991: 120). Kimbrough presents Kant in a survey of morality as the major proponent of an ethics grounded in pure reason and governed by the concept of the categorical imperative. However, he rather speciously describes it as 'certain as a mathematical proof' in its absolute nature and universal applicability, equating moral laws with the categorical imperatives [sic] obliging people unconditionally to do their duty (Kimbrough 1985: 33–34). Sergiovanni, in a brief survey of ethical traditions, identifies Kant as a characteristic representative of deontological ethics,[8] describing his position in the *Foundations of the Metaphysics of Morals*[9] as one maintaining 'that any action, in order to be moral, must be taken in the belief and because of the belief that it is right – from duty, not because of personal inclination, gain, or love' (1992: 20). Sergiovanni also appeals to Kant's dictum about the superiority of ordinary reasoning in practical matters, invoking the categorical imperative[10] as one of the tests of moral principles for building school community and guiding administration (1992: 106, 108). Kimbrough and Nunnery attribute Kantian ethical performance to only those 'well-educated persons of superior intellectual powers [who] can discern universally applicable, unchanging values' (1988: 399),[11] and assume that in order to ground ethics in pure reason one must disregard 'pleasure, human desires, happiness' (1988: 400).[12] It seems that Kant is associated with 'goodness' and, therefore, arguing for morality or ethics in administration and leadership must necessarily be consistent with Kantian principles and worldview.

Hodgkinson references Kant frequently in his books, using him as a touchstone in a variety of ways. First, the distinction between the desirable and the desired – or the good and the right (Hodgkinson 1978: 110) – and the categorical imperative are used, along with a number of other theoretical works, in constructing the categories of his value paradigm (1978: 113, 189; 1983: 208; 1991: 99; 1996: 118). The second formulation of Kant's categorical imperative (human beings as ends in themselves) is used to critique the organisational pathologies of egotism (1978: 161), careerism (1983: 153), and organisational authority (1991: 70; 1996: 153). However, Hodgkinson overdraws the distinction between the traditions of *Realpolitik* for which morality is relative and the absolute morality of the Kantian ethic (1983: 87; 1996: 94–95),[13] and rather speciously associates the Kantian notion of 'duty' with Taylorism (1983: 109), Marxist collectivity (1991: 133), and administrative duty (1996: 256).

One of the most extensive presentations of Kantian ethics in educational administration is Rebore's *The Ethics of Educational Leadership* (2001), where he surveys the major ethical traditions from which educational administrators must individually choose the basis of their decisions and actions. Each tradition is presented as equally relevant in identifying and resolving 'ethical problems and issues facing educational leaders' (2001: 16). It is assumed that all ethical traditions cohere, and that none has limitations, inconsistencies, or contradictions. The section on the Kantian conception of moral duty is located in a chapter contemplating the 'variables' of power and duty. This discussion, accompanied by a short excerpt from the *Foundations of the Metaphysics of Morals*, focuses exclusively on relating Kant's categorical imperative to the practical demands on administrators fulfilling their responsibilities. However, in an un-Kantian style, emphasis is placed on the consequences of actions rather than their intent and an interpretation of Kant's imperative only in so far as it supports existing administrative codes and responsibilities.

In general, Kant has suffered the same kind of transmission problem that Weber's writings have experienced in the field. A complex major theorist's work is cut to fit prevailing administrative ideologies. This practice is indicative of the general lack of influence of philosophy which, Fox argues, obtains in administrative ethics and the prevalent practice of famous philosophers being 'appropriated only as authoritative founts of principles rather than as colleagues in dialogic discovery' (2001: 107), often presented in an uncritical smorgasbord of ethical theories. This often takes the form of a superficial reference to the categorical imperative, using snippets from Kant's writings with no coherent and comprehensive treatment of his thought,[14] and compounded by an over-reliance on and isolated use of the *Foundations of the Metaphysics of Morals*. As Gregor (1963) demonstrates, an understanding of Kant's moral theory requires the consideration of his *Metaphysics of Morals* where the formal principles introduced in the *Foundations* and the *Critique of Practical Reason* are applied to everyday life. An additional problem is the variety of mis-characterisations of his work as overly abstract, as moral certainty, or as synonymous with existing rule, legal and constitutional regimes. The latter has produced confusion about Kant's concept of duty – some misinterpret it to mean political rather than moral duty, that is, obedience to the system or superiors. This treatment of Kant demonstrates the degree to which administration, as Luke and Hart claim, has lost touch with moral philosophy in its evolution as a distinctive discipline from political philosophy (2001: 529–530). In all these cases, Kant's moral theory is rendered impotent for administrative application, thereby reinforcing Menzel's 'morally mute manager' syndrome in the field.

There are, however, a few writers who have provided suggestive commentary upon which a Kantian ethic for administration can be built.

Greenfield referenced Kant as a proponent of subjectivity (Greenfield and Ribbins 1993: 7, 95), for whom the moral order originates within (1993: 98–99). Starratt locates Kant in the tradition of rational individualism, that is, clearly differentiated from affect and largely interpreted through Rawls's construct of rules by which a moral community can achieve justice (Starratt 1991: 192). Evers and Lakomski, although promoting Rawls's ethics as a 'more powerful and sophisticated version' of Kant's, do credit Kant for a conception of social justice grounded in reason (1991: 180–181). Bates (1984: 12–13) introduces Kant's second formulation of the Universal Principle of Justice – people should be treated as ends in themselves rather than as means – as part of a critique of bureaucracy in a discussion drawing on R. Denhardt (1981), Hummel (1982), and Weber (1958). Hodgkinson, too, contrasts the Kantian ethic of treating others as ends in themselves with the organisational imperative to treat others as means (1996: 153) with the Machiavellian administrator of *The Prince* (1996: 197) and Nietzschean ethics (1996: 201).[15]

Apart from Kant's dominant role in modern philosophy, there are additional reasons for considering his relevance to administration theory. First, his ethics was largely developed to political purpose. It informed his conception of the role and responsibilities of the state (and presumably the civil service) in creating the conditions and support for those activities that meet moral requirements, as Kant regarded politics to be an applied branch of right, and morality, the theoretical branch (1991a: 116). He understood his moral system to operate within a republic, the only kind of civil constitution he believed would ensure freedom, equality, and civil independence under a single common legislation (1991a: 74, 99; 1991b: 125),[16] in contrast to democracy, which he thought would inevitably lead to a despotism of the majority against the rights of the individual (1991a: 101). It is not through moral attitudes of the citizenry alone that a good political constitution is created; rather, it is through the latter that people will attain a high level of moral culture (1991a: 113). Kant's is a moral system predicated upon reciprocity, requiring an engagement in society and a duty to the political community. The role of ethics in this context is to provide a moral foundation to our political self-determination, our relationship with authority, and our ability to subordinate our self-interests to higher claims. The principles by which we should conduct our interpersonal and societal relations should equally serve as a guide in administrative relations and responsibilities, from policy development to its implementation, and in shaping the organisations that serve these purposes.

It is Sullivan's contention that Kant's ethical system grew more out of his political theory than out of a consideration of individual character and action. Thus it provides the underlying conceptual structure for community life, the ultimate moral norm which 'should measure the fundamental policies on which we act for their suitability to serve as impersonal laws for everyone' (Sullivan 1994: 1–2). Moral duties in Kant can, therefore, be organised under the following three basic questions (Sullivan 1994: 149–154): (1) What kind of political system should we have? That is, what are the requirements for a civil community? (2) What kind of person should each of us aim to become? Or, what qualities are necessary to exercising autonomy and achieving moral character? (For administrators this means what degree of independent judgement should exist within a system of obedience.) (3) What should our personal associations be like? Meaning, what moral obligations do we have in voluntary relationships that fulfil needs and enhance the quality of our lives (in management, the quality of treatment of staff and clients)?

The character of Kantian ethics

Kant regarded ethics as both objective and subjective, carried through in the interdependent relationship he posited between morality and anthropology. Separable analytically, they are necessary to one another: 'one must know human beings in order to know whether they are capable of performing all that is demanded of them. The consideration of a rule is useless, if one cannot make people prepared to fulfil it' (as quoted in Munzel 1999: 37).[17] While moral principles cannot be determined empirically, all morals 'need anthropology for their application to men' (Kant 1969: 33). They also require that moral politicians, whose task it is to educate people morally, have a 'higher anthropological vantage-point' (Kant 1991a: 119) and logically an administratively staffed instrument of government through which to carry this out. Viewing Kant's moral theory comprehensively, it is clear, as Munzel notes of more recent English-language scholarship,[18] that it is not solely deontological – an empty formalism – but is grounded in empirical reality. Louden (2000) contends that this is a result of a common emphasis of the *Foundations* at the expense of the *Metaphysics of Morals, Religion within the Limits of Reason Alone, Critique of Practical Reason,* and *Anthropology from a Pragmatic Point of View*. Kant also provides a phenomenological account of moral experience in the *Critique of Practical Reason*[19] with strong implications for his theory of moral education – particularly in the last section on methodology (Beck 1956: xiii) where basic pedagogical principles are discussed that could inform a programme of ethical education in administrative training. The phenomenological character of Kant's moral reasoning can also serve as a foundation from which to construct a practical ethics of administration alternative to the current predominant functionalism.

While Kant drew a distinction between 'pure' and 'practical' reason, he created a unity of them at odds with the dichotomy that has been imposed on his writings: 'Kant is trying to show that pure reason can be practical, and must be practical if morality is not an illusion; he is trying to show that it is practical of itself, and not merely as "the servant of the passions" (Hume), i.e., in connection with other, non-rational components of personality' (Beck 1956: xii). Where ethical theory must be based on rationality expressed through the principle of non-contradiction (Kant 1969: 64) instead of experience (1969: 26–33), pure practical reason considers the motives for duty to ethical values, the setting of ends of action, as well as the control of impulses – in effect a theory of agency and action.[20] One can extrapolate from Kant's distinction between the responsibility for *a priori* topics in the faculty of philosophy and practical ones of the faculties of theology, law, and medicine in *The Conflict of the Faculties* (1979), to the differing scholarly responsibilities of a critical philosophy and the professional discipline of administrative studies. Kant also drew a distinction between moral reasoning as pure practical reasoning, and prudential, or empirical, reasoning that has been confused in administrative literature. Kantian ethics rests on the respect for others as rational agents, allowing us, argues Hill, to weigh 'others' comfort relative to their projects in more or less the same way that those persons would do for themselves' and the 'rational value [of projects] to a person as ends depends on that person's deliberative choices' (1991: 188). This results in the standard that what to value in others 'should *prima facie* be *their own choices*, unless those choices cannot withstand their own critical scrutiny . . . and unless, on reflection, their choices are ones that we cannot aid without losing our own self-respect' (1991: 188).

It is important to distinguish between Kantian moral freedom and the psychological sense of freedom more common in managerial theory based on authors such as Maslow (1971) and Herzberg (1966), whose view of freedom derives from need, inclination, and desire.[21] For Kant, 'The autonomy of the will is the sole principle of all moral laws and of all duties conforming to them; *heteronomy* of choice, on the other hand, not only does not establish any obligation but is opposed to the principle of duty and to the morality of the will' (1956: 33). A radically free will is one that acts according to general maxims – free in the ability to initiate and not be subject to forces beyond rationality. Kant's notion of autonomy is more restrictive than the common current sense, as it is wholly morally derived:

> The idea of freedom functions not just as Kant's fundamental metaphysical presupposition, in the form of freedom of the will, but also as his most fundamental normative presupposition: according to Kant, freedom of choice and its natural expression in action are what human beings value most, and the fundamental principle of morality

and the rules for both public and private spheres constitute the laws that we must adopt and adhere to in order to preserve and promote freedom itself as our most fundamental value.

(Guyer 2000: 5)

Where there is no freedom, there is no obligation or responsibility, and therefore no occasion for moral blame or praise. Kant defended the principle of the *'public use* of one's reason in all matters', intended as the exercise of moral freedom against all forms of institutional authority (e.g. religion, government, military) in contrast to a more restricted form in private use, that is, when one holds a 'particular *civil* post or office with which he is entrusted' (1991a: 55, Kant's emphasis; see also 1933: 593–605; 1991a: 247–248).[22] The more administration programmes behaviour through rule-making and policies, the more it constricts the possibilities for choice-making and reduces the self-determination necessary for moral agency. In other words, administrative design, as ethical paternalism, works to relieve people of morality. Or, turning this around, if one wants administrators to function morally, then what organisational conditions have to be met (socially, psychologically, legislatively) to allow for rational free choice? As Berlin argues in his discussion of Kantian ethics (1969: xx), one can attribute responsibility and apply moral rules to individuals only when those in an organisational setting are capable of exercising choice.

Desire, or any motive other than duty to ethics (Kant 1969: 23), cannot be used to prop up our moral will. Doing so would only place us in the role of servant to our desires, as many ethical systems do,[23] producing only practical, and therefore hypothetical, rules excluding the possibility of categorical laws (Kant 1969: 71). This would produce only an empirical psychology and anthropology of hopes and fears (1969: 5), or a heteronymous, rather than autonomous, moral system (1969: 71). It is only through the power of reason that one can enact 'a law unto itself' regardless of any influences external to rationality. An ethics grounded in reason instead of human need and desire runs contrary to most managerial practices, including current leadership fads promoted in the New Public Management, based on preference, that is, individual desires and self-interest.

Moral disposition and character are described by Kant as the 'highest good in man' (1956: 161) identified with power of choice (*Willkür*), conduct of thought (*Denkungsart*), and comportment of mind (*Gesinnung*) – in other words, a 'good will'. The morally best character one can attain, or 'the good or dutiful or conscientious will', requires moral strength, courage, and self-mastery to have 'virtue'. This means demonstrating a continual propensity to act morally, that is, to act in accordance with moral laws and the maxims one derives from them. The moral worth of an act depends upon the capacity for autonomy, or free commitment to rationally chosen ends; if one acts under external influences or internal desires and passions, there is no moral value. The exercise of freedom through self-legislating powers is meant in both positive and negative senses: negatively in judging and acting independently from desires and inclinations; and positively in self-mastery by bringing our decisions under the moral law and motivating us to act from a dutiful attitude (Kant 1969: 11–15). The good will is still of value even if it accomplishes nothing through utmost effort (1969: 12). Such an ethical system in which motives count more than consequences violates managerial principles, particularly those of the New Public Management that place an exclusive emphasis on effectiveness and efficiency through performance measurement, cost–benefit analysis, and reward systems based on achievement regardless of the moral motivation.

Kant's concept of morality is also dependent upon his conception of radical evil, part of his anthropological, and therefore empirical, study of morality (Louden 2000: 132–133). Radical evil is defined in *Religion Within the Limits of Reason Alone* as the innate capacity in human beings for evil (as well as good) (Kant 1960: 16–17). Therefore, it does not mean, as Louden points out, 'beyond measurement', 'beyond comprehension', or 'qualitatively distinct from all else that has preceded it', in the sense that Hannah Arendt used the term to mean 'beyond the pale of human sinfulness' (Arendt 1951: 459). It is also not equivalent to the Christian concept of original sin, but meant in the etymological sense of 'root' – in that it is rooted in the nature of humanity and results from free choice (*freie Willkür*) (Louden 2000: 155–156). It is to radical evil that Kant alludes in the famous saying, 'Nothing straight can be constructed from such warped wood as that which man is made of' in 'The Idea for a Universal History' (1991a: 46), in his justification for the necessity of a 'law-governed social order' in creating a universally just civil society accompanied by the institutional supports to repress evil inclination and achieve a moral community.

The evil person is one who has deliberately adopted immoral policy to satisfy his inclinations (Sullivan 1994: 136): 'Consequently man (even the best) is evil only in that he reverses the moral order of the incentives when he adopts them into his maxim' (Kant 1960: 31). As for minor transgressions, while 'in the individual case, [their] consequence and effect may certainly be a small evil, the maxim adopted by the agent to perform the action, in his determination by the laws of freedom, still remains a large one, and unlimited in its consequences' (Kant 1997: 312). This Kant distinguishes from the '*monstra* of inhumanity' or 'maxims of viciousness' (1997: 420) – the 'devilish vices' of ingratitude, envy, and pleasure in the misfortunes of others (*Schadenfreude*) that evidence a mediate inclination to evil (1997: 197). Lying for Kant carries not only the potential for producing an evil result, but is also an act 'contrary to the condition, and the means, under which a society of men can come about, and thus contrary to the right of humanity' (Kant 1997: 203),[24] extended to secrecy when the intent is to deceive. While many bureaucratic corruptions may come within the realm of moderate vices, such as the occasional intrusion of personal problems in organisational life or promise-breaking under extenuating circumstances, most acts of maladministration exhibit a maximal consistency – 'dirty hands', lying, abuse of power, discrimination, deception, secrecy, conflicts of interest, and venality – aided by codes and conventions of anonymity and confidentiality. Discipline or punishment 'is the physical evil apportioned to someone because of moral evil' (Kant 1997: 304), and must be just, applied as the consequence of a morally bad act rather than 'inflicted to improve the criminal, or as an example to others' (1997: 309).

The logic of the *Critique of Practical Reason* in establishing the essence of Kant's moral theory, is identified by Beck to constitute: (1) the formula of the moral law; (2) the difference between moral law and maxims and rules of practice; (3) its necessary relationship to the autonomy, or freedom, of the will; and (4) the relationship between moral principles and moral concepts (of good and evil) (Beck 1956: xiii). This *Critique* presupposes (Kant 1956: 8) the establishment of the moral law in the form of three formulations of the categorical imperative described in the *Foundations*. The first, the 'Formula of Autonomy', expressed as a form of reciprocity means to 'Act only according to that maxim by which you can at the same time will that it should become a universal law' (Kant 1969: 44) without contradiction. Kant's 'dialectical rules' for guiding our moral judgements, or a procedural restatement of the Law of Autonomy, include: (1) thinking for oneself, (2) thinking from the standpoint of every other person, and (3) thinking consistently (Sullivan 1994: 109). This is not only a qualification of free, rational agents, but also an impersonal and social ideal, providing the foundation for political self-determination where correct moral judgements are most likely to emerge in the forum of open and public debate (the Principle of Publicity), in contrast to a life dominated by external authority.

The second formulation, the 'Universal Principle of Justice', rests upon a distinction between persons and things, the latter having value only extrinsically, conditionally, and subjectively for their utility or emotional value (Kant 1969: 59–61). It recognises that all rational beings have the same objective, intrinsic worth: 'every rational being exists as an end in himself and not merely as a means to be arbitrarily used by this or that will. In all his actions, whether they are directed to himself or to other rational beings, he must always be regarded at the same time as an end' (Kant 1969: 52). Here the notion of a person is impersonal in the same manner that the idea of universal law is: a disinterested and impersonal character of the notion of personhood provides the moral basis for a society in which the administration of justice is not skewed by personal relationships and law is administered impartially.[25] According to this principle, everyone has fundamental dignity as a person and lawful freedom with which no one has the moral right to interfere or use merely for their own purposes. The positive injunction of this principle is a duty to self to enhance one's own moral integrity, and a benevolent duty to contribute to the welfare of others by providing for their self-respect and furthering their responsibility and self-determination. The ends one chooses, governed by the 'rules of prudence', must through moral duty be brought into alignment with the ends one ought to choose, governed by the moral doctrine of ends (Kant 1991b: 190). However, Kant did acknowledge 'worldly wisdom' as 'the skill of a man in having influence on others so as to use them for his own purposes' (1969: 38n), providing others are not reduced only to this. The second formula also stipulates that we may not allow ourselves to be treated only as instrumentally valuable; we cannot renounce our right to respect, for to do so results in servility – the attitude or action where we treat ourselves merely as a means to curry another's favour, thereby disavowing self-respect (Sullivan 1994: 70). Respect is also distinct from honour that rests with organisational roles and distinctions. We have a duty to live up to our own, and others', moral worth, placing the 'organisational man' in a dilemma where obedience to authority is regarded as an end value, and where clients are reduced to calculable units.

And third, the 'Formula of Legislation for a Moral Community' is regarded by Kant as the most comprehensive since it combines the matter and form of our moral life (1969: 55–56, 61–62): 'Every rational being must act as if he, by his maxims, were at all times a legislative member in the universal realm of ends' (1969: 64). Each person is thereby ruler and subject, as each has the capacity to formulate and adopt laws. These formulations collectively suggest the type of moral world we should aim to create. Sullivan outlines three distinct forms of this social moral union. It consists first of a civil society in which the Principle of Justice is universally observed – the ideal political state in which juridical obligations are used to enforce legal behaviour preserving the outer freedom of others. Secondly, it is a community in which everyone observes the moral law out of dutifulness – the ideal religious or ethical community focused on the inner duties of virtue, ethical motivation, and ethical ends of respecting all persons, producing a community composed of those affirming each other's worth and supporting others' moral strivings. And finally, it promises a future in which the laws of nature conform to moral law – the ideal moral world in which everyone receives the happiness they deserve and the conditions necessary in achieving moral destiny in the 'final realm of ends' (1994: 85–88). Rawls argues that it is this principle, understood as 'public reason', that is realised when 'judges, legislators, chief executives, and other government officials, as well as candidates for pubic office, act from and follow the idea of public reason', thereby fulfilling 'their duty of civility to one another and to other citizens' (Rawls 2001: 576). Public reason also operates on the principle of universality, excluding biases based on any kind of group interest such as social role, class, sex, or race (Rawls 2001: 268). However, institutions are obliged to redress the negative effects of prejudice as it applies to individuals (Rawls 2001: 298). Such criteria would govern administration in its primary role of advancing citizens' legitimate rights, liberties, and responsibilities including the membership of bureaucracies. The most obvious problem for bureaucratic administration is the tendency to treat staff as means to organisational purpose, and demanding obedience to authority that cannot be grounded in the categorical imperative.

The categorical imperative has two functions: to command our obedience; and to test, through justification and derivation from the higher order principles of the categorical imperative (along with the principle of non-contradiction), possible maxims (such as truth-telling) as practical rules that can serve as policies for everyone. In other words, the moral worth of maxims and rules is not inherent, but derived only from their consistency with the categorical imperative. This also means testing maxims of self-interest or special interest for their moral acceptability and intention rather than consequences. Though the categorical imperative is objective, the fundamental maxims are 'subjective' in that they hold only for one person or subject and may be based on that person's ignorance or desires (Kant 1969: 43n), while taking into account special features such as time, place, and personal relationships. Though principles cannot be contextualised, operational maxims and rules are. The three maxims of 'ordinary human understanding' that underlie more specific maxims and rules are constitutive of character-formation and serve to orient and guide thinking: thinking for oneself, thinking consistently, and thinking from a universal standpoint (maxim of judgement) (Kant 1987: 160). In deriving and applying maxims, one must determine whether a policy is relevant to complex situations of ambiguity where there are conflicting grounds of obligation, and how the passage of time affects moral responsibilities (Sullivan 1994: 39–40).

Acting upon judgement Kant referred to as 'subjective determination of the will' (1969: 38), composed of two levels. The first is to test general maxims (or policies) for their moral acceptability, and the second involves deliberation over immediate decisions about how to act. Once it is determined that a maxim is not forbidden (that it does not violate the categorical imperative), we have 'moral title' to act or not act on the maxim. Most choices in everyday life are morally permissible; at any given moment there is usually an indefinite number of permissible maxims on which we may act, giving us what Kant calls 'play room'. Moral theory should reflect 'common and everyday responsibility', guarding against what he called 'fanaticism' in seeing duties everywhere when in fact there are many 'morally free' choices. This contrasts with bureaucratic administration in so far as the codifications of administrative regimes delude people into assuming that compliance is always morally permissible (substituting them for moral judgement), and in socialising civil service staff into a realm of duty-bound performance – what Kant regards as confusion of legality with morality (1991b: 46).

Given these moral requirements, what are the implications for being moral, that is, by using this judgement process, within organisational contexts? What are the appropriate foundations and limits of administrative reasoning, and what is the demand on administrators in terms of character and good will, particularly in the scientised world of management? Ethical judgement of administrators meeting Kant's standards would require critical, creative, and imperative faculties: critical, meaning to construct policies and rules on which to act (the role of moral philosophy); creative, meaning bridging the cognitive distance between principles and actions (the role of judgement); and imperative, meaning causing deliberations to issue in actions (the role of moral character) (Sullivan 1994: 40). It also requires the cultivation of conscience as a duty – as administrators, to subject our current and possible future actions to moral reflection at all times. The implications for the education and continued in-service training of administrators include theoretical training to use reasoning necessary to function in a sufficiently rational manner to apprehend the categorical imperative, to have enough 'mother-wit' to function in complex situation, and to have enough creative power to construct the maxims and duties necessary in daily professional life. While the essence of maxims is administrative – morally sound policies to guide action – moral duty and administrative duty are distinct. The 'good' Kantian administrator who uses the categorical imperative to measure moral integrity is different from the 'good' organisational man who follows organisationally and politically correct imperatives.

The ethical demand and impedimenta in administration

Even though conventional bureaucratic practices suggest that administration does not yield serious moral considerations, there are a number of ways in which administrators do have moral agency. First, the moral demand on administrators is multifaceted. The most common distinction made is that between individual and public morality, seen in Appleby (1952: 228) who recognises organisational conditions in public morality as more restricting, and Waldo (1980: 100), for whom the two may be in opposition.[26] Burke (1986) represents a moderate view, recognising that individual and institutional ethics can both make a claim, thereby limiting each other, but that through an understanding of individual responsibility one can reconcile the seemingly opposed demands of bureaucratic obedience and the duties and obligations of democratic institutions. His conception of individual responsibility, though, is that of a person in an official bureaucratic capacity, not in one's primary moral responsibility as a free agent (see Burke 1986: Chs 1 and 2). Are the moral obligations of government officials, though, restricted to their legal and organisational responsibilities, and the regulations, rules, and procedures designed to enforce these? Thompson (1981: 266) argues that they are not, citing cases where harmful consequences can result from legitimate decisions such as failing to warn of a crime someone is about to commit. In his interviews with a number of public managers in the US Federal merit system, Gortner found that all had felt constrained ethically by 'the law' in ways that sometimes required them to question specific statutes, rules, and regulations of their bureaucratic lives (1991: 6). Gortner describes 'the law' in this context as the enshrinement of fundamental principles of rights and responsibilities as embedded in constitutional frameworks, elevating them to a philosophical character as they serve as guiding political and moral values.[27]

Moral responsibility is also often regarded as coterminous with the degree of authority and correspondingly increasing obligations the higher one is placed in the organisational hierarchy. Waldo regards hierarchy as a pyramidal structure of responsibility, and therefore of ethics, noting that there has been strong support in administrative literature for representing it as a 'force for morality' (1980: 110–111).[28] Combined with this is the view, characteristically represented by Finer (1941), that 'the first commandment is subservience'. But, do loyalty, compliance, accountability, and obedience in the organisational machinery relieve one of moral responsibility? More cynically, Moore has argued that procedural innovations, such as sunshine and sunset laws, whistleblower legislation, rights to injunction and damages, requirements for public hearings, and mechanisms of coordination and consultation, have provided excuses for inaction and avoidance of responsibility on the part of public officials (1981: 3–4).

Further, in contrast to the conventional ethic of neutrality, holding that administrators 'do not exercise independent moral judgment' once a decision or policy is 'final' (Thompson 1981: 35),[29] some have argued that the considerable discretionary powers of administrators, regardless of the strictness of codes and regulatory systems, leaves room for moral agency (Moore 1981: 4–5; Richardson and Nigro 1987).[30] For Rohr, the central issue of ethical relevance is how bureaucrats practice the discretion inherent in their roles and the moral values from which they govern (1978:

15, 33, 38), since 'managerial innovations cannot change the fact that administration is governance' bound by constitutional foundations (2000: 203). Rohr notes that bureaucratic tradition has taught bureaucrats a self-image that is morally deplete: 'powerless and alienated . . . [b]ureaucrats frequently resist the idea that they have an impact on public policy until they see for themselves that they use the word "policy" to describe something that *by definition* is done by someone else' (1978: 39).[31] For Gawthrop, 'the logic of utility that still provides the basic rationale for the classical management tenets of efficiency and control' (1998: 87) informing the prevailing ethos, is simply not an adequate foundation. Bureaucrats must break out of 'the habits of the self-serving good which allows public servants to pursue a procedural, quasi-ethical life' (Gawthrop 1998: 139).

Berlin notes that Kant's free man needs no public recognition for his inner freedom (Berlin 1969: 156n). However, to what degree is moral principle in conflict with organisational demands and administrative responsibilities? There are a number of organisational constraints mitigating against a Kantian-style ethic grounded in autonomy, that instead enforce professional compliance. The first category of impedimenta is a bureaucratic mentality derived from the formal attributes of organisational design that reduces ethics to a strict adherence to codes, rules, and regulations, promoted through reward and discipline systems. The rational 'bureaucratic' approach to dealing with ethics is to proceduralise and standardise it. The New Public Management, in responding to changing demands on the public service, as Maguire notes, has caused many jurisdictions to develop new codes of conduct that 'set out more explicitly the standards of behaviour expected of public servants' as it is 'no longer sufficient to rely on public servants knowing the law and absorbing the professional norms as they go along' (1998: 31). This enforced conformity results in a moral inversion causing people to adapt their personal values, producing what Guy refers to as 'contradictory norms' that give rise to unethical behaviour (1990: 97). Ethics is thereby reduced to what Ciulla calls 'prescriptive' rules, supported by a naïve and uncritical belief in 'real world' practicality and the certainties promised by current organisational systems (1998: 373). In other words, morality is not allowed to disturb order in the 'real world' of administration (Ciulla 1998: 375). This prescriptive approach to administrative ethics also emphasises results or consequences at the expense of intentions, substituting morality with procedures and rules, or even constitutional standards.[32] Moore regards as morally problematic the way policies are conceived and treated: not seeing the consequences of policies; conceiving of the effects of a policy too narrowly; and mishandling the uncertainty of choices by either ignoring them or burying them in an over-reliance on science (1981: 10–12). In addition, bureaucratic organisations diffuse responsibility through their hierarchy and committee structures, rendering individual moral responsibility impossible to separate from a collective responsibility, particularly where individuals have little control over the moral atmosphere of an organisation.[33]

Morality is thereby reduced to what Kant refers to as 'Servility' (1991b: 230–231), motivated in some cases by avoidance of responsibility or the sheer hard work of moralising (1978: 95). Kant's concerns about servility are echoed in Hummel's more cynical terms: 'bureaucracy . . . has produced [a] dehumanized human fragment – socially crippled, culturally normless, psychologically dependent, linguistically mute, and politically powerless' (1977: 221). A less damning, but nonetheless sceptical view, is that of Denhardt, for whom the organisational milieu 'imposes a new set of obligations, pressures and constraints. The organization will in some ways determine who engages in ethical deliberation, what is considered ethical, as well as the range of options available to administrators who are attempting to make the "ethical" decision' (K. G. Denhardt 1988: 75).

One consequence of moral muteness is the moral silence, or passive evil, practised by officials witnessing unethical behaviour on the part of superiors. Raes identifies five avoidance strategies practised in such morally demanding situations, of some relevance to this essay: 'a) reducing the morally blameworthy to what is pragmatically necessary; b) uplifting the morally blameworthy into the morally required; c) toning down the morally required by reference to relativism; d) reducing ethics to what is legally required; e) de-ethicising the problem by making ethics into a mere "theoretical viewpoint"' (1998: 202). It is argued here that these practices have been institutionalised in the profession, and underlie what Menzel identifies as the three influences that produce moral muteness (Menzel 1999: 9): workplace prescriptions of modern organisations that produce docility through an emphasis on technical competence, 'practicality', objectivity, and impersonality; professional associations that prescribe narrowly limited behaviours and practices or promote general character traits; and graduate programmes of public administration that do not adequately teach and inculcate ethics. These sentiments on the negative effects of authority on administrators are echoed in Berlin's view that 'A world in which one man depends upon the favour of another is a world of masters and slaves, of bullying and condescension and patronage at one end, and obsequiousness, servility, duplicity and resentment at the other' – which for Kant was 'incompatible with choice, freedom, morality' (Kant 1991: 217).

The second type of impedimenta includes culture and socialisation that act as pressures in organisational life on the individual to obey external authority without subjecting their commands or directives to moral scrutiny. For Kant, the 'tendency to evil is already implanted by nature';

however, it requires 'nourishment' to develop (1997: 324). One could view officials as being socialised into relinquishing their moral duty – adopting a role morality (Thompson 1981: 278). Instead, Thompson argues that officials accept roles and choose to remain in them, making them morally responsible in any case (1981: 269). Professionalism itself operates culturally as a constraint on moral agency. It inculcates loyalty to one's professional organisation and membership as well as to administrative and political superiors, traditionally accompanied by neutrality and anonymity. Such loyalty can come into conflict with moral principles that are necessary, in Kant's view, for an adequately morally oriented commitment to the public interest and the welfare of clients.

There are two major issues here for administrators, given Kant's emphasis on autonomy. The first is the responsibility of individuals to achieve their own freedom of will by maintaining sufficient self-awareness to cultivate it and overcome organisational practices associated with recruitment, training, and promotion along with legal, political, and economic activities that promote conformity. Bureaucrats, however, do not think of themselves as ends (Kant 1969: 64), but rather as the anonymous and loyal 'organisation man' detailed in Whyte's now classic text (1957), in keeping with the bureaucratic ethos. The second requirement for administrators is in creating the social environment in which others' freedoms of will are not only respected, but supported. This requires perceiving others as ends in themselves and creating the organisational structures and processes that permit them to act freely on moral principle. It also requires the reconceptualisation of authority based on collegialism without, however, imposing the tyranny of groupthink through the teamwork and consensus that typifies much current administrative and leadership thinking.

A third category of constraint is educational. Kant regarded education as having a primarily moral purpose, composed of three dimensions necessary to free will: the discipline of inclination, cultivation of aptitudes, and the formation of character. Students should be taught to think about 'the worth of the things which they might possibly adopt as ends' and adopting free will (1969: 37).[34] Instead, administrative degree programmes are typically designed around managerial conceptions of administration to include primarily those courses replicating the functional dimensions of practice – for example, policy analysis and evaluation, financing and budgeting, strategic planning, and personnel development. In drawing upon programme, academic, and practitioner surveys, Fox demonstrates that philosophy plays a marginal role at best in public administration training (in the US) (2001: 106). Even though interest in ethics courses in educational administration and leadership programmes is increasing, as demonstrated in Beck and Murphy's mid-1990s survey of UCEA member universities (1994: Ch. 4), reflecting the increasing topicality of values and ethics in the scholarship, there is little evidence that philosophical texts underlying various professional and educational ethics are studied in any detail.

A final constraint, related to the one just mentioned, is the considerable 'scientisation' of administration in training, practice, and research, particularly in English-speaking countries. A recent OECD Symposium has reinforced an 'ethics infrastructure', illustrative of a technological mindset:

> The eight elements of infrastructure (namely political commitment, effective legal frameworks, efficient accountability mechanisms, workable codes of conduct, professional socialisation mechanisms, supportive public service conditions, co-ordinating body and public involvement) are complementary, and for optimal effectiveness they should be synchronised to provide coherent control, guidance and management.
>
> (OECD/PUMA 1997: 12)

Also characteristic is Selznick's mechanical turn of mind, regarding the moral elevation of administration to be an engineering problem: 'The great task of institutional design is to build moral competence into the structure of the enterprise. This is the key to corporate responsibility – private as well as public' (1992: 345). It is this organisational imperative that causes Selznick to attempt a reconciliation of the Kantian principle of regarding individuals as ends with instrumental requirements by proposing an 'operationalisation' of morality at the institutional level, attributing to organisations an 'internal morality' (1992: 324).

Worse from Kant's perspective than the use or abuse of people by each other, according to Berlin, is determinism, slavery to nature, and the law of causality (1999: 73). Substituting science for one's own moral understanding Kant regarded as immaturity, and the 'dogmas and formulas, those mechanical instruments for rational use (or rather misuse) of his natural endowments, are the ball and chain of his permanent immaturity' (1991b: 54–55).

> 'Science' was deemed by Kant to be a 'dangerous possession and to have the tendency to make one conceited, rude, and inhuman. Now it is just the task of the academic teacher of philosophy to guard against this,' to guard against the student becoming a mere 'Cyclops,' someone equipped with 'only one eye' who sees 'things only from a single standpoint', that of his specialty.
>
> (Paulsen 1963: 63–64)

Conclusion

What are the possibilities, then, for a Kantian-style ethic of administration? The 'frailties', 'impurities', and 'corruption' or 'wickedness' of mankind – the three degrees of capacity for evil Kant identifies in his theory of radical evil (1960: 24–25) – would appear through individual and institutional form to be insurmountable conditions for his moral system. While most administrative theory stresses rational decision-making models, it generally falls short of the reasoning employed by Kant. Administrative training programmes equally promote and enforce technical rationality encased in systems of obedience, discouraging individual autonomy. And administrative practice, too, has traditionally operated through a hierarchy of authority (including ethical), that has been intensified through the New Public Management on one hand, and modified through collaborative and 'learning' organisation approaches, substituting the authority of the group for that of a superior, on the other. Rather than the impractical inhering in Kant's system, it is administrative imperatives for external authority and instrumentality that create the conditions in which Kantian ethics is made impractical. One simply cannot reconcile Kantian ethics with conventional administration.

One could argue that the fault lies with Kantian ethics. Two major problems, identified by Sullivan, are that all reasoning individuals can know what morality requires of us without guidance from an authority, and that we are able to do what morality requires without being motivated by self-interest (that is by desire and need; or aversion of an unwanted outcome such as punishment) (1994: 160). These are partly answered by Kant in his writings on government in his political essays and in *The Metaphysics of Morals*. It is the duty of government and education to provide both the training and conditions for moral development, and, if necessary, for the populace to 'subject itself to a public lawful external coercion' until such time as 'a public lawful condition is established' (1991b: 124) – 'lawful' here meaning in accordance with the categorical imperative. An inherent problem more difficult to overcome for administration is a regime of coercion, however ethically motivated, in bringing a society to the public lawful condition that Kant outlines.

All of this, of course, begs the question as to the moral aptitude of the state, and its public service arm, to 'lawful' coercion. If the purpose of civil administration is to enforce standards of ethics, it must be based on organisational principles that do not undermine ethics. This would apply to administrative and organisational theory consistent with the categorical imperative, as well as to system designs, practices, and a conception of professionalism that do not subsume one's individual moral necessity. In particular, the authority an administrator should obey, and the actions an administrator should take with subordinates, must meet the tests of free will set by Kant. These are described by Guyer, from his reading of *Foundations of the Metaphysics of Morals*, to be the following:

> It is precisely the capacity to set and consent to ends and the capacities necessary for us to pursue those ends in which humanity as Kant conceives it consists; the idea of humanity as an end in itself, in other words, is identical to the idea of the incomparable dignity of human autonomy or freedom governed by the law that we give to ourselves.
> (Guyer 2000: 10)

It is towards an appeal to these basic precepts that much discussion of humanising bureaucracies, 'responsiveness', and diversity in administrative cadres is oriented.

Administration, by its very nature, requires contrary demands on the individual: responsibilities to oneself and responsibilities to others. However, as Berlin notes in his discussion of Kantian values, 'to sacrifice a man, you must sacrifice him to something higher than himself. But nothing is higher than that which is to be regarded as the highest moral value' (Berlin 1999: 72). Kant's conception of ethics is conceived to provide a standard, or ideal, to resolve what appears to be a dilemma, and which can serve as a guide to administrative reform:

> This dependence upon the will of others and this inequality is, however, in no way opposed to their freedom and equality as men, who together make up a people; on the contrary, it is only in conformity with the conditions of freedom and equality that this people can become a state and enter into a civil constitution.
> (Kant 1991b: 126)

Notes

1 Kant, from 'Idea for a Universal History with a Cosmopolitan Purpose' (1991a: 46), 'First Section' of *Foundations of the Metaphysics of Morals* (1969: 15), 'An Answer to the Question: "What is Enlightenment?"' (1991a: 56), and 'Second Section' of *Foundations of the Metaphysics of Morals* (1969: 52) respectively. The 'warped wood' has frequently, and famously, been alternatively translated as 'crooked timber'.
2 The amoral nature of administrative theory in this respect is due largely to the psychologisation of administration theory.
3 Interestingly, German public administration authors do not use Kant extensively for ethics either.
4 'Transcendental' in the Kantian sense means the system of *a priori* concepts and principles that make possible reason and our experience of empirical reality, not the popular or religious sense of the term meaning other-worldly or heightened perception, sometimes associated with charismatic experience.

5 Sheeran also confuses Platonic and Kantian idealism, assuming that the categorical imperative has the same ontological status as Platonic ideal forms.
6 Rawls departs from Kant in a number of significant ways, a number of these discussed by Sandel, the most important of which for administrative discussion is the adoption by Rawls of an empirical account of circumstances for justice, and a reliance on some generalised preferences and desires (Sandel 1998: 37–49).
7 Although he alters them to fit organisational imperatives.
8 However, Sergiovanni's concept of deontological here is idiosyncratic.
9 The title is also translated as *Groundwork of the Metaphysics of Morals*.
10 'Act so that you treat humanity, whether in your own person or in that of another, always as an end and never as a means only.' This is the second formulation of the categorical imperative, the Universal Principle of Justice. Most authors in administrative studies do not distinguish among the three formulations of the categorical imperative.
11 Presumably, though, if one cannot function cognitively on this level morally, one cannot assume the many taxing administrative responsibilities associated with policy, legislation, and organisational development.
12 However, they do introduce the distinction between the hypothetical and categorical imperatives as contrary guides to action (Kimbrough and Nunnery 1988: 400), an important characteristic of Kantian ethics not usually recognised in educational administration ethics.
13 Hodgkinson, as is common in administrative theory, regards the categorical imperative as 'a moral order in the universe' independent of human construction (1996: 94–95); in other words, he equates it ontologically with Platonic ideal forms. He places too much weight on the absoluteness of the categorical imperative, a common problem in the administrative representation of Kantian ethics.
14 Reflecting the general manner in which administrative studies demonstrates 'little compunction against picking out a hodge-podge of ideas, norms, and concepts from other more integrated literatures' (Fox 2001: 116).
15 However, Hodgkinson does not develop the Kantian position as a critique of organisational relations, but rather suggests that the Kantian ethic would have to be reinterpreted (and would thereby lose its fundamental quality) in order to bring it in line with organisational reality, which requires leaders to use followers to organisational ends (1996: 153, 172).
16 These criteria are discussed in 'On the Common Saying: "This May be True in Theory, but it Does Not Apply in Practice"' and 'Perpetual Peace: A Philosophical Sketch'.
17 See Munzel (1999: 35–39) for a discussion of the status of Kant's anthropology in Kantian scholarship and the relationship between his anthropological writings and his moral and political writings.
18 See Munzel (1999: 38n) for an overview of Kantian scholarship on this point.
19 See especially Chapter III of the 'Analytic of Pure Practical Reason'.
20 See 'On the Common Saying: "This May be True in Theory, but it Does Not Apply in Practice"' (Kant 1991a) for a detailed discussion of the relationship between theory and practice.
21 And that serves as the basis for managerial manipulation through reward and punishment systems and the moral infantilisation of the workforce – contrary to the moral educational aim of Kant's political theory.
22 The last essay is 'What Is Orientation in Thinking?'

23 For example, Aristotle, Machiavelli, and Hume who base their systems on experience, and the later development of utilitarianism.
24 For a detailed discussion of lying see Kant 1997: 200–209.
25 Analytic impersonality here is distinct from the impersonal, or more accurately the dehumanised, nature of bureaucratic organisations.
26 To these two fundamental ethical roles Waldo adds a 'map' of twelve types of obligation that must be considered: constitution, law, nation or country, democracy, organisational-bureaucratic norms, profession, family and friends, self, middle-range collectivities (e.g. party, class, race, church, interest group), public interest or general welfare, humanity or the world, religion or god (1980: 103–106).
27 However, Gortner places great, but not exclusive, emphasis on legal interpretations of administrative ethics following Rohr's lead in this respect (see Gortner 1991: Ch. 4).
28 Waldo identifies the proponents of this view as Appleby (1952), Bernstein (1972), and Thompson (1975).
29 Leaving them, from this perspective, little choice but to obey or resign.
30 This is one of the underlying reasons for the recent attempts in the NPM to rein bureaucrats in from their perceived policy-capture of their political masters.
31 Although Rohr himself has been critiqued for an uncritical over-reliance on 'regime values' as a grounding for administrative ethics (Wall 1991: 142–144) and elevating social contract theory to 'a Kantian level of abstraction' and legitimising the administrative state (Fox 2001: 113–115).
32 An example of 'ethical' grounding in constitutionalism is Chapman's examination of Sir Edward Bridges' tenure as Secretary to the British Cabinet during World War II and as Permanent Secretary to the Treasury for the succeeding eleven years (1988).
33 See Cooper (1968) for an extended discussion of this problem.
34 In the Appendix to *The Metaphysics of Morals* Kant includes a section on 'Teaching Ethics' that could serve as course design and methodological principles for administrative ethics (1991b: 266–268).

References

Appleby, P. (1952) *Morality and Administration in Democratic Government*, Baton Rouge: Louisiana State University Press.
Arendt, H. (1951) *The Origins of Totalitarianism*, New York: Harcourt, Brace and World.
Bates, R. (1984) 'Education, community and the crisis of the state', *Discourse* 4, 2.
Beck, L. W. (1956) 'Translator's introduction', in I. Kant, *Critique of Practical Reason*, New York: Macmillan.
Beck, L. and Murphy, J. (1994) *Ethics in Educational Leadership Programs: An Expanding Role*, Thousand Oaks: Corwin Press.
Berlin, I. (1969) *Four Essays on Liberty*, London: Oxford University Press.
Berlin, I. (1999) *The Roots of Romanticism*, Princeton: Princeton University Press.
Bernstein, M. (1972) 'Ethics in government: The problems in perspective', *National Civic Review* 6: 341–347.

Brown, P. (1981) 'Assessing officials', in J. Fleishman, L. Liebman and M. Moore (eds) *Public Duties: The Moral Obligations of Government Officials*, Cambridge, MA: Harvard University Press.

Burke, J. (1983) Book review of Peter A. French, *Ethics in Government* (Englewood Cliffs: Prentice-Hall, 1983), *American Political Science Review* 77: 1112–1113.

Burke, J. (1986) *Bureaucratic Responsibility*, Baltimore: Johns Hopkins University Press.

Chandler, R. C. (2001) 'Deontological dimensions of administrative ethics revisited', in T. Cooper (ed.) *Handbook of Administrative Ethics*, 2nd edn., New York: Marcel Dekker.

Chapman, R. (1988) *Ethics in the British Civil Service*, London: Routledge.

Ciulla, J. (1998) 'Business ethics as moral imagination', in G. R. Hickman (ed.) *Leading Organizations: Perspectives for a New Era*, Thousand Oaks, CA: Sage.

Cooper, D. E. (1968) 'Collective responsibility', *Philosophy* 49: 258–268.

Cooper, T. (1998) *The Responsible Administrator*, 4th edn, San Francisco: Jossey-Bass.

Denhardt, K. G. (1988) *The Ethics of Public Service: Resolving Moral Dilemmas in Public Organizations*, Westport: Greenwood Press.

Denhardt, R. (1981) *In the Shadow of Organization*, Lawrence: University Press of Kansas.

Dorbeck-Jung, B. (1998) 'Towards reflexive responsibility: New ethics for public administration', in A. Hondeghem (ed.) *Ethics and Accountability in a Context of Governance and New Public Management*, Amsterdam: IOS Press.

Evers, C. and Lakomski, G. (1991) *Knowing Educational Administration: Contemporary Methodological Controversies in Educational Administration Research*, Oxford: Pergamon Press.

Finer, H. (1941) 'Administrative responsibility in democratic government', *Public Administration Review* 1: 335–350.

Foster, C. and Greenwood, L. (1996) 'When state and federal obligations conflict', in L. Pasquerella, A. Killilea and J. Vocino (eds) *Ethical Dilemmas in Public Administration*, Westport: Praeger.

Fox, C. (2001) 'The use of philosophy in administrative ethics', in T. Cooper (ed.) *Handbook of Administrative Ethics*, 2nd edn, New York: Marcel Dekker.

Garofalo, C. and Geuras, D. (1999) *Ethics in the Public Service: The Moral Mind at Work*, Washington, DC: Georgetown University Press.

Gawthrop, L. (1998) *Public Service and Democracy: Ethical Imperatives for the 21st Century*, New York: Chatham House Publishers.

Gortner, H. (1991) *Ethics for Public Managers*, New York: Greenwood Press.

Greenfield, T. and Ribbins, P. (1993) *Greenfield on Educational Administration: Towards a Humane Science*, London: Routledge.

Gregor, M. (1963) *Laws of Freedom*, New York: Barnes and Noble.

Grundstein, N. (1981) *The Managerial Kant: The Kant Critiques and the Managerial Order*, Cleveland, OH: Weatherhead School of Management, Case Western Reserve University.

Guy, M. E. (1990) *Ethical Decision Making in Everyday Work Situations*, Westport, CT: Quorum Books.

Guyer, P. (2000) *Kant on Freedom, Law, and Happiness*, Cambridge: Cambridge University Press.
Herman, B. (1993) *The Practice of Moral Judgment*, Cambridge, MA: Harvard University Press.
Herzberg, F. (1966) *Work and the Nature of Man*, Cleveland: World Publishing.
Hill, T. (1991) *Autonomy and Self-Respect*, Cambridge: Cambridge University Press.
Hitt, W. (1990) *Ethics and Leadership: Putting Theory into Practice*, Columbus: Battelle Press.
Hodgkinson, C. (1978) *Towards a Philosophy of Administration*, Oxford: Blackwell.
Hodgkinson, C. (1983) *The Philosophy of Leadership*, Oxford: Blackwell.
Hodgkinson, C. (1991) *Educational Leadership: The Moral Art*, Albany, NY: State University of New York Press.
Hodgkinson, C. (1996) *Administrative Philosophy: Values and Motivations in Administrative Life*, Oxford: Pergamon.
Hummel, R. (1977) *The Bureaucratic Experience*, New York: St. Martin's Press.
Hummel, R. (1982) *The Bureaucratic Experience*, New York: St. Martin's Press.
Jos, P. and Hines, S. (1993) 'Care, justice, and public administration', *Administration and Society* 25, 3: 373–392.
Kant, I. (1933) *Immanuel Kant's Critique of Pure Reason*, 2nd edn, Houndmills: Macmillan.
Kant, I. (1956) *Critique of Practical Reason*, New York: Macmillan.
Kant, I. (1960) *Religion within the Limits of Reason Alone*, New York: Harper and Row.
Kant, I. (1969) *Foundations of the Metaphysics of Morals: Text and Critical Essays*, New York: Macmillan.
Kant, I. (1978) *Anthropology from a Pragmatic Point of View*, Carbondale: Southern Illinois University Press.
Kant, I. (1979) *The Conflict of the Faculties [Der Streit der Fakultäten]*, Lincoln and London: University of Nebraska Press.
Kant, I. (1987) *Critique of Judgment*, Indianapolis, IN: Hackett Publishing.
Kant, I. (1991a) *Political Writings*, 2nd edn, Cambridge: Cambridge University Press.
Kant, I. (1991b) *Metaphysics of Morals*, Cambridge: Cambridge University Press.
Kant, I. (1997) *Lectures on Ethics*, Cambridge: Cambridge University Press.
Kellough, J. E. (1999) 'Reinventing public personnel management: Ethical implications for managers and public personnel systems', *Public Personnel Management* 28, 4: 655–671.
Kimbrough, R. (1985) *Ethics: A Course of Study for Educational Leaders*, Arlington: American Association of School Administration.
Kimbrough, R. and Nunnery, M. (1988) *Educational Administration: An Introduction*, 3rd edn, New York: Macmillan.
Lewis, D. (1998) 'Theodore Lowi and the administrative state', in P. Lawler, R. Schaefer and D. Schaefer (eds) *Active Duty: Public Administration as Democratic Statesmanship*, Lanham, MD: Rowman and Littlefield.
Louden, R. (2000) *Kant's Impure Ethics: From Rational Beings to Human Beings*, New York: Oxford University Press.

Luke, J. and Hart, D. (2001) 'Character and conduct in the public service: A review of historical perspectives', in T. Cooper (ed.) *Handbook of Administrative Ethics*, 2nd edn, New York: Marcel Dekker.

Maguire, M. (1998) 'Ethics in the public service – Current issues and practice', in A. Hondeghem (ed.) *Ethics and Accountability in a Context of Governance and New Public Management*, Amsterdam: IOS Press.

Maslow, A. (1971) *The Farther Reaches of Human Nature*, New York: Viking Press.

Maxcy, S. (1991) *Educational Leadership: A Critical Pragmatic Perspective*, New York: Bergin and Garvey.

Menzel, D. (1995) 'Through the ethical looking glass darkly', *Administration & Society* 27, 3: 379–399.

Menzel, D. (1999) 'The morally mute manager: Fact or fiction?', *Public Personnel Management* 28, 4: 515–527.

Mitchell, C. (1999) 'Violating the public trust: The ethical and moral obligations of government officials', *Public Personnel Management* 28, 1: 27–38.

Moore, M. (1981) 'Realms of obligation and virtue', in J. Fleishman, L. Liebman and M. Moore (eds) *Public Duties: The Moral Obligations of Government Officials*, Cambridge, MA: Harvard University Press.

Munzel, G. F. (1999) *Kant's Conception of Moral Character: The 'Critical' Link of Morality, Anthropology and Reflective Judgment*, Chicago: University of Chicago Press.

OECD/PUMA (1997) 'Issues Paper No. 12', Symposium, Chateau de la Muette, Paris.

Paulsen, F. (1963) *Immanuel Kant: His Life and Doctrine*, New York: Frederick Ungar.

Raes, K. (1998) 'Moral powerlessness in relations of subordination: moral responsibility and organisational culture', in A. Hondeghem (ed.) *Ethics and Accountability in a Context of Governance and New Public Management*, Amsterdam: IOS Press.

Rawls, J. (1980) 'Kantian constructivism in moral theory', *Journal of Philosophy* 77, 9: 515–572.

Rawls, J. (2001) *Collected Papers*, Cambridge, MA: Harvard University Press.

Rebore, R. W. (2001) *The Ethics of Educational Leadership*, Upper Saddle River, NJ: Merrill Prentice-Hall.

Richardson, W. and Nigro, L. (1987) 'Administrative ethics and founding thought: Constitutional correctives, honor, and education', *Public Administration Review* 47, 5: 367–376.

Rohr, J. (1978) *Ethics for Bureaucrats: An Essay on Law and Values*, New York: Marcel Dekker.

Rohr, J. (1998) *Public Service, Ethics, and Constitutional Practice*, Lawrence: University Press of Kansas.

Rohr, J. (2000) 'Ethics, governance, and constitutions: The case of Baron Haussmann', in R. Chapman (ed.) *Ethics in Public Service for the New Millennium*, Aldershot: Ashgate.

Sandel, M. (1998) *Liberalism and the Limits of Justice*, 2nd edn, Cambridge: Cambridge University Press.

Selznick, P. (1992) *The Moral Commonwealth: Social Theory and the Promise of Community*, Oxford: University of California Press.

Sergiovanni, T. (1992) *Moral Leadership: Getting to the Heart of the School Improvement*, San Francisco: Jossey-Bass.

Sheeran, P. (1993) *Ethics in Public Administration: A Philosophical Approach*, Westport: Praeger.

Starratt, R. (1991) 'Building an ethical school: A theory for practice in educational leadership', *Educational Administration Quarterly* 27, 2: 185–202.

Stewart, D. (1991) 'Theoretical foundations of ethics in public administration', *Administration and Society* 23, 3: 357–373.

Strike, K., Haller, M. and Soltis, J. (1988) *Ethics of School Administration*, New York: Teachers College Press.

Sullivan, R. (1994) *An Introduction to Kant's Ethics*, Cambridge: Cambridge University Press.

Thomas, M. D. and Davis, E. E. (2000) 'Legal and ethical bases for educational leadership', in D. Walling (ed.) *Readings on Leadership in Education*, Bloomington: Phi Delta Kappa Educational Foundation.

Thompson, D. (1981) 'Moral responsibility and the New York City fiscal crisis', in J. Fleishman, L. Liebman and M. Moore (eds) *Public Duties: The Moral Obligations of Government Officials*, Cambridge, MA: Harvard University Press.

Thompson, D. (1992) 'The possibility of administrative ethics', in P. Madsen and J. Shafritz (eds) *Essentials of Government Ethics*, New York: Meridian.

Thompson, V. (1975) *Without Sympathy or Enthusiasm: The Problem of Administrative Compassion*, University of Alabama Press.

Van Wart, M. (1998) *Changing Public Sector Values*, New York: Garland.

Waldo, D. (1980) *The Enterprise of Public Administration: A Summary View*, Novato, CA: Chandler and Sharp.

Wall, B. (1991) 'Assessing ethics theories from a democratic viewpoint', in J. S. Bowman (ed.) *Ethical Frontiers in Public Management: Seeking New Strategies for Resolving Ethical Dilemmas*, San Francisco: Jossey-Bass.

Warwick, D. (1981) 'The ethics of administrative discretion', in J. Fleishman, L. Liebman, and M. Moore (eds) *Public Duties: The Moral Obligations of Government Officials*, Cambridge, MA: Harvard University Press.

Weber, M. (1958) *From Max Weber: Essays in Sociology*, New York: Galaxy.

Weingartner, R. (1999) *The Moral Dimensions of Academic Administration*, Lanham, MD: Rowman and Littlefield Publishers.

Whyte, W. (1957) *The Organization Man*, Garden City: Doubleday.

Wittmer, D. (2001) 'Ethical decision making', in T. Cooper (ed.) *Handbook of Administrative Ethics*, 2nd edn, New York: Marcel Dekker.

Wolf, C. (1981) 'Ethics and policy analysis', in J. Fleishman, L. Liebman and M. Moore (eds) *Public Duties: The Moral Obligations of Government Officials*, Cambridge, MA: Harvard University Press.

Woller, G. (1998) 'Toward a reconciliation of the bureaucratic and democratic ethos', *Administration and Society* 30, 1: 85–109.

Zajac, G. and Bruhn, J. (1999) 'The moral context of participation in planned organizational change and learning', *Administration and Society* 30, 6: 706–733.

Chapter 8

The new pragmatism and social science and educational research

Spencer J. Maxcy

Most social science and educational workers conducting research in universities and government offices are not very philosophical at all. These researchers tend to operate as 'bench experimenters' or 'methodologists', and are typically devoid of any interest in the theoretical underpinnings of their methods or purposes. Logical empiricists or naïve realists to the core, these thinkers believe that the essential philosophical questions driving enquiry are either uninteresting or an annoyance. As they see it, their job is to 'get it right', by which is meant to provide a spectator's report on the certainty of knowledge regarding the way the world operates (Phillips 1987, Lagemann 2000, Diesing 1991).

In addition to this majority, there is a fraction of researchers working in the social and educational spheres who do express a knowledge or interest in the philosophical warrants for enquiry. These thinkers are often leftover analytic philosophers, spent idealists, starry-eyed hermeneutians or phenomenologists, and a scattering of deconstructers (Baynes, Bohman and McCarthy 1987, Diesing 1991). Sensitive to theories and concepts fuelling research programmes, these thinkers cluster into communities that have little to do with one another. Whatever conversations go on about research and its methods, seem to remain within the respective groups. Policy makers and policy users see such philosophers 'speaking in tongues' and not much of a force for practical change.

But there is another, emerging section of thoughtful social scientists and educational researchers, for whom philosophy is a joy, working out the practical bearings of theoretical puzzles underlying research – a supreme thrill, and seeing concrete changes – an epiphany. These are pragmatists, or philosophers, who turn their lens upon social scientific and educational enquiries, and attempt to reform assumptions and their conduct. They tend to fall into three groups: scientists, politicians, or romantics. Of these philosophically sensitive, some ply their trade as scientist-pragmatists, or those fundamentally dealing with issues of the nature of modern science, methodological questions, and/or the function of theories in enquiry – all with an eye to pragmatic assumptions regarding truth, belief, and method.

A second group of pragmatists addresses concerns about social injustice, law, equity, and other social issues, and may be termed 'politicians' for our purposes. Their view is that the pragmatic take on politics and enquiry is the correct one. Romantics, or those pragmatists manifesting more sensitivity and feeling and who are identified with art and beauty, narrative, biography, and the drama of social transactions, form the third group.

All three of these pragmatic strands take their inspiration from the history of pragmatism and the major moves made by the so-called 'fathers' of the movement such as Charles S. Peirce (1839–1914), William James (1842–1910), John Dewey (1859–1952), George Herbert Mead (1863–1931), and Arthur F. Bentley (1870–1957). On the other hand, the strands, as they are focused and set within twenty-first-century conditions, carry with them contemporary vocabularies and twenty-first-century concerns (Maxcy 2003).

The fundamental question that emerges as these three pragmatisms vie for our attention is how may they be made pragmatically useful? Such divisions in pragmatic theorising affect the way we enquire into the issues of schooling and social life, polarising researchers of a pragmatic bent. What must be demonstrated is how this variety of practical reformulations of social and educational enquiry may yield pragmatically useful solutions for us.

There seems to be an emerging pragmatism, one that is more self-reflective and pluralistic, and speaks of reform and a better 'way of living'. This fourth strand has a practical attitude and multiple methods of dealing with the unknowns in society and education. Engaging in reconstructions of these social and cultural problems, this strand of pragmatists uses critique to reveal confusions and ambiguities in research itself, while keeping to the goal of making an improved culture and society.

What is pragmatism?

To understand the nature of these strands of contemporary pragmatism and their impact on social scientific and educational research, it is important to clarify what we mean by 'pragmatism'. This term has been used to name a variety of theories of meaning, method, and practice over the years. In addition, a large number of social scientists and philosophers have used 'pragmatism' to denote some or all of their theoretical positions. Amongst the founders of pragmatism, we see both agreement and difference. The different emphases were noted by Lovejoy (1963), who identified as many as thirteen distinct versions of pragmatism, many of which had no connection with its founder, Charles Sanders Peirce, but differed in emphasis and details.

For example, Peirce certainly stressed the role of the pragmatic in science. This divergence in the understanding of what pragmatism meant was complicated by a tendency not to view pragmatism as a full-blown philosophy, but rather as an open matter that would never be quite filled in. For Peirce, pragmatism was the method for fixing belief that was far more significant than the other methods. His pragmatic theory of meaning asserts that what the concept of an object means is simply that set of all habits (conditionals) involving the behaviour of that object under all conceivable conditions. Peirce further refined his definition of pragmatism in terms of belief, being the willingness to act, and abandoned 'pragmatism' for a new term 'pragmaticism' (Apel 1981).

William James departed from Peirce's 'pragmatism', and by so doing, prompted the latter to shift to the term 'pragmaticism' (Peirce 1931: Sec. 415). James took pragmatism to be common sense and a rather personal approach to questions of meaning. Pragmatism was the natural purposiveness of the stream of consciousness as it was directed rationally in the cause of making certain an idea was right. The search or method of enquiry was conceived of as looking at what followed, and not towards some ideal or some historic precedent. James wrote: 'Ideas [which themselves are but parts of our experience] become true just insofar as they help us to get into satisfactory relation with other parts of our experience' (Barzun 1983: 86). 'True' is equated with what is helpful or fruitful in a given situation. Highly individualistic, James came to see pragmatism as a common sort of device, psychological in nature, for describing how we think. And this ordinary process wove together abstract and concrete elements, obvious or not so obvious, known and imagined, into a tentative truth we can live by.

Dewey positioned his pragmatism (which he termed 'instrumentalism') as a way of reconstructing American democracy and education. In the preface of his book *Logic: The Theory of Inquiry* (1938), John Dewey confessed that the term 'pragmatism' did not occur, he thought, in his book. He confessed that 'Perhaps the word lends itself to misconception. At all events, so much misunderstanding and relatively futile controversy have gathered about the world that it seemed advisable to avoid its use'. Yet, he went on to give a general definition or proper interpretation of 'pragmatic' as 'namely the function of consequences as necessary tests of the validity of propositions, provided these consequences are operationally instituted and are such as to resolve the specific problem evoking the operation' (Dewey 1938: iii–iv).

George Herbert Mead came under the influence of John Dewey at the University of Michigan from 1891 to 1894, and later worked with him in the philosophy department at the University of Chicago. Mead made original contributions to social psychology, some of which are found in his posthumous writings in *Mind, Self and Society* (1934). Mead wrestled with the social science issues and primary questions of self, language, and the world in his popular 'Social Psychology' course at the University of Chicago from 1900 until 1930, when he fell ill and sought to leave for Columbia University to join his friend John Dewey. The illness led to his death on 26 April 1931 in Chicago, and he never made the trip (Miller 1973). Mead's emphasis oriented his pragmatism towards questions in social philosophy and social psychology (Miller 1973). While his articulation of theories of social interaction and the emergence of mind and self were notable and ground-breaking, his ideas do not seem to have been picked up by today's new pragmatists' social science or educational research communities. Hans Joas (1998) argues persuasively that Mead and the other pragmatists are not to be found in the recent treatises on sociological theory.

Arthur F. Bentley was interested in the language of social science and the practical effects of terminological use upon the conduct of enquiry. He developed a wholly new social science vocabulary in his efforts to unblock research. After making original pragmatist-like contributions to political science study, Bentley gradually embraced a more analytic form of pragmatism to aid him in unravelling a number of linguistic and psychological knots in social science methodology. His and Dewey's notion of 'transactionalism' came late in life (Dewey and Bentley 1949).

Each of the 'fathers' of pragmatism emphasised a different thrust. Today, second- and third-generation, and even fourth-generation followers tend to further dissect and re-alloy this rich heritage to form new 'strands' of pragmatic emphasis.

Pragmatism's strands

It is often assumed that pragmatism is more than a method, that it is in fact a 'paradigm'. It is suggested that all one needs to do is to select it as one of the standard paradigms of enquiry and apply it to social and educational research. Either hermeneutics or critical theory – or pragmatism will do. However, no philosophy voluntarily relativises its own discourse and hence no paradigm is capable of being disproved easily (Maxcy 1995a). It is in the nature of philosophers and their systems to see their beliefs as the one best window on truth and beauty. Critical theorists, positivists, grounded theorists, and the rest, all believe they have the most justifiable system for understanding and explaining social phenomena. There is a fundamental lack of openness to external and internal critique of enquiry once the status of 'a paradigm' is designated. This is not to deny that research paradigms have existed; and beyond this, exercised compelling impact upon people and practice. Since World War II, social science research has moved ever more aggressively towards the ideal of making itself into an ideology. This gravitation, in educational research for example, was effectively countered briefly in the 1980s (Greenfield 1984, Foster 1986, Bates 1990), with the result being the emergence of a variety of new perspectives and approaches mentioned earlier.

Of all these philosophic 'isms', pragmatists assert most loudly that being a follower of this approach is not to have membership in a paradigm or ideology, but rather simply to attempt to employ more intelligent ways of thinking. It vouches that owing to the fact that it is unencumbered by system allegiances, it may better contribute to the ongoing reformulation of research. Amongst pragmatists, pragmatism is, as Peirce conceived of it, like a rope of many strands, rather than a holistic belief system.

Early pragmatists accepted the piecemeal, incomplete, and practical nature of pragmatism. Hence, pragmatism did battle early on with modernist philosophy frameworks, such as positivism, rationalism, idealism, and so forth – but it also sought to avoid the charge of relativism being attached to its instruments of enquiry. By seeking their roots in nature and the embrace of the widest sort of practical intelligence, pragmatism became a proto-postmodernist venture (Dickstein 1998), a kind of free-standing non-dogmatic attitude.

From the start, North American pragmatists made up plural groups (Childs 1956). Inside each pragmatist beat the heart of an investigator who sought to use its tools to do his or her own particular version of useful work. Some of them were invested in attaching scientific thinking, *à la* Dewey's early work on logic, to education and social science (Hullfish and Smith 1961). A number of them sought pragmatic political reform (Mills 1964, Bernstein 1983, Putnam 1995). Others used pragmatism to fight for religious redemption or as a moral template for reform (West 1989, Rockefeller 1991, Maxcy 2002a). Still others proposed it as a means of community reunification, by reuniting the self and other (Smith 1978, Lavine 1998). Finally, a small group stressed the artistic responsibility embedded in the pragmatic agenda (Jackson 1997, Garrison 1998, Maxcy 1991, 1995a). The varieties of pragmatism noted by Arthur Lovejoy (1963) have not gone away over time.

Today, the strands of pragmatism informing researchers are of three kinds:

Scientific pragmatism

Those stressing pragmatism as a fruitful way to answer long-standing epistemological questions following Peirce, Dewey, and Bentley, soon shifted to a kind of scientific self-cleansing (Biesta 1994, 1995, Popp 1998, Rescher 1977, Tashakkori and Teddlie 1998, Evers and Lakomski 2000, Lakatos 1978) through a focus upon methodological, theoretical, or programmatic concerns facing the researcher. Their criteria for admissible issues were driven from inside the logic of their arguments and this strand tended to overlook connections with the political cultural milieu or culture and art. In addition, methodological and theoretical versions of pragmatism did not drop their interest in knowledge questions; rather, they dedicated themselves to resurfacing the foundations of epistemology. This narrowness tended to run against the grain of the mainstream pragmatism, which took the search for foundations of knowledge to be a waste of time (Margolis 1986, Kaplan 1961).

Scientific-oriented pragmatists fasten upon the realm of research and offer a pragmatic solution to the complicated and often heated competition between research techniques or methods (Tashakkori and Teddlie 1998). Here the emphasis is upon the practical utility of rival methods and their use in combination to achieve more 'effective' findings. Spurred by the effort to end the great war between quantitative and qualitative research advocates, a war that has somewhat simmered, if it has not gone flat, methodological pragmatism as a kind of political reality therapy has resulted in quantitative and qualitative methods being linked in single research projects under the rubric of 'mixed methodology'.

It follows that research reports and publications, whether they be surveys or very abstract statistical samplings, are not normative. However, studies of philosophy of science and philosophy of education are normative, because like shopping lists, they set out principles that regulate methods of enquiry and the activities or ends that such methods seek to achieve. Popp (1998) offers pragmatism as a means of naturalising epistemology, and by way of evaluation proposes a methodology for enquiry into education that allows us the means to chose between one good and another.

This scientific pragmatism is a result of the first expression of pragmatism, that which occurred as a result of a decisive encounter with idealism. Charles S. Peirce, William James, and John Dewey sought to define truth in terms not of descriptions of matches between ideas and things, but rather in terms of hunches and predictions. Pragmatists took issue with the empiricist belief that unless a proposition originated in either the sensations or else from reflective thought about the relationships among ideas, it was in error. Pragmatists looked not at the origins of the idea, but instead to its destination. What counted was not where you had been with an idea, but where it took you.

As Kaplan pointed out, 'It is not that the pragmatist is seeking a logic of discovery rather than a logic of proof, but rather that he refuses to identify the formalist reconstruction of scientific method with the procedures of discovery and of proof that the scientist actually employs' (1961: 33). This 'naturalising' of enquiry has continued to exercise an effect upon the conduct of scientific and social scientific research.

Science, and later social science, began to seriously consider its methods while at the same time becoming obsessed with grounding scientific knowledge upon logical proper names. Next, scientists shifted to examining propositions, statements, and descriptions in the form of sentences as the epistemological unit upon which to rest empirical knowledge. Following this period, science shifted to the consideration of conceptual schemes or frameworks as the proper unit of epistemology. Then, the focus was directed to conflicting theories, paradigms, and research programmes (Bernstein 1983).

Throughout most of its history, science and social science have been in the business of grounding research processes and products upon some foundation or core of knowledge, coupled with transcendental rules or algorithms like 'the scientific method', or 'rationality' to guide enquiry. Knowledge was constructed through an exercise of thought upon experience, catalysed by doubt and a desire to seek some kind of resolution or closure to a problem. For most of its existence, scientific pragmatism has engaged in a shift from the problem of knowledge and how it was to be obtained to a transaction with questions of methods, theories, and programmes of research.

Methodological pragmatists

The departure from a study of purely epistemological matters is found in the first spin-off of scientific pragmatism – 'methodological pragmatism'. It was Rescher (1977) who called for a 'methodological pragmatism' for research. In Rescher's view, the role of the philosopher of science was to move researchers from a quest for a pragmatic solution to the knowledge question, to an embrace of pragmatism as a criterion for method acceptance. Competing methods of enquiry were to be tested by how well they achieved their purported goals.

Rescher rejected epistemological pragmatism and embraced methodological pragmatism in its place. He asserted:

> It is thus clear that, with particular regard to methodology at any rate, the pragmatists were surely right: there can be no better or more natural way of justifying a method than by establishing that 'it works' with respect to the specific appointed tasks that are in view for it.
>
> (1977: 3)

A method is correct or appropriate if and only if it achieves its purposes. In fact, method and purpose are used interchangeably. It follows for Rescher that a method may be evaluated in rational terms if it succeeds.

In educational research today, methodologists are fairly sprinting towards a pragmatic characterisation of methodological decision-making.

That method or technique was best which produced the most 'useful results'. Tashakkori and Teddlie (1998), for example, argue for mixed-methods research strategies that combine quantitative and qualitative approaches, connected to a search for 'effectivism'.

What we get is an a-theoretical practicalism driven by cross-methodological justification rooted in combinational moves of a political sort. This is to say that to satisfy members of the qualitative researcher camp, such methods will be introduced into a decision model that allows them to be used. However, the ultimate arbiter remains that of a quantitative and essentially positivist numeric head count.

Theoretical pragmatism

The second iteration of scientist-inspired pragmatism was 'theoretical pragmatism'. Hans Reichenbach (1951) argued that theory is best which is more in agreement with observed facts than the other theories. By this test, the choice between equally valid theories (rational in their make-up) is to be made based upon the correspondence of the theory with the findings. This test, or induction by enumeration, allowed statistics to be used to justify the fruitfulness of a theory based upon its non-exhaustive repetition. That theory was best which worked most often.

Evers and Lakomski propose that theory choice must be made on the basis of certain extra-empirical virtues held by the theories themselves. They point to the virtues of coherence, simplicity, consistency, comprehensiveness, conservativeness, and fecundity (1991: 4). Walker and Evers (1994) speak of simplicity, comprehensiveness, elegance and explanatory power as properties of coherence. Essentially, coherency theorists like Evers, Lakomski, and Walker replace a justification scheme rooted in epistemological foundations by one located in a system of theory choice flowing from characterising virtues abiding in theory itself.

Theoretical research pragmatists believe that enquiry is best where it provides a pragmatic criterion for theory selection. Rather than using a correspondence theory of truth, they kick it up a level to the airy realm of theory. Theories compete relative to knowledge production. It was reasoned that the best theory was the one that cohered or pulled together truth claims. Evers and Lakomski (1991) argued that research on educational administration requires, on this ground, a pragmatic perspective.

Programmatic pragmatism

A third spin-off of scientific pragmatism is 'programmatic pragmatism'. Lakatos switched focus from methods and theories to entire research programmes. He wrote: 'According to my methodology the great scientific achievements are research programmes which can be evaluated in terms of progressive and degenerating problem shifts; and scientific revolutions consist of one research programme superseding (overtaking in progress) another' (1978: 110). The appraisal of research ought not to be made based upon one theory or a group of theories, but on the collective success of the research programme.

For Lakatos, methodological pragmatism is entirely too narrow, exchanging the struggle to know for the struggle over methods by which to find out. It is precisely due to a lack of an external history of research that theoretical pragmatism fails. The search for coherence is entirely too local and self-serving to give perspective and a balanced account. Both of the other forms of scientific pragmatism lacked a real criterion of usefulness.

However, before we all shift to methodological, theoretical, or programmatic pragmatism, a caution is necessary. As Paul Feyerabend has stated, a theory of rational choice whether regarding knowledge, methods, theories, or programmes is not essential for science of any kind to progress. Enquiry of individual creative research is all that is needed. And for this to work, a supportive climate or atmosphere is required which stimulates and recognises that creativity (Diesing 1991).

All enquiry methods engage in a kind of transformation in which old objects are changed into new ones. All discourse is transformational, whether it is statistical or poetic, as experience immediately had is made into objects of knowing and meaning for the purposes of acting.

Practical-minded philosophers of science have historically warned against 'formalism' in theories and methods. Systems of belief, whether they be patterns, paradigms, or schemes run the risk of becoming self-contained collections of beliefs that deflect criticism. A pragmatism that focuses upon theories but fails to consider their usefulness is not quite pragmatic. Sir Karl Popper proposed openness to falsification as the criterion for judging the adequacy of a theory, while Kuhn argued for a historical and 'conventionalist' approach in which theories build upon one another until the pigeon-holing of new findings falls apart and we get a 'scientific revolution'.

Hence, quite another consideration – political context and reconstruction of socio-political organisations – became the preferred strand for many pragmatists.

Political pragmatism

Those avowing a dedication to this strand of pragmatism may be distinguished in terms of an emphasis upon political context, with such matters as freedom, justice, and equity taking centre stage.

Political pragmatism of the kind embraced by John Dewey in his *Liberalism and Social Action* (1935) and *The Problems of Men* (1946), Richard Bernstein in his *Beyond Objectivism and Relativism* (1983), and Cherryholmes in his *Reading Pragmatism* (1999), bear little in common with Richard Rorty's recent *Achieving Our Country: Leftist Thought in Twentieth-Century America* (1998), and *Philosophy and Social Hope* (1999). The former set of writers examines the role of critical thought as a matter of shared consciousness regarding the conditions and prospects of human action, while simultaneously valorising the fact that 'pragmatism requires democracy' for it to work as a social philosophy (Cherryholmes 1999: 39). This group of scholars argues for practical decision-making to remedy social and cultural ills, with a keen eye to the role of individual choice in remaking a contextually better world. Social justice emerges as the criterion of pragmatic choice for these writers. In Rorty's project, on the other hand, we can detect that 'the poor will always be with us'. More compliant and resting upon social hope (Rorty 1999) and the continuous and unforgiving conditions of inequality and difference any democracy must breed, Rorty holds up literature, novels in particular, as inspirational sources for coping.

It would seem that the pragmatist revival has made the biggest impacts in the study of the law rather than politics, for it has made American jurisprudence, in particular, most aware of the fact that 'law is contextual: it is rooted in practice and custom, and takes its substance from existing patterns of human conduct and interaction. To an equal degree, law is instrumental, meant to advance the human good of those it serves, hence subject to alteration to achieve this end' (Grey 1998: 269). Deriving its thrust from Justice Oliver Wendell Holmes Jr, the great American legal expert, today's law school graduate in forty-nine of the fifty United States is more likely to be a practical lawyer than any other kind (Louisiana is the exception owing to the great impact of Napoleonic law there). As such, law is the study and practice of a group of practical ways of measuring social living, relying upon principles and rules to guide human conduct. Grey tells us no pragmatist worth his salt would not believe that the law operates without regard for general theories about its practice. And law, while offering no absolute moral claims to justify it, nonetheless asks of each individual that she or he weigh and consider law in their individual reflections and choices as to what they will in fact do (Grey 1998).

Perhaps, as Wolfe tells us, 'at its best pragmatism is not a politics but a sensibility, a reminder of the impossibility of thinking about human beings without putting humans at the center of the inquiry' (1998: 199). As a humanistic social science, political science in pragmatic hands may be interventionist, as it was for Jane Addams and her Hull House followers in Chicago in the late nineteenth and early twentieth centuries, and for C. Wright Mills (1964) and his brand of political sociology.

Romantic pragmatism

Finally, there is a strand that has much less in common with the scientised and political versions of pragmatism, and more in common with the strong poetry of Richard Rorty. This view argues for a version of pragmatism that is less grounded in the foundations of an epistemological paradigm and the formalism of method or theory choice, and more connected to aesthetic and moral–ethical values. This 'romantic pragmatism' has more in common with painting and tale-telling than positivist science (Alexander 1987, Shusterman 1992, Garrison 1997). When applied to the field of education and social research, this strand of pragmatism calls for attention to be directed at artistic criteria (Maxcy 1991, 1995a).

When we attempt to justify a particular programme, theory, or method, it may be in terms of its value rather than its choice matrix. When asked to justify a theory, method, or programme, we may argue that a theory is better than its rivals because it is more 'elegant', or beautiful in its organisation. But beyond this, when the latter is the case, we may mean that the aesthetic preference is the consequence of a certain way of life, or a sociocultural pattern. This is precisely what Hilary Putnam is saying in his *Pragmatism: An Open Question* (1995) when he points out that we need to address knowledge issues, but always with respect to the democratic way of living.

Oddly, pragmatists dedicated to explaining fundamental method effectiveness, theory coherence, or the overall progress of research programmes, are subject to having their narrower agendas held up to the light of communal values. Dewey early on reported that certain schools of philosophy (such as realism) had borrowed 'coherence' from aesthetic experience, and that the term was not meant to be applied as a category of the universe at large (Dewey 1939: 553). And, more recently, Putnam redefines 'coherence' as a kind of congealed social common sense, rather than an algorithmic mechanism for theory choice (1995: 14–16). When we look at John Dewey's contributions to pragmatic thought, we find current emphases to be spread between seeing his philosophy as driven by a theory of knowledge or methodological issues (Sleeper 1986) versus that of art and aesthetics (Alexander 1987). By focusing upon philosophy as a creative enterprise, pragmatism laid a trail for followers which cast each human being as in charge of building his or her own world view not from outside and inherited sanctions derived from religion, politics, or historical tradition, but from the ideas shaped by one's own experience. Nothing like it had been seen in philosophy before (Rockefeller 1991).

Pragmatism has historically sought to link theory and practice, but at the level of research methodology we find the practical bent to rest solely in testing the richness of research methods relative to outcomes in practice. Satisfaction results from matching theory choice with paradigmatic elegance. I wish to argue that such moves are aesthetic rather than logical and hence raise a number of as-yet-unaddressed issues for the researcher.

Yet, 'pragma' also invade the life of the researcher in educational and social science as she or he searches for a means of justifying the arrangement of competing meaning-making strategies. This is to say that while old-time pragmatists wrestled with the question of how to make their research more 'useful', contemporary researchers of a pragmatic strain seek to make their enquiries more beautiful.

How pragmatic should pragmatism be?

The adoption of any of these strands has introduced researchers to a further set of new issues. The fundamental question is: How useful is any one of these strands in dealing with social science and education enquiry into problems and prospects? The introduction of the criterion of 'use' seems to add a single quality to the status of pragmatism as the leading mode of philosophy in the present circumstances. For among all of the approaches identified in this volume, only pragmatism hinges all of its essential ingredients upon the matter of usefulness.

Examining the theme of significance of a theory of knowledge and the sources of knowing and doing, allows us to elevate questions of 'use'. A scepticism underwrites the more radical camp of pragmatists relative to the status of any *a priori* model of knowledge in enquiry. Certainly, new questions surrounding the falsification of research findings, use of animal subjects in experiments, and the consequences of research products on the environment, and so forth, have alerted us to the moral–ethical side of enquiry. Here, pragmatism offers us a number of moral–ethical considerations as the hard choices are made relative to such matters and sources. Questions of culture in its scientific and political dimensions also include issues of personal identity, themes of equality and difference, and concerns regarding the value glue that enables researchers and research organisations such as universities to prosper.

What is most important for us to realise is that the debates surrounding the 'new educational and social science' are essentially becoming a contest over values, both artistic and moral–ethical in nature. Pragmatism is up to the task, but only if we are flexible enough to grasp the individual threads of its stands and appropriate the mix for our treatment of current dilemmas in both research self-understanding and the concrete changes needed if society and culture are to prosper. What we need is an answer as to how pragmatic thought and practice may be reunited in the name of a more 'useful pragmatism'.

Critical pragmatism

A fourth strand of pragmatism, here called 'critical pragmatism' for want of a better term, may be emerging in response to the new age of chaos as well as the failure of logical empiricism to provide a connection between thought and practice, or a moral–ethical environment in which to live and work. While it may be more scientific, more political, or more romantic – the probability is that critical pragmatism displays a mixture of parts of all of these strands, with the emphasis being placed upon critical self-reflection plus the desire to reform and reconstruct social and cultural life (Maxcy 1991).

Critique has received a bad name. One positive critical element at work here is Hegelian, and finds today's new pragmatists surfacing the often hidden assumptions and meanings driving social science and educational research and exposing them to human intelligence. What is being critiqued is the idea that there are fully formed frameworks, structures, or methods which must be deployed upon any or every social or educational problem which may arise (Maxcy 1995a). Critique has a much more positive use in the newest strand of pragmatism: the critical pragmatist looks at values, but neither judges them in terms of their other-worldly source, nor attempts to see them read off of human nature or the natural world. Instead, there is a concerted effort to elevate human intelligence as the method by which they may be judged in terms of practical outcomes.

The second element in the critical dimension of pragmatism today is the reliance upon a rich sociocultural context as the setting within which to conduct pragmatic work in everything from art to school choice. Critical pragmatists speak of 'a way of life', or entire tradition informing investigation. Where that way of living is free and open as it is in a democratic society, it is more likely that research may prosper. When the social context is autocratic, dictatorial, immoral or amoral, pragmatic enquiry is less likely to yield fruitful results.

This approach to philosophy of research no longer claims some special privilege, as did non-pragmatic research, to determine the behaviours of researchers. The so-called 'professional standards' adopted by so many academic fields may continue to be applied to increasingly more professionals, in more states and nations, and may well continue to be used to judge the adequacy of work. But the new critical pragmatism sees nothing sacred in such standards. Yet, it can do nothing about this, for philosophy has no special insights as to how to come to know and how to use that knowledge for building the effective space of the school.

Once we understand these parameters and limits, it is possible to redefine the idea of enquiry, as Peirce, James, and the other pragmatist fathers attempted to do. James confesses that pragmatism is 'ticklish' and difficult to pin down. He likens the pragmatic attitude with searching for the 'particular go of it' (1907/1960: 131). And he goes on to make that famous pronouncement: 'The truth of an idea is not a stagnant property inherent in it. Truth happens to an idea. It becomes true, is made true by events' (1907: 133). Such a view differs significantly from the popular notion then (and now) that truth is some agreement or correspondence between things out there and ideas we hold in our heads. For 'rationalists', life is only capable of being conducted with the aid of 'principles' and 'standards' by which the truth of things is checked as to its connection and correct mapping of the turf or terrain of reality. It seems not to matter that this correspondence is between numerical symbols and linguistic reports of that world. Contemporary social and educational research is rife with studies of just this connection between 'standards' and practices (Maxcy 2002a).

Any new pragmatism will have to have something important to say about this common assumption as it drives social science and educational research today. There are some theorists helping the scientific side of any new pragmatism do this. Stephen Wolfram (2002) attacks that notion that getting the mathematical map of the world is the way science ought to proceed. He predicts that a quite simple, but elusive, computer programme and its running will generate the operating system for not just the world but the entire universe. Somewhere in the chaos of change, Wolfram finds an island of computing offering hope for truth to happen. But, whether he is correct or not, his solution is ultimately quite non-mathematical and quite pragmatic. It will be in the 'go' or testing that the truth will be found.

Efforts to reduce pragmatism to a political ideology are equally dangerous. Richard Rorty in *Philosophy and Social Hope* (1999) argues that we have had failed prophets in the past predict certain outcomes in our world. He fastens onto the *New Testament*, and Marx and Engels and the *Communist Manifesto* as examples: the world has awaited the second coming as it awaits the death of capitalism and the rise of the working class. The documents may be read for hope, but not necessarily for prediction, Rorty tells us. Nevertheless, he finds these writings to be inspirational and perhaps pragmatically useful, as they teach us that Christ's message of the need for human fraternity, and the Communist view that the divisiveness created by capitalism must be overcome, are both worthwhile. 'It would be best, in short, if we could get along without prophecy and claims to knowledge of the forces which determine history – if generous hope could sustain itself without such assurances' (Rorty 1999: 209).

So, too, our newest pragmatism will run the risk of descending into ideology and announcing the end or beginning of this or that. Such a tack may be uncomfortable as we in social science or education work to sell our homes and stand atop hills awaiting some cataclysmic event. This is perhaps why 'prophet pragmatism' as Cornel West describes it, has certain dire attendants. We do not need prophets telling us what social science and educational research must find. In so far as the scientific and political emphases in historic pragmatisms emerge, we need to have hope and an open mind to allow new meanings of characters and events develop in experience without shoving them through formal frameworks, grids, regressions, and supremely effective methods.

What then of the romantic version of pragmatising? Do we need more poetry, pictures, and dances to make things go? Despite the penchant for literature, and particularly novels and poems, to provide the methodological fodder to do pragmatism today, we seem not to need them. Whether or not Derrida's deconstructing is of any use to the social scientist or educationist is moot.

And, in these times of falling stock prices and anxious economy, going is just what is needed! We will come to believe what we believe about research findings, but our situations and our histories already colour the tone and direction of how we take certain kinds of evidence and what we use it for. There is no Rorty-like 'compliant pragmatist', unconcerned about the poor, and letting changing society move as it will. No room here for the postmodern poetic liberalism that flourishes in good times, but has rough-sledding in the tough ones. If we accept our fate to be that of making decisions about what we find through investigation into the chaos and disorder of contemporary culture and society, with an eye to discovering what will make things go, then it is important to set out certain post holes to pay attention to, not that they will serve to hold posts, but that if we do not we shall fall into one and have a horrible fate.

It is possible to locate three dominant guides operating within the critical pragmatism I am detailing, all of which have a bearing upon a working philosophy of educational leadership research. Following Dewey, it seems the following are important. First, communication is seen as vitally linked to leadership practice. Second, commonality of interests and desires, wishes and purposes, frames the interrogation of ends-in-view. Shared concerns mark the nature of our social transactions. Where we come to see common concerns as driving our investigations, only then will parents, students, teachers, administrators, school board members, and others be able to 'see' the knowledge which is used to underwrite policy and practice. Such a change in educational research scope would be significant.

Third, community forms out of the communication of shared interests and goals. And democratic community is the best form of social arrangement for realising the aims of educational leadership, as well as providing the most equalitarian base for its scrutiny. While 'democracy' has been most often treated as a political concept, for Dewey it was an entire way of living. And, if we come to life from an artistic perspective, democracy must been seen as the means for so organising social experience that persons find the best fruits realised in its conception. It entails the belief that a full and freely flowing stream of communication and information yields the best-prepared citizen. With the increasingly public character of information and access to information resulting from the Internet and computer technology, we can see the potential for visual displays of leadership actions being communicated to broad constituencies.

The act of enquiry is pragmatic, rather than abstract and theoretical in nature, when it is an active searching that is characterised by a desire to transform that knowledge into a qualitatively better and richer inherited meaning. A fully functioning research strategy for study, then, should engage its practitioners in active talk with a variety of constituencies, under the guidance of open lines of communication and guided by the values of full and free disclosure. Secrets, closed doors, and lack of affiliations and connections with others seem to work towards the opposite condition, one that favours rumour, tradition, closure, and slow death.

The pragmatic take on current trends in research depiction makes clear how the new critical pragmatism strand may affect leadership in all spheres of social life, from government to schools. To its credit, the pragmatic approach to research is prospective; what matters is not the origin of ideas as we have sensed and reported them in research studies, but rather outcomes yet to be realised and not yet measured (Kaplan 1964). Pragmatism is not so interested in explanations of anomalous cause–effect cases, but in the ways in which practical intelligence may push towards full and free settlement of chaos and discord (Maxcy 1995a).

Nothing pleases a pragmatist more than testing out a conception. For it is by tracing what an idea means in actual practice that we come to understand that idea. Peirce and Dewey stressed the importance of testing, but not in the formal manner we see deployed by educators. Most testing is highly formalised and amounts to an exercise that has little impact on either the problem at hand or the methods used. Instead of refining our tests and instruments of measure, we find educational leadership research using tests like the child with the hammer (everything is for pounding!).

Historically, pragmatism in the hands of the 'fathers' was a kaleidoscope of views. Some saw the knowledge questions, theory, and methods issues; another group viewed the political face of the kaleidoscope, with emphasis upon equality and opportunity, freedom and public communication; and still others saw the dramatic and poetic face. In most cases, the strand that dominated was the one that had the most pragmatic pay-off given the social and cultural conditions people encountered. Cremin (1961) argues this point, and he seems to have it correct. Today, we of the postmodern or poststructural generation must decide which pragmatism we shall use to solve our problems. And the answer should be to select the most pragmatic for current contexts. We must be pragmatic about our choice of pragmatic emphasis.

There are stark parallels with America and the West during these first decades of the twenty-first century and the sociocultural conditions we faced in the 1950s. We find a new cold war brewing, government efforts to tighten things up, a troubled stock market and economic uncertainty, and the 'Man in the Grey Flannel Suit' of the 1950s has become the 'Woman in the Grey Flannel Suit'. The economic values of America have been exported worldwide so that such problems as overly inflated CEO salaries are found throughout Europe, Canada, and Australia. Just as in the 1950s, we are struggling today with equity issues, access issues, and extremes in competition and puritanism.

Social scientists and educators are focused upon the orgy of testing that has been legislated and mandated by governments. Accountability is paramount. Teacher pay is still too low. Students continue to be ill-prepared for school. The costs of education are climbing at all levels. Gender and racial equality are not what they should be, and governments seem unable to do much about this. School buildings are in poor shape. In short, education is long overdue for reform.

If history repeats itself, then one scenario for the future may be a neo-progressive reform of education like that experienced in the US in the 1960s. We may see a reaction to the educational and social problems. The new pragmatic strand may be reformist with an emphasis upon change for the better (probably not 'deschooling'). The demise of formalism, however, is greatly exaggerated. There is still a tendency to solve problems with new laws, structures, and frameworks, rather than getting things done. Bureaucracy has not gone away.

A critical pragmatism may arise in which the assumptions are that things need to change, but there are no five-year plans that will make that happen. No recommendations from star panels or élite consultants. There are no straightforward rules that can guide us. Our decisions will be based on raw feelings, hunches, and guessing. We shall have to bet and wager more, and not expect high rates of return. Whatever our beliefs may be, we must see them as highly contextual. What we believe is caught up in the stories we tell. Efforts to stand outside our experiences and account for them are mistaken (Fish 1998: 420). The way to make our way through this world is to just keep going.

Two dangerous versions of pragmatism

Two dangerous strands of pragmatism may present themselves. First, we may find that the next pragmatism is nothing but 'naïve pragmatism'. This is to say that pragmatists will simply bumble along believing that things will take care of themselves. As Apel (1981) argued, Charles S. Peirce provided in his 'pragmaticism' a way to transcend the technical and instrumental rationality that dominated his day (and continues to dominate our own). Unless we reject the embrace of naïve pragmatism, or merely doing something practical for its own sake, we shall not see much improvement in social science or education research studies. Lured into embracing a non-reflective kind of value-free enquiry rooted in a belief in the private nature of values, we may well contribute to the breakdown in the very political and moral–ethical presuppositions that support pragmatic enquiry in the first place.

The second danger is that we find the new pragmatic version amounting to nothing but 'vulgar pragmatism'. This type of pragmatism is interested in expediency rather than quality. Getting the job done is getting what is fastest, easiest, and without pain. Vulgar pragmatism is vulgar as in the Vulgate version of scripture; it appeals to the lowest order of intelligence, masks an ideology, and portends lower levels of living. Here the tendency is to see social scientific and educational thinking as mere following of scripts. Standards, rules, checklists, and other protocols are set out as 'practical' guides to decision-making. As Brian Fay tells us: 'Acquiring the skills of a good research scientist is not reducible to learning a set of rules'. Rather, it is 'acquiring the practical sense of knowing what is appropriate research behaviour and knowing how to make judgements which express this understanding' (1987: 181). Removing reflective thinking from practical research work is to vulgarise it by dumbing it down.

Concluding suggestions

Ever since Peter Winch sought to attach philosophy to social science in his classic work, *The Idea of a Social Science* (1958), theoreticians have wrestled with the issue of which canons of rationality ought to provide the standards for justifying social science enquiry. If the pragmatic revival has made little imprint upon social scientists today (Wolfe 1998), it is at least within this long-standing effort to connect philosophy with social and educational enquiry that we may see evidence of a new pragmatism emerging. Once convinced of this, we must see what we may do to help it along.

My recommendation is that we may 'cherry pick' or select those elements within the strands of pragmatism operative today, that seem most pragmatically useful for addressing today's social and cultural dilemmas (Maxcy 1991, 1995a). Thus, the criteria for deciding what our new critical pragmatism will be are located in the fruitfulness of it in our researching. This effort is one with the current desire to achieve a methodological pluralism in social science and educational research (Roth 1987, Tashakkori and Teddlie 1998) so as to improve such activities and build a more varied and satisfying form of life (Bernstein 1983, Maxcy 1991). Along this line, I am convinced too that the scientist pragmatists have something to offer as they point to the need to connect our social and educational enquiry to some ends-in-view. This is to say that 'effectivity' is a value that increases the value of our tools as well as evokes beneficial changes in our social and cultural spaces. Our old-fashioned methods and techniques of investigation could be refined to test the outcomes we achieve. To rewrite social science and educational research assumptions and methods, as I see Tashakkori and Teddlie (1998) advocating, based upon their power to make some difference in the world, is not a bad idea.

From the politician pragmatists, there are powerful insights offered regarding the disequilibria of this universe in terms of the advantaged and disadvantaged human beings around the globe. Keeping our attention upon these discontinuities in social progress is worthwhile for all of us. Certainly, social justice needs to be focal. Gender, racial, religious, and other inequalities must be surmounted and increasingly more people given access to the best of all possible worlds.

Romantic pragmatists provide a poetic and artistic take on the universe. We may learn much from Garrison (1999) and others who follow Rorty's invocation of the 'strong poet' in us as a palliative for today's ills. Perhaps most importantly, we may take from the romantics their unalloyed pragmatic faith. Peirce and James valued religious attitudes in their science. Dewey sought to enlarge his democracy to that of a faith. Cornel West (1989) tells us that matters of the spirit are fundamental tares by which to weigh our pragmatic choices. Least likely to be embraced but perhaps the most important, pragmatic conceptions of spirituality may well provide both solace and understanding as we try to make our way in the post-9/11 world. My own work has focused on the artistic take on ethics and value as a solution to the moral and ethical malaise visited upon nations in the West (Maxcy 1991, 1995a, 1995b, 2002a, 2002b, in press).

A pluralistic and critical pragmatism seems to allow for persons involved in social and educational enquiry to draw upon a greater number of elements of tradition and to weave together unique combinations of these. Mixed and multiple methods may be used in research without running the risk of deciding in advance which are best, but rather in capturing new and more creative enquiry approaches as the problem becomes clearer and the objectives come more into focus. Using research in this multi-faceted way results in the amplification of what John Dewey called a fuller 'way of life'. To resolve disputes over rival understandings of terms, concepts, frameworks, paradigms, and finally programmes of research has yielded little of value (Bernstein 1983). Testing out a smorgasbord of pragmatic impulses in terms of an entire way of life needs to be attempted. If, as it did for Dewey, democracy turns out to be that complete way of living, a way that enables full and free enquiry and the dissemination of results (Dewey 1916), then fine, it will have to do until something better comes along.

A critically intelligent pragmatism for each of us, composed of threads from the strands outlined here, could be a solution to what has appeared to be overly scientised investigations and unsolvable personal and social difficulties, as well as providing a fuller release from the grip of popular and abject capitulationism and hand-wringing. Pragmatism as a whole does away with the 'middle man', or the mental monitor we think speaks to our actions and their consequences. And, today more than ever before, we long for just such a voice to interpret what is going on around us. But, were the new pluralistic pragmatism to gain a place in critical social and educational enquiry and practice, it would be a no-nonsense, direct, and practical engagement without the need for voices rehashing and soul-searching for justifications. A new pragmatism for social science and educational research, invested with a spirit of critique, armed with plural methods, linking theory to practice, and aimed at enhancing through art and morals our individual and collective social lives, is within our grasp. Time will tell if we fashion and use it.

References

Alexander, T. M. (1987) *John Dewey's Theory of Art, Experience and Nature: The Horizons of Feeling*, Albany, NY: State University of New York Press.

Apel, K. (1981) *Charles S. Peirce: From Pragmatism to Pragmaticism*, Amherst, MA: University of Massachusetts Press.

Barzun, J. (1983) *A Stroll With William James*, New York: Harper and Row.

Bates, R. (1990) 'Leadership and the rationalization of society', paper read before the American Educational Research Association, Boston, April.

Baynes, K., Bohman, J., and McCarthy, T. (1987) *After Philosophy: End or Transformation?*, Cambridge, MA: MIT Press.

Bernstein, R. J. (1983) *Beyond Objectivism and Relativism*, Philadelphia, PA: University of Pennsylvania Press.

Biesta, G. J. J. (1994) 'Education as practical intersubjectivity. Towards a critical-pragmatic understanding of education', *Educational Theory* 44, 3: 299–317.

Biesta, G. J. J. (1995) 'Pragmatism as a pedagogy of communicative action', in J. Garrison (ed.) *The New Scholarship on John Dewey*, Dordrecht, Boston, and London: Kluwer Academic Publishers.

Brickman, W. W. (1970) 'Dewey's social and political commentary', in J. Boydston (ed.) *Guide to the Works of John Dewey*, Carbondale, IL: Southern Illinois University Press.

Cherryholmes, C. (1988) *Power and Criticism: Poststructural Investigations in Education*, New York: Teachers College Press.

Cherryholmes, C. (1999) *Reading Pragmatism*, New York: Teachers College Columbia Press.

Childs, J. L. (1956) *American Pragmatism and Education*, New York: Henry Holt.

Cremin, L. A. (1961) *The Transformation of the School*, New York: Vintage.

Dantley, M. and Cambron-McCabe, N. H. (2001) 'Licensure of Ohio school administrators and social justice concerns', paper presented before the American Educational Research Association, Seattle, WA, April.
Dewey, J. (1916/2002) 'Democracy and education', in S. J. Maxcy (ed.) *John Dewey and Education*, vol. 3, Bristol: Thoemmes Press.
Dewey, J. (1938) *Logic: The Theory of Inquiry*, New York: Henry Holt.
Dewey, J. (1939) 'Experience, knowledge, and value: A rejoinder', in P. A. Schillp (ed.) *The Philosophy of John Dewey*, New York: Tudor.
Dewey, J. and Bentley, A. F. (1949) *Knowing and the Known*, Boston: Beacon.
Dickstein, M. (ed.) (1998) *The Revival of Pragmatism: New Essays on Social Thought, Law, and Culture*, Durham, NC: Duke University Press.
Diesing, P. (1991) *How Does Social Science Work? Reflections on Practice*, Pittsburgh, PA: University of Pittsburgh Press.
Evers, C. and Lakomski, G. (1996) *Exploring Educational Administration: Coherentist Applications and Critical Debates*, Oxford: Pergamon Press.
Fay, B. (1987) *Critical Social Science*, Ithaca, NY: Cornell University Press.
Fish, S. (1998) 'Truth and toilets: Pragmatism and the practices of life', in M. Dickstein (ed.) *The Revival of Pragmatism: New Essays on Social Thought, Law, and Culture*, Durham, NC: Duke University Press.
Foster, W. P. (1986) *Paradigms and Promises: New Approaches to Educational Administration*, Buffalo, NY: Prometheus Books.
Garrison, J. W. (1997) *Dewey and Eros: Wisdom and Desire in the Art of Teaching*, New York: Teachers College Columbia Press.
Greenfield, T. B. (1984) 'Leaders and schools: Willfulness and nonnatural order in organizations', in T. Sergiovanni and J. Corbally (eds) *Leadership and Organizational Culture*, Urbana, IL: University of Illinois Press.
Grey, T. C. (1998) 'Freestanding legal pragmatism', in M. Dickstein (ed.) *The Revival of Pragmatism: New Essays on Social Thought, Law, and Culture*, Durham, NC: Duke University Press.
Hodgkinson, C. (1991) *Educational Leadership*, Albany, NY: State University of New York Press.
Hullfish, H. G. and Smith, P. G. (1961) *Reflective Thinking: The Method of Education*, New York: Dodd, Mead.
Jackson, P. W. (1998) *John Dewey and the Lessons of Art*, New Haven: Yale University Press.
James, W. (1960) *Pragmatism and Four Essays from 'The Meaning of Truth'*, New York: Meridian.
Joas, H. (1998) 'The inspiration of pragmatism: Some personal remarks', in M. Dickstein (ed.) *The Revival of Pragmatism: New Essays on Social Thought, Law, and Culture*, Durham, NC: Duke University Press.
Kaplan, A. (1961) *The New World of Philosophy*, New York: Random House.
Kaplan, A. (1964) *The Conduct of Inquiry: Methodology for Behavioral Sciences*, San Francisco: Chandler Publishing Company.
Lagemann, E. C. (2000) *An Elusive Science: The Troubling History of Education Research*, Chicago: University of Chicago Press.
Lakatos, I. (1978) *The Methodology of Scientific Research Programmes*, Cambridge: Cambridge University Press.

Lavine, T. Z. (1998) 'The contemporary significance of the American philosophic tradition: Lockean and redemptive', in L. A. Hickman (ed.) *Reading Dewey: Interpretations for a Postmodern Generation*, Bloomington, IN: Indiana University Press.

Lovejoy, A. O. (1963) *The Thirteen Pragmatisms and other Essays*, Baltimore: Johns Hopkins University Press.

Maddock, T. H. (1996) 'Three dogmas of materialist pragmatism: A critique of a recent attempt to provide a science of educational administration', in C. Evers and G. Lakomski (eds) *Exploring Educational Administration: Coherentist Applications and Critical Debates*, Oxford: Pergamon.

Margolis, J. (1986) *Pragmatism Without Foundations: Reconciling Realism with Relativism*, Oxford: Blackwell.

Maxcy, S. J. (1991) *Educational Leadership: A Critical Pragmatic Perspective*, New York: Bergin and Garvey.

Maxcy, S. J. (1995a) *Democracy, Chaos, and the New School Order*, Thousand Oaks, CA: Corwin Press.

Maxcy, S. J. (1995b) 'Beyond leadership frameworks', *Educational Administration Quarterly* 31, 3: 473–483.

Maxcy, S. J. (2002a) *Ethical School Leadership*, Landham, MD: Scarecrow.

Maxcy, S. J. (ed.) (2002b) *John Dewey and American Education*, vols 1–3, Bristol: Thoemmes Press.

Maxcy, S. J. (2003) 'Pragmatic threads in mixed methods research in the social sciences: The search for multiple modes of inquiry and the end of the philosophy of formalism', in A. Tashakkori and C. Teddlie (eds) *Handbook of Mixed Methods in the Social and Behavioral Sciences*, Thousand Oaks, CA: Sage.

Mead, G. H. (1934) *Mind, Self and Society: From the Standpoint of a Social Behaviorist*, Chicago: University of Chicago Press.

Miller, D. L. (1973) *George Herbert Mead: Self, Language, and the World*, Chicago: University of Chicago Press.

Mills, C. W. (1964) *Sociology and Pragmatism: The Higher Learning in America*, New York: Paine-Whitman.

Peirce, C. S. (1931) *Collected Papers of Charles Sanders Peirce*, vol. 6, Cambridge, MA: Harvard University Press.

Phillips, D. C. (1987) *Philosophy, Science, and Social Inquiry*, Oxford: Pergamon.

Popp, J. A. (1998) *Naturalizing Philosophy of Education: John Dewey and the Post-analytic Period*, Carbondale, IL: Southern Illinois University Press.

Putnam, H. (1995) *Pragmatism: An Open Question*, Oxford: Blackwell.

Reichenbach, H. (1951) *The Rise of Scientific Philosophy*, Berkeley: University of California Press.

Rescher, N. (1977) *Methodological Pragmatism: A Systems–Theoretic Approach to the Theory of Knowledge*, New York: New York University Press.

Rockefeller, S. C. (1991) *John Dewey: Religious Faith and Democratic Humanism*, New York: Columbia University Press.

Rorty, R. (1998) *Achieving Our Country: Leftist Thought in Twentieth Century America*, Cambridge, MA: Harvard University Press.

Rorty, R. (1999) *Philosophy and Social Hope*, London: Penguin.

Roth, P. A. (1987) *Meaning and Method in the Social Sciences: A Case for Methodological Pluralism*, Ithaca, NY: Cornell University Press.

Shusterman, R. (1992) *Pragmatist Aesthetics: Living Beauty, Rethinking Art*, Oxford: Blackwell.

Sleeper, R. W. (1986) *The Necessity of Pragmatism: John Dewey's Conception of Philosophy*, New Haven: Yale University Press.

Smith, J. E. (1978) *Purpose and Thought: The Meaning of Pragmatism*, Chicago: University of Chicago Press.

Tashakkori, A. and Teddlie, C. (1998) *Mixed Methodology: Combining Qualitative and Quantitative Approaches*, Thousand Oaks, CA: SAGE Publications.

West, C. (1989) *The American Evasion of Philosophy: A Genealogy of Pragmatism*, Madison: University of Wisconsin Press.

Winch, P. (1958) *The Idea of a Social Science*, London: Routledge and Kegan Paul.

Wolfe, A. (1998) 'The missing pragmatic revival in American social science', in M. Dickstein (ed.) *The Revival of Pragmatism: New Essays on Social Thought, Law, and Culture*, Durham, NC: Duke University Press.

Wolfram, S. (2002) *A New Kind of Science*, Champaign, IL: Wolfram Media.

Chapter 9

Heidegger's 'question concerning technology'
Implications for responsible school leadership in an era of restructuring

Carol Harris

Martin Heidegger, in declaring that 'the essence of technology is by no means anything technological' (1977: 4), invites the question: If not something technological, then what? Philosophers, scientists and, yes, organisation theorists, have debated for many years the 'real world of technology' (Franklin 1991/1999). In the 1960s, Canadian philosopher Marshall McLuhan declared in unequivocal terms that each person's understanding of the world is changed, not so much in the exchange of messages but, rather, in tandem with the technical devices through which messages are transmitted (McLuhan 1994).[1] More recently, in a series of Massey Lectures for the Canadian Broadcasting Company, physicist Ursula Franklin (1991/1999) explored the social and moral impacts of technology, distinguishing between 'holistic' technologies which leave workers in control of particular processes or creations, and 'prescriptive' technologies which encourage a one-best route to efficient and effective practice. Both approaches to technology deal with tools, products and an accompanying mind-set. And both are pursued by educators who, in exploring the politics of technology and educational reform, question the assumption that computer technology can be 'only a tool!' (Moll 2001). Moll, for instance, advances strong arguments against the tool metaphor, maintaining that each new technology changes the way we think about the world, others and ourselves, as it delimits possibilities for action. This question of the relationship between thought and action, like all philosophical questions of significance, can be traced historically to the earliest known writings.

In this chapter, I pick up the conversation drawing on Martin Heidegger's ontological critique of technology. I assume, with McLuhan (1994), Noble (2002), Parker (2001), Rose (2000), and Moll (2001), that each new technological tool changes the way we interact with our surroundings. A moment's reflection on the use of computers, for example, reveals new modes of information-gathering and communication, social arrangements in classrooms, and visible signs of physical stresses and strains. My question, addressed here to school leaders, concerns technology as a way of thinking: What is the nature of the drift, noted by many (e.g. Berman 1984, Franklin 1991/1999, Greene 1995, Weber 1978), towards ever-greater technological (or instrumental) reasoning in our everyday work lives? The question is asked in the general context of the neo-liberal ideologies that dominate school restructuring in many regions of the world, and is considered in the specific context of three Canadian provinces, Ontario, Alberta and British Columbia,[2] where new political regimes have effected dramatic cuts to all social services, including education and family welfare. In such contexts, school leaders face especially difficult decisions as they are asked to comply with cuts that adversely affect the very people they are responsible for helping – children, teachers, support staff, and parents.

While it may seem strange to call upon Martin Heidegger, who for a brief time supported fascism and the National Socialist Party in Germany,[3] to clarify issues of administrative ethics, I contend that the field has much to gain from his examination of human and non-human essences. Heidegger reminds us of what living a life, not as a solo performance but rather as a social endeavour, can mean. He advocates action in the world over contemplation of it, and he touches upon our empathetic Being, our ability and desire to care for others. Holding neither utopian nor dystopian views of technology (Thomson 2000), Heidegger provides a clearing wherein we may live with technology so that its imperatives work for, rather than against, our relationship with other sentient beings, the environment, and art and science.

In drawing connections between Heidegger's preoccupation with Being, and the practical everyday tasks of school leadership, I explore four concepts – enframing, concealment, freedom, and agency. These together illuminate, theoretically speaking, what some have called the problem of technical rationality (Habermas 1971, Weber 1978, Smyth 2001). My purpose is to suggest that educational leaders, who enter teaching with empathy for the human condition and a desire to make a positive difference (Connell *et al.* 1982), may find in Heidegger's ontological perspectives reminders of their own social and educational commitments that, in turn, will encourage resistance to present-day imperatives of technological thought and action.

My reference to *leaders and leadership* is intentional for several reasons. In the belief that discourse both reflects the world and changes it, I find talk of administration to be unnecessarily limited and limiting. My observation of those who work within schools supports Gronn's (1999, 2002) view of effective leadership as more often distributed throughout the organisation, than as emanating from a single role incumbent. While many decisions are made solely by school administrators, important decisions about curriculum content (both explicit and hidden), individual students, and community action also involve teachers, and sometimes support staff.

The unfortunate tendency, well documented in the literature of educational administration and leadership, to separate conceptually, and sometimes physically, administrators from teachers (Young and Levin 1998), administrative issues from those of pedagogy (Bates 1984, Evans 1992, Foster 1986, Greenfield and Ribbins 1993), teachers from their larger communities (Dillard 1995, Harris 1998), and teachers and administrators alike from developing 'culturally relevant value systems' (Foster 1986: 22), demonstrates the very technological approaches addressed here.

In the first section of the chapter, I review concepts of technological rationality, and how they have played out in North America in cyclical patterns of application and resistance in education since the early years of the twentieth century. Next, I briefly outline features of restructuring – globally, locally, and educationally – that challenge educators' core values today. In the third section, I explore selected features of Heidegger's critique[4] and, in the discussion, I consider his philosophy as applied to leadership in everyday school situations. My argument is that school practice has become seriously derailed from the intended purposes of early and present-day educators, a derailment all the more damaging as it accompanies, draws on, and fortifies larger market forces which, in turn, carry the potential to sweep all before them into a maelstrom of technological rationality. Heidegger, I believe, can direct us back to the 'celebration' and 'wonder' that lies at the heart of teaching and learning.

Technology and the steady pace of disenchantment

> Celebration . . . is self-restraint, is attentiveness, is questioning, is meditating, is awaiting, is the step over into the more wakeful glimpse of the wonder – the wonder that a world is worlding around us at all, that there are beings rather than nothing, that things are and we ourselves are in their midst, that we ourselves are and yet barely know who we are, and barely know that we do not know all this.
>
> (Heidegger in Polt 1999: 1)

These words of philosopher Martin Heidegger (1889–1976) convey a sense of mystery, not simply because of his invented vocabulary, but also because of the questioning mode in which he formulates his message. Within Heidegger's most profound statement is embedded a space for the listener or reader to move forward, assisted only by her reflective thoughts and her engagement with the world. The 'world' that captivates Heidegger's imagination is proffered in opposition to the Cartesian conception of one inhabited by entities self-evidently fixed in time and space. To Descartes, who ushered in the Enlightenment with his famous proposition, 'I think, therefore I am', thought, existence, and certainty were simply notions that provided the launching pad for more important investigations. Descartes begins with self-evident truths and, from these, explores and accepts the reality of phenomena that can be verified by reason. As the modern age progressed, and control of the environment through science became ever more importantly a mark of progress, verification by experiment was added to the warrant of reason. Heidegger rejected such single-minded preoccupation with calculations of control and progress, maintaining that in their pursuit, essential features of the world would be ignored and, ultimately, lost.

Heidegger was not alone in his critique of an all-dominating private, public, and professional attentiveness to science and technology. Weber (1978), for instance, drew attention to the inexorable tendency for technically rational thought and action (*Zweckrationalität*) to overshadow motivations based on societal and cultural values (*Wertrationalität*). He warned of the imbalance inherent in a worldview that ignores truth claims, and of the corresponding limits of technical rationality to deliver on calculations of effectiveness and efficiency (Brubaker 1984). While both sets of thought and action are rational, one favours end states and the other, means to achieving a given end. In organisational terms, one set deals with administrative decisions about what an institution should do, while the other addresses management issues of utility (see Hodgkinson 1991: 51). Weber joins a long line of continental philosophers who note the human distress and alienation that occur as the grounds for Wertrational activity become destabilised, and inherited 'truths' become less absolute – perhaps as family and community traditions fade from our horizons, perhaps as science eclipses religion, or possibly as a postmodern scepticism about absolute truth replaces a modern adherence to verifiable facts.

Habermas (1971), in his early writing, also explores the dangers inherent in a one-dimensional adherence to science and technology over other ways of knowing. He argues that humans are motivated by three interests: first, by science and technology whereby we can gain a measure of control over the environment; second, by communication through which we can relate to others; and third, by emancipatory pursuits. I understand the latter as people's search for increasingly deeper understandings of the things they have formerly taken for granted, but now begin to question. Habermas talked of expanding one's everyday understanding of personal meaning (the Lifeworld) as distinct from, yet embedded within, the meanings extracted from the larger world of work, state, media, administration, and so on (System). While in no way denigrating the importance of science and technology, Habermas argued later that, in a broader approach to 'communicative action' (Habermas 1984), people's obsession with science/technology must be mitigated by discursive and emancipatory (including artistic) modes of expression.

Undoubtedly, the achievements of science and technology in the modern era have lightened the burden of human existence. At the same time, they accompany the gradual move of people from traditional communities to purposeful societies (Tönnies' (1955) *Gemeinschaft* and *Gesellschaft*), and they exacerbate two less comfortable features of modernity. Weber names these two related features as 'disenchantment with the world' (*die Entzauberung der Welt*) (Weber 1958: 155) and, within organisations of all kinds, as a tightening 'iron cage' of bureaucratic control (Giddens 1985: 235, 243). Disenchantment, as the term implies, indicates a state of human understanding in which the magic (*die Magie*), or mystery, of living has dissipated. In this state, people tend to distance themselves from traditional beliefs in the forces of nature, in deities, and in social cohesion. Emanating from the birth of Enlightenment, and from Cartesian rationalism and science, Weber also sees that this process has accompanied a dichotomisation of facts (what *is* in the world) from values (what *ought* to be). As the process applies to the work of educators, this bifurcation of facts/values discourages the sort of risk-taking and mental acrobatics required for an active imagination, certainly for the 'sociological imagination' advocated by Mills (1959), if one is to envision a world that has not yet materialised. In other words, adherence to 'what is' precludes thoughts of making a difference, as well as efforts towards its achievement (Greene 1995).

The 'iron cage' of organisational life metaphorically symbolises disenchanted thinking at work. It refers to the tension 'between the demand for technical efficiency of administration on the one hand, and the human values of spontaneity and autonomy on the other' (Giddens 1985: 235), and it encompasses the bureaucratic division of labour in which, in Weber's view, modern man is compelled to live. Such a cage of existence conjures up images of enclosure and imprisonment, a condition defying escape. In exploring the manner of thought and action that could lead to this, I move between Callahan's (1962) explication of efficiency, as it affected school administrators from the turn of the twentieth century until the 1960s, and the present-day 'cult of efficiency' (Stein 2002). While Callahan writes in an American context, today's efficiencies are viewed here as global impacts on school lives in Canada.

Back to the future

It would be a mistake to think of technology and its impact on education without placing it in a context that today, in North America and much of the Western world, is one of advanced capitalism. Nowhere are the connecting links between the past and present better displayed than in Callahan's *Cult of Efficiency*. In his study of school administration, Callahan sets out to understand how administrators, initially the defenders of a free and open public school system, came to assume 'the posture of the business executive' (Callahan 1962: vii), and to adopt business values and practices that were crippling to equality and equity in education. Callahan's investigation, beginning at the turn of the twentieth century, clearly demarcates the parallel movement between scientific management, which dominated the corporate world from about 1910, and the business of schooling (see Gronn 1982). In tracing the powerful pressures from the business world upon school leaders, Callahan names four major 'lost opportunities':

> That educational questions were subordinated to business considerations; that administrators were produced who were not, in any true sense, educators; that a scientific label was put on some very unscientific and dubious methods and practices; and that an anti-intellectual climate, already prevalent, was strengthened.
> (Callahan 1962: 246)

He adds that 'countless educational decisions were made on economic or on non-educational grounds' (Callahan 1962: 246–247). Of course, not all administrators obeyed the market imperatives of their time. Callahan approvingly quotes Superintendent Jesse Newlon, whose experience spanned many years of high school teaching, school and district administration, and university teaching. Newlon warns that 'the greatest danger than besets superintendents . . . is that they will become merely business managers'. Many, Newlon asserts, 'are more concerned about the purchase of pencils and paper . . . and about business routine, than they are about the educative process that goes on in the schoolroom' (Callahan 1962: 203).

Apropos the 'anti-intellectualism' in the ranks, Callahan maintained that educational leaders, despite their rhetoric about science and scientific methods of enquiry, were not really interested in research. This could be seen in frequent references to 'mere book learning', maintained Callahan, and in their impatience with philosophical discussion. Their models were the corporate leaders of the day, rather than philosophers such as Dewey and James.

Quoting from an article in *Fortune* magazine, Callahan noted that the schools were portrayed as 'no different from General Motors for their job was to "optimize the number of students and to minimize the input of man-hours and capital"' (Callahan 1962: 256). The author did not attempt to assess the quality of schools. His main point, claimed Callahan, 'was to show that whereas the productivity per worker had increased in the steel industry', 'the productivity of the education industry had declined'. The important aspect of this thinking is that per-pupil costs, easily available, became the 'most relevant measure' of success or failure.

By the early 1960s, when the New Theory Movement in administration was in full sail, Callahan's observations of schooling had not changed. He observed pressures facing school leaders similar to those of the early twentieth century. Callahan contended that school administrators 'are still vulnerable to public opinion and to all kinds of pressures, and their perennial problem is how to get enough money to operate the schools from a nation that is reluctant to spend money in the public sectors of the economy' (1962: 255).

While Callahan appreciates the pressures posed by inadequate budgets, he also views administrators as responding to each new wind that blows across the social landscape:

> [Administrators] are being urged, often with the hope of economizing, to introduce new panaceas such as teaching machines and educational television. Unfortunately their training does not enable them to understand the *educational aspects*, advantages and limitations, of these devices; so if they are adopted it is apt to be for public relations purposes. In American education it is important to be able to say that one's school system is abreast of the latest developments.
> (Callahan 1962: 255–256)

The same can be said of Canada today. Following the respite from an obsession with business enjoyed by post-Depression educators (after the 1930s collapse of the market economy) and World War II, Canada has taken up the market models once more. Post-war images of a humane and compassionate state have slowly given way to a kind of egoistic individualism. The term 'me generation' exemplifies this turn, while the youth of 'generation X' suffer the benefits. Now there is a new generation of children to consider.

Little doubt remains that the focus of educational leadership, whether of school administrators or of classroom teachers, over the past decade in Canada as elsewhere, has edged steadily from considerations of pedagogy, curriculum, and community action to tasks of collective planning, standardised testing, and visible accountability. This is hardly surprising for educational administrators who, historically, have received their theoretical grounding as generically administrative rather than as educative (Bates 1984). For teachers, judging by the succession of strikes launched in Canada's most radically market-driven provinces, the transition appears to be more problematic. As Callahan claimed, however, we have taken our educative models from business. In doing so, we have veered sharply to consider consensus over the full consequences of our actions (Hodgkinson 1991). Financial issues have historically dominated thoughts of what stands for quality in education in North America (Greene 1995, cf. Warnock 1973). The administrative tendency to favour budgets over teaching and learning, or management over leadership, flows from our roots in business, and is fed today by tributaries of global, national, and local public policy.

While each era, within a capitalistic society, pits market interests against social welfare, a qualitative difference inheres in the present struggle. Once more we have the ascendancy of market logic in economics, but this time the stakes are higher. Global or 'new' economic transactions of finance and communication take place within compressed dimensions of time and space. Transactions can now be conducted instantaneously, anywhere in the world. Powers once held by nations, in the post-war era for example, now reside in transnational organisations and banks. Companies pull up stakes in one country only to relocate where labour laws are less stringent. For the most part, 'global corporations now outstrip most nation states when it comes to wielding economic and political clout' (Clark and Dopp 2001: 97). Characteristics of this new economy can be seen in a lessening of state influence and an increase in the power of international trade and banking agreements. These agreements, though still adamantly opposed by many citizens, threaten the autonomy of social services, as well as national and local businesses.

Global changes are registered at the national level in an obsession with deficit and debt reduction (McQuaig 1995), economic competition, amalgamation and/or closure of companies, smaller government, and putative efficiencies in every sphere of activity. Financial belt-tightening, however, falls differently on different groups. Women, for instance, have been disproportionately affected by cuts in both the private and public sectors of business and government, leading to unacceptable levels of unemployment, part-time jobs (Young 1999, 2002) and new positions without benefit of pension and medical insurance (Bakker 1996, Brodie 1995). The effect of economic restructuring, overall, has brought with it a dramatic increase in the gap between Canada's wealthy and poor (Jackson and Robinson 2000, Hanly 1998, Burke, Mooers and Shields 2000). Porter's (1967) 'vertical mosaic' of class distinction now more closely resembles an hourglass. In 1989, the wealth of the top 10 per cent of families with children was 39 times that of the bottom 10 per cent. By 1997, this gap had grown to nearly 110 times (Jackson and Robinson 2000: 122).[5]

An examination of restructuring within education, which in Canada remains under provincial jurisdiction, reveals patterns of disparity similar to those noted in other countries (Smyth 1993, 2001). Changes include amalgamation of school districts, larger class sizes, reduction in supports for special needs children, growth of private and home schooling, partnerships between public and private businesses, a dramatic intensification of teachers' work, and a devolution of fiscal management from Ministries of

Education to local districts and schools (Griffith 2001, Kachur and Briton 1998, Sears 2000). Exacerbating the effects of restructuring are cuts in social services, such as school meals and special grants to inner-city schools (Harris 2002), that formerly supported poor families and children.

Underlying each level of restructuring, as well, is the rationality of efficiency born of capitalism unfettered by state control. At the expense of protection to the individual, society, and the environment, new trade and banking agreements actually protect and fortify what Linda McQuaig (2001), writing in the popular press, calls 'an ethic of greed'. McQuaig, drawing liberally on Karl Polanyi's classic text *The Great Transformation*, points to the gradual substitution in contemporary society of this ethic for the more traditional ethic of responsibility. Underlying the changing ethic are two views of human nature: one, of humans as constantly acquisitive and self-serving, and the other of humans as social beings. As Polanyi states, we do not aim to safeguard individual interests in 'the acquisition of material possessions, but rather at ensuring social good will, social status, social assets' (McQuaig 2001: 14; also see Macpherson 1969).

It is this social impetus that teachers bring to their work within schools. It is also the impetus indicated by Foster in his description of administrators as critical humanists:

> Humanists because they appreciate the usual and unusual events of our lives and engage in an effort to develop, challenge, and liberate human souls. They are critical because they are educators and are therefore not satisfied with the status quo; rather, they hope to change individuals for the better and to improve social conditions for all.
>
> (Foster 1986: 18)

The ethic of responsibility for society is implicit, as well, in Hodgkinson's contention that leadership, 'while it has at its disposal a managerial quasi-technology, it is essentially a philosophical endeavour, a kind of humanism. Its overriding mission is the civilization of power' (1978: 100).

Complementing philosophers and social scientists who have mounted critiques of the unbalanced attentiveness shown to science and technology in the modern age, Heidgegger turns our attention to the inherent danger of a mind-set that conceives of everything as open to calculations of control and, at the same time, that fosters feelings of personal and collective helplessness. This tendency – to think of everything as controllable by technology, and the conviction that everything has been taken care of by others – assails our educational systems at every level of leadership.

Essences and enframing

According to Heidegger, an all-encompassing emphasis on technological thinking has led to an 'enframing' that essentially turns all it touches, including people and inanimate objects, into resources to be optimised.

> We shall never experience our relationship to the essence of technology so long as we merely conceive and push forward the technological, put up with it, or evade it. Everywhere we remain unfree and chained to technology, whether we passionately affirm or deny it. But we are delivered over to it in the worst possible way when we regard it as something neutral; for this conception . . . makes us utterly blind to the essence of technology.
>
> (Heidegger 1977: 4)

Heidegger claims we should think of something's essence as a very coming–to–being, as 'essencing'. In this way, we would think of the essence of technology as the way it happens to us these days, to our intelligibility, and to our ways of relating to others.

To understand further Heidegger's sense of a thing's 'essence', we must examine the problems he found with traditional ontological claims and the direction of his own thinking. Heidegger's questions concerning technology emerged relatively late in his overall project which, by his own declaration (Frede 1993), was to clarify the nature of being (*Seinsfrage*, or questions of being).

Deeply influenced by the ancient Greeks, as well as by the phenomenological scholarship of his day, Heidegger nevertheless formed his own theory of Being largely as a critical opposition to both. Concerning the Hellenic tradition, Heidegger rejected the Platonic hierarchical positioning of contemplation of the world (as a Form of the Good) over *techne* (acting *in* the world, as in artistic expression), as well as Aristotle's categories of meaning which would divide substantial entities, existing in the natural world, from their attributes of quantity, quality, relation, place, time, action, affection, possession, and position. Heidegger held that such hierarchies of being, and of categories of substance and attributes, emanated from a false belief that one can read reality from nature. Instead, he argued, one reads meaning into nature. One imposes meaning. He felt that it was a mistake to confuse the act of judging with what is judged, that is, the act with the entity itself. With this, Heidegger moves towards the phenomenological position that meaning as a whole is embedded in the actual life of the person who entertains it.

Yet Heidegger, indebted to Husserl for guidance in phenomenology, later became equally critical of an ego-centred science that would furnish all disciplines with an *a priori* mode of knowing. According to Husserl, 'every object is to be interpreted as it is grasped by an act of comprehension in consciousness; it is something thought of, wished for, doubted, imagined, seen, heard, or known. If we want to understand the nature of all phenomena, we . . . have to work out the precise way in which consciousness intends its object' (Frede 1993: 52; see Heidegger 1996: 32). While Husserl did not deny an actual world that lies beyond consciousness, it was bracketed or kept out of consideration; only the experience of the subject and the content of intentional acts of consciousness were worthy of study. Frede outlines three objections to Husserl's position, as held by Heidegger. First, he objected to the assumption that subjects can adequately know the workings of their own consciousness. Second, Heidegger questioned the possibility of 'bracketing' the world. He saw this as coming dangerously close to turning the objects *of* consciousness into objects *in* consciousness – that is, of ignoring ties to the world that transcend consciousness. Heidegger's third objection was to Husserl's view of reality whereby objects of consciousness are simply given in the stream of consciousness to be studied in a detached manner, a view all too prevalent in the Cartesian world of contemplative rationality centred on the ego. From this position of 'systematic suspicion' (Frede 1993: 53) both of essential forms and of ego-centrism, Heidegger worked towards a holistic conception of human existence as 'Dasein' (as being-in-the-world).

If we are to understand anything, be it a subject (including oneself) or an inanimate object produced or naturally existent, we must explore where it has come from, what it has done or been used for, and where it is going in terms of human purpose and desire. With this demand for temporal continuity, Heidegger (1977) makes his famous statement that the essence of technology is nothing technological. It is not found in the device or machine but, rather, in the overweening mind-set of the modern world that considers all problems to be soluble through rational thought and action.

(Un)Concealment

When one way of seeing overshadows all others, much is hidden from view. For instance, the everyday existence of others, and of objects, is passed over. Heidegger calls this their 'concealment', and its opposite state is one of coming-into-presence, 'unconcealment'. Unconcealment involves the appearance of entities and the role of human practices (e.g. speaking, painting, dancing, teaching) in articulating what shows up as fundamental to understanding. Heidegger's important insight lies in the positive nature of the reliance unconcealment has on its counter-state. As Guignon points out, 'concealment inevitably accompanies every emerging-into-presence . . . [yet] insofar as humans are oblivious to the fact that every disclosure involves concealment, they fall into the illusion of thinking that nothing is hidden and that everything is totally out front' (1993: 19). For example, the emergence of individualism and, latterly, the overwhelmingly enthusiastic attention shown it in our society by some politicians, corporate interests, and the media, tends to conceal the role of shared social practices. The emergence of computer technology as the panacea for communication and learning, conceals what has been lost, for example, eye contact in face-to-face dialogue, non-verbal signs and symbols, and other embodiments of discourse. When 'what shows up at a particular time presents itself as the last word about reality, the only game in town' (Guignon 1993: 19), we lose sight of our own history and close off our imaginations from conceiving alternatives.

Heidegger, in looking for venues through which to illustrate unconcealment – of ways to see the world both historically and imaginatively as it might become – turned to poetry and visual arts. He felt that artworks were capable of formulating and bringing to realisation 'what is definitive of a people's form of life' (Guignon 1993: 23). For Heidegger, certain works of art act as focal point for meditation; their beauty lies in the pleasure people take from understanding existence more clearly. This they are able to do when art, encapsulating its own history as well as its appearance, reveals truth as coexistent with lived experience. As an example, Heidegger points to Van Gogh's painting of wooden clogs. The well-worn texture of these clogs, speaking of dawn-to-dusk labour in the field, of a weary home-coming, of village life, draws the viewer beyond the painting itself to contemplate lived experience, not only of the peasant woman who wore the clogs but of other labourers in other conditions. The artwork, in revealing the shoes as 'they function in and embody her life and world', shows us more than 'a truth of a merely particular thing like a pair of shoes'; the painting's truth is a truth of all that is (Heidegger 1976: 648). Heidegger describes this going beyond everyday reality in several ways. In addition to unconcealment, he talks of coming-to-light, or of entering-the-clearing. Each descriptor signifies a greater understanding of the world and of the individual's place within it.

These are examples of how we can think outside the boundaries of what is immediately before us. As this chapter focuses on the relationship between school leadership and technology, let us examine how an understanding of it, in its essence, can lead to greater freedom.

Achieving a free relationship

If Heidegger is correct in his claim that a modern understanding of technology, in rendering everything calculable, carries with it the potential to 'warp, confuse, and lay waste our nature' (1966: 54), we may ask where the danger lurks and what we can do to avoid it. Drawing a parallel from art, it would seem that freedom from the harmful effects of technology lies in reflecting consciously and purposely, first, the essence of technology itself, and then, non-technological ways of world-disclosing. This implies attending closely to what we, ourselves, bring to technology. What is our history, and what do we hope to accomplish with the equipment now before us? Such questions embody a 'meditative' existence.

Heidegger describes two kinds of thinking, each justifiable in its own way: calculative and meditative. Calculative thinking, though it may or may not work with numbers or machines, 'computes ever anew, ever more promising and at the same time more economical possibilities' (Heidegger 1966: 46). By assuming a distance from life (i.e. objectivity), we exclude uncomfortable thoughts about the ethical dimensions of our acts; in many cases, this distancing comes to signify a *'flight from thinking'* (Heidegger 1966: 45, original emphasis). Heidegger points out that meditation upon our role in everyday events (our subjective involvement) calls for great effort and practice, and requires 'more delicate care than any other genuine craft' (1966: 47). But, without such meditation, we lose our 'rootedness', pursue superficial goals, and experience anxiety. As we become shackled to computers, for example, we 'fall bondage to them' (Heidegger 1966: 54).

Heidegger clearly is concerned with the human *distress* caused by the technological understanding of being, rather than with the destruction caused by specific technologies (Dreyfus 1995). The distress is only exacerbated by the unrealistic belief that nature can be controlled and that science and technology will solve all our problems – even those of physical disability, illness and aging, market misfortune, and accidental harm. Heidegger roundly condemns the 'view that man, by the peaceful release, transformation, storage, and channeling of the energies of physical nature, could render the human condition . . . tolerable for everybody and happy in all respects' (1991: 53).[6]

Heidegger's first suggestion, in avoiding this falsely based optimism, is to diligently seek understanding through the difficult process of questioning what lies immediately before us. Rather than clinging 'one-sidedly to a single idea', or running 'down a one-track course of ideas', we should 'engage ourselves with what at first sight does not go together at all . . . It is one thing to have heard and read something, that is, merely to take notice; it is another thing to understand what we have heard and read, that is, to ponder' (Heidegger 1966: 54). In finding a route through what does not appear as straightforwardly clear, we come to Heidegger's second suggestion, that we become engaged in the world around us. In action, Heidegger distinguishes between the rational and the engaged approach – between 'knowing that' and 'knowing how' (Taylor 1993: 327).

Agency as a way beyond

When we shift our gaze from the 'what is' of technology, however, to 'what it does', we begin to ask different questions. For a start, we ask about history. As we examine a particular tool and our experience with it, we need to be aware of 'what we are attending from' (Taylor 1993: 325). Then, too, we ask questions about our use of the tool in relation to where we are going. The student at her computer, surfing the web for material suitable for her history assignment, for instance, may reflect upon her life and studies when she visited a library and picked from the shelf, not only the desired article but also several additional texts on her topic. Then, too, she may reflect upon her purpose in writing the article. Is it to satisfy her teacher? Or is it because she is truly curious about exploring all aspects of her chosen subject? If the latter, she may come to think of her computer-accessed web sites in an entirely fresh context. She may, indeed, come to see objectively presented information as contrary to what she considers to be worthy of her attention. This Taylor, after Heidegger, would identify as her escape from 'atomism' – the separation of facts from their having some role to play in one's goals (Taylor 1993: 319; also Feenberg 1999).

The young girl at her computer bears an optimistic message. While Heidegger holds that we are always already in conditions of concealment, we are at the same time in the process of coming to understanding. This coming-to-the-light takes place as we listen and hear, and act. We are not 'simply constrained to obey' (Heidegger 1977: 25).

School leadership as essencing

While there are those who consider Heidegger to be essentially deterministic concerning technology (Feenberg 1999, 2001; Thomson 2000), he more accurately contends that the challenge is to use technologies, yet keep ourselves free to let go of them at any time:

> It would be foolish to attack technology blindly. It would be short-sighted to condemn it as the work of the devil. We depend on technical devices; they even challenge us to ever greater advances. But suddenly and unaware we find ourselves so firmly shackled to technological devices that we fall into bondage to them.
>
> (Heidegger 1966: 53–54)

In his discussion of technology, albeit often circuitous and littered with newly minted words, Heidegger tosses down the gauntlet before educational leaders. He states most emphatically that the ultimate meaning of calculative thinking leads to an avoidance of what is most essential to humankind. In his discussion of 'thinking' – what surely must stand as the most important educational tract in his work – Heidegger declares that the very foundation of what it means to be human has been overlooked in the modern world where applied science and calculative thinking dominate our lives (1966: 20).

I believe that Heidegger's approach to what he defines as the problem of technology, that is, its impulse to frame sentient and non-sentient entities as ever open to manipulation and calculation, takes three routes that can assist school leaders who seriously seek ethical direction. The first invites one to consider broadened horizons of knowing; the second surrounds the complementary nature of concealment and unconcealment; and the third is embedded in the concept of temporality. Heidegger does not establish a map that will guide a smooth passage, or even promise a safe harbour at the end of the journey. The routes suggested by Heidegger are rather like a braid. Each twists in and around, crossing over and under the other two.

The most important message of Heidegger, for the present analysis of school leadership, is ontological – the essence of being human presupposes an inhabited world, and contemplation of that world. The person understands her world in various ways, theoretically, practically, and caringly. To Heidegger, these ways represent different kinds of knowing the world. But among these, he selects the unifying term – care – to designate the basic feature in us that constitutes all our involvements in the world. As Frede describes this,

> The decisive characteristic in our relation to the world as such, which includes ourselves as our ultimate point of reference, is conditioned by the care that allows us to treat everything as part of our *project* in the largest sense of the world . . . We project ourselves, our whole existence, into the world and understand ourselves as well as everything in the world in terms of the *possibilities* within the design or projection that we make of ourselves.
>
> (Frede 1993: 63, original emphasis)

Heidegger's message encourages educators to consider a 'project' and, in so doing, to prepare a clearing in which children may discover art, numeracy, language, science and technology, and other approaches to the world. In each discovering, the child moves beyond the object immediately before her, and even beyond her own evaluation of the object, to engage in meanings shared with others about where it has come from, how it comes to be, and where and how it may continue to be.

School administrators tend, especially in the present climate of Canada's most radically market-oriented provinces, to view their tasks as distinct from those of teachers. In addition to traditional distinctions between the two roles, teachers and vice-principals of British Columbia have belonged since the late 1980s to separate professional bodies. Bill 160 in Ontario recently formed a similar division of administrators from teachers in that province. This tactic not only ensures internal divisions within schools and a fading of democratic participation in decision-making, but also contributes to the added distancing of administrators from pedagogical and curricular responsibility referred to by Callahan and others. Yet, in my own research of restructuring within coastal communities (Harris 2002), I have found leaders (administrators, teachers, and parents) who adhere to Ministry orders, regardless of the impact this will have on children. They are not happy to suspend their core values in this manner, but they see no alternative. These leaders exhibit a technological rationality in that they perceive their duty as following the rules and regulations of a higher authority.

I also see school leaders who resist what they consider to be the most damaging changes, yet work to fulfil what they perceive as their responsibility to children in their care. These leaders provide students with as many cushions as possible against the worst excesses of economic restructuring and social upheaval. They ensure that school lunches are served, they maintain close ties with parents, and they oversee safe school environments. Like leaders in the other cohort, they expect and usually realise steadily improving academic levels of student achievement. These educators continue to speak out against the changes they see to be unjust, fully aware of the professional risks they run. It is not that good intentions, and even good acts, will close the gap between those who enjoy privileged lives, and those who live in poverty. We can all, in the spirit of Heidegger, however, examine our reasons for becoming teachers, our fulfilment of initial goals, and where our present choices may lead.

Concerning the choices we face, Heidegger insists always on an oppositional reality whereby each moral act assumes significance only in relation to its counter-possibilities. We can grow thoughtless only because we can think; we can become deaf to the words of others only because we can hear; we can hate only because we are capable of loving. Heidegger expresses each condition in terms of becoming, of growth. Each thought and action, in this view, can be considered together with its alternative, for both have flourished in the past. The drive for competition today, for example, can be weighed in its historical struggle to dominate those who argue for cooperation. In other words, neither competition nor cooperation are imperatives of human nature. Following Heidegger's lead, we would view these two together, for cooperation flourishes in so far as competition is a possibility. As Heidegger points out in the larger context, each human life is sweeter for facing its finitude (Hatab 2000).

Heidegger would not have us dichotomise phenomena in order to place them in opposition to one another. Rather, he tells us that, by holding them both at once, we avoid the 'flight from thinking' that would accept one and ignore the other. In administrative terms, this would be equivalent to the leader who, considering herself a 'thinker', spurns organisational tasks of management. It appears far more common that school leaders engage in the opposite practice; they concern themselves with management tasks of solving immediately urgent problems, but often before they consider the worth of the problem to be solved. We need to ask ourselves about each choice – to meditate, according to Heidegger, on what each conceals and reveals. Such questioning often opens up a space for insight and imagination. Heidegger indicates that this attitude of openness to the world – what he calls Releasement – once awakened, becomes habitual.

Summary

In exploring my initial question, about the effect of technology as calculable thought and action on our everyday lives, I turned to school leaders who, having chosen teaching and related leadership action to make a difference, find themselves cast in management roles. By this, I mean that organisations – and those who work within them at all levels – in responding to the emergent political context of neo-liberalism, increasingly focus on profit margins, down-sizing of the work force, ever-expanding tasks for those who remain, and other business imperatives. Their task has become one of effecting means as determined by others, rather than of deciding upon ends or goals. The work of educational leaders, in this manner, takes on the mantra of efficiency and effectiveness (Stein 2001), often at the cost of human health and well-being. Unfortunately, such work is often cloaked in a mystic veil of necessity, leading to perceptions of no alternative, referred to by critics as the TINA (there is no alternative) Syndrome. In searching for a way past such technological knowledge and action, Heidegger advocates incremental interventions supportive of 'technological democratisation' in which entities and actions may emerge from their former mysterious embodiment, or, as Heidegger puts it, from their concealment.

In this chapter, I have identified barriers to humane interaction with technology as:

1 a belief in the power of science and technology to solve all human problems (*enframing*);
2 an involvement with the here-and-now (as part of labour intensification) to the point where much of what stands before one is hidden

(*concealed*) while the essential properties of pedagogy (its *unconcealment*) increasingly come under siege;
3 an *un-free relationship* to technology whereby one's self-assessment becomes dependent upon the purposes and intentions of others; and
4 a state in which the embodiment of technology becomes that of failure and the avenues for *agency* – e.g. school and community leadership, political action – recede.

These are some of the danger points that affect school leaders with particular virulence. Each can be traced in the everyday lives of educators at work. The challenge for educators in British Columbia's 'new era' and Ontario and Alberta's not-so-new era, will be to mount small but persistent resistances to each feature of technological thought and action, and to show by example that alternative ways of Being are possible.

Notes

1 McLuhan's claim, specifically, was that the '"message" of any medium or technology is the change of scale or pace or pattern that it introduces into human affairs' (1994: 8) and that it is the 'medium that shapes and controls the scale and forms of human association and action' (1994: 9).
2 Education in Canada falls under provincial jurisdiction. One finds wide variations, thus, in curriulum content, forms of governance, and economic policy and supporting social services.
3 A discussion of Heidegger's flirtation with fascism is beyond the scope of this chapter. To pursue this complex affiliation, see, for example, Bourdieu's (1991) dismissal of Heidegger because of his links with fascism and his later failure to apologise, and Hatab's 'Epilogue' which traces several threads in Heidegger's later writing that would indicate the West's (and perhaps Heidegger's own) failure in perpetrating the project of willful domination that led to catastrophe and the extermination camps (Hatab 2000: 205).
4 Primary citations draw on the later Heidegger as recorded in his *Question Concerning Technology* and *Discourse on Thinking*, both of which explore the uses and abuses of technology and its accompanying rationality by people as they interact with the contemporary world.
5 These estimates are based on the Statistics Canada report for 1997. Like most statistics, they give the direction of change rather than its exact details. While the market income of the poorest 10 per cent of families with children fell by 66 per cent between 1989 and 1997, for example, their actual cash income fell 'only' 11 per cent when government transfers are computed into the statistic.
6 Marcuse, one-time student of Heidegger and a spokesperson for the brief renaissance of critical awareness in 1960s USA, picks up on this theme when he names as an example of Western 'Happy Consciousness' the numbing inability of American society to realise the limitations inherent in their Good Life, or to become more politically involved in the distribution of its bounty (Marcuse 1968: 80).

References

Bakker, I. (ed.) (1996) *Rethinking Restructuring: Gender and Change in Canada*, Toronto: University of Toronto Press.

Bates, R. (1984) 'Towards a critical practice of educational administration', in T. Sergiovanni and J. Corbally (eds) *Leadership and Organizational Culture: New Perspectives on Administrative Theory and Practice*, Chicago: University of Illinois.

Berman, M. (1984) *The Reenchantment of the World*, New York: Bantam Books.

Bourdieu, P. (1991) *The Political Ontology of Martin Heidegger*, Stanford: Stanford University Press.

Brodie, J. (1995) *Politics on the Margins: Restructuring and the Canadian Women's Movement*, Halifax: Fernwood.

Brubaker, R. (1984) *The Limits of Rationality: An Essay in the Social and Moral Thought of Max Weber*, London: George Allen & Unwin.

Burke, M., Mooers, C. and Shields, J. (eds) (2000) *Restructuring and Resistance: Canadian Public Policy in an Age of Global Capitalism*, Halifax: Fernwood.

Callahan, R. E. (1962) *Education and the Cult of Efficiency*, Chicago: University of Chicago Press.

Clark, T. and Dopp, S. (2001) *Challenging McWorld*, Ottawa: Canadian Centre for Policy Alternatives.

Connell, R. W., Ashendon, D. J., Kessler, S., and Dowsett, G. W. (1982) *Making the Difference: Schools, Families and Social Division*, London: George Allen & Unwin.

Dillard, C. (1995) 'Leading with her life: An African American feminist (re)interpretation of leadership for an urban high school principal', *Educational Administration Quarterly* 31: 539-563.

Dreyfus, H. L. (1995) 'Heidegger on gaining a free relation to technology', in A. Feenberg and A. Hannay, *Technology and the Politics of Knowledge*, Bloomington: Indiana University Press.

Evans, R. (1992) 'From applied science to hermeneutics: Requirements of a normative science of educational administration', in E. Miklos and E. Ratsoy (eds) *Educational Leadership: Challenge and Change*, Edmonton: University of Alberta.

Feenberg, A. (1999) *Questioning Technology*, New York: Routledge.

Feenberg, A. (2000) 'The ontic and the ontological in Heidegger's philosophy of technology: Response to Thomson', *Inquiry* 43: 445–450.

Foster, W. (1986) *Paradigms and Promises: New Approaches to Educational Administration*, New York: Prometheus Books.

Franklin, U. (1991/1999) *The Real World of Technology*, Toronto: Anansi.

Frede, D. (1993) 'The question of being: Heidegger's project', in C. Guignon (ed.) *The Cambridge Companion to Heidegger*, Cambridge: Cambridge University Press.

Giddens, A. (1985) *Capitalism and Modern Social Theory: An Analysis of the Writings of Marx, Durkheim and Max Weber*, Cambridge: Cambridge University Press.

Greene, M. (1995) 'What counts as philosophy of education?', in W. Kohli (ed.) *Critical Conversations in Philosophy of Education*, London: Routledge.

Greenfield, T. B., and Ribbins, P. (1993) *Greenfield on Educational Administration: Towards a Humane Science*, London: Routledge.

Griffith, A. L. (2001) 'Texts, tyranny, and transformation: Educational restructuring in Ontario', in J. Portelli and R. P. Solomon (eds) *The Erosion of Democracy in Education: From Critique to Possibilities*, Calgary: Detselig.

Gronn, P. (1982) 'Neo-Taylorism in educational administration?', *Educational Administration Quarterly* 18, 4: 17–35.

Gronn, P. (1999) 'Systems of distributed leadership in organizations', Paper presented to the Organization Theory Special Interest Group, American Educational Research Association, 22 April, Montreal, Canada.

Gronn, P. (2002) 'Distributed leadership as a unit of analysis', *Leadership Quarterly* 13, 4: 423-451.

Guignon, C. (1993) 'Introduction', in C. Guignon (ed.) *The Cambridge Companion to Heidegger*, Cambridge: Cambridge University Press.

Habermas, J. (1971) *Knowledge and Human Interests*, Boston: Beacon Press.

Habermas, J. (1984) *The Theory of Communicative Action: Reason and Rationalization of Society*, Boston: Beacon Press.

Hanly, K. (1998) 'Restructuring and the welfare state: Learner, meaner, and inequitable', in L. Groarke, *The Ethics of the New Economy*, Waterloo: Wilfried Laurier University Press.

Harris, C. E. (1998) 'Administration as pedagogy or as new management: Principles and practices in an era of restructuring', in E. Cramer and J. Panagapka (eds) *Teacher of Teachers: Papers in Honour of Lois Choksy*, Langley, BC: Tall Timbers.

Harris, C. E. (2002) 'Community schools fulfil different needs', Victoria *Times Colonist*, February 11, A 7.

Hatab, L. J. (2000) *Ethics and Finitude: Heideggerian Contributions to Moral Philosophy*, Oxford: Rowman & Littlefield.

Heidegger, M. (1966) *Discourse on Thinking*, New York: Harper & Row.

Heidegger, M. (1976) 'The origin of the work of art', in A. Hofstadter and R. Kuhns (eds), *Philosophies of Art and Beauty*, Chicago: University of Chicago Press.

Heidegger, M. (1977) *The Question Concerning Technology and Other Essays*, New York: Harper & Row.

Heidegger, M. (1991) *Poetry, Language, Thought*, trans. A. Hopstadter, New York: Harper & Row.

Heidegger, M. (1996) *Being and Time*, New York: State University of New York Press.

Hodgkinson, C. (1978) *Towards a Philosophy of Administration*, Oxford: Basil Blackwell.

Hodgkinson, C. (1991) *Educational Leadership: The Moral Art*, New York: State University of New York Press.

Jackson, A. and Robinson, D. (2000) *Falling Behind: The State of Working Canada 2000*, Ottawa: Canadian Centre for Policy Alternatives.

Jonas, H. (1984) *The Imperative of Responsibility: In Search of an Ethics for the Technological Age*, Chicago: University of Chicago Press.

Kachur, J. L. and Briton, D. (1998) 'Alberta education: Retooling through deschooling', in L. Groarke (ed.) *The Ethics of the New Economy: Restructuring and Beyond*, Waterloo: Wilfried Laurier Press.

Macpherson, C. B. (1969) *The Political Theory of Possessive Individualism*, Oxford: Clarendon Press.

Marcuse, H. (1968) *One-Dimensional Man*, Boston: Beacon Press.

McLuhan, M. (1994) *Understanding Media: The Extensions of Man*, Cambridge: MIT Press.

McQuaig, M. (1995) *Shooting the Hippo: Death by Deficit and Other Canadian Myths*, Toronto: Viking.

McQuaig, M. (2001) *All You Can Eat: Greed, Lust and the New Capitalism*, Toronto: Penguin/Viking.

Mills, C. W. (1959) *The Sociological Imagination*, London: Oxford University Press.

Moll, M. (ed.) (2001) *But It's only a Tool!: The Politics of Technology and Education Reform*, Ottawa: Canadian Centre for Policy Alternatives.

Noble, D. (2002) 'Digital diploma mills: The automation of higher education', http:www.firstmonday.dk/issues/issue3_1/noble/index.html.

Parker, I. (2001) 'Absolute PowerPoint: The software that tells you what to think', *New Yorker*, May, 76-87.

Polt, R. (1999) *Heidegger: An Introduction*, Ithaca: Cornell University Press.

Porter, J. (1967) *The Vertical Mosaic: An Analysis of Social Class and Power in Canada*, Toronto: University of Toronto Press.

Rose, E. (2000) *Hyper Texts: The Language and Culture of Educational Computing*, London, ON: Althouse.

Sears, A. (2000) 'Education for a lean world', in M. Burke, C. Mooers and J. Shields (eds), *Restructuring and Resistance: Canadian Public Policy in an Age of Global Capitalism*, Halifax: Fernwood.

Stein, J. G. (2002) *The Cult of Efficiency*, Toronto: Anansi Press.

Smyth, J. (ed.) (1993) *A Socially Critical View of the Self-Managing School*, New York: Falmer.

Smyth, J. (2001) *Critical Politics of Teachers' Work: An Australian Perspective*, New York: Peter Lang.

Taylor, C. (1993) 'Engaged agency and background in Heidegger', in C. Guignon (ed.) *The Cambridge Companion to Heidegger*, Cambridge: Cambridge University Press.

Thomson, I. (2000) 'What's wrong with being a technological essentialist? A response to Feenberg', *Inquiry* 43: 429-444.

Tönnies, F. (1955 [1887]) *Community and Association*, London: Routledge & Kegan Paul.

Warnock, M. (1973) 'Toward a definition of quality in education', in R. S. Peters (ed.) *The Philosophy of Education*, Oxford: Oxford University Press.

Weber, M. (1958) *Max Weber: Essays in Sociology*, Oxford: Oxford University Press.

Weber, M. (1978) *Economy and Society: An Outline of Interpretive Sociology*, Berkeley: University of California Press.

Young, B. (1999) 'Is it just a matter of time? Part-time teaching employment in Alberta', in T. Harrison and J. Kachur (eds) *Contested Classrooms: Education, Globalization and Democracy in Alberta*, Edmonton: University of Alberta Press.

Young, B. (2002) 'The "Alberta advantage": "DeKleining" career prospects for women educators', in C. Reynolds (ed.) *Women and School Leadership: International Perspectives*, New York: State University of New York Press.

Young, J. and Levin, B. (1998) *Understanding Canadian Schools: An Introduction to Educational Administration*, Toronto: Harcourt Brace.

Chapter 10

Vice and virtue
The value of values in administration

William Foster

In this chapter I intend to explore several topics. One is a brief analysis of the history of the field of educational administration, and its reliance on a form of scientism. Then I intend to look at the recent popularity of moral theory in the field, and how a return to the development of virtue might be useful for the field. This is followed by an analysis of the strengths and weaknesses of the communitarian argument, followed finally by a review of alternative thought that might help to reorient educational administration.

The early years: Starting with a mission

The early history of the field of administration in education was a history inspired by positivism, scientism, and progressivism. While the early practitioners of the administrative art, in the nineteenth century at least, tended to be seen as, and see themselves as, statesmen (Callahan 1962: Ch. 1), by the turn of the century it was the business executive who had become the model for educators. And, as cottage industry became replaced by large-scale industrial concerns, business turned towards ways to rationalise the production process. Scientific management, as developed by F. W. Taylor (1947), became an influential movement in the United States. It had as a fundamental purpose increasing efficiency in the workplace, and did so through time and motion studies, routinisation, and planning.

Through the influence of a newly established professoriate in educational administration, scientific management became a model for administering schools. One of its academic proponents – Cubberley – found that with scientific management 'it will be possible for any school system to maintain a continuous survey of all the different phases of its work, through tests made by its corps of efficiency experts, and to detect weak points in its work almost as soon as they appear' (Cubberley 1916: 325). Tyack found that these professors of educational administration 'tried to develop "scientific" ways of measuring inputs and outputs in school systems as a tool of management' (Tyack 1974: 136). Many practitioners and scholars of educational administration, then, in an attempt to be seen by the business and other communities as being 'progressive', made scientific management their mantra.

An unrelated but supporting epistemology arose around the same time. Logical positivism, which had a tremendous impact on 'administrative science', made a number of claims regarding 'true' knowledge. One was that truth could only be determined if it could be demonstrated logically, as in a statement such as 'an apple is not a pear', or empirically, through publicly demonstrable and falsifiable knowledge obtained through scientific experiment. Values, ethics, and moral theory became, then, a function of the emotions, neither scientific nor logical; while important, values were extra-scientific and not a subject of concern for administrators who wished to impose a rule of efficiency on their organisations.

This form of positivism was carried through the writings of administrative theorists and influenced generations of scholars interested in the practice of administration. A leading proponent – perhaps *the* leading proponent – of this way of thinking was Herbert Simon, whose text, *Administrative Behaviour* (1965 [1947]), published in the post-war period, impacted administrative preparation programmes in all types of fields. Simon took the position that once policy-makers had decided on policy for an organisation it was up to administrators to carry out that policy in the most efficient manner possible. To do so, the administrator should turn to the tools of science, and utilise them in an objective and value-free manner.

In educational administration, the positivist emphasis and the legacy of Taylorism led to the *theory movement*, wherein theorists in administration tried to find the behavioural attributes of administrators that led to success. The theory movement and its attendant respect for social science and the value of prediction and explanation led to the rejection of what Halpin, himself a leading proponent of an administrative science, called 'the heritage of the humanities' (Halpin 1966: 296), and to preparation programmes that stressed the technical and mechanical aspects of the field.

The failure of the mission: Predictability and social science

Social science and the resulting administrative science are based on what might be a myth: that human behaviour and actions are ultimately predictable. If such prediction is achievable, such a science will develop the laws and procedures for correct administrative action within organisational situations; such a science will account for the positive definition of laws for managerial behaviour. Simon put it this way:

> In so far as decisions can be said to be 'correct', they can be translated into factual propositions. Their ethical element must be eliminated before the terms 'true' and 'false' can be applied to them. Similarly, the propositions of a practical science must be put in hypothetical form in order to eliminate the ethical element.
>
> (Simon 1965: 248)

Simon was thus able to transport both the emotivist and positivist doctrines into an administrative 'science', providing thereby the grist for the mill of those social scientists concerned with the management of organisations.

If we turn to the work of Alasdair MacIntyre (1984), we can find the historical context for this claim. He suggests that this move to science was largely supported by the emergence in the twentieth century of the modern corporation and the transition from the model of the owner/entrepreneur to that of the manager/bureaucrat. The administrator in public service and the manager in private organisations became two of the major archetypes of modern society. This means that the manager/bureaucrat became a moral symbol for society, a *character*. A character, as developed by MacIntyre (1984), is a symbolic representation of the moral order. MacIntyre identifies three characters in modern society: the rich aesthete, the therapist, and the manager/bureaucrat (1984: Ch. 3). Each carries his own way of ordering the moral world, and each presents to us the priorities and values of social life.

As a character, the manager/bureaucrat becomes one of the central roles upon which the rest of social life is modelled. But it is this role that is now an emotivist one: it is a role to which we impute power and control, and it is a role sculpted by a managerial or administrative science. The manager in the corporation and the social scientist in the university together work to develop a science of management based on the prediction and control of human behaviour. Such a science is based on an instrumental rationality where humans are seen as 'resources', or as means to the achievement of organisational ends. It also develops a language of technique through which managers and administrators learn to motivate, inspire, control, reward, and punish employees. Educational administration, itself replete with dogmas drawn from administrative science, is but a more specific example of this general feature of Western social life.

The manager/bureaucrat is a role endemic to the modern organisation, and one to which we impute certain strengths. Among these is the ability to predict organisational behaviour and development. However,

> Consider the following possibility: that what we are oppressed by is not power, but impotence: that one key reason why the presidents of large corporations do not, as some radical critics believe, control the

United States is that they do not even succeed in controlling their own corporations; that all too often, when imputed organizational skill and power are deployed and the desired effect follows, all that we have witnessed is the same kind of sequence as that to be observed when a clergyman is fortunate enough to pray for rain just before the unpredicted end of a drought; that the levers of power – one of managerial expertise's own key metaphors – produce effects unsystematically and too often only coincidentally related to the effects of which their users boast.

(MacIntyre 1984: 75)

The reason for this lack of administrative power lies in the nature of systematic predictability for the social sciences. Such predictability is probably possible within certain natural scientific disciplines, but in the social sciences it remains elusive.

The moral turn

Given the failure of social science in general, and educational administration in particular, to develop generalisable laws of human and managerial behaviour, it is not surprising that there was a rediscovery of ethical and moral arguments. However, such arguments themselves became in some ways reductionist ones, where moral theory and valuation could be put on top of conventional administrative behaviour. Sergiovanni (1990), for example, became a proponent of something he labelled 'value-added leadership', wherein traditional management models were to be reconceived through an emphasis on those values that might lead to extraordinary performance. Modern texts on educational administration do, in a similar fashion, make reference to the importance of values. They will often, for example, reference transformational leadership where Burns (1978), in his seminal work, suggested that leadership that resulted in the transformation of a person or group was ultimately based in morality.

Vices and virtue

At issue here, however, is that the emphasis on value is often located in rule-based systems where the culture of the system is expected to reflect rules of behaviour. This proves to be unsatisfactory because such rules often cannot resolve fundamental moral questions. Thus, to take a Kantian stand that 'lying is always wrong' cannot help in a situation wherein a lie might be morally obligatory (e.g. to save an innocent life). MacIntyre (1984) addresses the incommensurability of various moral arguments made in contemporary times. His point, at least as I take it, is that the various moral debates that occur and the adding of value to institutional life cannot substitute for the understanding of vice and the development of virtue.

MacIntyre suggests that it is through the formation of character that virtues are developed, and character is dependent on *particular* friends, families and communities. He writes that

> what we have to learn from heroic societies is twofold: first that all morality is always to some degree tied to the socially local and particular and that the aspirations of the morality of modernity to a universality freed from all particularity is an illusion; and secondly that there is no way to possess the virtues except as part of a tradition in which we inherit them from a series of predecessors in which series heroic societies hold first place.
>
> (MacIntyre 1984: 127)

The virtues are, then, those attributes that lead, when fully developed, to the achievement of excellence in a society, and that excellence, for MacIntyre, depends on the development of *a practice,* defined as

> any coherent and complex form of socially established cooperative human activity through which goods internal to that form of activity are realized in the course of trying to achieve those standards of excellence which are appropriate to, and partially definitive of, that form of activity, with the result that human powers to achieve excellence, and human conception of the ends and goods involved, are systematically extended.
>
> (MacIntyre 1984: 187)

In light of the previous discussion, then, the achievement of excellence in schools, for example, depends not on adding value or changing cultures, but on the development of a community of practitioners who encourage virtuous activity in each other. The modernist agenda, however, tends to counteract communitarian efforts at achieving practices of excellence because of emphases on individualistic achievement driven by economic forces.

The development of community

In this way, the school organisation came (and continues) to be seen in an almost totally instrumental way: as a tool to achieve those social goals deemed important in a particular period, but almost always focusing on the development of a productive and employable citizen. This instrumental view would, then, often relegate schools to being tools of the economy, and, while education itself seemed to remain universally valued as an inherent good, the school-as-organisation became valued for what it could or should accomplish in relation, largely, to the economy.

This situation, of course, was not unique to schools as institutions. Rather, it seemed to be a phenomenon inherent in the development of the modern Western state, and has been commented on by thinkers as diverse as Tönnies, Durkheim, Weber, and Habermas. Each of them suggested in some fashion or other that a bureaucratic society advanced an instrumentalist notion of being that often led to anomie and disenchantment. MacIntyre (1984) goes so far as to suggest that the bureaucratic/instrumentalist orientation has in fact corrupted moral language entirely.

The instrumental orientation is also a contractual one, wherein the use of persons for instrumental ends is achieved through the establishment and enforcement of contracts. This reflects the type of *Gesellschaft* society Tönnies (1957) wrote about, a society based on enforced obligation. *Gemeinschaft* – the contrast he used – becomes a condition attenuated by the ever-increasing dominance of instrumental and contractual social logic. The *Gemeinschaft* condition, of course, refers to the community spirit that pervaded most social groupings prior to the industrialisation of the world.

One can imagine a time in history when the term 'community' was not problematic: taken for granted and a part of the cultural landscape, there was no need to 'create' or 'build' community. But the apparent erosion of community in much of our world has us looking to define it and, by naming it, develop it. There are multiple ways of investigating the term, and it has become common to use it somewhat indiscriminately, particularly with regard to building a school community.

Ways of looking

Approaches to community and notions of community have a history of being based on specific philosophical and even metaphysical assumptions. In administration, in particular, the idea of community has had several orientations and expressions. But it is important to note that community is determined more by social structure than by administrative fiat; the best administrative intentions can be inadequate to overcoming the structural properties of large systems. Merz and Furman make this point when they observe that

> Simply *thinking* of schools differently, as communities rather than as organizations, does not alter the deep structures of the school as organization, structures that are institutionalized and that help create the *gesellschaftlich* climate of schools.
>
> (Merz and Furman 1997: 86)

Indeed, the structural variable of size itself might be an overriding consideration in the establishment of community (Merz and Furman 1997). As complex systems increase in size, organisational theorists tell us that mechanisms for both differentiation and integration are required (Burns and Stalker 1961); these, in turn, can diminish the face-to-face vitality of communities by establishing hierarchies of *distance* (e.g. *central* office, *local* control), or create artificial ways of bonding and loyalty-formation (e.g. creating corporate 'culture' through performance awards).

This is not to say that educational or other administrators cannot participate significantly in the reformation of structure. The leading proponents of this way of thinking aimed, in fact, to provide conditions for the emergence of community, but this may take a substantial reworking of basic administrative and organisational assumptions and not just the renaming of organisational characteristics. It may take both *rethinking* and *proaction.*

Rethinking suggests the reconceptualisation of schools, not as organisations but as communities. This is to say, to consider changing our metaphors-in-use regarding schools, as Sergiovanni (1994) and others have suggested. Adopting the metaphor of community to describe schools has, of course, enormous implications. Among these could be included a restructuring of classroom organisation, a redefinition of the role of administration, and a review of the relationship between stakeholders.

Restructuring classroom organisation along the lines implied by a metaphor of community might mean that, for example, age-graded classrooms, originally begun to facilitate bureaucratic efficiency (Goodlad and Anderson 1987), would be recast in terms of service dimensions. Various options, such as those explored in Meier (1995), could be investigated. These could include teachers who stay with pupils beyond the one grade level, students grouped according to criteria other than age, and a curriculum determined by community standards.

Redefining the administrative role is also a complex endeavour. The historical development of administration has been a reflection of systems of control, and the legacy of scientific management is not unimportant in attempting to understand the field. It could be claimed, with some legitimacy, that the field has been founded on some base assumptions of the importance of efficiency, the value of impartiality, and the dominance of individualism. Efficiency has been an end-state of the administrative initiative, as Tyack (1974) and others have shown. This means that the role of administration was not the articulation of values but their implementation in the most efficient manner: administrators put into practice what policy-makers decree, and they do so in a rational (some would say rationalistic) manner, where rationality is the most efficient/effective path of moving from the current state to the desired one. This, in many ways, is inimical to a communal focus on value articulation and the often necessary subversion of means to ends; that is, to often take the more inefficient path if its meanderings seem to accomplish more important results.

Administration, as this has emerged as a discipline, has not only been committed to efficiency but has also valued the idea of impartiality: that is, there are no special cases and an ethos of equal justice is the goal. This, as Perrow (1979) has noted, is a hallmark of bureaucratic systems and establishes the basis of systemic rewards on achievement rather than ascription. It tends to prevent, for example, nepotism, and attempts to provide for equal opportunities for success within large-scale systems. This, in a word, reflects an ethos of justice (Gilligan 1993). The impartiality of such an endeavour can, however, substitute rules and procedures for personal judgements. In so doing, the ethos of care can be devalued. Formulating an ethic of care as a guiding principle is not necessarily to abandon rules of procedure, but rather to prioritise systems so that administrative judgement takes precedence over the universal application of rules. Such normative standards, it could be claimed, provide a framework for those communal environments (e.g. the family, the neighbourhood) that administer justice in a caring way. They also provide, certainly, the basis for a theological orientation that allows for forgiveness and redemption. To redraw administration upon *this* particular template is, however, a daunting task given both the historical orientations of the field and the characteristics of the greater system of which it is a part.

And the system of which it is a part is one that values (beyond, perhaps, what is necessary) the concept of individualism. Individualism is expressed in educational systems through many ways, including norms of achievement, reward structures, career paths, and other sociologically dense phenomena. Individualism is not necessarily *contra* community; however, the values and norms of systems can be effected by the way the terms are nested, and for the most part in this age the community concept tends to be nested within a more dominating notion of individualism. The building of community has always been in a contest with the building of the person. This tension is not unexpected, nor entirely unwelcome, for communities can be as domineering and disenfranchising of the person as the person can be over communities. When, however, entire systems are devoted to the advancement of the individual with the subsequent fragmentation of the community, then the programmatic development (by which I mean the funding and implementation of particular programmes, often associated, interestingly enough, with well known individuals) of community faces certain obstacles and their success (often measured, again, by individualistic norms) is jeopardised.

Adopting a metaphor of community in place of that of organisation is beset with a number of issues. None are insurmountable, for it is possible, I believe, to both learn from the past and reconstruct the future. Thus, organisational structures that have been created can be changed, and administrative preparation programmes modified. But perhaps more problematic is the actual substitution of metaphor itself. For it is metaphor that resides in the deep structures of thought, and which often guides our action. While it has been claimed that the Whorfian hypothesis is overstated, it nevertheless seems to be true that in many cases action follows language. And our language seems to be replete with metaphors that value individualism, efficiency, and impartiality. Or, to be somewhat more accurate, our prototypical, public language values these, and is, indeed, quite separate from the more private language of love and care. In their small and classic work, Lakoff and Johnson (1980) show, indeed, how our language is based on metaphors of battle, struggle, and dominance. They find, for example, that 'in the area of politics and economics, metaphors matter more, because they constrain our lives . . . [a] metaphor in a political or economic system, by virtue of what it hides, can lead to human degradation' (1980: 236). The treatment of educational networks as organisational systems *is* the use of a political metaphor, and the use of the metaphor does hide the optional construction of such networks as communal systems. However, because the larger social system is built upon metaphors of often militaristic organisation (e.g. 'fighting the *battle* of the bulge', 'the computer *revolution*', 'the teaching *corps*'), it is difficult to consistently reorganise our thinking to project different metaphors of consequence.

The reorganisation of thinking to reflect a more communal orientation is in itself a political quest. Yet this often remains unacknowledged. Sergiovanni, in a chapter designed to encourage us to 'change our theory of schooling', raises these important questions:

> As we seek to build community in all three of its forms [kinship, place, mind], we might ask: What can be done to increase the sense of kinship, neighborliness, and collegiality among the faculty? How can we become more of a professional community where we care about each other and help each other to be and to learn, and to lead more productive work lives? What kind of relationships need to be cultivated with parents that will enable them to be included in our emerging community? How can we help each other?
>
> (Sergiovanni 1994: 7)

But, underlying these questions about community and how it is to be achieved, are basic political and economic issues; each question presupposes the prior resolution of such issues and this, indeed, is something of a stretch. In much of the community-building literature aimed at school administrators there is hardly, if any, mention of politics, even though the classic form of communal thought is basically a political statement.

Two emergent demi-gods: Critical theory and the postmodern

In the past few decades, the discipline of educational administration has seen the emergence of alternative, counter-approaches to what were the dominant metaphors and ways of thinking in the field.

Critical theory is a Marxist-derived sociological body of thought that found its most widely known expression in the work of the Frankfurt School in the 1920s and later. Its ideas have been upheld and developed in the contemporary work of social philosophers like Habermas. This approach, as the name implies, has been critical of modern governance structures and concerned particularly with the demise of the individual. In brief, Habermas (1973, 1975) posited three species-specific human interests: the technical, the practical, and the emancipatory. These he labels 'cognitive interests', meaning that they are anthropologically driven parts of a human need to know more about the species. The technical interest is related to the need to control one's environment, to engage in labour processes that are, in a word, productive. It is reflected in the binding of individuals to form organisations that are designed to function productively in some fashion. The practical interest, on the other hand, has to do with the practical management of human interaction and affairs of the state; in other words, it has to do with how communities form and learn processes of self-governance. The emancipatory interest, finally, concerns the need for self-determination, the sharing of power, and the need for freedom.

These interests are grounded and expressed through forms of rationality, that is, reasoning processes and ways of thinking to arrive at the 'reasonable'. Habermas argues that two forms of rationality dominate: purposive rationality and communicative rationality. The technical interest uses purposive rational action, that is, a goal-oriented, means–ends way of thinking serves the technical interest best. In order to be productive in any given fashion, a purposive rationality would suggest that ends be established (the 'why' of the organisation) and means selected (the 'how' of the organisation). Rationality ensues when these are matched, if not perfectly, then consistently. Communicative rationality, on the other hand, has to do with deciding the best course, what the 'good' is, and how we should live together. It is not based on accomplishing a task, but on selecting norms that bind us to each other. It is a communicative process of discourse and debate. Technical rationality is oriented to rules, communicative rationality – to norms.

The argument now takes a twist. In traditional societies, it is argued, purposive rationality was embedded within communicative rationality; labour and production, in other words, served the needs of the community's formation of self-governance and emancipation. The processes of production were subordinated to and served the processes of interaction and the normative context of the community. In modern societies, however, this pattern becomes reversed, and now social norms are established and changed to meet the needs of the production apparatus. This reversal thwarts the emancipatory interest to some extent, which leads to the need for a dominant administrative structure, explaining the rise of the administrative state in modern times.

For Habermas (1975), this process of reversal resulted in several crises in the modern state, including a crisis of motivation and of legitimation. That is, without the normative beliefs in communities of participation, and with lives directed largely towards producing goods in order to earn a wage, people began to lose motivation and began to question the legitimacy of the system.

In educational administration, this set of arguments was instrumental for some scholars in suggesting that the administrative process had become too concerned with achieving technical superiority and organisational efficiency, rather than with educational communities examining, discussing, and debating their norms and bases for improving their quality of life. Thus, a critical theory of administration emerged, not at all reluctant to question the structures and processes of the dominant model. Not all critical theorists in this field were influenced by Habermasian arguments; many were educated in critical sociology and brought those ideas into the field. Much of the emphasis here was on the distribution of power and then on the democratisation of the school. The specific issue, then, with a critical approach to administration lies in an ongoing analysis of attempts to put the technical goals of efficiency and productivity over the practical goals of democracy and equality in the school. A critically aware administrative theory sets itself to a goal of being educative and transformative, rather than to a goal of control and manipulation. Obviously, I have polarised these issues, though, like administration itself, they are complex and even fuzzy.

The second emergent demi-god is that of postmodernism. This is a wide-ranging group of often conflictual theories which are of a large, social nature, but which can be used to some extent in the analysis of administration. In brief, some aspects, but certainly not all, of the arguments made include an analysis of modernity, an analysis of truth and power, and a critique of the state administrative structure. It should be noted here that postmodernism, like perhaps all the models and theories discussed, presents itself in (somewhat) pure forms, and then in derivative forms.

From a postmodern perspective modernity is characterised by science and technology, by industry, by rational models of thought, by the certainty of the truth used to explain, and by the power of the state. Postmodernity, not surprisingly, questions all of these. It suggests, first, that science is not a monolithic enterprise that convincingly marches towards the truth, but is rather a series of false starts and then learning. Technology can dominate us as well as serve us. Rationality can be a false god used to reify relations of power, and truth is intimately tied to power itself. There are many competing 'truths', and it is those in power who can say what *the* truth is. And the state may not be the expression of democracy and freedom for all, but only the expression of democracy and freedom for some – those who by virtue of their status and power can define how the state serves the people.

Postmodernism, I think, can be more loosely defined not as a theory but as a set of concerns about modernity. If one takes the modern life to reflect a vision of certainty, happiness, and a regular order, postmodernism asks what about the chaos, the multi-cultures, the intersections of industrial life with family life, the many forms of what counts as 'art', the many forms of what counts as 'schooling', medicine and 'alternative' medicine, and so on. In education, we see debates about order and discipline, national standards, schools as organisations versus schools as communities, alternative schools, home schooling, the curriculum as presenting fundamental values and the curriculum as exploration, and so on. Postmodernism recognises that there is no one 'way' by which other such ways might be judged; rather, modernity presents a conflict of interests.

For the administrator, postmodernism means a sensitivity to the fractures of the modern age, to the differences that surround us, and to the relationship between administrative power and the profession of truth to others. It could be paralysing, or liberating.

Conclusion

It appears, then, that there are many developments in educational administration. While postmodernism and critical theory provide analytical possibilities for the examination of the modern state and its impact on education, the concept of reexamining the building of character through an emphasis on the virtues as traditionally developed holds a promise for the development of a community of learning that might disregard the individualistic emphasis of so much of today's education. The development of an educational *practice* that takes leadership as its exemplar holds considerable meaning in the attempt to achieve virtuous excellence.

References

Burns, J. M. (1978) *Leadership*, 1st edn, New York: Harper and Row.
Burns, T. and Stalker, G. M. (1961) *The Management of Innovation*, London: Tavistock Publications.

Callahan, R. E. (1962) *Education and the Cult of Efficiency: A Study of the Social Forces that have Shaped the Administration of the Public Schools*, Chicago: University of Chicago Press.

Cubberley, E. P. (1916) *Public School Administration: A Statement of the Fundamental Principles Underlying the Organization and Administration of Public Education*, Boston: Houghton Mifflin.

Gilligan, C. (1993) *In a Different Voice: Psychological Theory and Women's Development*, Cambridge, MA: Harvard University Press.

Goodlad, J. I. and Anderson, R. H. (1987) *The Nongraded Elementary School*, rev. edn, New York: Teachers College, Columbia University.

Habermas, J. (1973) *Theory and Practice*, Boston: Beacon Press.

Habermas, J. (1975) *Legitimation Crisis*, Boston: Beacon Press.

Halpin, A. W. (1966) *Theory and Research in Administration*, New York: Macmillan.

Lakoff, G. and Johnson, M. (1980) *Metaphors We Live By*, Chicago: University of Chicago Press.

MacIntyre, A. (1984) *After Virtue*, 2nd edn, Notre Dame, IN: University of Notre Dame.

Meier, D. (1995) *The Power of their Ideas: Lessons for America from a Small School in Harlem*, Boston: Beacon Press.

Merz, C. and Furman, G. C. (1997) *Community and Schools: Promise and Paradox*, New York: Teachers College Press.

Perrow, C. (1979) *Complex Organizations: A Critical Essay*, 2nd edn, Glenview, IL: Scott Foresman.

Sergiovanni, T. J. (1990) *Value-added Leadership: How to get Extraordinary Performance in Schools*, San Diego: Harcourt Brace Jovanovich HBJ Leadership.

Sergiovanni, T. J. (1994) *Building Community in Schools*, 1st edn, San Francisco: Jossey-Bass.

Simon, H. A. (1965 [1947]) *Administrative Behaviour: A Study of Decision-making Processes in Administrative Organization*, 2nd edn, New York: Free Press.

Taylor, F. W. (1947) *Scientific Management, Comprising Shop Management, the Principles of Scientific Management [and] Testimony before the Special House Committee*, New York: Harper.

Tönnies, F. (1957) *Community and Society (Gemeinschaft und Gesellschaft)*, East Lansing: Michigan State University Press.

Tyack, D. B. (1974) *The One Best System: A History of American Urban Education*, Cambridge, MA: Harvard University Press.

Chapter 11

Thinking through moral values

Putting Bourdieu to work within the field of education management[1]

Helen M. Gunter

An intellectual journey

The project reported in this chapter is to develop intellectual histories of the field of education management by researching field members in higher education institutions (HEIs) in the UK from the 1960s. This has been attempted through gathering professional biographies, searching the literature, and analysing the archival papers of the British Educational Leadership, Management and Administration Society (BELMAS).[2] While I have previously reported on aspects of theory and research design (Gunter 1997, 1999, 2000, 2001), this chapter marks the early stages of reporting the theorisation of the empirical work through Pierre Bourdieu's theory of practice.

I approached the empirical work with a number of questions regarding knowledge production by field members located in HEIs. What is a field and how do individuals come to locate and position themselves within a particular field? How does membership of a field affect the nature of professional practice and how do field members understand and shape their professional identity through this practice? How are choices within professional practice made, and in what ways are values valued in how ethical dilemmas are worked through? In what ways is a field a space where debates about moral purposes within theory, practice, and research are created and resolved? These are ambitious but necessary questions because they enable a productive conceptualisation of the interplay between the agency of the individual knowledge worker to make choices about research and teaching, and the structuring context in which that activity is shaped and controlled.

In this chapter I intend to draw mainly on oral texts constructed through interviews with sixteen people who are or have been located in an HEI, and have or currently seek to position their work within the field. These people are significant in their contribution to developing the field as a legitimate area of study and practice for members of an HEI. I intend to show that an intellectual history of the field of education management can be theorised using Bourdieu's theory of practice so that habitus can be revealed through an understanding of field position and positioning. Particular attention will be given to Bourdieu's approach to reflexivity and, by thinking through values, challenging questions are raised about practice. A central purpose of such an enquiry is to explore ways in which knowledge is produced, because the field sits between professional 'practice' and the 'academy'. This problematises associations and boundaries between the two, and so the chapter will examine the formation of BELMAS as a field network.

Creating and developing the field

Christopher Hodgkinson is emphatic in telling us that 'values, morals and ethics are the very stuff of leadership and administrative life, yet we have no comprehensive theory about them and often in the literature they receive very short shrift' (1991: 11). While he has made a major contribution to rectifying this situation, we do not have a culture and practice of reflecting and theorising about knowledge production that enables us to ask why knowledge can be both preferred and marginalised.[3] Reflecting on the professional practice of field members in the UK enables us to ask questions about the orientation and scope of what is done and why it is done. A study of public outputs affords us the opportunity to ask why we have networks such as BELMAS, journals such as *Educational Management and Administration*, postgraduate provision through Master's and Professional Doctorate degrees, and research studies that focus on organisational practice. Through practice, knowledge workers have a sense of being members of a field, and by virtue of their entry are involved in giving purpose and identity to that field. Field activity becomes a shared territory where members are able to use the space to create meaning through taking action such as publishing a book, and through describing and labelling action in particular ways by how they respond to that book. However, are decisions about worth and worthiness of activity a product of a clearly worked-through ethical position about knowledge and how to engage in dialogue about and through knowledge, or is it a product of political opportunism to attack and seek advantage? Knowledge production takes place within the complex networks that are developed within dynamic power structures such as the university, and are themselves a powerful structure determining who is and is not included.

An important resource in creating intellectual histories is the study of field outputs such as the publication in 1969 of Baron and Taylor's book *Educational Administration and the Social Sciences*. The theme of their collection is to establish the connection of the social sciences to the meaning and practice of educational administration, defined 'as all that makes possible the educative process, the administration of education embraces the activities of Parliament at one end of the scale and the activities of any home with children or students at the other' (Baron and Taylor 1969: 6). This inclusive approach set the agenda for the next decade and enabled the field to draw on the social sciences to explore, with practitioners through postgraduate study and research, the interface between theory and practice. Recognition was also sought from the academy, and Baron argues that the production of the edited collection 'was motivated by the political need to legitimate the study of educational administration in the university world in this country' (Baron 1980: 18).

The heirs to this social science tradition (e.g. Bottery 1992; Bush 1986, 1995; Bush *et al.* 1999; EMA 1999; Greenfield and Ribbins 1993; Gunter 1997; Hall 1996; Hoyle 1982, 1986, 1999; Hughes, Ribbins and Thomas 1985a; Strain *et al.* 1999) have worked for a focus on *educational* management, and continued to build on Baron and Taylor (Bolam 1999; Gunter 1999; Ribbins 1999a; Strain *et al.* 1999). Illustrative of this is Hughes *et al.*'s position on the importance of 'critical analysis' so that the reader has access to 'a powerful and flexible conceptual tool, which will be of use over a longer period than an approach stressing description or managerial guides to action' (1985b: xiii). What is valued is more than pragmatic utility because the intellectual work needed to undertake critical analysis within activity is an enduring process of being and doing in the world. The purposes of education are never finally settled and constantly generate new challenges for our moral commitment to children and adults. While choices in day-to-day practice in education require sensible decisions, and often a strong pragmatic recognition for what seems to be the right thing to do, they do need to be located in a struggle over enduring moral questions. As Hodgkinson has argued, 'unreflexive action is degenerative . . . It is entropic' (1996: 11). Winkley, in conversation with Pascal, confirms this point by arguing that the government-controlled training courses for head teachers in England may mean that the person has learned a lot of technical matters but may 'still not be terribly good as a head' (1998: 236). As a head teacher, what matters for Winkley is the importance of reflexivity within an 'ideas-creating school', in which questions are asked which 'require you to think about yourself as a person'. Such questions are about 'creating an ambience and a culture within the school, within the people in the school, within the children, a deeper sense of what you're trying to do as an organisation. What is it? What is a learning environment?' (Winkley 1998: 236). He goes on to argue: 'it doesn't matter how many courses you've been on, and how much you actually know intellectually about the process of being a head, unless you can get to grips in depth with those two areas of philosophy and your own emotional understanding, in a sense of how to get from A to B, you will never . . . make a good head' (Winkley 1998: 236).

While Winkley's arguments show that the legacy of Baron and Taylor lives on, at some point in the 1980s some field members stopped citing Baron and Taylor. They sought to modernise education through the transference of private sector models in which the emphasis was on having the right leadership language, behaviours, and strategies rather than on how the leader was enabled to think through the tough questions about educational issues (Gunter 1997). For those disposed towards entrepreneurial activity, Baron and Taylor were representative of another age, and philosophical debates about knowledge production were seen to hinder the urgency of making site-based performance management operationally efficient and effective.

In seeking to understand these developments, we need to engage with a theory of practice that enables the interplay between agency and structure to be described and explained. We need to have a way of investigating the link between lived lives and the choices made in intellectual work within the context, both institutional and social, that structures and shapes those choices. We need both a language and conceptual tools to be able to investigate how research and theory contributed to how field members were able to gain access to the HEI curriculum and course provision, and how this connected with the professional needs of educationalists. What we also need to engage with is how researchers, such as myself as author, connect their own intellectual projects with what they are writing about, and so how our own orientation to select this or that, to cite or silence, is central to how we create an understanding of who we are and what matters to us. Intellectual histories of the field can be written only by giving attention to these matters. Theorising through Bourdieu's theory of practice provides the opportunity to think out loud about what we observe, describe, and understand as current through what is past.

Theorising professional practice

A central aim in Bourdieu's sociology is to attempt to remove the dichotomy between the individual and society. This requires a theory of practice that enables complexity to be worked with rather than masked by simplistic monochrome accounts. Bourdieu argues for and uses observations and interviews to create accounts of life which are a 'multi-layered representation capable of articulating the same realities but in terms that are different and, sometimes, irreconcilable' (Bourdieu 1999b: 3). Since transcriptions of field notes and tape-recorded discussions can objectify the subject, the task for the researcher is to enable the interviewee to speak about who they are and what their position is without either collaborating or 'setting up the objectivising distance that reduce the individual to a specimen in a display case' (Bourdieu 1999a: 2). Such reflexivity enables researchers to challenge and to seek to overcome the limits of their intellectual work. While it aims to open up hidden assumptions about what we do and why we do it, it also confronts the power structures that condition our work. Research as critical reflective struggle needs thinking tools to challenge the tidiness of thought about the range of possibilities for how what is known and can be known is to be known about.

Bourdieu uses habitus as a means of explaining how the agent is not engaged in a rational calculation (a subject) or obeying externally defined and driven behaviour demands (an object). Habitus is described by him as:

> systems of durable, transposable dispositions, structured structures predisposed to function as structuring structures, that is, as principles which generate and organize practices and representations that can be objectively adapted to their outcomes without presupposing a conscious aiming at ends or an express mastery of the operations necessary in order to attain them.
>
> (Bourdieu 1990b: 53)

Habitus is learned more by experience than by teaching, and through a socialisation process remains durable. In this way the individual has a 'practical sense' or is an 'acting agent' (Bourdieu 1990a: 13, 10). Doing is not just doing, and neither is it determined to be done – instead, doing is related to the struggles that you are in: your position, your expectations, or 'the only thing to do'; put another way, 'agents to some extent *fall into* the practice that is theirs' (Bourdieu 1990a: 11, 90).

During the socialisation process, the objective social conditions in which the agent lives are inculcated, and so the habitus is 'structured structures' (Bourdieu 1990b: 53). Furthermore, as the agent develops practice related to different contexts, then the dispositions within the habitus are 'structuring structures' (Bourdieu 1990b: 53). An agent can operate in a range of fields of activity and practice still linked to the core habitus, and so habitus is *transposable*. In this sense, Bourdieu talks about a 'generative habitus':

> I am talking about dispositions acquired through experience, thus variable from place to place and time to time. This 'feel for the game', as we call it, is what enables an infinite number of 'moves' to be made, adapted to the infinite number of possible situations which no rule, however, complex, can foresee.
>
> (Bourdieu 1990a: 9)

The generative aspect of habitus is also illustrated in the reproductive capacities of agents, but Bourdieu avoids the pitfalls of objective determinism through the development of the concept of field.

A field is a dynamic concept as shifts in power relations and position change the structure, and so a field is a 'social arena within which struggles or manoeuvres take place over specific resources or stakes and access to them . . . Fields are defined by the stakes which are at stake' (Jenkins 1992: 84). What brings people together is a 'social magic' (Bourdieu 1990a: 88) in which agents have similar dispositions developed under similar social conditions and have specific stakes and interests. For example, lifestyle, education, politics, and prestige can be summed up by the struggle over values in which each can have rival claims to truth. Central to understanding the individual–collective dynamic interactions is the *position* that is achieved by access allowed to *capital* or goods/resources: economic, social, cultural, and symbolic. Symbolic capital can be invested in, for example, citation, invitations to speak, and book reviews. Distinction is about taste, and perception is about who is and is not worth reading, or listening to (Bourdieu 1984).

Bourdieu argues that we should guard against objectifying this into a 'totalising system', and so we should investigate this as 'products of *habitus*' (Bourdieu 1988: 49–50). An intellectual who is located within the bureaucracy of the university is not simply a person type, but entails a way of seeing and being within the world. Participating in the intellectual game requires a habitus that secures an interest in ideas rather than economic necessities, combined with the cultural capital to be able to invest (Swartz 1997). Language is part of this struggle: 'words are both currency and commodity in the academic marketplace' (Jenkins 1992: 157). The struggle is over legitimacy reflecting vested interests in a field, illustrated by those who classify in the field versus those who are in the classified products of the field. Consequently, Bourdieu advises the sociologist to take care in the words she or he uses, arguing that practice is objectified because of the tradition of rational categorising in science. A simplification of language and style supports conservative thinking because it sends out the message that 'everything is just fine as it is', and this makes us vulnerable to manipulation:

> When it comes to objects of inquiry as overladen with passions, emotions and interests as those of social life, the 'clearest', that is, simplest discourses, are probably those which run the greatest risks of being misunderstood, because they work like projective tests into which each person imports his or her prejudices, unreflective opinions and fantasies. If you accept the fact that, in order to make yourself understood, you have to work at using words in such a way that they say just what you wanted them to say, you can see that the best way of talking clearly consists in talking in a complicated way, in an attempt to transmit simultaneously what you are saying and your relationship to what you are saying, and in avoiding saying, against your will,

something more than and different from what you thought you were saying.

(Bourdieu 1990a: 52–53)

While agents may seek to dominate within one field, they can also be dominated by others such as the political and economic fields. Bourdieu has much to say about whether intellectual work is concerned with cultural power that is indifferent to the market, or whether this activity is more about temporal power allied with political and economic interests (Bourdieu 1988). Struggle within a field is not just about pragmatic reactions to external pressures with direct cause and effect responses: Bourdieu argues that to understand, you must look at the 'whole logic of the field' (1990a: 43). What is significant is how and why agents within a field, linked to their habitus, give legitimacy to particular claims for recognition.

Positions and positioning

An analysis of the oral texts collected for this study shows evidence of a habitus formed through professional work as a practitioner, evidencing a 'structured structure' (Bourdieu 1990b: 53) in which dispositions in current professional practice are linked to prior experiences. Before moving into middle and/or senior management roles in higher education, twelve of the sixteen interviewees had been practitioners in schools. The impact of this background has a strong influence on moral purpose within the field and is illustrated by the following biographical account:

> (09) I was in education for 16 years before I became an academic, 4 years as an assistant master teaching mathematics in a grammar school in (place name), for 4 years as a head of a maths department, that was in (place name) . . . Then 8 years as a headmaster in (place name) . . . and up to fairly late in that period of 16 years, I had no specific reason to think of myself as doing this on the way to an academic career. I was appointed headmaster at the age of 35 of a four form entry grammar school which was expanding to become a five form entry grammar technical school of about 900 pupils. When I went into that headship I certainly had no idea at all of changing career in a few years. I enjoyed being a headmaster and the opportunities that it gave me, but after the first 4 years or so I began to wonder whether I would want to be doing it for another 25 years or so . . . and an opportunity came to go on a school master fellowship to (institution name) and that term in (place name) was a term I enjoyed very much. It gave me a chance to look back at what I had been achieving and to start reading, in a way I hadn't read before,

about management and consider to what extent is this relevant to schools and so on. I became aware of the American literature – this would have been about 1961. The new theorising in the States was taking place in the late (19)50s. I learnt about what was happening in the States and it interested me very much. When I went back to school I still hadn't really developed the idea but quite soon after that I began to think well is there a way to be involved in this other than as a headmaster. And an opportunity came in 1965 to take up an academic post as a lecturer at (institution and place name). It was quite a big step in a way and particularly for my wife and young family, because it would involve a drop in salary of about 20% I think, with no guarantee of future advancement on the university side . . . because it was just an ordinary lectureship and with no promise of anything beyond that. I was particularly interested in looking at headship at that time, and a widening of interest came later, but at the time I was interested in critically examining the job that I had been doing myself as a headmaster.

Claims for legitimacy are rooted in credentials as a practitioner and the ability to present the self as a person who knows and understands this context, and so has a 'feel for the game' (Bourdieu 1990a: 9):

> (09) . . . it was a case of organising short courses. I still had a fair amount of credibility with a lot of the heads in (place name) because I had been one of them, and that gave me credibility and access also in connection with my research on headship which was taking place at this same time.

The professional biographies show a consensus in the need to go beyond action by seeking out new ideas and insights regarding the ethical dilemmas underpinning such realities of practice. Raising questions and intellectualising practice are central features of all the field participants interviewed – many had begun to write and research about management issues before moving into an HEI:

> (11) I have been working in Higher Education and in schools. I have worked for 21 years in universities but I am not really interested at all in HE, but for me those 7 years in teaching in a secondary school were seminal. I have spent twenty years working to understand secondary schools, and education management is just one way of doing it. Education management was protean in its early days both in methodology and at a practical level. You can make of it what you wish. The emphasis was on trying to understand school: how and why we do things. How schools are managed is very strong within

education management as practice, and theory is designed to enable, and to be clear what might be done and how might it be done. However, we need to be careful as we can start to believe that management has a purpose of its own! My own model is that we aim to: 1. Understand, 2. Enable, 3. Identify what can be better, and 4. Change and improvement. I have concerns about Critical Theorists who begin by change as the aim, we need to understand first, and to act as enablers.

Thus, the academic habitus that supported entry into an HEI, shaping both research and teaching activity, was revealed during the time as a teacher and manager. This impacts on how the practitioner is conceptualised; when practitioners are in a postgraduate session, or writing an assignment, or reading an article from a journal, they are positioned as being simultaneously distant from and close to practice. They are close because they can think through the tough issues in their work, but they are also distant because they have the space afforded by study where they can affirm their past practice, develop new insights into their current practice, and open up possibilities for alternative practice. They are working with field members in higher education who were practitioners in schools and local administration, and who are now not only lecturers and researchers but also managers in higher education. This academic-practitioner habitus is 'generative' through the growth of networks between field members in higher education, local administration, schools, and colleges. This disposition towards doing and an understanding of that doing is not dichotomised into theory and practice, or academic and action, but is theory within practice, and practice within theorising. These field members could have been trainers or private consultants, but in the debates about knowledge claims and the central focus on the practitioner there is clear understanding of why field members are located in HEIs:

> (05) So what I've been trying to do here is to say we are academics and I'm constantly saying this to people, we are not management trainers although we do management training, but we are not management trainers who don't think about the bigger issues. We are academics. We are constantly wanting to ask questions and to look at the long-term outcomes of what we do . . . I think we are about working with teachers to enable them to be more reflective and to put some skills in that reflection. I don't think you can sit round and contemplate your navel. I think you do have to have some skills. You do have to have knowledge. You do have to have research and expertise. You have to have analytical tools. You have to have all of those things that universities are concerned with . . . So on one hand I want to be in there and working with the practitioners. On the other hand I want

to be standing back from them and thinking about what education managers are doing, and why, and how . . .

Professional practice is centred around a number of activities: the creation and development of short and long-term courses (particularly Master's and more recently Ed.D.s); undertaking management and leadership roles within their institutions; the supervision of research students/staff, including bidding for research grants; writing and editing of books and journals; membership and undertaking officer roles in national and international networks; and the development of consortia and the writing of bids for contracts for professional development funding. Talking with the interviewees about their professional practice within HEIs shows that there are similar types of work related to the particular configuration of the field combined with the structural influences of the nature and purpose of an HEI. Some of the interviewees talk about their work primarily in relation to teaching, others more about particular disciplines and the knowledge claims that both interest them and have validity within the field.

It seems that locating work within the HEI and working with practitioners in schools and colleges become 'structuring structures' (Bourdieu 1990b: 53) in which ongoing learning confirms and builds on academic–practitioner oriented dispositions. The interplay between knowledge generated both within and distant from practice is seen as productive and is the basis on which the field makes claims for distinction. One of the early field leaders states:

> (03) . . . the basis of my thinking was we had to convert practice into teachable forms. In other words, it wasn't just a case of learning from Nelly, but of systematising it and building up a body of knowledge, a discipline if you like, which could be passed on through courses, developed to some extent through research but I felt that the main thing was to develop courses for practising administrators whether Heads, or Local Authority people or Department of Education people or whoever and the more academic side would develop through the normal teaching (such as the) MA.

One of the current field leaders argues that in the past forty years the contribution of field members working in HEIs in partnership with practitioners in schools and colleges has been to establish it as a valid area of activity:

> (15) . . . in its own right and is not in my view now dependent on the earlier established disciplines from which it was derived . . . I think what's happened progressively, and again it's much easier to backward

this than it is to look forward on it, is the development of an indigenous literature and underpinned increasingly by research of education and management specific to the UK context . . .

Networks and networking

This academic-practitioner habitus can be revealed through an exploration of formal networks that have been created and sustained over the past forty years. These networks include, for example, the British Educational Leadership, Management and Administration Society (BELMAS); the Commonwealth Council for Educational Administration and Management (CCEAM); the European Forum on Educational Administration (EFEA); the International Intervisitation Programme (IIP); and the Standing Conference for Research in Educational Leadership and Management (SCRELM). Knowledge claims about the interplay between the academy and practice are played out in these spaces, meanings are created through position, and boundaries are contested through positioning. Illustrative of tensions and dilemmas arising in the positions and positioning of field members in lived professional practice is how the academic-practitioner habitus has been simultaneously promoted and challenged.

The oral texts contain field member experiences and views about the formation and development of the British Educational Administration Society (BEAS). Field leaders sought to establish networks at home and abroad to ensure that the teaching and research of education administration had both academic and practitioner respectability. The network engaged in particular activity to facilitate the intellectual development of the field: establishing a journal, organising conferences, and supporting contacts at home and abroad. There is a clear moral commitment to the practitioner within a wide range of educational institutions, and the original aim was to seek members from Local Education Authorities (LEAs), and the then Department for Education and Science (DES), as well as from schools and colleges. BEAS became a forum for the attempt to link field members across educational institutions so that the academic-practitioner habitus could flourish. This had the potential to break down boundaries between institutional location in ways that could challenge the power structures underpinning the university as the main location for authentic knowledge production. Illustrative of this approach is the change of name in 1980 with the inclusion of 'management' in the title. A key participant describes the events and the inclusive approach to the network:

> (09) . . . He was a Headmaster who turned up at annual meetings and he was stirring things up a bit from the practitioner point of view,

beginning to say that BEAS was becoming rather an academic organisation, wasn't taking sufficient account of the practitioners and so on. So we got him on to Council. I mean in a way that could be regarded as a way of dealing with the opposition by bringing them in. But, quite genuinely we wanted people on the Council who had views of their own . . . It shows that we accepted it very readily, considering it was such an important decision . . . but the discussion didn't take very long either in the meeting. It certainly wasn't a meeting where people were sort of taking sides and against it or that sort of thing. I think we were glad to be prodded into doing something which we felt probably it was time to do something about.

However, while field members were seeking to build activity around the academic-practitioner position, there were also challenges to this. Practitioners in schools and colleges were increasingly being positioned through policy changes in ways that challenged the relevance of intellectual work within practice habitus. While BEAS (and later BEMAS/BELMAS) symbolised and facilitated the field's claim to be about practitioner concerns, agreed notions about accountability were being redefined as central government began to intervene more in policy implementation through direct involvement in professional development and through the promotion of preferred models of leadership and management practice (Gunter 2001). Consequently, while field members became increasingly aware of the value of their symbolic capital of having been practitioners themselves, the network continued to find practitioner recruitment challenging. The shift of employment into higher education had created an important opportunity to work with practitioners in innovative ways, but that distance also raised questions about relevance. As one field member states:

(14) . . . But there has been another division . . . between those with responsibility for something and those who were commentating on something or analysing it or teaching it. And that division has always been a serious one for BEMAS . . . People who had the luxury of analysing and commenting and who could look back afterwards and say that's undoubtedly a mistake . . . But, you know, at the time somebody had to make a decision with politicians breathing down their neck and they, these people found it hard to believe that BEMAS had something to offer. Of course, its members did have something to offer and the dilemma then, and I think still now, was to somehow make a contribution to national policy making while recognising that you don't have the responsibility, you don't have to live with the consequences, you're not answerable directly to the Minister or the Prime Minister.

While the academic-practitioner position was shared territory within the field, there were also tensions. The founders of BEAS see the word 'administration' as being an obvious label, used in England and Wales in direct response to the common international use of the term. The politics of international recognition affected the initial labelling of this network: the introduction of 'management' into the title revealed a struggle for competing understandings of how the practitioner was conceptualised in the universities compared with polytechnics and colleges. There were issues of status, power, and validity between leading field members and their different locations within HEIs. For those located in universities in which there were Departments or Institutes of Education, the emphasis is more on 'administration' compared with those who were located in polytechnics and colleges, who often began their work on educational management within departments focused on business management:

> (06) . . . and here I am echoing the concerns of people who were very critical of me in the early seventies, and what I represented to them, as being almost amoral. People at (name) university at the time, for example, often used to charge me privately and publicly with leading an amoral movement of sheer instrumentalism, simply doing what the employer wants sort of thing, and not paying attention to issues of policy, values and these sorts of things. Now that was because they had a view that management was purely instrumental, if it was anything else, you called it administration, but management was being purely executive, it was simply doing as you were told, but being efficient about it . . . Now this, of course, was a complete misunderstanding of the way in which the word 'manager' was used in context. We talk about the general manager, the managing director. These are not purely instrumental things, these are the guys who decide where the place is going to go, or what the mission is going to be, and so we had a problem for a long time of people being constrained with the particular traditions, and I found it particularly interesting having moved from one tradition – the school teacher, administrator, university don at (name) of all places, into the dirty handed, low status world of the poly(technic).

Critical reflection on the development of the field has led one field leader from a university to argue that there is something more subtle going on, as the drive to reposition themselves as managers is central to the profession's struggle for status in a world in which public sector services were coming under pressure to be more accountable:

> (02) We didn't actually use the word 'management' until well into the (19)70s . . . It may be that what we do now has pretty well always

been done. But we've created a language . . . somebody ran schools, but there was no management. I started teaching in 1953 a school of 500 and there was a Head, a Deputy who had a full timetable and a secretary. And that was it. I mean there were no scale posts until the Burnham agreement of 1956. That's when we created a great hierarchy. Management jobs were done and then eventually management became a bigger thing, partly as a result I think of comprehensivisation and larger schools – people started to attend to that. But we still weren't using the term. Then we began to use the term 'management' and then we began to create all kinds of management positions and the question for me is the pull/push question – did we create all these management positions and of course some of these, the titles, particularly in higher education, are now hilarious . . . Now then, are those jobs to be done? Are those roles for people to be filled for salary purposes? . . . So I think there was a push there in terms of money to be spent and roles to be created rather than a pool of jobs to be done. Now I'm not dismissing the fact that there are many more jobs to be done. I'm not denying that, but I think it was much push than pull . . . We have created a language for this and people are inventing jobs for themselves.

This type of analysis comes within the tradition of the field's engagement with the social sciences as a way of enabling reflective understanding of the interface between policy and practice. Field members are very much aware that there are positions where the academic-practitioner habitus is being reworked around entrepreneurial approaches to knowledge as a commodity. While the pragmatic tradition within the field is seen as supportive of practitioners facing difficult challenges, it can also been seen as a limitation: (11) 'education management is very much a "magpie discipline"' and 'in the nest there are many silvery things which have been pinched'. It seems that the structures of the market-place are shaping professional practice more than the location within the academy, and as one interviewee stated: (08) 'Well it gives people a lot of jobs, doesn't it? And a sort of cynic in me would say, you know, it's total social invention. Its a business, its a way of working'. The field members who were interviewed disassociate from this trend through emphasising values and how they underpin management development and practice. Nevertheless, the dominance of political and economic demands on HEIs to become entrepreneurial challenges intellectual work and amplifies the instrumental reworking of the practitioner habitus. Field members, like members of other fields in HEIs, are located in a bidding culture, in which a direct policy intervention to make HEIs just one player in the education market-place affects practice. At the same time, academic culture remains strong, still shaping the aims of field members who locate themselves within an HEI out of a desire to research into and to critically understand professional educational practice.

Thinking with Bourdieu

The relevance of thinking with Bourdieu for conceptualising field professional practice is in both the breadth as well as the depth of his theorising. There has been a rapid growth in the number of articles and books that are about and make use of his ideas (Calhoun, LiPuma and Postone 1993, Grenfell *et al.* 1998, Robbins 1991, 1993). There have been studies using habitus (Harker and May 1993, Hodkinson and Sparkes 1997, Nash 1990, Reay 1995), and field (Fitz 1999, Ladwig 1994), in which writers are often experimenting with the theory, working on their understanding of it, and developing new insights into educational practice. However, educational studies have been censured for engaging in the 'adulation of great thinkers' (Tooley with Darby 1998: 56) such as Bourdieu. In reply, Nash argues that Bourdieu 'forces one to think', and creates 'a place for "thinking aloud"', and the resulting dialogue 'is a long one and if it moves ahead, two steps forward and one step backwards, then so be it' (Nash 1999: 185–186).

This argument supports critical reflection about the moral dilemmas underpinning our job as knowledge workers. Bourdieu's epistemology works against adulation of any type. According to him, intellectual work is about 'argument and refutation', and we need to guard against what is happening in 'political life' where there is 'denunciation and slander, "sloganization" and falsification of the adversary's thought' (Bourdieu 1998: 9). Consequently, a sociological investigation enables us to conceptualise the interplay between agency and structure in ways that illuminate what he calls 'the illusion of freedom' (Bourdieu 1990a: 15). Bourdieu talks about 'social determinants' or the conditions which have 'made a particular way of being or doing possible', arguing that the 'specific determinant' of an intellectual is thinking and acting as if we are free from this. He also argues for the importance of sociology in enabling freedom from this 'illusion of freedom' because of its role in understanding the relationship between the 'instruments of knowledge of the instruments of knowledge' (Bourdieu 1990a: 16). Such approaches can cause trouble because 'freedom is not something given: it is something you conquer – collectively' (Bourdieu 1990a: 15), and so thinking with Bourdieu helps us to problematise rather than spin a position, and open up dialogue about activity rather than move directly to either condemn or to prescribe action.

Wacquant (1993) argues that Bourdieu is subject to more criticism because he is dealing with the context where knowledge workers in higher education are living and working. So, one is not dealing with a theoretical model developed by someone else about someone else, but rather engaging in a discussion of empirical data, observations, and theoretical concepts which have been developed by another academic with and about academics (Bourdieu 1988). Reflexivity has revealed the development of a values-driven commitment to, and longevity of, an academic-practitioner habitus within field-member professional practice, and the field as an arena where dialogue about moral choices takes place is evident through the pages of journals as well as within the postgraduate seminar room and research. However, as the empirical data show, there is an ongoing struggle to keep this space open for the creative interplay of theory about and from practice. Recent dialogue through the ESRC-funded Seminar Series Redefining Educational Management is illustrative of how the field is engaging in questions about its knowledge claims and renewal. The continued importance of working for the academic–practitioner habitus, at a time when the field is open to domination by the field of power, is revealed through papers on knowledge, research, policy, professional development, and pedagogy (see Bush *et al.* 1999).

Thinking through the empirical data shows a range of 'career trajectories' (Fitz 1999: 314), where field members may shift employment location and the emphasis in their professional practice in ways that can simultaneously create both contradiction and complementarity in the shaping of identities. Revealing habitus enables us to see that identity is not just what role you inhabit, that is, head teacher or professor, but is about what you do, how you do it, and why you do it. Complementary identities can be seen through how both the head teacher and the professor are practitioners in the leadership and management of educational activity, and so there are relatable issues about practice and the research of that practice. Contradictions for these practitioners are observable in how the demands for a particular kind of practice and accountability are required in different employment locations, and this has implications for working through what can and should be done, and the learning that comes from it. On the surface, the demands of the Research Assessment Exercise for the professor may seem far removed from the everyday practice of the head teacher preparing for inspection, but quality processes is the terrain on which all in education are located, and all face the possible detrimental effects on educational values.

Bourdieu's theory of practice could be seen as limiting because it enables us to see habitus and positioning within fields, but does not directly provide a strategy for change (Connell 1983). However, Bourdieu has recently commented on the importance of revealing the difficulties in people's lives and, while this does not directly solve problems or guarantee the longevity of what is admirable, 'one does have to acknowledge the effect it can have in allowing those who suffer to find out that their suffering can be imputed to social causes and thus to feel exonerated' (Bourdieu 1999c: 629). In other words: 'what the social world has done, it can, armed with this knowledge undo' (1999c: 629). So, through productive struggle, field members can work through what Connell (1983) describes as the 'possibilities' for action and the 'traps' that can limit action.

The possibilities are within the intellectual heritage of the field, and this remains an important resource for how field members create and sustain the future. For example, Fitz argues that the field does not have an 'ology' (Fitz 1999: 317) that enables it to analyse power and authority; however, the social science tradition exists, for example, in Greenfield's humanist values orientation (Greenfield and Ribbins 1993), Hall's (1996) work on gender, and Hoyle's (1982, 1999) work on micropolitics. Field members have a fund of knowledge about adult learning and the pedagogy of professional development through which the academic-practitioner habitus is developed. Many thousands of postgraduates working in practice are consequently able to productively work through the dilemmas created by the drive for action and the broader understandings they have generated (Hoyle 1986). As the empirical data show, the academic-practitioner habitus is shaped by the conceptualisation of the practitioner as engaging in intellectual work, and hence the leader not only uses knowledge but also produces it. Nevertheless, the link with the classroom has remained a problematic area for the field, often because of the unreflexive assumption that improving strategic organisational management directly causes better teaching and learning. This is regarded as an important area for field members to engage with (Bolam 1999, Cordingley 1999, Fitz 1999) and this could revitalise field traditions through exploring the relationship between teaching and learning with organisational and systemic policymaking (Baron and Taylor 1969, Gronn 2000).

Nevertheless, the traps also appear, and while some might be particular to this field, much is also relevant to knowledge workers in other fields in educational studies, not least the impact of neo-liberal policies manifested in site-based performance management, and the implications this is having for the intensification of work. The traps are not just opposites of the possibilities in which field members fail to go to particular places and so do not draw on the past in order to create the future. The traps are also linked to knowledge production within the field in which the entrepreneurial approach to prescribed action is characterising practice as instrumental rather than intellectual activity. This can be seen through the widespread, and normally unreflexive, adoption of particular types of language such as 'improvement', 'effectiveness', 'fitness for purpose', without debate over what this might do to our ability to engage in meaningful dialogue. Problematising language does not stop us from making a difference to teaching and learning. It is not an esoteric 'academic' pastime for those with nothing better to do, but, as Bourdieu (1996) argues, it is essential to democratic development. If we can only talk about school improvement as a 'good thing' and not question whether it is about *educational* improvement, then we do not cause any trouble. A consequence of this is that we all feel good about our efficiency, but we are left powerless to shape alternative agendas and theories.

For this field in particular, the trap lies in the busyness of the terrain, and how particular field members in HEIs may be positioned in particular ways. The challenge to the academic-practitioner habitus is currently coming from policy sociologists who have focused on field members as entrepreneurial knowledge brokers (Grace 1995, Ozga 1992) in which preferred strategies for leader and management action are disconnected from the social, economic, and policy context. While this challenges the 'academic' claim of appropriate distance within the academic-practitioner habitus, Thomson (2000) questions the closeness to practice claim:

> If education management and/or administration academics want to avoid being positioned as entrepreneurial content providers by governments, and dismissed as elitist and irrelevant by the profession, then some other accommodation with headteachers and their practical and empirical knowledges will have to be found.
>
> (Thomson 2000: 728)

It seems that the challenge for the field is that while it has established a claim for distinction through an academic-practitioner habitus, it is being positioned as trapped between the academy and practice. Boundary scanning is in the tradition of the field (Glatter 1979), but replies and making connections are few (see Bolam 1999, Glatter 1999, Ribbins 1999b). Thinking with Bourdieu does mean that the political position of the knower can be opened up to scrutiny, enabling field members to take a more robust approach to questioning the territory inhabited by others and their claims for distinctiveness. The academic-practitioner habitus is one that is shared by other fields (e.g. School Improvement) and has the creative potential to revitalise networking with practitioners in ways that are central to the purposes of the field. But in order to do this, the field is going to have to revisit its moral purposes and commitment to intellectual work so that the realities of day-to-day practice are located in wider philosophical questions. Site-based performance management has and is continuing to create huge tensions for field members in schools and colleges. The question is, who do they turn to for help in working this through? The expansion and diversification of the field creates an arena for productive struggle over this, and thinking with Bourdieu facilitates an engagement with how claims and counter-claims can be described, understood, and explained.

Conclusion

Bourdieu's thinking tools have revealed the dynamics of an academic-practitioner habitus within field-member professional practice. This is the basis of claims for distinction – it is what structures activity and is a structuring outcome of that activity. We know much more, but not enough, about the moral dilemmas faced within the realities of everyday practice. This habitus has been under pressure from within the field, and this has been creative through dialogue about new places where field members have gone and need to be going to such as Hall's (1996, 1999) work on opening up the gender dimension. However, there have been serious challenges from both within and outside of the field to separate the 'academic' from the 'practitioner', and without socio-historical analysis supported by Bourdieu's theory of practice these patterns and positions could go unnoticed or unsaid, and so particular positions become or remain privileged. The productive struggle for alternative spaces and places of enquiry is open to the ridicule of irrelevance, but unless knowledge workers pack and repack their intellectual suitcases, they, as Bourdieu argues, 'cross the borders with empty suitcases – they have nothing to declare' (quoted in Harker, Mahar and Wilkes 1990: x).

Acknowledgements

I would like to thank the sixteen people who have so far participated in this research.

Notes

1 This chapter is based on a paper 'Purposes and positions in the field of education management: Putting Bourdieu to work' (Gunter 2002).
2 BEAS was formed with a Foundation Meeting in London on 23 October 1971. Professor Sir George Baron and Professor Sir William Taylor brought together interested people. See Hughes (1997) for an account of the formation. BEAS became BEMAS in 1980 following a vote at an Extraordinary General Meeting at the Annual Conference. See Bolam (1981) and McHugh (1979) for an account of the debates. In 2000 BEMAS became BELMAS following a vote at the Annual Conference.
3 Professor Peter Ribbins and I have been working on developing approaches to mapping knowledge production within the field of leadership studies. See Gunter and Ribbins (2002), Ribbins and Gunter (2002), Ribbins and Gunter (2002).

References

Baron, G. (1969) 'The study of educational administration in England', in G. Baron and W. Taylor (eds) *Educational Administration and the Social Sciences*, London: Athlone Press.
Baron, G. (1980) 'Research in educational administration in Britain', *Educational Administration* 8, 1: 1–33.
Baron, G. and Taylor, W. (eds) (1969) *Educational Administration and the Social Sciences*, London: Athlone Press.
Bolam, R. (1981) 'Editorial', *Educational Administration* 9, 3: i–ii.
Bolam, R. (1999) 'Educational administration, leadership and management: towards a research agenda', in T. Bush, L. Bell, R. Bolam, R. Glatter and P. Ribbins (eds) *Educational Management: Redefining Theory, Policy and Practice*, London: Paul Chapman.
Bottery, M. (1992) *The Ethics of Educational Management*, London: Cassell.
Bourdieu, P. (1984) *Distinction*, London: Routledge.
Bourdieu, P. (1988) *Homo Academicus*, Cambridge: Polity Press in association with Blackwell Publishers, Oxford.
Bourdieu, P. (1990a) *In Other Words: Essays Towards a Reflexive Sociology*, trans. Matthew Adamson, Cambridge: Polity Press in association with Blackwell Publishers, Oxford.
Bourdieu, P. (1990b) *The Logic of Practice*, trans. R. Nice, Cambridge: Polity Press.
Bourdieu, P. (1993) *The Field of Cultural Production*, Cambridge: Polity Press.
Bourdieu, P. (1996) *On Television and Journalism*, London: Pluto Press.
Bourdieu, P. (1998) *Acts of Resistance*, Cambridge: Polity Press in association with Blackwell Publishers.
Bourdieu, P. (1999a) 'To the reader', in P. Bourdieu *et al.*, *The Weight of the World*, Cambridge: Polity Press, in association with Blackwell Publishers, Oxford.
Bourdieu, P. (1999b) 'The space of points of view', in P. Bourdieu *et al.*, *The Weight of the World*, Cambridge: Polity Press in association with Blackwell Publishers, Oxford.
Bourdieu, P. (1999c) 'Postscript', in P. Bourdieu *et al.*, *The Weight of the World*, Cambridge: Polity Press in association with Blackwell Publishers, Oxford.
Bush, T. (1986) *Theories of Educational Management*, London: Paul Chapman.
Bush, T. (1995) *Theories of Educational Management*, 2nd edn, London: Paul Chapman.
Bush, T., Bell, L., Bolam, R., Glatter, R. and Ribbins, P. (eds) (1999) *Educational Management: Redefining Theory, Policy and Practice*, London: Paul Chapman.
Calhoun, C., LiPuma, E. and Postone, M. (eds) (1993) *Bourdieu: Critical Perspectives*, Cambridge: Polity Press in association with Blackwell Publishers, Oxford.
Connell, R. W. (1983) *Which Way Is Up? Essays on Sex, Class and Culture*, Sydney: George Allen & Unwin.
Cordingley, P. (1999) 'Pedagogy, educational management and the TTA research agenda', in T. Bush, L. Bell, R. Bolam, R. Glatter, and P. Ribbins (eds) *Educational Management: Redefining Theory, Policy and Practice*, London: Paul Chapman.
EMA (Educational Management and Administration) (1999) *Special Edition: Redefining Educational Management and Leadership* 27, 3.

Fitz, J. (1999) 'Reflections on the field of educational management studies', *Educational Management and Administration* 27, 3: 313–321.

Glatter, R. (1979) 'Education "Policy" and "Management": One field or two?', in T. Bush, R. Glatter, J. Goodey and C. Riches (eds) (1979) *Approaches to School Management*, London: Harper Educational Series.

Glatter, R. (1999) 'From struggling to juggling: Towards a redefinition of the field of educational leadership and management', *Educational Management and Administration* 27, 3: 253–266.

Grace, G. (1995) *School Leadership: Beyond Education Management*, London: Falmer.

Greenfield, T. and Ribbins, P. (eds) (1993) *Greenfield on Educational Administration*, London: Routledge.

Grenfell, M. and James, D., with Hodkinson, P., Reay, D. and Robbins, D. (1998) *Bourdieu and Education*, London: Falmer Press.

Gronn, P. (2000) 'Distributed properties: A new architecture for leadership', *Educational Management and Administration* 28, 3: 317–338.

Gunter, H. (1997) *Rethinking Education: The Consequences of Jurassic Management*, London: Cassell.

Gunter, H. (1999) 'Researching and constructing histories of the field of education management', in T. Bush, L. Bell, R. Bolam, R. Glatter and P. Ribbins (eds) *Educational Management: Redefining Theory, Policy and Practice*, London: Paul Chapman.

Gunter, H. (2000) 'Thinking theory: The field of education management in England and Wales', *British Journal of Sociology of Education* 21, 4: 623–635.

Gunter, H. (2001) *Leaders and Leadership in Education*, London: Paul Chapman.

Gunter, H. (2002) 'Purposes and positions in the field of education management: Putting Bourdieu to work', *Educational Management and Administration* 30, 1: 3–22.

Gunter, H. and Ribbins, P. (2002) 'Leadership studies in education: Towards a map of the field', *Educational Management and Administration* 30, 4: 387–416.

Hall, V. (1996) *Dancing on the Ceiling*, London: Paul Chapman.

Hall, V. (1999) 'Gender and education management: Duel or dialogue', in T. Bush, L. Bell, R. Bolam, R. Glatter and P. Ribbins (eds) *Educational Management: Redefining Theory, Policy and Practice*, London: Paul Chapman.

Harker, R. and May, S. A. (1993) 'Code and habitus: Comparing the accounts of Bernstein and Bourdieu', *British Journal of Sociology of Education* 14, 2: 169–179.

Harker, R., Mahar, C. and Wilkes, C. (eds) (1990) 'Editors' Introduction', in R. Harker, C. Mahar and C. Wilkes (eds) *An Introduction to the Work of Pierre Bourdieu*, London: Macmillan.

Hirst, P. (1974) *Knowledge and the Curriculum*, London: Routledge and Kegan Paul.

Hodgkinson, C. (1991) *Educational Leadership: The Moral Art*, Albany, NY: State University of New York Press.

Hodgkinson, C. (1996) *Administrative Philosophy*, Oxford: Elsevier Science (Pergamon Press).

Hodkinson, P. and Sparkes, A. C. (1997) 'Careership: A sociological theory of career decision-making', *British Journal of Sociology of Education* 18, 1: 29–44.

Hoyle, E. (1982) 'Micropolitics of educational organisations', *Educational Management and Administration* 10: 87–98.

Hoyle, E. (1986) 'The management of schools: Theory and practice', in E. Hoyle and A. McMahon, *World Yearbook of Education 1986: The Management of Schools*, London: Kogan Page.

Hoyle, E. (1999) 'The two faces of micropolitics', *School Leadership and Management* 19, 2: 213–222.

Hughes, M. (1997) 'From bulletin to journal', *Educational Management and Administration* 25, 3: 243–263.

Hughes, M., Ribbins, P. and Thomas, H. (1985a) *Managing Education: The System and The Institution*, Eastbourne: Holt, Rinehart and Winston.

Hughes, M., Ribbins, P. and Thomas, H. (1985b) 'Introduction', in M. Hughes, P. Ribbins and H. Thomas, *Managing Education: The System and The Institution*, Eastbourne: Holt, Rinehart and Winston.

Jenkins, R. (1992) *Pierre Bourdieu*, London: Routledge.

Johnson, R. (1993) 'Pierre Bourdieu on art, literature and culture – Editor's Introduction', in P. Bourdieu, *The Field of Cultural Production*, Cambridge: Polity Press.

Ladwig, J. G. (1994) 'For whom reform? Outlining educational policy as a social field', *British Journal of Sociology of Education* 15, 3: 341–363.

McHugh, R. (1979) 'Notes from discussions in the plenary sessions', *Educational Administration* 7: 43–47.

Nash, R. (1990) 'Bourdieu on education and social and cultural reproduction', *British Journal of Sociology of Education* 11, 4: 431–447.

Nash, R. (1999) 'Bourdieu, "habitus", and educational research: Is it all worth the candle?', *British Journal of Sociology of Education* 20, 2: 175–187.

Ozga, J. (1992) 'Review essay: Education management', *British Journal of Sociology of Education* 13, 2: 279–280.

Reay, D. (1995) '"They employ cleaners to do that": Habitus in the primary classroom', *British Journal of Sociology of Education* 16, 3: 353–371.

Ribbins, P. (1999a) 'Editorial: On redefining educational management and leadership', *Educational Management and Administration* 27, 3: 227–238.

Ribbins, P. (1999b) 'Understanding leadership: Developing headteachers', in T. Bush, L. Bell, R. Bolam, R. Glatter and P. Ribbins (eds) *Educational Management: Redefining Theory, Policy and Practice*, London: Paul Chapman.

Ribbins, P. and Gunter, H. (2002) 'Mapping leadership studies in education: Towards a typology of knowledge domains', *Educational Management and Administration* 30, 4.

Ribbins, P. and Gunter, H. (2002) 'Leadership Studies in Education: Maps for EPPI Reviews?', in L. Anderson and N. Bennett (eds) *Evidence Informed Policy and Practice in Educational Leadership*, London: Paul Chapman.

Robbins, D. (1991) *The Work of Pierre Bourdieu*, Buckingham: Open University Press.

Robbins, D. (1993) 'The practical importance of Bourdieu's analyses of higher education', *Studies in Higher Education* 18, 2: 151–163.

Strain, M., Dennison, B., Ouston, J. and Hall, V. (eds) (1999) *Policy, Leadership and Professional Knowledge*, London: Paul Chapman.

Swartz, D. (1997) *Culture and Power: The Sociology of Pierre Bourdieu*, London: University of Chicago Press.

Thomson, P. (2000) 'Move over Rover! An essay/assay of the field of educational management in the UK', *Journal of Education Policy* 15, 6: 717–732.
Tooley, J. with Darby, D. (1998) *Educational Research, a Critique,* London: Office for Standards in Education.
Wacquant, L. (1993) 'Bourdieu in America: Notes on the transatlantic importation of social theory', in C. Calhoun, E. LiPuma and M. Postone (eds) *Bourdieu: Critical Perspectives,* Cambridge: Polity Press in association with Blackwell Publishers, Oxford.
Winkley, D. with Pascal, C. (1998) 'Developing a radical agenda', in C. Pascal and P. Ribbins (eds) *Understanding Primary Headteachers,* London: Cassell.

Chapter 12

Naturalising ethical judgement: A neuro-computational view

Colin W. Evers

This chapter outlines and defends a naturalistic view of ethical judgement in both its descriptive aspects and its normative aspects. The first aspect concerns what amounts to the problem of developing a theory of moral cognition, of how people reason about ethical issues when they make ethical decisions. The second deals with the question of how people ought to reason in order for those decisions to be normatively appropriate. Addressing these matters within a naturalistic framework involves, roughly speaking, adopting the epistemology and ontology presumed to obtain in natural science, as a sufficient explanatory resource. Finally, some key corollaries of using this framework will be a blurring of the initial descriptive/normative distinction, a denial of the autonomy of ethics, a model for how ethics is part of, and continuous with, our knowledge conceived as a seamless web, and a view of the growth of moral knowledge. (For background to this position, see Evers and Lakomski 1991: 166–191, 1996: 142–153, 2000: 104–120.)

Moral cognition and norms: The example of hedonistic utilitarianism

Utilitarianism, in both its hedonistic varieties and its modern preference forms, provides a helpful example of how the descriptive and the normative comport to yield a systematic theory of moral judgement. Consider a simple moral judgement. A dear friend of questionable aesthetic perception asks how you like their new jacket. To tell the truth is to risk causing hurt. As a utilitarian (Smart 1956: 344–354), who appraises each moral issue according to the amount of happiness it entails as a consequence of acting upon it, you tell a lie: 'It's a splendid jacket.'

The core of the theory of value at work here, the normative aspect, is the equating of good with the natural quality of maximising human happiness (or minimising pain). That is, hedonistic utilitarianism lies within the naturalistic tradition of ethical theorising. How might one attempt to justify this theory of value? A descriptively oriented epistemological approach is to argue that the resulting elaborated ethical theory provides an excellent systematisation of actual moral practice. That is, when we examine the moral decisions people make, under the conditions in which they are made, we argue that there is an excellent fit, or at least the best possible fit given the diversity of judgement that obtains in many cases, with the judgements of the theory.

But why should a best possible fit serve as evidence for the normative merits of a moral theory such as utilitarianism? After all, a community's collective moral practice may not itself be morally praiseworthy (Sterba 1996: 252–253). One standard response is to argue that the community's moral practice is, in fact, rational, or the outcome of sound reasoning processes. Consider the most widely used folk theory of rational decision-making: belief-desire theory. On this analysis, a person's actual decision-making is the result of a coordination of particular beliefs and desires. So, someone's decision to buy a lottery ticket is rationally explained by claiming that they desire to have a chance at winning the lottery and they believe that buying a ticket gives them that chance. Similarly, in the case of telling lies about the aesthetic merits of someone's jacket, you desire not to hurt their feelings and you believe that this can be achieved by dissembling.

Unfortunately, this descriptive account of reasoning, whatever its merits as an empirical theory, fails to explain why we should regard the facts about what people desire as revealing what is desirable. Indeed, some have argued that J. S. Mill (1861–1962), the major figure in the development of hedonistic utilitarianism, made precisely this error of running together the desirable with the desired (see Mabbott 1956: 115–120).

But if an entire moral community enjoys a consensus in its judgements of what is desired, why cannot we just equate that with the desirable? Why not just say that that is what desirable *means*, namely, to be desired consistently by everyone? And if ever there were a candidate for this kind of consensus it would surely be, as Mill thought, the case of happiness. For happiness is something that everyone desires. Indeed, this would be the basis for any explanatory fit between moral theory and actual moral practice.

This form of naturalistic ethics, therefore, has three key methodological components. First, a theory of value that is required to generate a good explanatory fit between actual ethical judgement and what the elaborated theory produces. Second, an account of cognition that explains how people engage in moral reasoning. And third, a theory of meaning that defends the moral premises used in moral reasoning by appeal to the conditions that make for the explanatory fit.

Problems with a naturalistic ethics: The naturalistic fallacy

Largely in response to hedonistic utilitarianism, Cambridge philosopher G. E. Moore raised what he and many others regard as a fundamental objection to the whole enterprise of a naturalistic ethics. Writing in 1903, Moore, in his *Principia Ethica* (pp. 5–15) argued that all naturalistic definitions of moral terms – 'good' in particular – commit a fallacy, which he called the naturalistic fallacy. His argument is complex (see Evers and Lakomski 1991: 169–172 for a discussion), but the central strategy is to pit a theory of meaning against utilitarianism's theory of value. Essentially, he argues that for any naturalistic definition of good, say in terms of human happiness, we can always ask: 'But is good really that which promotes human happiness?' Indeed, he claims that any purported definition of good can be met with this 'open question'. The contrast Moore has in mind is with so-called analytic definitions, definitions of terms whose truth is guaranteed by meanings. Thus the definition of 'bachelor' as an unmarried adult male does not sensibly admit of an open question since the sentence 'a bachelor is an unmarried adult male' is analytic. In fact Moore concludes that good is a simple non-natural property.

It is hard to underestimate the impact of this argument on moral philosophy. 'Moore's use of the open-question argument generally has been accepted by philosophers, although over the years some cogent criticisms have been directed at it' (Arrington 1989: 8). Lycan (1988: 198–204) also singles out Moore's open-question argument as having a profound (but unfortunate) influence on twentieth-century moral philosophy.

My view, in common with Lycan's (1988: 199–201), is that this argument is much overrated. In particular, it has little purchase on ethical theorising that denies any clear demarcation between analytic and synthetic statements. If, under the influence of Quine's (1951, 1960, 1981, 1990) arguments, we accept a form of semantic holism, then we can say, first, that the meaning of a term is given in part by its conceptual role within a theory, and second, that it can be a matter of methodological choice which statements of the theory to hold true, come what may, thus giving them the apparent character of analytic claims.

To see how this works, consider the term 'force'. In ordinary usage, it has a variety of meanings: 'power' or 'influence' as a noun, 'compel' or 'push' as a verb, to give just a few. And querying these – 'does "force" really mean "power"?' – may indeed run counter to our intuitions of analyticity. But within Newtonian mechanics, where it means 'mass times acceleration (F = ma)', matters are different. In response to the question 'is "force" really "mass times acceleration"?' the answer is: that depends on the merits of the theory. If Newtonian mechanics is a true theory, then science has told us something very important about the way the world is, namely that $F = ma$. Within this theory, 'force' derives its meaning from the conceptual role it plays, notably its systematic links with other terms in the theory, and the conditions under which the theory as a whole enjoys empirical support.

Notice that this provides one reason for thinking that it is the scientific theory as a whole that enjoys empirical support rather than particular individual statements. Because the statements of the theory are systematically interconnected, empirical content is distributed across the entire theory (or those topic-specific parts where the interconnections may be strongest), thus making it possible to insulate any particular claim against empirical refutation by making adjustments to other parts of the theory. So, if we decide to protect $F = ma$ from empirical refutation, regardless of observation, we can do so, thus giving it the appearance of an analytic statement.

The same point can be made on behalf of hedonistic utilitarianism's account of good. Equating good with the maximising of human happiness (or the minimising of human suffering) is to make a theoretical claim that is a central organising principle of an ethical theory designed to explain moral behaviour and judgement, and to prescribe what is to be done. The merits of this particular definition are therefore linked to the merits of the theory as a whole. Asserting that a naturalistic fallacy is being committed uses intuitions of what is, or is not, a suitable definition in advance of any adjudication of the merits of the particular moral theory. But this is to give unwarranted privilege to the theories embedded in ordinary language and usage – the principal source of our analyticity intuitions – ahead of alternatives that may turn out to be epistemically more justified.

Substance and property anti-naturalism

For the utilitarian, ethical claims can be true or false. There is a fact of the matter, albeit one that is often difficult to determine, concerning whether human happiness is advanced or retarded. Moore's anti-naturalism, coupled with a belief that ethical claims could be true or false, led him to what is nowadays regarded as a rather exotic view of moral cognition, namely intuitionism, a doctrine that asserts there is a special moral realm that can be known only by some correspondingly special faculty of moral perception. In educational administration, Christopher Hodgkinson (1978, 1983, 1991, 1996, 1999), who has written the most on ethics, comes close to such a view for his highest level of values. Unfortunately, little is known about this faculty. Moreover, the place where enquiry might most profitably be pursued is empirical psychology, suitably constrained to cohere with models of how the human brain perceives and learns. The result is that the methodology and ontology of a theory of moral cognition will most likely part company with the methodology and ontology of the theory of value with which it is supposed to mesh to form an explanatory unity.

Such a consequence is not unusual in philosophy. Realist views of mathematics that posit an ontology of abstract objects need to address the question of how humans could ever become acquainted with these objects. Plato's solution was to posit an equally abstract object to be the centre of cognition: the soul. Although this kind of substance dualism has few defenders nowadays, property dualism flourishes. There is no shortage of people who accept both a naturalistic ontology of substance and are willing to defend the view that, say, mental properties such as belief, desire, knowledge, or intention, are entirely different from, or not reducible to, physical properties such as mass, length, or electric charge (Chalmers 1996). Similarly, the autonomy of ethics as an account of an irreducible set of moral properties is maintained while accepting a naturalistic ontology also describable in terms of naturalistic predicates (Blackburn 1984).

Property anti-naturalism in ethics (and in the philosophy of mind) is not without its costs. Indeed, there is a huge literature around the theme of 'supervenience' that is devoted to dealing with the problem of explaining how autonomous sets of properties can influence each other. In ethics 'The supervenience of ethical predicates on natural predicates is the thesis that if two actions (or two people) are indistinguishable with respect to their natural predicates, the same ethical predicates apply to them as well' (Drai 2000: 1). However, in rejecting the naturalistic fallacy, this issue can be bypassed in favour of accepting the theoretical identities of ethical and (possibly complex) natural properties arising out of an epistemically defensible account, or theory, of phenomena in general. Let us turn, then, to the question of epistemology and its role in justifying ethical claims.

Naturalistic epistemology

One of Frege's lasting contributions to logical theory was to separate out clearly the features of logical systems from concerns over the psychology of thought. As Tversky and Kahneman (1981) have been able to demonstrate through their investigation of cognitive illusions – systematic errors in human reasoning – there is an important distinction to be drawn between descriptive decision-making, which is the province of psychology, and normative decision-making, which is about how we ought to make decisions. This distinction turns up in epistemology, too, as the distinction between 'context of discovery', presumed to be a matter of psychology, and 'context of justification', which is concerned with the logic of preferring one theory over another. Karl Popper's epistemology, which provides a prominent and well formulated instance, is instructive.

In his first major work, *The Logic of Scientific Discovery* (1934/1959), Popper attempted to extend anti-psychologism even further. Discovery itself was a matter of logic. More precisely, he argued that the growth of knowledge had a particular logical structure, notably that which applied to the process of conjecture and refutation. Popper later theorised this aspect of his position in epistemology as 'epistemology without a knowing subject', being the title of one of his papers. Schematically, the logic of discovery could be represented by the schema P1 → TT → EE → P2, where P1 is an initial problem, TT a tentative theory for dealing with the problem, EE a process whereby errors in that theory are eliminated and revisions made, and P2 a new problem to be dealt with as the start of a new cycle (Popper 1972: ch. 3). A succession of 'Popper Cycles' constitutes epistemic progress if, roughly speaking, successive tentative theories solve more problems than their predecessors while surviving ever more powerful tests of refutation. Formulated thus, the logic of discovery makes no explicit reference to any theory of human cognition.

Opposed to this sort of position are some strong reasons for thinking that, in epistemology, an understanding of the powers of the mind matters a great deal. Consider Popper's discussion of Hume's epistemology (Popper 1934/1959: 420–425, 1963: 43–48). For Hume, the identification of patterns in the flow of experience occurs through a psychological process of induction. For example, a black raven is observed on one occasion, and then another, and then another, and so on, leading to the expectation – not logically justified – that all ravens are black. Popper attacks this modest learning theory on logical grounds, arguing that the identification of successive objects as ravens presupposes an antecedent mechanism for classifying objects as instances of the same thing. Judgements of similarity are always relative to the observer; they always presuppose a point of view; they are similarity for us. (For a formal proof, see Watanabe 1969: 376–379.) But similarity ratings are therefore functioning as antecedent hypotheses that we bring to experience. Unlike Kant's view of the synthetic *a priori*, Popper thinks that these prior hypotheses, initially beginning as innate dispositions, are subject to correction and improvement through the process of refutation. They are the original conjectures necessary to commence the learning process, motivated by the need to solve problems, for us to navigate at better than chance through the world we inhabit (Popper 1963: 47).

It seems to me that this schema is broadly correct (Evers and Lakomski 1991: 37). However, Popper's orientation towards anti-psychologism prevents recourse to an important source of necessary refinement: the empirical study of successful 'epistemic engines', namely creatures (or machines) that extract patterns from the passing show of experience, building up, in the process, maps or representations of the world that improve their chances of problem-solving and predicting with some measure of success the consequences of events and actions. And some refinement is certainly needed in order to fit together holism with falsification. Because when it comes to explanation, problem-solving, or prediction, it is the conjunction of statements making up the relevant part of the theory that carry the burden of implication, not individual singular hypotheses. So when a refutation occurs, the problem could lie with any one of a number of hypotheses. Moreover, since observations themselves are laden with theory, there is the additional complexity of adjudicating whether it is the theory at fault or whether there is something wrong with the alleged refuting observation. And then there is the need to make changes to accommodate new recalcitrant data while conserving that which accounts for past success.

The task of determining how to revise a theory in the light of competing considerations of holism and empirical adequacy may be regarded as coming up with a way of maximising the satisfaction of a set of multiple epistemic constraints on theories. In line with Thagard and Verbeurgt (1998), I see this task as equivalent to providing a coherence theory of knowledge justification. In addition to squaring with theory-laden observation, a theory should enjoy the virtues of consistency, simplicity, comprehensiveness, explanatory unity, fecundity and, to do justice to its past successes, some measure of conservatism.

While it has proved extremely difficult in the past to specify with precision how epistemic justification operates with all these constraints acting in concert, work done over the past fifteen years or so on the descriptive study of successful epistemic engines has had a number of important normative implications for epistemology. In particular, it has been argued by a number of writers in the tradition of scientific naturalism, for example Churchland (1989, 1995) and Thagard (1992), that neuro-computational models of how the human brain represents and acquires knowledge can provide significant details on how the cognitive dynamics of successful epistemic practice might operate. One virtue of these models is that they provide an example of the microprocessing that goes on in learning that is driven by the satisfaction of multiple epistemic constraints.

Before discussing these models and how they operate to justify ethical claims, some general features should be mentioned. First, in commenting on his conjectured process of how moral progress occurs, Churchland has this to say about the unity of moral and scientific knowledge growth:

> From the neurocomputational perspective, this process looks different only in its ontological focus – the *social* world as opposed to the *natural* world – from what we are pleased to call *scientific progress*. Our conceptual development in the moral domain, I suggest, differs only in detail from our development in the scientific domain.
>
> (Churchland 1998: 92)

Likewise, Thagard links together ethics, naturalism and coherentist epistemology, as follows:

> This paper shows how justification of ethical principles ... and particular judgments ... can be accomplished by taking into account a wide range of coherence considerations. Cognitive naturalism is currently the dominant position in the philosophy of mind, and it has made substantial contributions to epistemology and the philosophy of science. By applying a psychological/computational theory of coherence, this paper demonstrates the relevance of cognitive naturalism to ethics.
>
> (Thagard 1998: 406)

Cognitive naturalism, epistemology, and the justification of ethics

Thagard's view

The argument in this section has a number of parts. First, following Thagard, I shall sketch how a theory that combines naturalism and coherentism – my own preferred orientation – can be elaborated to yield a neuro-computational model for ethical decision-making. As this is not without difficulties, I then discuss Churchland's complementary account of the acquisition of moral knowledge as a way of resolving these difficulties. Finally, I shall suggest why a naturalistic epistemology can be used to justify the normative appropriateness of moral knowledge acquired under its prescriptions. The result will be what Dewey saw with clarity many years ago: that the good is linked to the virtue of promoting the growth of knowledge.

The operation of Thagard's naturalistic coherentism in a computational model can be seen most clearly with the aid of one of his own examples, the Necker cube (Figure 12.1). In this figure, the face at the front is ambiguous; it can be either ABCD or EFGH. But whichever interpretation is made, it has systematic or holistic consequences for interpreting all the other vertices. These two interpretations can be represented as clusters of related hypotheses (Thagard 1992: 70–71; Evers 2000: 218–219). So the hypothesis 'A is at the front', Af, coheres with the hypothesis 'B is at the front', Bf, and also hypotheses Cf and Df, and the hypothesis 'E is at the back', Eb. Similarly, hypothesis Ab coheres with hypotheses Ef, Db, Cb, and Bb. Now it is possible to represent these hypotheses as nodes in an artificial neural network, with their truth or falsehood being represented by node activation values, a_i, of 1 and 0 respectively, and the level of coherence, or incoherence, between hypotheses as positive or negative weights, w_{ij}, between nodes. (Weights are the model's mathematical analogue of synaptic junctions between neurons.) The network is said to

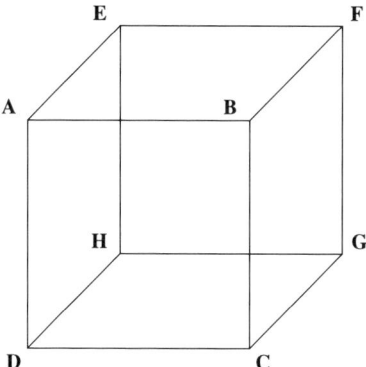

Figure 12.1 The Necker cube

settle into an interpretation of the evidence, to decide on a conceptual scheme, when coherence is maximised, and this is defined as maximising the sum of all the products of weights and their adjoining node activation levels, thus:

$$\text{Global coherence, } G = \Sigma_i \Sigma_j w_{ij} a_i a_j$$

Since for the Necker cube, the two possible interpretations are incompatible – they incohere – when the network settles on one interpretation, the activation values of nodes representing hypotheses for the other interpretation are switched off, or zero. (For a fuller treatment of these 'harmony nets' and their theory, see Smolensky 1986.)

This model can be used to make decisions about choice among theories. Let us suppose, in a simplified universe, that we have five items of evidence, E_1, E_2, E_3, E_4, E_5, and that this evidence is more or less supporting two competing theories, T, and T', composed of two sets of hypotheses, t_1, t_2, t_3, and t'_1, t'_2, respectively. Then the harmony net that represents the coherence maximisation decision process is given by Figure 12.2.

For Thagard's program ECHO that computes this simulation (and is available on his website), typical initial default values would be 0.01 for all activations, 0.04 for excitatory links, and −0.06 for inhibitory links. For each cycle of processing through the net, activations are updated according to the formula:

$$a_j(t+1) = a_j(t)(1-\phi) + I_j(1-a_j(t))$$

where t is the time of update, I_j is the input to the j-th node and ϕ is a decay constant. Weights between nodes are adjusted in order to maximise global coherence. These small harmony nets usually stabilise into a decision between alternative theories or clusters of cohering hypotheses, after about 100 cycles.

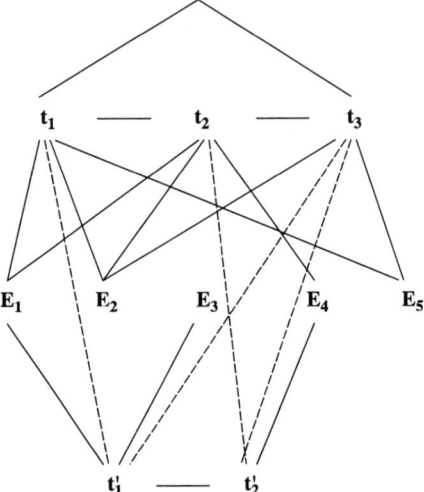

Figure 12.2 Harmony network for choosing the most coherent theory: T (composed of hypotheses t_1, t_2, t_3) or T' (composed of hypotheses t'_1, t'_2). Solid lines indicate excitatory links, dotted lines indicate inhibitory links.

Something like this processing can also be applied to ethical decision-making since, when it comes to the identification of coherence or incoherence relations among hypotheses, there is no principled difference between ethical hypotheses and other hypotheses. To illustrate this, Thagard (1998) considers the case of whether the state is justified in executing a person who commits a serious crime. Hypotheses and their connections within the network might include the following selected from Thagard:

> 'Capital punishment is wrong' incoheres with 'Capital punishment is sometimes justified'.
>
> 'Preventing serious crime is good' coheres with 'Capital punishment helps to prevent serious crime'; both of these hypotheses cohere with 'Capital punishment is good'.
>
> 'Evidence' may cohere with 'Capital punishment helps to prevent serious crime'.
>
> 'Capital punishment is wrong' coheres with 'X should not be executed'.
>
> (Thagard 1998: 416)

The point is that it is possible to find a maximally coherent set of hypotheses that involve ethical claims that are also linked to empirical evidence.

There are, nevertheless, some difficulties. For example, notice that the value premises are already given, and the task of the theory of cognition is to maximise coherence among them. But why should the result be a morally acceptable set of value claims? Why is not a coherently evil result possible? The parallel case in empirical science is, why cannot a piece of fiction be more coherent than a scientific theory? The answer that tells against fiction is that in the model the activation levels of some nodes representing empirical hypotheses are subject to direct 'evidence' inputs. Because coherence includes empirical adequacy, the net is presumed to be expandable in the direction of theory-laden evidence inputs. That is, a theory should cohere with a suitable account of how it is acquired, and at this point, if not earlier, fiction becomes discernible. But there are empirical evidence inputs into the capital punishment example, too. Evidence is relevant to the claim 'Capital punishment is a deterrent' and this, in turn, coheres with 'Capital punishment is sometimes justified'. In line with our view that semantics should be viewed holistically, as involving considerations of conceptual role, the apparent distance of cohering ethical claims from empirical evidence would be due to their position towards the centre of our web of belief. They may be as accessible to observation as the scientific claim 'protons are made up of two u-quarks and one d-quark'.

The web of belief, a metaphor cashed out as a harmony net, needs to be added to substantially if the justification of the ethical claims is to be borne by the maximisation of global coherence. As Thagard explains:

> when dealing with difficult ethical issues such as capital punishment and abortion we should feel obliged to take into account all the different kinds of issues that have been taken to be relevant to the morality of such practices.
>
> (Thagard 1998: 417)

Unfortunately, when this is done, when the simplified universe is scaled up, the computation of global coherence becomes formally intractable. Shorn of technicalities, what this means is that for even modest increases in the number of hypotheses to be considered, the amount of computation time required to solve the theory choice problem becomes enormous. Or as Millgram (2000: 87) colourfully puts it, 'there are reasonably sized inputs for which you will not be able to solve the problem – at any rate, not before the universe freezes over . . .'.

An obvious fallback strategy is to explore possible approximation techniques. However, the computed next best coherent result could be a

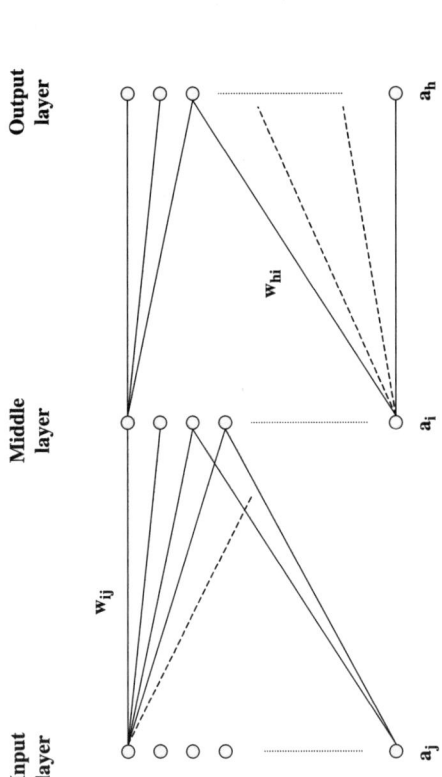

Figure 12.3 Three-layer feedforward net that learns by backpropagation

theory that is clearly wrong (Millgram 2000: 87–88). What grounds are there for having confidence in approximation techniques? In the case of modelling theory choice in science, we can check the approximate calculation of global coherence results against real competing theory outcomes. According to Thagard, 'The simulations show that the theory of explanatory coherence is coherent with important cases in history' (2000: 4). While within this framework of knowledge and justification there may be good reasons for thinking that the same kind of approximations will work for ethical judgements, appeal to the moral equivalents of science's Newton, or Darwin, or Einstein is more problematic.

A more promising approach, in my view, is to lessen the demands on computation by scaffolding the problem developmentally, through the incorporation of learning. Moral values are presumably learned along with other features of the social world we inhabit. The question is whether an epistemically progressive procedure exists for making the learning of these values self-correcting, for transforming any learned bad values into good ones.

Churchland's view

The sort of naturalistic coherence decision procedures modelled by harmony nets are an example of unsupervised learning. If this could be supplemented with a form of supervised learning that is also naturalistic and coherentist, it would provide a more realistic and incremental approach to the development of a normatively suitable moral perspective. Here the work of Paul Churchland (1989, 1995, 1998) is relevant. Consider, again, the Popper Cycle learning schema proposed for explaining the growth of scientific knowledge. Learning, in the form of theory revision, is driven by the process of error elimination, which requires making adjustments to a theory in response to a mismatch between theory-based feedforward expectations (in the form of, say, predictions, or proposed solutions to problems) and feedback from experience (in the form of disconfirmations of predictions, or proposed solutions that fail to solve anything). Feedback is a form of supervision and learning from it can be modelled within the naturalistic, neuro-computational framework by using feedforward nets that learn by backpropagation of error. Figure 12.3 provides an example of such a network.

With this network, information flows from the input layer, through the hidden layer and on to the output layer. (For a detailed account, see Evers 2000.) Each node is an artificial neuron, with the input layer being activated by an input vector representing information from experience. The input then leads to output being produced by the first layer, the a_j in Figure 12.3, and transmitted on to the next layer. During the transmission process, these activation values are multiplied by weights, w_{ij}, summed, and then inputted into the relevant middle layer nodes. Node a_i thus receives as input $\Sigma w_{ij}a_j$. In response, the middle layer nodes become activated (the level of activation being determined in most models by a non-linear function of the received input known as a sigmoid function) and transmit a signal along to the next layer, the output layer. Once again the signal is weighted and summed. Supervised learning takes place when there is a difference between the net's output and the 'target' output. Initially, the net's output will be determined by a random assignment of weight values. The model then learns by making a series of adjustments to all of the weights according to a learning rule that reduces the error difference – thus instantiating a form of coherentist learning. Assuming there is pattern in the input data and the net has sufficient resources, the error will gradually converge to a set minimum amount, say, 5 per cent or 10 per cent. In this way, the net learns to produce the correct output for given inputs, its knowledge residing in the weights distributed across the net's architecture.

An example will illustrate how learning can occur. Some years ago, I trained a small three-layer feedforward net to extract patterns of wins and losses from the previous four weekends of games in a football competition. There being sixteen teams in the competition, each could be represented by a four-digit vector comprised of binary numbers, e.g. [0,0,1,1] or [1,0,1,0], and so on. A game between two teams could thus be represented by an eight-digit vector, e.g. [0,0,1,1,1,0,1,0]. If the team playing on its home ground is put first, we can code that additional piece of information by putting that team's four-digit representation first. The outcome for each game can be represented by the vectors [0,1] or [1,0] (or, in the case of rare draws, by [0.5,0.5]), where the first number gives the result for the first team, a '1' for a win, a '0' for a loss, and the second number gives the result for the second team. Training up the net therefore involved feeding in thirty-two input vectors of eight digits, one at a time, and for the net's output on each vector to be checked against the true, or target, result. After about half an hour of processing, the net would manage to extract what pattern there was in the data, correctly calculating learned output vectors for corresponding inputs. (I allowed the program to halt when the net's output came within 10 per cent of the target.) With the net trained on recent past results, I could then feed in vectors corresponding to games to be played in the next round and the net would compute an output, being a prediction of a win or a loss. The net, which had a total of fourteen neurons (eight input, four hidden, and two output) managed to gain third place in the faculty's football tipping competition!

For each input vector, the net eventually managed to exhibit one of two characteristic patterns of activation across the neurons in its penultimate layer (in this case the middle layer): one pattern corresponding to a perception of a win/loss result, the other corresponding to loss/win. These are called prototypical activation patterns. If you can imagine each of the n neurons of this layer being able to take on a range of numerical values, then the n-space 'volume' of theoretically possible activation configurations, the conceptual space, will be partitioned into two parts: win/loss and loss/win. (I assume draws are unpredictable.)

Now, Churchland treats the elements of moral learning in the same fashion:

> In living creatures, learning also consists in the repeated adjustment of one's myriad synaptic connections, a process also driven by one's ongoing experience with failure.
> (Churchland 1998: 87)

and

> the suggestion here advanced is that our capacity for *moral* discrimination also resides in an intricately configured matrix of synaptic connections, which connections also partition an abstract conceptual space, at some proprietary neuronal layer of the human brain, into a hierarchical set of categories, categories such as 'morally significant' vs. 'morally nonsignificant' actions; and within the former category, 'morally bad' vs. 'morally praiseworthy' actions; and within the former subcategory, sundry specific categories such as 'lying', 'cheating', 'betraying' . . . etc.
> (Churchland 1998: 86)

In this kind of learning from experience, feedback comes from one's social world. But it is not only specific responses from parents or teachers or friends or other particular individuals that provide feedback and additional inputs. The structure of moral behaviour, implicit in the pattern of practices in which the learner is engaged, forms a significant source of experience to be scanned implicitly along with the rest of the passing show. This is an important point and helps us deal with a common objection to Churchland's account of moral knowledge. The objection is simply that there is no reason for supposing that what a person learns under these conditions is morally praiseworthy. The social context in which moral learning occurs may, itself, be corrupt or morally bankrupt.

The ethics of learning

Nevertheless, we should note that the social relations of learning also embody a moral framework. The social relations of rote learning provide one example. And the social relations of implementing the sort of fallibilist, Popperian model of learning, provide another. Popper understood this point perfectly well when he came to develop the implications of his epistemology for political philosophy and policy-making. For wherever we assume that our knowledge is provisional and fallible, the making of epistemic progress requires a social, political and moral infrastructure that can nurture and sustain something like the process of conjecture and refutation, the testing of ideas and the acknowledgement and communication of error. For Popper (1945), herein lay the cornerstone of his defence of the 'open society' against its enemies (Plato and Marx), for his defence of democracy against the totalitarianisms of the left and the right.

Similarly, the *moral* infrastructure required for fallibilist learning would include tolerance of divergent viewpoints, freedom of speech, freedom of association, and support for the right to be able to participate in the learning community as an active enquirer. Although these are modest moral resources, their acquisition as moral prototypes arising out of ongoing experience will be greatly augmented when further developments of moral perspective are required, by the demands of epistemology, to cohere with them. Scaffolding upwards, we can envision a cohering politics, educational philosophy, legal system, and a host of preferred social arrangements. The best example of such an elaborately articulated framework can be found, of course, in the work of Dewey. In fact, for Dewey (1916), with his coherentist approach to knowledge and his naturalistic ontology, good was identified with the growth of knowledge.

But why, to echo Moore, should we promote the growth of knowledge? Our holistic semantics enables us to bypass the assumptions that give rise to the charge of committing a naturalistic fallacy. Moreover, holism also prompts a coherentist response to epistemology. In being allowed to cohere with natural science, epistemology itself can be naturalised within a theory of cognition that draws on recent work in computational neuroscience. Fitting together the coherence approach of Thagard with the learning approach of Churchland provides suggestions for a normative theory of moral learning that resists the computational intractability problem while opening the way to resolving the charge that moral learning cannot be normatively self-correcting. (Adaptive resonance neural network models developed by Grossberg (1982, 1988) come closest to combining these two features in a biologically realistic way.) The defence of such an ethic is both general and piecemeal. It is general in so far as humans need to solve problems, and to navigate around the world doing better than chance or, better, to flourish in civilisations, knowledge is required. But such knowledge is hard to come by and is always fallible. By scaffolding upwards from the empirical conditions for best meeting the epistemic demands of life, we find implicit in the practices and policies entailed by these conditions a set of moral values. It is piecemeal in the sense that there is debate over what constitutes the problem, over what we know and do not know about solving it, and over the social conditions for resolving those debates and for acquiring the knowledge we do not have. My epistemology gives one kind of answer. My conjecture, subject to refutation, is that rival views will need to end up competing for theoretical adequacy within the epistemic and moral framework I defend, if we are to make progress on the particularities.

References

Arrington, R. L. (1989) *Rationalism, Realism, and Relativism,* Ithaca: Cornell University Press.
Blackburn, S. (1984) *Spreading the Word,* Oxford: Oxford University Press.
Chalmers, D. J. (1996) *The Conscious Mind,* Oxford: Oxford University Press.
Churchland, P. M. (1989) *A Neurocomputational Perspective,* Cambridge, MA: MIT Press.
Churchland, P. M. (1995) *The Engine of Reason, the Seat of the Soul,* Cambridge, MA: MIT Press.
Churchland, P. M. (1998) 'Towards a cognitive neurobiology of the moral virtues', *Topoi* 17: 83–96.
Dewey, J. (1916) *Democracy and Education,* New York: Free Press.
Drai, D. (2000) 'Moral supervenience and moral thinking', *Disputatio* 8: 1–10.
Evers, C. W. (2000) 'Connectionist modeling in education', *Australian Journal of Education* 44, 3: 209–225.
Evers, C. W. and Lakomski, G. (1991) *Knowing Educational Administration,* Oxford: Pergamon.
Evers, C. W. and Lakomski, G. (1996) *Exploring Educational Administration,* Oxford: Pergamon.
Evers, C. W. and Lakomski, G. (2000) *Doing Educational Administration,* Oxford: Pergamon.
Grossberg, S. (1982) *Studies in Mind and Brain,* Boston: D. Reidel.
Grossberg, S. (1988) *Neural Networks and Natural Intelligence,* Cambridge, MA: MIT Press.
Hodgkinson, C. (1978) *Towards a Philosophy of Administration,* Oxford: Blackwell.
Hodgkinson, C. (1983) *The Philosophy of Leadership,* Oxford: Blackwell.
Hodgkinson, C. (1991) *Educational Leadership: The Moral Art,* Albany: State University of New York Press.
Hodgkinson, C. (1996) *Administrative Philosophy,* Oxford: Pergamon.
Hodgkinson, C. (1999) 'The triumph of the will: An exploration of certain fundamental problematics in administrative philosophy', in P. Begley and P. E. Leonard (eds) *The Values of Educational Administration,* London: Falmer.
Lycan, W. G. (1988) *Judgement and Justification,* Cambridge: Cambridge University Press.
Mabbott, J. D. (1956) 'Interpretations of Mill's *Utilitarianism*', *Philosophical Quarterly* 6: 115–120.
Mill, J. S. (1861/1962) *Utilitarianism,* London: Collins.
Millgram, E. (2000) 'Coherence: The price of the ticket, *Journal of Philosophy* 97, 2: 82–93.
Moore, G. E. (1903) *Principia Ethica,* London: Cambridge University Press.
Popper, K. R. (1934/1959) *The Logic of Scientific Discovery,* London: Hutchinson.

Popper, K.R. (1945) *The Open Society and its Enemies*, vols 1 and 2, London: George Routledge and Sons.
Popper, K. R. (1963) *Conjectures and Refutations*, London: Routledge and Kegan Paul.
Popper, K. R. (1972) *Objective Knowledge*, Oxford: Oxford University Press
Quine, W. V. (1951) 'Two dogmas of empiricism', *Philosophical Review* 60: 20–43.
Quine, W. V. (1960) *Word and Object*, Cambridge, MA: MIT Press.
Quine, W. V. (1981) *Theories and Things*, Cambridge MA: Harvard University Press.
Quine, W. V. (1990) *Pursuit of Truth*, Cambridge, MA: Harvard University Press.
Smart, J. J. C. (1956) 'Extreme and restricted utilitarianism', *Philosophical Quarterly* 6: 344–354.
Smolensky, P. (1986) 'Information processing in dynamical systems: Foundations of harmony theory', in D. E. Rumelhart and J. E. McClelland (eds) *Parallel Distributed Processes*, vol. 1, Cambridge, MA: MIT Press.
Sterba, J. P. (1996) 'Justifying morality and the challenge of cognitive science', in L. May, M. Friedman and A. Clark (eds) *Mind and Morals*, Cambridge, MA: MIT Press.
Thagard, P. (1992) *Conceptual Revolutions*, Princeton: Princeton University Press.
Thagard, P. (1998) 'Ethical coherence', *Philosophical Psychology* 11, 4: 405–422.
Thagard, P. (2000) 'Coherence: The price is right', http://cogsci.uwaterloo.ca/Articles/Pages/coh.price.html.
Thagard, P. and Verbeurgt, K. (1998) 'Coherence as constraint satisfaction', *Cognitive Science* 22, 1: 1–24.
Tversky, A. and Kahneman, D. (1981) 'The framing of decisions and the psychology of choice', *Science* 211: 453–458.
Watanabe, S. (1969) *Knowing and Guessing*, New York: John Wiley.

Chapter 13

Greatness and service
Antinomies of leadership?

Peter Gronn

The purpose of this chapter is to discuss a broad ethical tradition which has played a significant role in legitimating the formation and ongoing work of generations of educational and other leaders. For want of a better term, this ethic may be described as a philosophy of practical, working idealism. It is an approach to moral leadership with which the man to whom this collection of essays is dedicated has recently linked himself and his writings (Hodgkinson 1996: 264). Historically, this working ethic formed a loose worldview comprising a diet of wisdom and insights, distilled mainly from biblical, classical sources and other writings which, in many cases, formed part of what is now referred to as the Western literary and philosophical canon. The intention of this curriculum was to imbue the products of schooling (in particular boys) with 'character' as a foundation for their future moral leadership of society. This idealism was most closely associated with the doctrine of *noblesse oblige* – the idea that such schooling carried with it a duty on the part of its privileged recipients to willingly take on future social roles and responsibilities. In practical terms, acceptance of responsibility meant service to society, one of the two main themes of this chapter, in a range of institutional spheres. Service, and the willingness to serve others, was imbibed by young people as part of the formal school curriculum, and was a virtue extolled and proselytised by heads of schools in numerous speech day addresses and chapel sermons. It was also a message mediated throughout the wider society, in literature, newspaper editorials and in pulpits, and by the products of the schools themselves as they assumed their eventual roles as part of the organs of government, business, the church, the civil service and the universities.

The ideal of service was part of an implicit social contract in which a (mostly male) minority, by virtue of a unique combination of birth, upbringing, circumstance and social standing, was groomed for, and monopolised, leadership. In both the Victorian and Edwardian eras, this broad approach to leader formation was most closely associated with an English public school education, the ideals of which were transported as part of a civilising mission throughout the Empire by a diaspora of ex-public school and Oxbridge-educated graduates. While there were few attempts to try to systematise this broad public school ethos (although see Norwood 1929), it was acknowledged by its proponents and critics alike that the institutional practices informed by it produced a leadership type known as the gentleman. This approach to leadership and service to society had its various continental European equivalents (Armstrong 1973) and Confucian parallels (Wilkinson 1964), and, in the new world, entire cohorts of educational leaders were schooled in, and subsequently modelled, 'character' as 'managers of virtue' (Tyack and Hansot 1982). The ethic of service was closely associated with the second theme of this chapter, greatness, through the range of exemplary heroic, mythic and warrior deeds of the figures of history modelled in the texts and stories forming the school curriculum. The heads of the schools themselves also exemplified greatness, both in their self-chosen image as 'very superior men',[1] for example, and in the thriving literature of school novels and magazines which proved popular with the rising middle classes (Protherough 1984). As most students of leadership would be aware, the theme of greatness also exercised a significant and pervasive influence on teaching and research in the field of leadership, in the guise of trait theory, right up until Stogdill's important landmark critique in the late 1940s (Bass 1990: 59–88).

Despite the circumstances of their origin, over time both service and greatness have been democratised by being stripped of most of their traditional aristocratic, imperial and paternal assumptions. In the case of greatness, for example, while there may be few contemporary commentators, perhaps apart from Simonton (1994), who are prepared to extol the virtues of greatness in an overt and unabashed way, this theme is very much alive and well in a much more muted and domesticated form in the neo-trait theories of leadership which underwent a renewed interest during the 1980s and 1990s. These include a number of transformational, charismatic and visionary leadership approaches. Each of these embodies a democratised sense of greatness in the sense that the 'super-leader' and institutional 'turn-around' behaviour, which they model and commend as both desirable and feasible, has ceased to be restricted to persons of a particular gender, social background or stratum, and can be acquired through training and development programmes by, potentially, any individual (Gronn 1995, Yukl 1999). Likewise, with service, the notion of a 'service class' of hired, usually working-class, menial labourers has mostly disappeared in the industrialised and post-industrialised world,[2] and during the twentieth century a secularised 'service' ideal became institutionalised in the corporate, public and not-for-profit sectors in the form of notions of customer service, public service and community service (through a plethora of voluntary 'service clubs') respectively. Just as the last two decades or so of the second millennium witnessed a resurgence of greatness as part of a hero paradigm in leadership theories, so the organisation of services as public goods has been recently reconstructed. Former notions of vocation and altruism which, as will be shown, were the traditional legitimations for 'service', have been jettisoned as outmoded in favour of commodification and the reconstitution of service delivery as a market transaction.

Against this background, I consider some current writings on the themes of greatness and service. I begin with a discussion of the more recent work of Christopher Hodgkinson. In the passage in *Administrative Philosophy* in which he gives voice to his own idealism, Hodgkinson (1996: 264, original emphasis) asserts that, as a philosophy, idealism 'remains pristine in all its classical glory', for it is 'in the last analysis the *only* philosophy – all other philosophies being merely commentaries upon it or reactions to it'. Perversely, however, idealism has been corrupted into a mere ideology by modernity and post-modernity. Thus, 'Justice becomes a demand for rights, Truth becomes opinion, Beauty whatever the eye beholds, Goodness political correctness' (Hodgkinson 1996: 264). With these sentiments, I suggest, Hodgkinson has taken his readers to the heart of an important dilemma confronting anyone who is committed to the attainment of social ideals. Briefly, this dilemma (to be considered in more detail shortly) is admirably captured in the two popular lines from Robert Browning's poem, *Andrea Del Sarto*: 'Ah, but a man's reach should exceed his grasp, / Or what's a heaven for?' This dilemma is concerned with how idealists cope with the unattainability of their ideals in the face of human imperfectability (i.e. when human reach exceeds its grasp). I then contrast Hodgkinson's thinking with a recent and increasingly popular leader prototype which, prima facie, appears to be the antithesis of greatness: the idea of the leader as a servant, as manifest in the writings of Robert Greenleaf (1977, 1996). This contrast raises the question of whether, despite their historically close association, the connection between service and greatness has been severed, so that they now represent diverging polarities or antinomies of leadership.

My argument shall be that the various ways in which idealists try to reconcile the hiatus between the real and the ideal provide the wellsprings of their stance towards leadership and its ethical foundations. In essence, the preference for greatness may be understood as a commitment to transcendence, of trying to find ways, as it were, of bending an obdurate reality in the pursuit of desired ends. The service impulse, by contrast, while it may sometimes function as a way of clothing greatness or as a vehicle for its attainment (the subtitle of Greenleaf's *Servant Leadership* is, after all, *A Journey into the Nature of Legitimate Power and Greatness*), is a different impulse. Here, the commitment may still be to particular ends, except that the pursuit of ideals entails immanence rather than transcendence, or a disposition towards working with and within the necessities of life imposed by reality. While leadership commentators or practitioners may be temperamentally disposed towards either greatness or service, these two polarities should not be dismissed as a crude binary distinction or dualism, for some ethical idealists will no doubt find themselves pulled in both directions simultaneously or on separate occasions. That is, they experience a mix of psychological optimism and pessimism. In the following discussion, therefore, I will attempt to explicate some of the overlap, as well as differences, between these two alternatives.

Another Bethlehem?

It is inconceivable that anyone even remotely familiar with the writings of Christopher Hodgkinson would be unaware of his distinction between Type 1, 2A, 2B and 3 values. This ascending arrangement of values types, grounded in justifications ranging from preferences (Type 3) to principles (Type 1), comprises a values paradigm. With this axiological apparatus, Hodgkinson's purpose is to show that, in a world of value pluralism, commitments to human values are far from being all of a piece. Originally outlined in *Towards a Philosophy of Administration* (Hodgkinson 1978), his most recent statement of the paradigm has appeared in *Administrative Philosophy: Values and Motivations in Administrative Life* (Hodgkinson 1996). Arguably, this paradigm has been Hodgkinson's major contribution to the fields of educational administration and leadership over more than two decades, for he has tried to show that the decisions and actions of administrative and leadership practitioners, at all levels and in all spheres of action, are informed by one or the other of these three value types. Despite the centrality of the values typology, the focus of this section is on a different and, in some ways, equally important dimension of Hodgkinson's writings: his view of leadership. Previously (Gronn 1993), I have indicated how, within Hodgkinson's hierarchy of value types, is embedded a conception of leadership as personified by the deeds of great men and grounded ethically in Type 1 values. In making this earlier appraisal, I concentrated my analysis for the most part on *Towards a Philosophy of Administration*, *The Philosophy of Leadership* (Hodgkinson 1983) and *Educational Leadership: The Moral Art* (Hodgkinson 1991). Here I update this theme of greatness and show how it continues to underwrite Hodgkinson's view of leadership, particularly as it has been developed in *Administrative Philosophy* and other recent writings (e.g. Hodgkinson 1997, 2001). With his final words in *Administrative Philosophy*, Hodgkinson (1996: 270) makes a plea for the return of his preferred leader prototype, his embodiment of idealism, the Platonic guardian. This is a type, he concedes, that is 'totally unsuited to our times' yet 'crying out to be reborn'. 'Can it be', he speculates, 'that this rough beast, its hour comes [*sic*] around at last, shuffles towards another Bethlehem?'

Hodgkinson's preference for 'Bethlehem' is intriguing. While one should be wary of reading too much into the choice of particular discursive symbols, Bethlehem expresses Hodgkinson's own personal hope for a leadership reincarnation. Bethlehem, in the well rehearsed form of the holy family and the animals surrounding the infant Christ in the manger, has always been a powerful religious symbol of hope for Christians. To some extent, this imagery has even been domesticated and made palatable for non-believers through its absorption into a range of secularised symbols that package Christmas as an occasion for general festivity and indulgence. This same religious symbol of Bethlehem also functions as a vehicle for Christian idealists to reconcile greatness and service through the idea of the kingship of the Christ. That is, Christ, as God incarnate, is both Lord and king, and his message is not the pursuit of earthly power and dominion (after all, he was born into impoverished, migratory family circumstances in an insignificant town in Judea), but the path of discipleship (through crucifixion, death and resurrection) in the attainment of the kingdom of heaven. There are, of course, other alternative symbols and images of hope. Unlike Hodgkinson, William Blake, the English romantic poet, for example, nominated Jerusalem, the holy city, rather than Bethlehem, as the title for his famous poem, and as the symbol of a new heaven for a new earth. There may be a risk in overstating the differences between these two place names in the Holy Land. Nonetheless, the contrast between them is instructive. If Bethlehem suggests an annual renewal of hope at Christmas, it also denotes a state of innocence, whereas Jerusalem, on the other hand, symbolises an unending journey and a battle still to be won. Significantly, then, while it may not be a kind of idyllic and harmonious Eden to which Hodgkinson wishes to return, Bethlehem, for him, seems to stand for a past that has been forsaken. On this reckoning, utopia is to be found in a return to the true path shaped by one's cultural roots, rather than in a forward movement into an unknown tomorrow and still to be determined future.

But there is another, perhaps slightly less innocent, side to Hodgkinson's ethical idealism. Garbed in frequent allusions to a so-called malaise of postmodernism, and taking the German philosopher Friedrich Nietzsche as his inspiration, his recent thinking asserts the need for leadership strength, not so much of character (a traditional theme amongst idealists), but of will. This is evident in his choice of 'the triumph of the will', with its unmistakeable resemblance to the title of Leni Riefenstahl's famous film of the 1934 Nazi Party Congress in Nuremberg, as his solution for contemporary leadership ills (Hodgkinson 1997). Beset by cultural value incoherence amidst the collapse of old certainties, contemporary administrators and leaders (and for Hodgkinson these are one and same) have, for the most part, lost their nerve. Will and the ability to impose one's will in such circumstances mean everything. Thus, 'on the darkling plain victory is a function of will' (Hodgkinson 1997: 384). To will something, following Nietzsche, he sees as the equivalent of commanding it to happen. But there are wills and wills: superior wills and lesser wills. When each confronts the other in a battle of wills, he reasons, the superior of the two wills, because it is a charismatic will that draws its strength solely from Type 1 values ('technical competence or expertise doesn't enter into it'), will prevail, with the result that the lesser of the two wills is 'psychologically disempowered' into submission. Eventually, this subdued will learns to draw new strength through its identification with the commanding charismatic leader's will (Hodgkinson 1997: 385). A failure of nerve, however, is a failure of will and, as such, a failure of will is a pathology of the individual leader, evidence of which can be found in

> The declension of leadership towards pragmatic mediation of interests, in pandering to designated minorities and vocal activists, in the compulsive search for consensus, in the reluctance or inability to say no, in the endless oiling of squeaky wheels, in meek surrender to groupthink or politically correct orthodoxy.
>
> (Hodgkinson 1997: 388)

Alongside the gentleness, sweetness and light of Bethlehem, then, is juxtaposed a rather strident appeal to strength of will. However, Hodgkinson's brief flirtation with will, which was foreshadowed in *Administrative Philosophy*, may be nothing more than that, for in his more recent work (e.g. Hodgkinson 2001), where there is a similar candid expression of his well rehearsed and pessimistic loathing for modern-cum-postmodern social developments, the alleged need for a display of leadership will has given way to a much tamer test for his familiar 'know thyself' injunction to leaders: the A3M3 quiz (or the Administrative Arrogance And Managerial Modesty Measure).

As should be obvious by now, both from the cited extracts and paraphrasing of his arguments, Hodgkinson is casting about for an appropriate way of positioning his perspective on the role of leaders in cultural circumstances which, for him, are proving elusive and largely unamenable to control. But this search for different possibilities creates a number of problems for Hodgkinson's view of leadership. For a start, the idea of strength of will may not sit as easily as he would like to think with the role of his preferred guardian leader. As a charismatic guardian, the Type 1 leader or poet who carries the fire brings 'something other' to leadership than rational technology, a something that is religious, so that 'poetry, ideology and religion run together hand in hand' (Hodgkinson 1996: 216–217). And yet, while each of these things can be forces for good or evil, Hodgkinson is unable to provide his readers with criteria for distinguishing between good or bad Type 1 leaders, despite his own mention of leaders who are good and virtuous. This task is made doubly difficult for Hodgkinson due to his claim that all poets live and die by their values, such is the depth and strength of their axiological commitments. In short, how defensible is a category of leadership values that simultaneously embraces not only Christ and Buddha, but also Adolf Hitler (Hodgkinson 1996: 218)? Hodgkinson's answer is twofold: first, that the judgements of history about leaders are written by the winners, and for that reason can be disregarded – for, had Hitler and Germany savoured victory, then they, rather than liberal democracy, would have been celebrated by history; and second, 'for the purposes of theory', moral judgements do not apply to Level 1 leadership and can be 'bracketed out' (Hodgkinson 1996: 220). For these reasons, the Christs, Buddhas, Hitlers, along with the Gandhis, Pol Pots and Stalins (Hodgkinson 2001: 306) and every other Level 1 leader throughout history, inhabit a shared axiological terrain, and each leader may score 7 (or a perfect score) on his hypothetical seven-question A3M3 test.

With these kinds of justifications, I suggest, Hodgkinson has transported his readership to a somewhat ethereal, transcendental realm from where, in an effort to shore up his values paradigm, his reasoning invokes a range of historical supports, although in a somewhat curiously inconsistent manner. In regard to his first claim, that history has been written solely by the winners, this assertion, of course, may be queried on the grounds of its accuracy. Quite apart from this objection, supposing his claim were once historically accurate, it is surely less true of the recent past for, within the very cacophony that he dismisses as cultural values pluralism are to be heard a range of new, but previously historiographically marginalised, voices of difference. These include women, minorities, post-colonial peoples, the exploited, the powerless, the oppressed and so on; in short, all of those human beings whose journeys through the suffering, pain and drama of life only come to light when historians refuse to privilege the lives and deeds of the 'big' and powerful figures of the past. Further, even were Hodgkinson's hypothetical example of historical reversal to be the case (e.g. the feting of Hitler and a victorious Reich), there is no guarantee that this posited celebratory outcome would transpire. Instead, under Nazism there would probably not be any history, for this was a totalitarian regime notorious, among its other grotesque horrors, for the burning of books. There is another inconsistency in this example, for Hodgkinson's assertion about the alleged irrelevance of history's judgement for leadership rests on what is, in reality, merely one more judgement (which, on this occasion, happens to be his own) about a historical likelihood or possibility (i.e. a so-called 'if' of history).

Hodgkinson's second claim, that his theoretical purposes are somehow impervious to judgements anyway, is also rather odd, given his strong emphasis on administrative praxis, or values-infused action, for it affords his paradigm an air of practical unreality. On the one hand, history does not seem to count for him. Thus, the paradigm can simply be justified philosophically as logically neat, with its categories discrete and as an analytically immune classificatory template, quite apart from the actualities of any real-world judgements. But this same arms-length strength may simultaneously be the paradigm's inherent weakness, for real-world judgements of the actors of history are made independently of the paradigm's values category imperatives. That is, in the cut and thrust of real-world praxis, people do evaluate the Christs, Buddhas, Hitlers and so on of this world as good, evil or as falling somewhere in between, often, it has to be said, according to the consequences of a particular leader's values (i.e. a Level 2A criterion). On the other hand, in articulating the relationship between praxis and what the paradigm decrees to be philosophically legitimate, there are places in Hodgkinson's explanation where history does appear to count after all. In the battle of would-be triumphant wills over contending Level 1 values, for example, conflicts may indeed be resolved over time, as Hodgkinson (1996: 239) concedes, through a 'pseudo-solution', 'grudgingly' coexisting factionalism or values degeneration from Type 1 downwards. But why, one might ask, need pseudo and grudging outcomes be the only possibilities, when historians can no doubt point to numerous other enduring instances of the successful reconciliation of different values and interests? Next, when Level 1 values are claimed to degenerate downwards to Level 2, precisely what does Hodgkinson have in mind? And how is it, on such occasions, that history is somehow able to mediate the movement between these switches in categories?

In Hodgkinson's idealist account, then, it is possible to detect tensions within his leadership imagery and also to query the absence of any clear ethical discrimination between leaders inhabiting the higher realms of his values paradigm. Despite these qualms, he remains insistent that the ethical motivation of his guardian leaders is a 'self-denying spirit of service' (Hodgkinson 1996: 189) and that leadership more generally is to be seen as a 'vocation' (Hodgkinson 1997: 392). My purpose in the next section is to consider how these exact same terms have been used to underwrite a very different, but equally idealistic, moral perspective on leadership.

Eastward with Leo

'Vocation' has clear religious origins and idealist ethical overtones. Historically it was synonymous with the idea of a 'calling' or religiously inspired endeavour, but more recently its meaning has been secularised. In the sphere of occupational employment, it came to refer to 'the emotional attachment of man [sic] to his work', in particular to 'explain his sense of dedication and the commitment of his personality and his talents to his working task for purposes beyond his own material benefit' (Reid 1969: 155, original text emphasised). According to this definition, the locus of motivation for action lies outside of, and beyond, oneself and is geared towards securing the well-being of others and the attainment of ideals. Essentially, the actions of persons in this frame of mind are to be understood as motivated by a sense of altruism rather than egoism.

Herman Hesse's (1956) *Journey to the East* offers a glimpse of the idea of vocation through service in the character of Leo. Hesse's story is about an enigmatic brotherhood of believers known as the League, who are on a meandering pilgrimage eastward through Europe and backwards in time. The group is accompanied by Leo, a young servant, whose demeanour and presence buoys the group's morale. Suddenly, however, in the depths of Europe, the unobtrusive and supportive Leo vanishes without trace. The impression left by Leo on Hesse's narrator (presumably Hesse himself) was profound:

> 'The law?' I asked curiously. 'What law is that, Leo?'
> 'The law of service. He who wishes to live long must serve, but he who wishes to rule does not live long.'
> 'Then why do so many strive to rule?'
> 'Because they do not understand. There are few who are born to be masters; they remain happy and healthy. But all the others who have only become masters through endeavor, end in nothing.'
> 'In what nothing, Leo?'
> 'For example, in the sanatoria.'
> I understood little about it and yet the words remained in my memory and left me with a feeling that this Leo knew all kinds of things, that he perhaps knew more than us, who were ostensibly his masters.
>
> (Hesse 1956: 34–35)

At one level, Hesse's *Journey* is the story of his narrator's inability to recount the actual story of the pilgrimage. This is due mainly to his obsessive search, for years afterwards, for the lost Leo. Eventually, Hesse's narrator succeeds in locating Leo, but he is surprised to discover that, all along, Leo has been the President of the League. At another level, then,

Journey is about the leadership of those who seek to serve. This, certainly, was the impact of Hesse's tale on Robert Greenleaf.

Like Chester Barnard before him, Greenleaf (1904–1990) was a scholar practitioner who, in his 38 years at ATandT (the motto of which, incidentally, was 'The Spirit of Service'), had responsibility for management education and research, rather than performing executive roles. His two major publications were *Servant Leadership* (1977) and *On Becoming a Servant Leader* (1996), the latter published posthumously. Each is a compilation of essays, pamphlets and speeches, rather than a systematic treatise or exposition in the manner of Barnard's (1982) classic, *The Functions of the Executive*. The vividness of Leo's example stimulated Greenleaf to develop the idea of the servant as leader. 'This story clearly says that *the great leader is seen as servant first*, and that simple fact is the key to his greatness'. Leo was a leader for what he was, *'deep down inside'* (Greenleaf 1977: 7–8, emphases in the original). From this starting point, Greenleaf assembled a corpus of writings on various dimensions of servanthood that, in some ways, provides a perfect illustration of Hodgkinson's (1997: 389) much sought-after 'practical wisdom'. Greenleaf's commitment to servanthood has been enshrined, since his death, in the ongoing work of the centre in Indianapolis, USA, which he founded and which bears his name: the Robert K. Greenleaf Center for Servant-Leadership. The Center's mission is to 'fundamentally improve the caring and quality of all institutions through a new approach to leadership, structure, and decision making'. The emphasis of servant-leadership is on 'increased service to others', 'a holistic approach to work', promotion of 'a sense of community' and 'the sharing of power in decision making' (Robert K. Greenleaf Center for Servant-Leadership 2002). Finally, Greenleaf's writings have begun to influence the design and delivery of leadership development programmes in higher education (Polleys 2002).

Greenleaf's view of leadership is suffused with paradoxes. On the one hand, it reflects much of the current orthodoxy of the scholarly community. To begin with, his conception of leadership is grounded in an unreconstructed individualism which, complete with the faint intimations of 'great' reasoning evident in the following extract, he views as the causal locus of social change and progress:

> In the end, it is the *person*, the leader as an individual, who counts. Systems, theories, organization structures are secondary. It is the inspiration and initiative of individual persons that move the world along.
>
> (Greenleaf 1996: 334, emphasis in the original)

As will be seen in a moment, however, the leadership of Greenleaf's individual servants is far from open-ended. His view of leadership is also articulated within the conventional binary distinction of leaders and followers. These categories are not hard and fast for him, for 'everyone in an institution is part leader, part follower' (Greenleaf 1977: 240). Further, his leadership embodies a range of other conventional assumptions, such as: leaders influence and persuade, rather than impose their wills; they possess foresight, awareness and an intuitive feel for events and circumstances; and they show the way to others and elicit their trust, provided those others have confidence in their values and competence. They are also inspired and inspiring, although not necessarily charismatic, individuals, notwithstanding Graham's (1991: 107) recent claim that servant leadership is a variation of charismatic leadership. The final key dimension that Greenleaf shares with many theorists is a similar working distinction between leaders and administrators (or managers) which, with the initial stimulus provided by Zaleznik (1977), attained the status of an orthodoxy amongst US leadership scholars during the 1980s. Organisational administrators, for Greenleaf, are creatures of order and consistency, while leaders are creative statespersons who take initiative.

Most of these attributes are standard fare within the scholarly community. On the other hand, however, what helps set Greenleaf's perspective on leadership apart is its grounding in an ethic of service, an ethic which is realised through social institutions. 'It is difficult', he writes, 'for the influence of an individual to go very far without the mediation of an institution' (Greenleaf 1996: 330). For this reason, the servant-leader is first and foremost an institution builder, and a servant of institutions, a dimension that aligns Greenleaf with writers in the institutional leadership tradition of Barnard (1982) and Selznick (1957). At the core of this idea of the servant-leader, for Greenleaf (1977: 13), is a 'natural feeling that one wants to serve'. That is, first comes the disposition to serve and only then to lead, rather than the reverse. To establish the difference in practice between these two impulses, Greenleaf suggested a two-fold test:

> Do those served grow as persons? Do they, *while being served*, become healthier, wiser, freer, more autonomous, more likely themselves to become servants? *And*, what is the effect on the least privileged in society; will they benefit, or, at least, not be further deprived?
> (Greenleaf 1977: 13–14, emphases in the original)

The idealist sense of 'doing good' and what it means to be the recipient of that moral goodness which is evident in this passage will be dealt with shortly. Greenleaf's other unique contribution concerns the social role and governance of those institutions to be built by servant-leaders, for institutions are to be the servants of society. 'If a better society is to be built', he writes, 'one that is more just and more loving, one that provides creative opportunity for its people', then the most open course is to *raise both the capacity to serve and the very performance as servant* of existing major institutions by new regenerative forces operating within them.

(Greenleaf 1977: 49, emphasis in the original)

This dual servant-leader role for individuals and institutions turns on Greenleaf's revision of the important concept of trusteeship.

The failure of institutions to create the kind of good society envisaged by Greenleaf is mostly a failure, or betrayal of trust, on the part of trustees. At the heart of the concept of trusteeship is an ethic of care, which means that trustee bodies 'care for *all of the people the institution touches*, and that they are determined to make their caring count' (Greenleaf 1977: 55, emphasis in the original). Central to the attainment of due care is the creation of a system of uneasy and ongoing tension between an institution's essentially part-time trustees and its full-time employees, in which trustees, as the bodies with legal authority, are motivated by the need for distinctive institutional performance and impose very high demands on those whom they hold accountable for that performance. Crucial here is the role of trustee chairs, whose principal objective 'is to make demands on the administration for performance that the trustees understand and that meets the standards they set' (Greenleaf 1977: 56). The failure of many trustees to do as Greenleaf would have them bid, lies with a widespread acceptance (in the US, certainly, but also elsewhere) of a flawed institutional structure that privileges what he calls 'the lone chief atop a pyramidal structure' (1977: 61). Individual leadership of CEOs and of board chairs, then, has its limits and its limitations. In each case, instead of a chief, a *prima donna*, Greenleaf proposes a 'primus', or first among equals (i.e. *primus inter pares*). That is, instead of the delegation of authority to a lone individual, to whom as CEO (or its equivalent) all subordinates report, for example, and who is in turn accountable to a governing board of trustees, Greenleaf substitutes the idea of an executive (number and composition unspecified) headed by a primus, or spokesman or spokeswoman. The resulting organisational design is a management and governance structure comprising two teams which confront each other, in which 'no single person has unchecked power', but in which all the members, possessing complementary expertise, 'may be both restrained and encouraged by their peers' (1977: 71).

With these ideas, Greenleaf, has in effect, created a kind of collectivised guardianship role for trustees, in the sense that the concept of trusteeship has been redefined to mean the pursuit and maintenance of institutional interests by all trustees, as opposed to delegating them to the chair. Moreover, with his assumption (at the time of writing in 1972) that such interests include a range of constituencies: 'owner, creditor, student, customer, or client, employee, government, supplier, administrator, parishioner, etc.' (1977: 86), he was able to anticipate part of the recently awakened concern with stakeholder capitalism and stakeholder democracy. In summary, then, Greenleaf may be said to have augmented the traditional and, it should be added, exclusive idealist concern with individual leadership character with a collectivised view of leadership character. With this perspective in mind, he has sought to expose the flaw in the widespread belief in the power of one: that 'only with luck in finding a "chief" with miraculous powers will the institution perform better' (1977: 111). However, despite all of his reservations about omniscient chief appointments (e.g. that, *inter alia*, it is corrupting and lonely, overburdensome, creates painful departures and replacements), this remains the preferred practice of most large organisations.

A disposition to serve

Trusteeship, then, is an example of servanthood. But whence cometh such a disposition or motivation to serve? Greenleaf acknowledges the importance of both formal and informal learning pathways and experiences in the development of a service orientation. However, he offers only a rather cursory critique of US education, along with a few sporadic ideas for engineering (what are for him) more desirable outcomes. One suggestion for dealing with disadvantage resonates with the notion of *noblesse oblige* referred to earlier. Here, Greenleaf proposes, in the case of 'the poor', that students from disadvantaged backgrounds who succeed educationally might be encouraged to 'return to their roots and become leaders among the disadvantaged'. His reasoning is that:

> The best service a school can render to these people may *not* be to homogenize them into the upper classes but to help those who have a value orientation that favors it to develop their ability to lead their people to secure a better life for many.
> (Greenleaf 1977: 164, emphasis in the original)

Thus, education would help those with the opportunity 'to learn to lead their own people'. While such a suggestion might provide an opportunity to understand how idealism works in practice, Greenleaf, unfortunately, does not support his claim with any empirical evidence. One writer who does, however, is the psychoanalyst Robert Coles in his book *The Call of Service: A Witness to Idealism* (1993).

For Coles, service to others is a vocation, in the altruistic sense distinguished earlier, in which, ostensibly, the motivation for, and the pursuit of, personal gain is minimal, non-existent or of secondary importance.

As socially legitimated motivational sources for action, both altruism and gain (or self-interest) have coexisted in uneasy historical tension. During the period referred to by Polanyi (1975) as the 'hundred years peace' (i.e. 1815–1914), gain, in the form of monetary gain, legitimated for the first time the idea of a self-regulating global market for trade as part of the *laissez-faire* credo of economic liberalism. This global market was one of four pillars (along with the gold standard, the balance of power system and the liberal state) on which nineteenth-century (European) civilisation rested, and with the vitiation or collapse of each pillar in the decades following the Versailles settlement, that civilisation crumbled. Half a century or thereabouts later, gain once again began to emerge as a principle of social and economic organisation. With the current popularity of marketisation as a governance principle and the resort to commodification of public sector service delivery, for example, access to public and not-for-profit sector services has been redefined as a market transaction. (A telling example of the consequences in Greenleaf's (1996: 273–276) case was his own experience in a blue-chip, retirement village where, in the absence of a theology of retirement life-care, none of the administrators ever talked to the residents and responsibility for the provision of community centre services fell to the residents themselves, so that overall centre management was divorced from any responsibility for the building of a sense of community.) This market development, because it is predicated on the reconstitution of citizens as consumers, portends, among other things, a diminution of the vocational ethic, a weakening of the traditional service ideal and a waning of volunteerism. Such possibilities have helped fuel a growing concern about the erosion of social capital (Putnam 2000).

While the popular view of the idealist mindset may be that it is something experienced most acutely as part of the psychological and emotional challenges in the transition of young people to adulthood, the disposition to serve is far from a monopoly of the young. The numerous testimonies of volunteerism documented by Coles, for example, encompass all age groups, from small children to the elderly. His observations and interviews include examples of people's engagement across the lines of class and racial division in the US civil rights movement of the 1960s; college students tutoring youngsters in deprived social communities, visiting the elderly and the sick in nursing homes, and running camps; citizen involvement in charity work; a variety of Big Brother and Big Sister mentoring roles; and participation in such government-sponsored programmes as the Peace Corps and Head Start. For Coles (1993: 75), 'all service is directly or indirectly ethical activity, a reply to a moral call within, one that answers a moral need in the world'. Invariably, those individuals who feel moved to respond to such a call, who enter the world of the other and work hard to establish their trust, at some point are asked a question, as a young Harvard undergraduate tutoring children in a poor area of Boston was, along the lines of: 'Hey, what's in it for you?' (Coles 1993: 91). When asked a similar question by an 11–year old ('Why do you come here?') years beforehand while also tutoring as an undergraduate, Coles was too embarrassed and tongue-tied to reply (1993: 175). Subsequent reflection on this experience with his own college adviser convinced him that the moral encounter with other people is always symmetrical, so that a variety of needs of both donor and recipient are satisfied. For the donor, these needs may be diverse (e.g. pursuit of a political or social agenda, sense of moral satisfaction, duty, accomplishment, the making of friendships, an overall sense of 'good' done) and, depending on the answer to the recipients' questions about motivation, the responses run the risk of being perceived as condescending, patronising, priggish, do-gooderish or dismissed as plain 'damn charity' (Coles 1993: 54).

These insights into the subjectivity of idealism are far from unique to the US cases documented by Cole, for this discursive phenomenonology is universal. Every public schoolboy and girl from the aspiring middle classes during Polanyi's new nineteenth-century era of gain, for example, no matter whether they were in England or in the far-flung corners of the British Empire, experienced precisely the same kind of moral auditing as they ran youth clubs, worked in settlement houses, arranged harvest and summer camps or later on delivered food parcels during the Great Depression, as part of the dynamics of *noblesse oblige*. In Coles's case, this sense of *noblesse oblige* was 'the conviction that I was sharing certain intellectual riches with "them", the children I tutored' (1993: 147). Depending on the depth of their belief in their moral rectitude, nobility of motives, lofty high-mindedness, and the security of their social position, these young men and women were also likely to have felt impelled from time to time to impose their wills, perhaps after the manner described by Hodgkinson, due to the presumed rightness of their cause. However, despite outward appearances of firm resolve and demeanour, either then or in the more recent period documented by Coles, the psychological norm for the idealist donor seems to consist of a wavering inner sense of uncertainty:

> even in communities where reasonably comfortable people are able to do reasonably conventional work without harassment, beatings, ostracism, or jailings, a measure of hesitation, of tiredness, of relative apathy can begin to take root. Of course there are fluctuations – a spell of the old, unqualified optimism will prevail yet again – but all in all, many doing service comment on their second thoughts, their lagging interest in the work being done, their feelings of being winded or out of breath, footsore or just plain beaten.
>
> (Coles 1993: 124)

A number of these impulses were experienced by 'Alan', the son of a black Atlanta, Georgia, postal worker, in what is perhaps a litmus test of Greenleaf's leadership of the poor by those who were previously poor, for Alan's attempt to live up to his ideals in the late 1960s had forced him to 'stare myself in the face' (Coles 1993: 186). A vivid formative encounter demonstrated for him the difficulty of empathising with the needs of a fellow human being.

Alan had visited one desperately poor black tenant farmer, with a wife and seven children to support, in an effort to persuade him to register to vote. He was making very little progress and was suddenly taken aback by being asked by the farmer to state his ideals. Alan, all the time getting more impatient with his interlocutor, responded with 'equality'. The farmer concurred, suggesting that this was the very same idea that Jesus had had, and that he would dearly love to be able to live up to this ideal, except that '*his* boss-man', the rich landlord who controlled his life, 'would have him killed'. For Alan, on the other hand, the only rich man he had ever known in his life, he had confessed when pressed, was the father of a former girlfriend, who, the farmer insisted, would merely have taken his girlfriend away, and 'that's the difference'. Subsequently, Alan reflected on how 'snotty' he had been with the farmer, for he had mentally dismissed him 'both psychologically and intellectually' in his attempts to 'bring equality to him', as part of an effort to notch up a few names of people he had 'rounded up' (Coles 1993: 190–191, emphasis in the original).

Greatness, leading and serving

Despite Coles' strictures about the inherent moral symmetry between donor and recipient, the tensions in the relationship just documented highlight an important potential flaw in the armoury of the practical idealist: a compulsion, as part of the act of serving others, to seek to 'rescue' them for their own presumed moral good. This is especially evident when Greenleaf (1977: 241) refers to the desire of 'natural servants' to 'lift others so that others become healthier, wiser, freer, more autonomous, and more likely themselves to become servants'. This discourse of ethical uplift resonates closely with that to be found in what is, arguably, the most significant recent idealist reconstruction of leadership. Although in his magisterial book, *Leadership*, Burns (1978: 19) couches the leader–follower relationship in terms of a reciprocal striving for 'the wants and needs, the aspirations and expectations' of both parties, this ethical engagement is informed by a parallel sense of saving mission. Leadership, for Burns, may well be 'inseparable from followers' needs and goals', but the question is: who bestows the label 'followers' and who makes the decision about followers' needs: the Alans or the impoverished tenant farmers of this world?

This caveat aside, with his concept of the servant-leader Greenleaf has gone some way towards severing the historic connection between the act of service and the attribution of 'great' to those who both model service and do the serving. A leader, to Greenleaf's way of thinking, is 'any person who wields influence' (1996: 287) no matter how mightily or lowly positioned, and is therefore a potential servant-leader. Moreover, the only greatness that matters for Greenleaf, in the end, is the greatness acquired by those enduring social institutions which are the fruits of the labours of servant leaders. Within the scholarly community, however, this view still runs against much of the current tide of opinion for, as with Hodgkinson, many commentators continue to hanker after great charismatic leadership. Shamir is a good illustration:

> the great majority of people in lower echelons of the organization are not in a position to evaluate proposals for major organizational changes in detail or to judge the merits of organizational policies. Therefore, they will turn to the great leader whose perceived character, strength, and skill give them assurance that policies are sound or the problem will be solved.
>
> (Shamir 1995: 23)

One of the difficulties with this kind of reasoning, as Graham (1991: 109), among others, has noted, is that charismatic leadership, due to its well documented mesmerising consequences, weakens the critical capacity of followers and thereby prejudices their moral autonomy. Perhaps this possibility accounts for the extraordinary passion with which so many leadership commentators assert the virtue of follower 'empowerment' as a so-called leader 'effect'. (It is worth recalling, at this point, that one of Hodgkinson's key propositions is that leadership is 'an incantation for the bewitchment of the led': see Gronn 1993.) Similar questions concerning agent autonomy have recently prompted Bass (Bass and Steidlmeier 1999), the leading proponent of transformational leadership, to shore up the ethics of transformational behaviour by invoking a distinction between pseudo and authentic transformational leaders. Prompted in part by a concern similar to that voiced in the early part of this chapter (viz., whether, given that the verdicts of history may be biased in the direction of the victors, as claimed by Hodgkinson, there is any other basis for discriminating between the moral worth of leaders), Bass relies on Sartre's notion of bad faith. Authentic transformational leaders are asserted to be those who remain true to self, whereas pseudo transformational leaders act in bad faith (Bass and Steidlmeier 1999: 184).

In the end, the alleged 'greatness' of an act or actions proves to be an elusive and purely arbitrary judgement. The Australian historian, the late Russel Ward (1990: 1), reported on his experiences as an editorial panel member along with four others who were asked to nominate the fifty greatest Australians of all time. The task proved impossible and there was no consensus. This frustrating experience convinced Ward that, 'the more I argued the question . . . the more I was driven to the conclusion that only one definition would stand up: Greatness is the attainment of lasting fame – or infamy – no matter how, when, where or why'. The one factor which bestowed greatness was not the possession of 'great virtue, intellect, power, even generosity of spirit and other "good" qualities', but the passage of time. Despite Ward's scepticism, Simonton (1994: 3–4) has asserted that 'the world we live in today bears the indelible stamp of the actions and thoughts of . . . figures who are now long dead', although his illustration of the point in his next breath ('this impact is implicit in the national boundaries we defend, the laws we live by, the religious beliefs we practice, the languages we use, and the recreations we seek') would seem to reinforce Ward's point about time taking its course. Simonton (1994: 415) assembles an impressive corpus of data from psychological assessments, surveys, experimental simulations and archival material in an effort to establish 'behavioral laws' of statistical probability that the attainment of greatness correlates with the possession of a range of genetic, psychological and other attributes. In the case of leaders, these include 'genetic endowment; integrative complexity, power, achievement, and affiliation motives; developmental experiences such as birth order, orphanhood, education, and marginality; a leader's age and intelligence; and such assorted traits as dogmatism, explanatory style, dominance, extroversion, morality, and psychopathology' (Simonton 1994: 403). This particular list, of course, begs a host of questions concerned with who gets to be a leader and the nature of the social processes by which leaders come to be attributed with that status.

This point can be illustrated with one of Simonton's (1994: 116) examples, the seventeenth-century English gentleman chemist, Robert Boyle, after whom Boyle's Law of Gases is named. At the back of Boyle's house in Pall Mall, London, was his scientific laboratory. The support personnel employed there, all of them male, were known as 'chemical servants'. The identity and exact number of these people employed by Boyle at any one time is difficult to ascertain, principally because in Boyle's account of the laboratory and in the historiography of laboratory science, they are absent. And that invisibility is precisely Shapin's (1989: 557) point, for the reality was that 'a very substantial proportion of Boyle's experimental work was done through prolonged experimentation and very hard labour on his behalf by paid assistants'. Indeed, Boyle was doubly dependent on the judgements of the hands and eyes of these people because both his eyesight and his health were poor. Thus, what in reality was a distributed regime of shared work, became masked by a Western individualistic bias as 'a solitary individual in contact with reality or with sources of inspiration' (Shapin 1989: 561). On the foundation of the (historically invisible) division of labour and moral economy of the seventeenth-century scientific laboratory, then, was erected the myth of a 'great' scientist, so-called. Ward (1990) provides another example. The subject of his discussion of greatness was John Macarthur, the man who earned his claim to fame (e.g. prominence in Australian school texts, pictorial commemoration on currency notes) for his role in the foundation of the Australian wool industry, but who also, as a subaltern in the Officer Corps in the young colony of New South Wales, hatched a plot to arrest the Governor (the 'Rum Rebellion'). As Ward (1990: 7) shows, however, it was not the irascible and haughty Macarthur, but his wife Elizabeth, who worked to eradicate the stain of treason and sedition resulting from his actions, and managed to stabilise the family fortunes. Indeed, it was she who 'bred his merino sheep, educated his daughters and cultivated good relations with the new governor, Macquarie, far better than he could have done himself'.

There are two points of general significance in these examples. The first, ironically, is the endorsement they provide for Hodgkinson's claim that it is the powerful and victorious, even if they do not necessarily write history, who are able to benefit from it. On the other hand, this point is two-edged, for the examples also show how historical realities may be veiled as much as revealed, in a way which does not necessarily operate in Hodgkinson's favour, for history helps sustain the myth-making that fuels a 'greatness industry'. The second point is that the distributed work pattern in Boyle's laboratory uncovered by Shapin has important implications for contemporary conceptions of leadership, the vast majority of which are individualistic and view leadership as the property of individuals. Just as Boyle was the sole author of his published work, but which was attributable in large part to other contemporaries (e.g. his assistant Denis Papin), 'because Boyle had *authority*' (Shapin 1989: 560), so many leaders come to be viewed as leaders automatically by virtue of their positional authority as managers. The reality of the division of leadership labour, however, as I have tried to show elsewhere (Gronn 2002b), is more likely to be in the dispersed or shared direction indicated by Shapin. That is, if distributed, rather than focused, leadership tends to be the organisational norm, then not only is 'greatness' exposed as a source of mystification but so also is much of 'leadership', at least as it is currently understood. Finally, despite his individualism, there is also an unanticipated consequence of a distributed work perspective for Greenleaf's sense of service and servanthood. If the relationship between the two juxtaposed groups (trustees and executives) in his preferred governance model is to work as he clearly intends, then each will have to negotiate their way to shared ethical standpoints, in which case servant leadership may also turn out to be a form of distributed leadership practice.

Conclusion

As should be evident from the discussion in this chapter, the idea of service has had a close association with leadership, principally through its historic connections with a culturally endorsed archetype of the deeds of 'great' men, and latterly through the idea of the leader as a servant. These connections have been illustrated by reference to the work of two writers, Christopher Hodgkinson and Robert Greenleaf, both of whom emphasise the centrality and significance of ethics in the work of educational and other leaders. Both writers have been acutely conscious of the recent transformation in contemporary Western social values, with Hodgkinson adopting a slightly more pessimistic view of the implications of these changes for leaders, and Greenleaf a more optimistic position. 'I am hopeful', wrote Greenleaf (1996: 330), in the early 1970s, 'because of the restlessness of the abler young people. I believe they are going to take us at a pretty fast clip to a new and nobler level of values'. Unlike Hodgkinson's paradigm, Greenleaf's servant leadership does not represent a fully developed theory or model as those terms are understood in academic circles. It lacks a systematic epistemology and is not informed by the justificatory apparatus of theory and research normally expected of scholarly writing. Quite apart from the reasons already given, however, it is also notable if only because of the steady trickle of interest it has begun to generate in leadership circles (Farling, Stone and Winston 1999: 50).

Each author's corpus of writings has taken on added significance in light of one other recent and interesting development. This is the prominence now being accorded to values and ethical criteria for action in the growing number of national sets of standards for school leaders (see Gronn 2002a). Taking the US *Standards for School Leaders* (Interstate School Leaders Licensure Consortium 1996) as an illustration, the preface to the *Standards* highlights the importance, along with knowledge and performances, of one of the key terms considered in this discussion: 'dispositions'. Their inability to define and assess dispositions proved vexing for the drafters of the standards, but eventually they settled on the idea of a disposition as a proclivity to act in a preferred direction within the individual's ambit of choice. In the standards, disposition statements enshrine values and beliefs. The only direct mention of service is to be found in Standard 4 which says, as part of a leader's anticipated performances, that 'the school and community serve one another as resources'. In Standard 5, there is a presumption that educational leaders will have knowledge of various ethical frameworks and community values; they will be disposed to develop a caring school community; and will demonstrate values, beliefs and attitudes 'that inspire others to higher levels of performance'. While it may be too early to know whether and how such standards might redefine the daily work of educational leaders, the inclusion of ethics and values in national accountability policy framework documents is an indication of the official recognition now accorded to the values-infused nature of school leaders' actions. This, of course, is a large part of the message which the author to whom this volume of essays is dedicated has been seeking to communicate to his scholarly peers for about a quarter of a century. For much of this time, he was a lone protesting voice in a behavioural theoretical wilderness. In no small measure, then, might the recent legitimation of ethical standards be due, perhaps ironically in the light of what has just been said about distributed leadership (but no doubt an irony which would delight him), to the pioneering work and influence of Christopher Hodgkinson.

Notes

1 The phrase used by Edward Thring, the headmaster of Uppingham, to describe his headmaster peers at the first meeting convened in 1869 to found the English Headmasters Conference.
2 Although recent publicity has focused on how the rising aspirations of dual working parent families in one of the so-called 'tiger economies' (Singapore), for example, are increasingly dependent on the employment of growing numbers of young, indigent domestic women from neighbouring Asian countries.

References

Armstrong, J. A. (1973) *The European Administrative Elite,* Princeton, NJ: Princeton University Press.
Barnard, C. I. (1982) *The Functions of the Executive,* Cambridge, MA: Harvard University Press.
Bass, B. M. (1990) *Bass & Stogdill's Handbook of Leadership: Theory, Research and Managerial Applications,* 3rd edition, New York: Free Press.
Bass, B. M. and Steidlmeier, P. (1999) 'Ethics, character and authentic transformational leadership behavior', *Leadership Quarterly* 10, 2: 181–217.
Burns, J. M. (1978) *Leadership,* New York: Harper and Row.
Coles, R. (1993) *The Call of Service: A Witness to Idealism,* New York: Houghton Mifflin.
Farling, M. L., Stone, A. G. and Winston, B. E. (1999) 'Servant leadership: Setting the stage for empirical research', *Journal of Leadership Studies* 6, 1–2: 49–72.
Graham, J. W. (1991) 'Servant leadership in organizations: Inspirational and moral', *Leadership Quarterly* 2, 2: 105–119.

Greenleaf, R. (1977) *Servant Leadership: A Journey into the Nature of Legitimate Power and Greatness*, New York: Paulist Press.

Greenleaf, R. (1996) *On Becoming a Servant Leader*, ed. D. M. Frick and L. C. Spears, San Francisco: Jossey-Bass.

Gronn, P. (1993) 'Bewitching the led: Hodgkinson on leadership', *Journal of Educational Administration & Foundations* 8, 1: 29–44.

Gronn, P. (1995) 'Greatness revisited: The current obsession with transformational leadership', *Leading & Managing* 1, 1: 29–44.

Gronn, P. (2002a) 'Designer leadership: The emerging global adoption of preparation standards', *Journal of School Leadership* 12, 5: 552–578.

Gronn, P. (2002b) 'Distributed leadership as a unit of analysis', *Leadership Quarterly* 13, 4: 423–451.

Hesse, H. (1956) *Journey to the East*, trans. H. Rosner, New York: Noonday Press.

Hodgkinson, C. (1978) *Towards a Philosophy of Administration*, Oxford: Basil Blackwell.

Hodgkinson, C. (1983) *The Philosophy of Leadership*, Oxford: Basil Blackwell.

Hodgkinson, C. (1991) *Educational Leadership – The Moral Art*, New York: State University of New York Press.

Hodgkinson, C. (1996) *Administrative Philosophy: Values and Motivations in Administrative Life*, Oxford: Pergamon.

Hodgkinson, C. (1997) 'The triumph of the will: An exploration of certain fundamental problematics in administrative philosophy', *Educational Management & Administration* 25, 4: 381–394.

Hodgkinson, C. (2001) 'Tomorrow, and tomorrow, and tomorrow: A post-modern purview', *International Journal of Leadership in Education* 4, 4: 297–307.

Interstate School Leaders Licensure Consortium (1996) *Standards for School Leaders*, Council of Chief State School Officers, available from http://www.ccsso.org/isllc.html (accessed 20 August 2002).

Norwood, C. (1929) *The English Tradition of Education*, London: John Murray.

Polanyi, K. (1975) *The Great Transformation*, New York: Octagon Books.

Polleys, M. S. (2002) 'One university's response to the anti-leadership vaccine: Developing servant leaders', Columbus State University, *Journal of Leadership Studies* 8, 3: 117–128.

Protherough, R. (1984) 'Shaping the image of the great headmaster', *British Journal of Educational Studies* 32, 3: 239–250.

Putnam, R. D. (2000) *Bowling Alone: The Collapse and Revival of American Community*, New York: Simon and Schuster.

Reid, G. (1969) 'Vocations, including the public service', *Public Administration* 28, 2–3: 153–163.

Robert K. Greenleaf Center for Servant-Leadership (2002) *About Us*, available from http://www.greenleaf.org/leadership/about-us (accessed August 2002).

Selznick, P. (1957) *Leadership in Administration: A Sociological Interpretation*, Evanston, IL: Row, Peterson.

Shamir, B. (1995) 'Social distance and charisma: Theoretical notes and an exploratory study', *Leadership Quarterly* 6, 1: 19–47.

Shapin, S. (1989) 'The invisible technician', *American Scientist* 77, 6: 554—563.

Simonton, D. K. (1994) *Greatness: Who Makes History and Why*, New York: Guilford Press.

Tyack, D. and Hansot, E. (1982) *Managers of Virtue: Public School Leadership in America, 1820–1980*, New York: Basic Books.

Ward, R. (1990) 'Human greatness', *Journal of Australian Studies* 27: 1–7.

Wilkinson, R. (1964) *The Prefects: British Leadership and the Public School Tradition*, London: Oxford University Press.

Yukl, G. (1999) 'An evaluation of conceptual weaknesses in transformational and charismatic leadership theories', *Leadership Quarterly* 10, 2: 285–305.

Zaleznik, A. (1977) 'Managers and leaders: Are they different?', *Harvard Business Review* 55, 3: 67–78.

Bibliography of Christopher Hodgkinson's writings

Compiled by Eugenie Samier and Kristina Mihailova

Chronological bibliography of books

(1978) *Towards a Philosophy of Administration*, Oxford: Basil Blackwell; New York: St. Martin's Press, reprinted 1982.
(1983) *The Philosophy of Leadership*, Oxford: Basil Blackwell; Toronto: Oxford University Press; New York: St. Martin's Press, reprinted as paperback 1984.
(1991) *Educational Leadership: The Moral Art*, Albany, NY: State University of New York Press.
(1996) *Administrative Philosophy: Values and Motivations in Administrative Life*, Kidlington, Oxford: Pergamon.

Translation of his books

(1983) *Proposicoes para uma filosofia da administracao*, Portuguese translation of *Towards a Philosophy of Administration*, S. Paulo, Brazil: Atlas.
(1985) *Xing Zheng Zhe Xue*, Chinese translation of *Towards a Philosophy of Administration*, trans. Li Chuang-ting, New York: St. Martin's Press.
(1988) Japanese translation of *The Philosophy of Leadership*, Tokyo: Keiso Shobo.
(1989) *Lin Dou Zhan Xie*, Chinese translation of *The Philosophy of Leadership*, trans. Li Chuang-ting, Lanzhou University and University of Calgary.
(nd) Korean translation of *Towards a Philosophy of Administration*, Seoul: University of Korea.

Book chapters

(1975) 'Values in the preparation of educational administration', in A. Myhre, R. Bruce and G. McIntosh (eds) *Administration and the Valuing Process*, pp. 118–125, Edmonton: ATA.
(1980) 'Redefinition of the school', in E. Hodgson, J. J. Bergen and R. Bryce (eds) *The Organization and Administration of Education in Canada*, rev. edn, Edmonton: University of Alberta Press.
(1981) 'Disrepair in the study of administration: Philosophical observations', in B. Catron (ed.) *From Management to Culture*, Festschrift für Sir Geoffrey Vickers, Washington, DC: George Washington University Press.

(1985) 'Foreword', in Leslie R. Gue, *An Introduction to Educational Administration in Canada,* 2nd edn, Toronto: McGraw-Hill Ryerson.
(1992) 'Foreword', in Thomas B. Greenfield, *Greenfield on Educational Administration: Towards a Humane Science*, London: Routledge and Kegan Paul, pp. 2–9.
(1993) 'With James Cutt. Iniquity of equity,' in E. Miklos and E. Ratsoy (eds) *Educational Leadership: Challenge and Change*, Edmonton: Department of Educational Administration, University of Alberta Press.
(1999) 'Foreword', in Paul T. Begley (ed.) *Values and Educational Leadership*, Albany: State University of New York Press.
'The will to power', in Paul T. Begley (ed.) *Values and Educational Leadership*, Albany, NY: State University of New York Press.
'The triumph of the will', in Paul T. Begley and Pauline E. Leonard (eds) *The Values of Educational Administration*, London: Falmer Press.

Selected essays and articles

(1968) 'Values and value judgements in the control of public education', *Proceedings of Conference of B.C. Educational Administrators*, Vancouver, BC: University of British Columbia Press.
(1970) 'Organizational influence on value systems', *Educational Administration Quarterly* 6, 3: 46–55.
(1971) 'A practical program for preparing administrators', *Education Canada* 11, 1: 19–21.
'Changing the perspective: A first note towards a field theory of administration', *Journal of Educational Administration* 9, 2: 200–206.
'The concept of value: An analysis of models', *Journal of Religious Humanism* 4, 3: 131–135.
'Educational goals: An analysis', *B.C. Teacher* 51, 2: 52–56.
(1972) 'The politics of management', *Proceedings of Conference for B.C. Superintendents of Schools*, Victoria, BC: University of Victoria.
'Change and common sense', *B.C. Teacher* 51, 7: 256–261.
'Discipline and dissent', *B.C. Teacher* 52, 1: 12–14.
'About books', *Bulletin of National Association of Secondary School Principals* 56, 388: 111.
'Accountability', *B.C. Teacher* 52, 1: 12–14.
(1973) 'Myths and realities in local control', *Proceedings of Conference for B.C. Superintendents of Schools*, Victoria, BC: University of Victoria.
'Why democracy won't work', *Phi Delta Kappan* 54, 5: 316.
(1974) 'The superintendency at the crossroads', in C. Hodgkinson (ed.) *Proceedings of Conference for B.C. Superintendents of Schools.* Victoria, BC: University of Victoria.
(1975) Pedersen, K. George with Alex Bavelas, Thomas G. Fleming, Christopher E. Hodgkinson and Arthur Kratzmann, *Report to the Minister of Education: A Study of Research and Development in British Columbia,* 31 August, Victoria, BC.

'Philosophy, politics and planning: An extended rationale for synthesis', *Educational Administration Quarterly* 11, 1: 11–20.
'Democracy and responsibility in education', in C. Hodgkinson (ed.) *Proceedings of Conference for B.C. Superintendents of Schools,* Victoria, BC: University of Victoria.

(1976) 'The junior secondary school in Victoria', *B.C. Teacher* 55, 8: 154–158.
'Values education at one remove', *Phi Delta Kappan* 58, 3: 269–271.

(1977) 'A crack in the monolith', *CSSE News* 4, 2: 1.
'Critique of administrative preparation in B.C.', in T. Fleming (ed.) *Symposium on Graduate Programmes in Educational Administration in British Columbia,* Victoria, BC: University of Victoria.
'The public funding of private education in British Columbia, *Nouvelles de la Société Canadienne pour l'Étudede l'Éducation* 4, 2.
'Curriculum at the crossroads', in C. Hodgkinson (ed.) *Proceedings of Conference for B.C. Superintendents of Schools,* Victoria, BC: University of Victoria.

(1978) 'The law and the superintendent', in C. Hodgkinson (ed.) *Proceedings of Conference for B.C. Superintendents of Schools,* Victoria, BC: University of Victoria.
'The failure of organizational and administrative theory', *McGill Journal of Education* 13, 3: 271–280.
'Re-evaluating Canadian education in a time of constitutional crisis', Paper presented at the Canadian School Trustees' Association Congress on Education, Toronto, Resources in Education.

(1979) 'The unspeakable curriculum: Moral education from a non-Aristotelian standpoint', *Canadian Journal of Education* 4, 2: 15–22.
'Quasi-ownership and the changing relationship between superintendents and boards', Paper presented at the International Congress on Education, Vancouver, Resources in Education.
'The two cultures in administration', *Canadian Association for the Study of Educational Administration Newsletter.*
'The local employment of superintendents', in C. Hodgkinson (ed.) *Proceedings of Conference for B.C. Superintendents of Schools,* Victoria, BC: University of Victoria.

(1980) 'Pathologies in education', in C. Hodgkinson (ed.) *Proceedings of Conference for B.C. Superintendents of Schools,* Victoria, BC: University of Victoria.

(1981) 'School law in action', in C. Hodgkinson (ed.) *Proceedings of Conference for B.C. Superintendents of Schools,* Victoria, BC: University of Victoria.
'A new taxonomy of administrative process', *Journal of Educational Administration* 19, 2: 141–152.
'Educational administration in Canada: A conspectus', *School Organization and Management* 1, 2: 61–67.

(1982) 'Wealth and happiness: An analysis and some implications for education', *Canadian Journal of Education* 7, 1: 1–14.
'Greed, dyspepsia and despair: A confutation of Professor Anderson', *Canadian Journal of Education* 7, 2: 90–93.
'Ominous trends in Canadian culture', *Orbit* 13, 2: 13–14.

(1984) 'Aristotle versus Plato: Round 2347', *The Yellow Papers* 3, 2.
(1985) 'The value bases of administration and leadership', *Research in Education.*
(1986) 'The value bases of administrative action and administration theory', *Research in Education.*

'New directions for research and leadership. The triplex value bases of organization theory and administration', *Journal of Educational Administration and Foundations* 1, 1: 4–15.

'The value bases of administrative action', Paper presented at the Annual Meeting of the American Educational Research Association, San Francisco, Resources in Education.

With J. J. Jackson. 'Peace education: A sophisticated approach', *Education Canada* 26, 4: 44–49.

'Beyond pragmatism and positivism', *Educational Administration Quarterly* 22, 2: 5–21.

'Values of agitprop', *Ethics in Education* 6, 2.

With E. Richards and J. J. Jackson. 'Peace education in the schools', *McGill Journal of Education* 22, 3: 317–326.

With J. J Jackson. 'Peace education: A sophisticating approach', *McGill Journal of Education* 22, 3: 327–332.

'Managing uncertainty: Administrative theory and practice in education', *Educational Administration Quarterly* 24, 1: 83–86.

'The value bases of administrative action', *Journal of Educational Administration and Foundations* 3, 1: 20–30.

(1989) 'Principals for tomorrow', *Canadian School Executive,* February.
(1990) 'Malaise in educational administration from an intercultural perspective', *Educational Sciences* (Journal of East China Normal University), published in Chinese (January).
(1992) With J. Cutt. 'Equity and excellence in the university', *Policy Options* 13, 7: 6–10.

'Pathology in educational administration', *Educational Sciences* (Journal of East China Normal University), 3 (December): 7–16.

(1993) 'The epistemological axiology of Evers and Lakomski: Some un-Quineian quibblings', *Journal of Educational Management and Administration*, 21, 3: 177–184.

'Taking political correctness seriously', *Fraser Institute* (March).

(1994) 'Towards an axiology of leadership', Paper presented to the Special Interest Group on Organizational Theory, Division A, Educational Research Association, New Orleans, April.
(1995) 'How not to Schweigen (A response to my colleagues)', *Educational Management and Administration* 23, 2: 135–140.
(1996) 'The triumph of the will: An exploration of certain fundamental problematics in administrative philosophy', *Educational Management and Administration* 25, 4: 381–394.
(1999) 'Theoria (sex, sin and seduction). Part 1 of 3', Paper presented to the British Educational Management and Administration Society, University of Manchester, September.

'Tomorrow and tomorrow and tomorrow: A post-postmodern view', Paper presented to the Barbados Conference of the Centre for the Study of Values and Leadership, OISE, University of Toronto and University of Virginia, Barbados.

(2000) 'Then-now-next: A postmodern peek at everything', *Journal of Educational Administration and Foundations* 15, 1: 10–22.

With R. S. Abella, D. Husband, H. Boisvert, J. Greenberg, P. Resnick, J. Cutt, J. Novek, R. J. Romanow and J. Graham. '20 years of educational policy in *Policy Options*', *Policy Options* 21, 7: 37–42.

'Tomorrow, and tomorrow, and tomorrow: A postpostmodern view', *International Journal of Leadership in Education* 4, 4: 297–308.

Selected reviews of his work

(1979) Vickers, Sir G. 'Review of *Towards a Philosophy of Administration*', *Public Administration* 57: 229–230.

(1985) Uhr, J. 'Review of *The philosophy of leadership*', *Canberra Bulletin of Public Administration* 12, 2: 135–162.

(1992) Barlosky, M. '*Educational leadership:* A non-prescriptive moral vision', *Curriculum Inquiry* 22, 4: 409–423.

Rizvi, F. A. 'Review of *Educational Leadership: The Moral Art*', *Educational Studies* 23, 4: 472–477.

(1993) Evers, C. 'Review of *Educational Leadership: The Moral Art*', *Journal of Educational Management and Administration* 21, 4.

Name index

Acton, J. E. 64
Addams, J. 164
Adler, A. 35, 84, 94
Albrow, M. 45
Alexander, T. 165
Alexander the Great 87–8
Allen, W. 20
Alvey, J. 97–9, 107
Ames, R. 99
Anderson, R. 205
Apel, K. 171
Appleby, P. 141, 150n
Aquinas, T. 29–30, 75
Ardrey, R. 49
Arendt, H. 137
Aristotle *xiv*, 29–30, 82–3, 95n, 150n, 187
Armstrong, J. 254
Arrington, R. 54, 237
Ashbaugh, C. 40
Attila the Hun 67n
Aurelius, M. 35
Austin, J. 17

Bailey, G. 30
Bakioglu, A. 14
Bakker, I. 185
Ball, S. 118
Barker, P. 17
Barnard, C. 29–30, 36, 42, 44–6, 50–1, 59, 64–6, 67n, 91, 127–8, 262–3
Baron, G. 213–15, 228, 230n
Barzun, J. 157
Bass, B. 89, 91, 254, 269

Bates, R. 75–6, 133, 159, 180, 184
Baynes, K. 155
Beck, L. *xiv*, 75, 134–5
Begley, P. 19, 40, 118
Bentley, A. 156, 158–9
Berlin, I. 136, 143–4, 146, 148
Berman, M. 179
Bernstein, M. 150n
Bernstein, R. 159, 161, 164, 172–3
Biesta, G. 159
Blackburn, S. 239
Blair, A. 14
Blake, W. 257
Blanchard, K. 90–1
Bloom, A. 129
Boethius, A. 21
Bohman, J. 155
Bolam, R. 214, 228–9, 230n
Boorstin, D. 30, 80
Borges, J. L. 25–6
Bottery, M. 214
Bourdieu, P. 76–7, 195n
Boyle, R. 270–1
Bridges, E. 150n
Briton, D. 185–6
Brodie, J. 185
Brown, P. 129
Browning, R. 255
Brubaker, R. 181
Bruhn, J. 129
Buckman, R. 95n
Buddha (Gautama, S.) *xiv*, 50, 67n, 259–60
Burke, J. 74, 129–30, 142

Name index

Burns, J. M. 49, 65, 87, 89–91, 268
Burns, T. 202, 205
Bush, T. 214, 227

Caesar, J. 11
Calhoun, C. 226
Callahan, R. 182–4, 193, 199
Carroll, L. 41
Cartland, B. 17
Chalmers, D. 239
Chamberlain, P. 95n
Chandler, R. 128
Chapman, R. 77n, 150n
Cherryholmes, C. 164
Chubb, J. 97, 116–18
Churchland, P. 77, 241–2, 247–50
Ciulla, J. 143
Clark, T. 185
Clinton, W. 14
Coker, E. 97
Coles, R. 265–8
Confucius 84, 254
Connell, R. 179, 227–8
Cooley, C. 99
Cooper, D. 150n
Cooper, T. 74, 78n
Cordingley, P. 228
Covey, S. 89
Cubberley, E. 199
Cunningham, A. 65

Dahl, R. 73
Darwin, C. 247
Davis, E. 131
Dawkins, R. 18, 20
Day, C. 14
Denhardt, K. 75, 77n, 144
Denhardt, R. 133
Dennett, D. 20–1
Derrida, J. 8, 169
Descartes, R. 180–1
Dewey, J. 76, 85, 156–60, 164–5, 167–70, 173, 183, 242, 250
Dickstein, M. 159
Diesing, P. 155, 163
Dillard, C. 180
Dopp, S. 185

Dorbeck-Jung, B. 129
Drai, D. 239
Dreyfus, H. 190
Durkheim, E. 204
Dye, T. 47

Easton, B. 118
Einstein, A. *xiv*, 247
Ellett, F. 54
Engels, F. 168
Evans, R. 180
Evers, C. *xii*, 12, 54, 56, 67n, 75, 91, 133, 159, 162

Farling, M. 272
Farquhar, R. 75
Fay, B. 172
Fayol, H. 44, 50
Feenberg, A. 191
Feyerabend, P. 163
Fiedler, F. 31, 89, 91
Finer, H. 142
Fish, S. 171
Fitz, J. 226, 228
Forsyth, P. 40
Foster, C. 128
Foster, G. 118
Foster, W. 76, 159, 180, 186
Foucault, M. 8, 52
Fox, C. 132, 150n
Frank, R. 99
Franklin, U. 178–9
Frede, D. 187–8, 192
Frederickson, H. 77n
Frege, G. 239
French, P. 77n
Freud, S. 5–6, 19
Friedman, M. 116
Furman, G. 204–5

Gaarder, J. 17
Galilei, G. 30–1
Gamble, A. 114–15
Gantry, E. 36
Gardner, H. 5
Garofalo, C. 73, 129
Garrison, J. 159, 165, 173

Gaugin, P. 13
Gawthrop, L. 77n, 143
Geertz, C. 53
Gendler, T. 118
Geuras, D. 73, 129
Gibson, R. 75
Giddens, A. 182
Gilligan, C. 206
Glatter, R. 229
Gödel, K. *xiv*
Goldring, E. 118
Goodlad, J. 205
Gortner, H. 130, 142, 150n
Goss, R. 78n
Grace, G. 118, 229
Graham, J. 263, 269
Gray, J. 122–3
Greene, M. 179, 182, 184
Greenfield, T. *xii–xiii*, 4, 6, 23–4, 26, 40, 59–60, 63, 73, 75, 91, 133, 159, 180, 214, 228
Greenfield, W. 118
Greenleaf, R. 77, 255, 262–6, 268–9, 272
Greenwood, L. 128
Gregor, M. 132
Grenfell, M. 226
Grey, T. 164
Griffith, A. 185–6
Gronn, P. 14, 77, 91, 93, 179, 183, 228, 254, 269, 271–272
Grossberg, S. 250
Grundstein, N. 127–8
Guignon, C. 188–9
Gunter, H. 23–6, 76
Guy, M. 143
Guyer, P. 135–6, 148

Habermas, J. 179, 181, 204, 208–9
Hacking, I. 40, 52–4
Hall, V. 214, 228, 230
Haller, E. 75, 130
Halpin, A. 200
Hannah, W. 75
Hansot, E. 254
Harker, R. 226, 230
Harris, C. 76

Hart, D. 130, 132
Hart, H. 44
Hatab, L. 195n
Hawkings, S. 18, 27
Hayek, F. 113–116
Hegel, G. W. F. 52
Heidegger, M. 21, 76
Herder, J. G. *xiv*
Hersey, P. 90–1
Herzberg, F. 57, 135
Hesse, H. 261–2
Hill, P. 118
Hill, T. 135
Hines, S. 129
Hitler, A. 67n, 90, 259–60
Hitt, W. 130
Hodgkinson, C. 85, 86, 88–9, 91, 97, 131, 149n, 181, 184, 186, 213–14, 238, 253, 255–60, 262, 269, 271–3
Hodgkinson, M. 14, 17, 21
Hodkinson, P. 226
Holmes, G. 34
Holmes, M. 54–5
Holmes, O. W. 164
Hoy, W. 91
Hoyle, E. 214, 228
Hughes, M. 4, 214, 230n
Hullfish, H. 159
Hume, D. 54, 120, 135, 150n, 240
Hummel, R. 133, 144
Husserl, E. 187–8

Isherwood, C. 18
Isherwood, G. 34

Jackson, A. 185
Jackson, P. 159
James, W. 76, 85, 156–7, 160, 167–8, 173, 183
Janis, I. 82, 95n
Jaques, E. 45–6, 51
Jenkins, R. 217
Jesus Christ 50, 168, 257, 259–60
Jevons, W. 98
Joas, H. 158
Johnson, M. 207
Jos, P. 129

Joyce, J. 17
Jung, C. 35, 82

Kachur, J. 185–6
Kahneman, D. 239
Kant, I. *xiv*, 35, 52, 76, 86, 90, 93, 240
Kaplan, A. 160, 170
Kaufmann, W. 86
Kasten, K. 40
Keegan, J. 88
Kellough, J. 74
Kets de Vries, M. 5–6
Kimbrough, R. 131
Kirby, P. 75
Kley, R. 115
Kohlberg, L. 129
Kuhn, T. 53, 163

Lacan, J. 8
Ladwig, J. 226
Lagemann, E. 155
Lakatos, I. 159, 162–3
Lakoff, G. 207
Lakomski, G. *xii*, 34, 54, 56, 67n, 91, 93, 133, 159, 162, 235, 237, 240
Lang, D. *xiii*, 75
Latour, B. 53
Lavine, T. 159
Levin, B. 180
Lewin, K. 82
Lewis, D. 128
Leys, W. 130
Lobb, W. 56, 67n
Lodge, D. 18
Longfellow, H. W. 38
Louden, R. 134, 137
Lovejoy, A. 156, 159
Luke, J. 130, 132
Lycan, W. 237

Mabbott, J. 236
Macarthur, J. 271
McCarthy, T. 155
McCourt, F. 18
McDermott, J. 85
Machiavelli, N. *xiv*, 90, 150n
McHugh, R. 230n

MacIntyre, A. 76, 201–4
McLuhan, M. 178, 195n
McQuaig, M. 185–6
Magee, B. 8
Maguire, M. 74, 77n, 143
Mann, L. 82, 95n
Manson, C. 67n
Marcuse, H. 195n
Marganis, F. 118
Marginson, S. 97, 116
Margolis, J. 52, 160
Marland, M. 12
Mars, A. 91–3, 95n
Martin, Y. 5, 7, 9–11
Marwell, G. 99
Marx, K. 50, 168, 250
Maslow, A. 35, 57, 135
Maxcy, S. 76, 131
May, S. 226
Mead, G. H. 99, 156–8
Meier, D. 205
Menzel, D. 74, 126, 132, 144
Merz, C. 204–5
Mill, J. S. 236
Miller, D. 158
Millgram, E. 245–7
Mills, C. W. 159, 164, 182
Mintzberg, H. 44, 67n
Miskel, C. 91
Mitchell, C. 129
Mitchell, J. *xiii*
Moe, T. 97, 116–18
Moll, M. 178
Moore, C. 84–5
Moore, G. E. 30, 52, 54, 67n, 83–4, 91, 237–8, 250
Moore, M. 142–3
Morfitt, G. 66n
Morris, A. 84–5
Moses 67n
Muller, J. 99, 110, 112, 116
Munzel, G. 134, 149n
Murdoch, I. 17
Murphy, J. 97

Nash, R. 226
Newlon, J. 183

Newton, I. 237–8, 247
Nietzsche, F. *xiii–iv*, 6, 14, 19, 21, 33, 52, 86, 133, 257–8
Nightingale, F. 38
Nigro, L. 142
Nixon, R. 14
Noble, D. 178
Norwood, C. 254
Nunnery, M. 131

Olivieri, N. 80
Ormerod, P. 115
Ozga, J. 229

Pal, L. 47
Paradise, L. 75
Parker, I. 178
Parker, L. 118
Parsons, T. 45
Pascal, B. 85
Paton, H. 84
Paulsen, F. 186
Peirce, C. S. 76, 156–7, 159–60, 167, 171, 173
Perrow, C. 206
Peshkin, A. 121
Philby, K. 32
Phillips, D. 155
Pickering, A. 53
Planck, M. *xiv*
Plato *xiii–xiv*, 44, 130, 149n, 239, 250, 256
Polanyi, K. 186, 266–7
Pol Pot 259
Polt, R. 180
Popp, J. 159–60
Popper, K. 163, 239–40, 247, 249–50
Powell, A. 17
Preston, N. 74
Protherough, R. 254
Protti, R. 75
Ptolemy, C. 30
Putnam, H. 159, 165
Putnam, R. 120–1, 266

Quine, W. 237
Quinn, N. 53

Raes, K. 144
Rawls, J. 129–30, 133, 139–40, 149n
Rayner, S. 5
Reay, D. 226
Rebore, R. 132
Reichenbach, H. 162
Reid, G. 261
Rescher, N. 159, 161
Ribbins, P. *xii–xiii*, 52, 180, 214, 228–9, 230n
Richardson, W. 142
Riefenstahl, L. 257
Robbins, D. 226
Robinson, D. 185
Rockefeller, S. 159, 165
Rohr, J. 74, 77–8n, 128–9, 142–3, 150n
Rokeach, M. 86
Rorty, R. 52, 164–5, 168–9, 173
Roth, J. 85, 172
Rothschild, K. 98
Rose, E. 178
Rosenberg, N. 107
Russell, B. 18, 84

Samier, E. 34, 75
Sandel, M. 149n
Sartre, J.-P. 269
Schilpp, P. 84
Schrödinger, E. *xiv*
Scott, W. 44
Sears, A. 185–6
Selznick, P. 129, 146, 263
Senge, P. 89–90
Sergiovanni, T. 75, 89, 91, 97, 118–19, 121–2, 131, 149n, 202, 205, 207
Seth, V. 14
Shamir, B. 269
Shapin, S. 270–71
Sheeran, P. 128, 149n
Shusterman, R. 165
Simon, H. 44, 61, 200–1
Simonton, D. 270
Sleeper, R. 165
Small, A. 99
Smart, J. 235
Smith, A. 9, 75–6

Smith, P. 159
Smolensky, P. 243
Smyth, J. 179, 185
Sola, P. 75
Soltis, J. 75, 130
Sowell, T. 97–8
Sparkes, A. 226
Stalin, J. 259
Stalker, G. 205
Starratt, R. 118, 133
Steidlmeier, P. 269
Stein, J. 182
Sterba, J. 236
Stewart, D. 129
Stogdill, R. 254
Stone, A. 272
Strain, M. 214
Strauss, C. 53
Strike, K. 75, 130
Sullivan, R. 134, 137–41
Sun Tzu *xiv*, 90
Swartz, D. 217

Tashakkori, A. 159–60, 162, 172–3
Taylor, C. 190–1
Taylor, F. 199
Taylor, W. 213–15, 228, 230n
Teddlie, C. 159–60, 162, 172–3
Tennyson, A. 90
Terry, L. 77n
Thagard, P. 77, 241–5, 247, 250
Thomas, H. 4
Thomas, M. 131, 142
Thompson, V. 44, 46, 129, 145, 150n
Thomson, I. 179
Thomson, P. 229
Thring, E. 273n
Tinder, G. 95n
Tönnies, F. 182, 204
Tooley, J. 226
Trevor, W. 17
Tucker, S. 15
Tversky, A. 239

Tyack, D. 199–200, 205, 254

Van Gogh, V. 189
Verbeurgt, K. 241
Vickers, G. 44, 46, 51, 64
Voltaire (Arouet, F. M.) 112

Wacquant, L. 226
Waldo, D. 141–2, 150n
Wall, B. 150n
Ward, R. 270–1
Warnock, M. 184–5
Warwick, D. 128
Watanabe, S. 240
Weber, M. 45, 50–1, 53, 57, 60–3, 66n, 107, 127, 133, 179, 181–2, 204
Weil, S. *xiv*
Weingartner, R. 130
West, C. 159, 173
Whitehead, A. 84
Whyte, W. 145
Wilkinson, R. 254
Williams, R. 12
Willower, D. 18, 40, 56
Wilson, E. 19–20
Winch, P. 172
Winkley, D. 214–15
Winston, B. 272
Wittgenstein, L. *xiv*, 21, 23, 34, 41, 53
Wittmer, D. 130
Wolf, C. 128–9
Wolfe, A. 164, 172
Wolfe, T. 17
Wolfram, S. 168
Woller, G. 128

Young, B. 185
Young, J. 102, 106–7, 180
Yukl, G. 254

Zajac, G. 129
Zaleznik, A. 263

Subject index

academic role 15
Achieving Our Country 164
administration: administration/management distinction 41–5; as 'value-free science' 26, 73
administrative: character 141, 201–3, 210, 254, 258; codes 132, 141–3; compliance 75; duty 131; generalism 46; ideologies 132; judgement 127, 206; communication 49–50; personality 127–8, 135; politicisation 74; power 201–2; reasoning 76, 141; reform 74; responsibility 11, 64, 66, 68n, 74, 76, 132, 140, 142–4; roles 74, 201; staff 45, 66n; theory 24; training 141, 145, 147, 214, 220–1, 262; vision 65, 67n
Administrative Behaviour 200
Administrative Philosophy xii, 22, 36, 39, 256, 258
administrators 66n, 184, 192–3, 201
aesthetics 57, 165–6, 173, 189, 235–6
agency 76, 135–6, 141–2, 191, 195, 215–16, 226
altruism 113, 265–6
ambition 109
American Educational Research Association (AERA) 13
Angela's Ashes 18
anthropology 6, 134, 136, 149n, 208
Anthropology from a Pragmatic Point of View 134
apprehension 82
archetypes 60–3, 65, 67n
aristotelianism 74, 130
authority 62, 117, 133, 142, 145, 147, 228, 264, 271; line of 46, 67n, 147; obedience to 40, 139–40, 147; Weber's types 50, 61, 63
autobiography 6
autonomy 86, 135–6, 138, 143, 182, 235, 239, 268–9

being 19, 187
beneficence 103–5
benevolence 100–1, 104–7, 123–4, 139
Beyond Objectivism and Relativism 164
Bhagavad-Gita xiv, 18, 84
biography 6, 212, 219
biology 20
British Educational Administration Society (BEAS) 222–4
British Educational Leadership, Management and Administration Society (BELMAS) 212, 222–3
bureaucracy 8, 74, 204, 217; Weberian ideal type 45
bureaucrat 60, 201; bashing 74
bureaucratic: control 182; corruption 8; efficiency 182, 205, 209, 224; ethos 145; mentality 143; necessity 73; obedience 142

The Call of Service 265
Canadian Association for Studies in Educational Administration (CASEA) 15

Subject index

Canadian Broadcasting Corporation 178
Canadian Psychological Association 33
Capital: cultural 217; symbolic 217, 223
capitalism 182, 185, 265
categorical imperative 35, 90, 128, 130–2, 138, 140, 147, 149n
Catholic Catechism 19
charisma – *see* leadership
civil society 137, 139
coherentism 162, 165, 241–4, 247, 250
Columbia University 158
commerce 123; contracts 103, 107, 204; exchange/transactions 106–7, 185, 266; property 102–3
commercial society 103, 105, 107–8, 110
commitment 32
Commonwealth Council for Educational Administration and Management (CCEAM) 222
communism 168
Communist Manifesto 168
community 76, 119, 133, 169, 179–80, 195, 203–7, 236, 254, 262, 267, 272–3
competition 185, 193
computers 168, 170, 178, 189–91, 207
conation 57
condottiere 5
Confessions of a Philosopher 8
The Conflict of the Faculties 135
confucian *jen* 84
conscience 130
Consciousness Explained 21
consequentialism 128–9
consilience 19–20
constitutions 133, 142–3, 150n
conviction 64
creativity 64, 66, 128, 141, 163, 165
critical analysis 214
critical theory 158, 208–10
Critique of Practical Reason 132, 134, 138

A Dance to the Music of Time 17
decision-making 50, 59, 235–6, 239, 242, 244, 262

democracy 121–2, 133, 157, 164, 167, 169, 173, 194, 209–10, 229, 254, 265
democratic institutions 142
desirable 236
determinism 6, 19, 36
discourse 163, 208
Discourse on Thinking 195n
disenchantment 14, 180, 182, 204
division of labour 105–6, 108–9, 116, 182
dramaturgy 52

economics 7–10, 15, 76, 97–9, 101, 113, 185, 202–3, 207, 217–18
education 53, 93–4, 110–13, 116, 123, 145, 147, 157, 165–6, 265; consumerism in 117–18; market principles in 117–18, 183–4, 192–4, 215, 225; networks 207, 220–2, 224, 220; reform 178
Educational Administration and the Social Sciences 213
Educational Management and Administration 23, 213
Educational Leadership xii, 12, 26, 39, 41, 47, 256
educator as leader 94, 179, 191–4
El Quaeda 121
Emma 17
emotion 57, 135, 200, 217, 261
empiricism 160, 167
entrepreneurialism 215, 225, 228–9
envy 109
epistemology 235–6, 239–41, 249–50, 272
equality 65, 148, 170
equity 163
ethical: dilemmas 77, 212, 226, 255; judgement 235, 245
ethic of: care 206; justice 129; neutrality 142; responsibility 186; service 253–5, 263
ethics 57, 173; administrative 39–41, 44, 63–5, 73–4, 124, 272; bioethics 19; deontological 128–9, 131, 134, 149n; of leadership 255; of learning 249–50; programmes 74, 145, 272–3;

Subject index   289

rule ethics 130; teleological 129; virtue ethics 130–1
The Ethics of Educational Leadership 132
ethnography 6, 121
European Forum on Educational Administration (EFEA) 222
Evil 35, 56, 61, 75, 81–4, 86, 94, 138, 147, 245, 259; passive 144; radical 126, 128, 137, 147
Eye in the Door 17

facticity 86, 162
fact/value distinction 53, 55, 85, 182
fallacies: homogenetic 26, 57; naturalistic 54, 67n, 237–9; paradigmatic 58, 62–3
fascism 179, 195n
fatalism 15
Foundations of the Metaphysics of Morals 131–2, 134, 148
formula of autonomy 138
formula of legislation for a moral community 139
Frankfurt School 208
freedom 19, 76, 86, 103, 114, 116, 126, 133, 135–8, 144, 148, 163, 170, 190, 210, 226, 250
free rider 130
free will 36, 135, 145
Freudianism 19
The Functions of the Executive 29, 262

Gemeinschaft 204
Gesellschaft 204
Ghost Road 17
globalism 8
good 56, 59, 80–1, 85, 87, 91, 131, 235, 237; and art 84; and passion 86; apparent good 82–3, 89
good will 130, 136–7, 141
governance 45, 77, 208, 272; self-governance 208
government 108, 115, 117, 123, 133, 134, 136, 147, 170–1, 181, 223; Alberta 195; British Columbia 193, 195; British Department for Education and Science 222; British Parliament 213; Canadian Federal 9, 32–3; Canadian Ministry of Defence 31, 33; civil 102–3; Ontario 195; responsibilities 102; US 142
The Great Transformation 186
Greenfield on Educational Administration xii, 4
habitus 216–18, 220, 222, 225–7
Handbook of Administrative Ethics 74
Headteachers and Leadership in Special Education 5
Heideggerian: bracketing 188; calculative thinking 190–2; consciousness 188; releasement 194; unconcealment 188–9, 194–5
Henry Luce Chair 11
hermeneutics 158
historiography 25
history 165, 191, 199, 212–13, 253–4, 259, 271
humanism 25–6, 186, 228
human relations theory 126

idealism 77, 127, 130, 149n, 159, 253, 255–7, 263, 266–7
The Idea of a Social Science 172
individualism 113, 116, 133, 206, 271
indoctrination 48
instrumentalism 25, 127, 204, 224–5
intention 75, 81–3, 129, 143, 195, 239
interests 44, 127, 208, 210, 217–18, 264–5
International Intervisitation Programme (IIP) *xiii*, 222
intuitionism 238

The Journal of Educational Administration and Foundations 5
The Journey to the East 261–2
jurisprudence 101, 103, 164
justice 76, 101–2, 104–5, 123–4, 139, 163, 206, 255

kantianism 74, 202
Knowing Educational Administration xii
Ku Klux Klan 121

law 123, 164, 261
law of autonomy 138
Leadership 268
leadership 64–5, 87–8, 253, 260; acts of 48–9; and climate 90–1; and culture 90–1; and education 25, 36, 180, 253–4, 262; and ideology 90–1; and the good 80, 88, 90; business of 89; charisma 50, 61–3, 65, 67n, 148–9, 254, 258, 263, 269; concept of 36, 40, 47, 51–2, 77, 88, 91, 180, 262–3, 268–9; forms of 49, 51–2, 67n; individuals 88; learning 25, 93; research 169–70; responsibilities 48, 66; roles 94, 221, 254; science of 31, 89; theories of 51, 254–5, 272; transactional 65, 68n; transforming 49, 65, 68n, 89–90, 202, 254, 269; tyrannical 68n
Lectures on Jurisprudence 101, 110
legitimacy 77, 217, 219
legitimation 209, 273
liberal education 17–18
liberalism 122, 169, 179, 194, 228, 266
Liberalism and Social Action 164
lifeworld 181
literature 169, 261
Local Education Authorities 222
logical positivism 41, 200
The Logic of Scientific Discovery 240
Logic: The Theory of Inquiry 157
lying 137–8, 150n, 202

McGill University 10
machiavellianism 129
Mafia 121
maladministration 138
management 194, 201, 221, 224–5
managerialism 4, 126, 141, 149n, 181, 186, 224
The Managerial Kant 127
Managing Education 4
A Man in Full 17
market: model 76; order 115, 123–4
markets 97, 180, 266
marxism 131, 208
mathematics 18, 27, 131, 168, 239

Matsushita School 10
mentorship *xiv*, 12, 266
Metaphysics as a Guide to Morals 17
Metaphysics of Morals 132
military 32–3, 46, 48–9, 91–4, 136, 207, 254
Mind, Self & Society 157
Minnowbrook conferences 73
modernity 210, 255
moral: avoidance strategies 144; character 134, 136, 145; cognition 235, 238–40; codes 59, 61, 64, 73; conduct 65; duty 130–5, 139, 145, 267; education 134; engineering 146; freedom 135–6; inquiry 165–6; judgement 73, 75, 77, 82, 134, 140–1, 236, 238, 249; knowledge 235, 241; law 138–9; learning 248–50, 253; maxims 136–7, 140–1; muteness 126, 132, 144; order 41, 60, 66, 201; purpose 46, 77, 218, 266; reasoning 64, 74, 77, 134–5; relativism 122; responsibility 82, 87, 136, 142, 148; values *xiii*, 165
morality 60, 65, 67n
motivation 57, 62, 67n, 209, 261, 266
motives 88
MPA programmes 74

naturalism 237, 239, 242, 247, 250
nazism 48, 257, 259
Necker cube 242–3
New Public Management 73–4, 76–7, 136–7, 143, 147, 150n
New Testament 168

On Becoming a Servant Leader 262
Ontario Institute for Studies in Education 10, 21
ontology 76, 179, 187, 192, 238–9
organisation 129; behaviour 201; cognitive complexity 45, 66n; constraints 144–5; culture 58, 63, 127, 166, 202; design 264; functional specialisation 46; hierarchy 40, 43–45, 48–9, 142–4, 205; means/ends 43; nomothetic/idiographic

Subject index   291

dimensions 54; norms 73; pathology 131; politics 127, 165, 228; purpose 140; requisite organisation 45

Pergamon Press 22
phenomenology 187
philosophy 4, 8–9, 19, 21, 24, 43, 62, 73, 75, 84, 129, 132, 155, 158, 160, 180, 183, 186, 204, 214, 237, 239, 242, 250, 255
Philosophy and Social Hope 164, 168
'philosophy-in-action' *xiii*, 4
The Philosophy of Leadership xii, 39, 47
physics 18, 27
platonism 12, 187
policy 32, 34, 43, 46–7, 50, 77, 140, 143, 149n, 155, 205, 223, 228–9, 249–50
political: correctness 13, 27n, 58, 141, 258; ideology 168
politics 14, 43, 47, 73, 133, 207, 250
political science 158, 164
positivism 76, 98, 158–9, 165, 200
postmodernism 20–1, 23, 159, 170, 181, 209–10, 255, 257–8
power 61, 67n, 86, 127, 132, 209, 213, 216–18, 224, 227–8, 237, 265, 270
pragmatism 62–3, 65, 76, 155–7; critical 167–74; methodological 161–3; political 163; programmatic 162–3; romantic 165; scientific 159–61, 172–3; theoretical 162; vulgar 172
Pragmatism: An Open Question 165
Pride and Prejudice 17
The Prince 133
Principia Ethica 237
principle: of justice 139; of publicity 138
The Problems of Men 164
professional: identity 212–3, 227; practice 65, 212–3, 215, 221, 226
professionalism 76, 127, 145, 167, 215
prudence 101–2, 105, 123–4, 127, 139
psychological testing 33
psychology 80, 99, 135–6, 148, 157–8, 239–40, 270
public scrutiny 74

Question Concerning Technology 195n

rational individualism 133
rationalism 159, 182
rationality 172, 208; communicative 208; instrumental/technical 57, 171, 179–81, 187, 201, 208; purposive 208; Weber's types 57, 181
Reading Pragmatism 164
Realpolitik 128–9, 131
reason 57, 75, 82–3, 85–6, 127, 129, 131, 133–4, 136, 235–6, 240
reflexivity 213–16, 227
Regeneration 17
relativism 75, 129
religion 18, 27, 57, 84–5, 89, 119–21, 136, 148, 165, 173, 257, 258–9, 261
Religion within the Limits of Reason Alone 134, 137
research 160–1, 165–6, 173, 221–2; ideology 158–9; mapping 24–5; paradigm 158
Royal Roads Military College 29, 31

Santa Filomena 38
school: community 131; leaders 94, 192, 218–19, 253; restructuring 185–6
schools 118–19, 170, 199–200, 210, 219–21, 265; as businesses 183–4, 194, 202–3; communal 121; convenantal 119–21
science 16, 18, 20, 53, 146, 155–7, 159–61, 179, 181, 190, 194, 200, 209, 217, 237–8
scientific: method 85; management 183, 199, 201, 205; programmes 241; theory 237–8, 241, 245, 247
scientism 146
secrecy 138, 170
self-command 104–5, 123–4
self-interest 113, 116, 133, 140, 147, 186
Servant Leadership 255, 262
social: action 62, 85; capital 120; inequality 109; justice 76, 114–15, 133, 156, 164, 173

socialisation 53, 216
sociobiology 19
sociology 99, 158, 209, 226
Sophie's Choice 17
speech 107–8
Standards for School Leaders 272
Standing Conference for Research in Educational Leadership and Management (SCRELM) 222
subjectivity 133, 140
A Suitable Boy 14
supervenience 239
system 181

taylorism 131, 200
teaching 4, 9–10, 30, 33–6, 111, 183
technology 3, 76, 178, 187–8, 190, 194, 209–10
theology 19
Theory Movement 75, 184, 200
The Theory of Moral Sentiments 99–100, 102, 110
Therapy 18
Towards a Philosophy of Administration xii, 24, 29, 39, 53, 256
trusteeship 264–5
truth 168

universal principle of justice 133, 138, 149n

University of: British Columbia 7, 10; California at Berkeley 7, 10; Cambridge 10; Chicago 158; London 7; Michigan 157; Victoria 4, 10, 12–13, 31
Upanishads xiv
utilitarianism 74, 128, 235–8

value: analysis 31, 33, 167, 245; audit *xiii*, 32; choice 73; definition 32, 67n, 172; hierarchy 43, 54–5, 256, 259–60; paradigm 19, 31–6, 60–3, 66–7, 86–7, 131, 256, 258–60, 272; theory 237
values *xii*, 39, 52, 76, 85–6, 122, 143, 145–6, 170, 202, 227, 238, 247; and leadership 25; conflict 34, 123; cultural 53; democratic 73; economic 76, 171, 183; organisational 10, 43–4, 58–9, 63–4
vedantism 19
virtues 119, 203, 270
vision statement 63

Watergate 74, 78n
The Wealth of Nations 97, 99–100, 102, 110
Whorfian hypothesis 207
Will 57, 64, 75–7, 82, 84–6, 127, 135–6, 138, 148, 257–8, 263